Humanizing Childhood in Early Twentieth-Century Spain

LEGENDA

LEGENDA is the Modern Humanities Research Association's book imprint for new research in the Humanities. Founded in 1995 by Malcolm Bowie and others within the University of Oxford, Legenda has always been a collaborative publishing enterprise, directly governed by scholars. The Modern Humanities Research Association (MHRA) joined this collaboration in 1998, became half-owner in 2004, in partnership with Maney Publishing and then Routledge, and has since 2016 been sole owner. Titles range from medieval texts to contemporary cinema and form a widely comparative view of the modern humanities, including works on Arabic, Catalan, English, French, German, Greek, Italian, Portuguese, Russian, Spanish, and Yiddish literature. Editorial boards and committees of more than 60 leading academic specialists work in collaboration with bodies such as the Society for French Studies, the British Comparative Literature Association and the Association of Hispanists of Great Britain & Ireland.

The MHRA encourages and promotes advanced study and research in the field of the modern humanities, especially modern European languages and literature, including English, and also cinema. It aims to break down the barriers between scholars working in different disciplines and to maintain the unity of humanistic scholarship. The Association fulfils this purpose through the publication of journals, bibliographies, monographs, critical editions, and the MHRA Style Guide, and by making grants in support of research. Membership is open to all who work in the Humanities, whether independent or in a University post, and the participation of younger colleagues entering the field is especially welcomed.

ALSO PUBLISHED BY THE ASSOCIATION

Critical Texts
Tudor and Stuart Translations • *New Translations* • *European Translations*
MHRA Library of Medieval Welsh Literature

MHRA Bibliographies
Publications of the Modern Humanities Research Association

The Annual Bibliography of English Language & Literature
Austrian Studies
Modern Language Review
Portuguese Studies
The Slavonic and East European Review
Working Papers in the Humanities
The Yearbook of English Studies

www.mhra.org.uk
www.legendabooks.com

STUDIES IN HISPANIC AND LUSOPHONE CULTURES

Studies in Hispanic and Lusophone Cultures are selected and edited by the Association of Hispanists of Great Britain & Ireland. The series seeks to publish the best new research in all areas of the literature, thought, history, culture, film, and languages of Spain, Spanish America, and the Portuguese-speaking world.

The Association of Hispanists of Great Britain & Ireland is a professional association which represents a very diverse discipline, in terms of both geographical coverage and objects of study. Its website showcases new work by members, and publicises jobs, conferences and grants in the field.

STUDIES IN HISPANIC AND LUSOPHONE CULTURES

Humanizing Childhood in
Early Twentieth-Century Spain

ANNA KATHRYN KENDRICK

Studies in Hispanic and Lusophone Cultures 30
Modern Humanities Research Association
2020

Published by Legenda
an imprint of the Modern Humanities Research Association
Salisbury House, Station Road, Cambridge CB1 2LA

ISBN 978-1-78188-541-3

First published 2020

Copy-Editor: Charlotte Brown

CONTENTS

❖

For my parents,
Elizabeth and Stephen Kendrick

LIST OF ILLUSTRATIONS

ACKNOWLEDGEMENTS

Every book has its own upbringing. While this one developed from a dissertation completed at the University of Cambridge in 2015, it was shaped over many years by countless chance encounters and the generosity and grace of many. As an undergraduate, recently returned to Harvard from a semester in Granada filled with poetry, hikes, and cycle rides into the foothills of the Sierra Nevada, I began to understand that education was not a series of books or arguments, but a lived engagement with people and places. After graduation, as a teacher at the Shrewsbury School in Shropshire, a tightly-knit community of teachers provided me with an embracing model of a holistic vocation. My developing interest in both internationalism and education came together over the coming years. Stumbling across prodigious writings on pedagogy by figures such as Miguel de Unamuno and José Ortega y Gasset, I saw how education came to constitute a larger intellectual, literary, and cultural project. The questions I encountered led me toward, firstly, this project, but also more broadly the transnational endeavour in which I have been invested for the past years. Teaching within a liberal arts framework at NYU Shanghai, the first degree-granting Sino-American university in China, I am watching new waves of international and progressive education unfold. While individual national and historical contexts are decisive, the recurring questions of humanistic education I examine in this book — between technical skills and creativity, quantitative and qualitative measures, knowledge and lived experience — continue to frame debates across borders on how and why we educate.

Such origin stories can be told in many ways, but one thread is constant: the role of those who contributed, materially, physically, or emotionally, along the way. Alongside individuals, I wish to acknowledge the institutions that made this work possible. Facilitating my first foray into Spanish fieldwork, Harvard's Minda de Gunzburg Center for European Studies and the Real Colegio Complutense provided early encouragement. The Abraham Lincoln Brigade Archives' Watt Prize and Harvard's Francis H. Burr Prize offered funds which made my MPhil study a reality, while a scholarship from the Gates Cambridge Trust allowed me to carry the doctoral research forward. I benefitted immeasurably from the scholarship's interdisciplinary lens, which holds the arts and humanities as crucial to its mission of improving the lives of others. The collegiality of Provost Barry Everitt, Jim Smith, and fellow scholars including Vaibhav Bhardwaj, Erica Cao, Andrés Castro Samayoa, Catherine Gascoigne, Kevin Grove, Andrew Gruen, Mona Jebril, Katrin Pfeil, Devani Singh, and many others made these years a joy, as do my colleagues on the Gates Cambridge Alumni Association board today. The Bibliothek für Bildungsgeschichtliche Forschung in Berlin offered a postdoctoral stay, during which I was warmly received by Sabine Reh and colleagues. The *Bulletin of Spanish Studies* and *Modern Language Review* has kindly granted permission to adapt articles published in these journals as portions of Chapters One and Six respectively. I am grateful to my anonymous reviewers, as well as to Duncan Wheeler, for their comments. Finally, I wish to acknowledge the Association of Hispanists of Great Britain and Ireland as well as the Office for Cultural and Scientific Affairs of the Embassy of Spain in the United Kingdom for their awarding of the 2016 Annual Publication Prize. This opportunity brought me into contact with Graham Nelson at Legenda, who steered the editorial process with aplomb and good humour. Thanks are due also to Charlotte Brown for her editorial attention and Audrey McClellan for her masterful indexing work.

At the University of Cambridge, profound thanks are due first and foremost to my supervisor Alison Sinclair, who oversaw the dissertation from which this book grew. Reports from her spring garden or the Cam, meetings in the Tea Room, and miraculously swift replies, even from the remotest reaches of Andalucía: it was a privilege to have not only an eminent Hispanist but also a wholly engaged and caring teacher as my guide. Across a decade and two Cambridges, Brad Epps introduced me to Catalan art and literature through inspired undergraduate teaching and, at the viva stage, crucially encouraged my 'catholic' readings of holism. David Midgley helped me to think through biological holism in German thought, while Sarah Wright provided thoughtful insight into Hispanic studies of childhood. Within the Department of Spanish, David Jiménez Torres, Daniel Gutiérrez Trápaga, Parker Lawson, Samuel Llano, Stuart Davis, and Coral Neale made the faculty an ideal place to work, while Luis Castellví Laucamp earned my lasting gratitude for his attentive reading of the manuscript. At Emmanuel College and elsewhere, friends including Alice Blackhurst, Ruth Blackshaw, Elizabeth Brickley, Yuna Han, Helen Hatch, Leah Katzelnick, and Krzysztof Kozak brought the sun, while Dame Fiona Reynolds, Rev. Jeremy Caddick, and the Chapel Choir fostered beauty and, as befits this book, sustenance of the spirit.

But this work is first and foremost about Spain, and my gratitude to scholars across the country runs deep. From our first meeting in a London pub to the archives of the Universitat Autònoma de Barcelona, Annette Mülberger enthusiastically welcomed me into the world of the history of psychology. Through her, I met the treasure that is Mònica Balltondre, whose benevolence extended from Gràcia to the shores of Altafulla. With inimitable care, Noemí Pizarroso López and Enrique Lafuente Niño greeted me warmly at my first symposium of the Sociedad Española de Historia de Psicología and introduced me to colleagues at the Universidad Nacional de Educación a Distancia (UNED); Noemí graciously shared her Lavapiés with me. Gabriela Ossenbach connected me to key colleagues in the history of education, including the late Antonio Molero Pintado, my visit to whose lovingly curated house-museum I remember fondly. María del Mar del Pozo Andrés discussed her work on Justa Freire with me, while Encarnación Martínez opened up the Instituto-Escuela's history at IES Isabel La Católica. In Berlanga de Duero, Agustín Escolano Benito and Purificación Lahoz Abad of the majestic Centro Internacional de la Cultura Escolar (CEINCE) received me with great hospitality, while José

Antonio Gallardo Cruz, Roberta Quance, and Eamon McCarthy pointed me toward key sources. I am indebted to the staff of the Residencia de Estudiantes and the Fundación Ángel Llorca, the Museo Patio Herreriano, the Patronato Carmen Conde-Antonio Oliver, the Casa-Museo Unamuno, the Associació de Mestres Rosa Sensat, the Museo Sorolla, as well as Andrew H. Lee of NYU. Miguel de Torre Borges and Xosé Luis Suárez Canal graciously granted permission to share drawings and photographs, respectively, from their family heritage. Finally, Fanny Rubio was a serendipitous guide to Madrid's literary, poetic, and cultural heritage, from exuberant Casa Patas invitations and book readings to thoughtful and open reflections on the Civil War, generations, and the course of history.

While Spain exerted a continual pull, much of this book was written beyond its borders. In Berlin, and across Germany, I was welcomed by Friederike Mehl, Ahmet Korubay, Till Kössler, Tom Reichard, and Adelheid and Christian Geppert. In Boston, Sarah Hill, Kathleen Creel, Elissa Berwick, Annie Chen Andersson, Justine Kastan, and Anne Stetson shared poetry and ideas. I am grateful for the investment of my own teachers, including Jim Jer-Don and Tyler Knowles at the Winsor School, as well as Jeanne Follansbee, Liz O'Leary, Michele Martinez, and Sabrina Sadique at Harvard. Shrewsbury colleagues including Laura Wakeling, Nicholas Wakeling, Charles Oakley, and others modelled living and teaching well, as did Dermot Walker and Dawn Tibbetts along many a hill and mere. Today, I am fortunate to work alongside NYU colleagues around the world including Diane Geng, John Robertson, Maria Montoya, and Joanna Waley-Cohen in Shanghai; Kristofor Larsen, Malina Webb, and Almaz Zelleke in New York; and Doug Cutchins in Abu Dhabi; and the many students who share their stories with me.

Across these many continents, days and years, Alexander Geppert has been my interlocutor at all stages of this endeavour, in mind, body and spirit (and many a footnote). There is no one with whom I would rather build one life, let alone our three, in New York, Shanghai, and Berlin. From my childhood, Marie Vernlund taught me what generosity and faith in another look like. Though in truth, I already knew: my family — my parents, Elizabeth and Stephen Kendrick, my siblings Paul and Elizabeth, and each of my Gotlieb, Moorman, and Kendrick relatives — shaped with love a childhood that, as in Jorge Guillén's 'luz y esa niñez', projects its light onto the present.

A.K.K., New York City, July 2019

NOTE ON TRANSLATION

In translating the language of early twentieth-century education and child development, several choices should be noted. The first concerns the 'child' and the pronouns it engenders in English. While the singular *niño* (as in the oft-used 'mundo del niño') stood for an entire field of scientific and pedagogical discourse, pedagogues were also discussing and influencing the lives of real children with real consequences. While I have sought context for each instance, given advances in co-education, I consciously tend toward a masculine 'he', particularly in texts focused on 'el hombre' as a metonym for the development of future society. The second concerns terms for the mind, spirit, and the soul. In *fin-de-siècle* and early twentieth-century contexts, both the 'alma del niño' and the 'espíritu del niño' were liberally employed in psychological texts as well as broader expressions of religiosity, morality, and transcendence. In cases where these latter aspects are paramount, I have held to more literal translations of 'soul' and 'spirit' respectively; within clearly clinical or empirical contexts, I represent the child's *alma* and *espíritu* as the 'mind' and 'mental' development. All translations are mine unless otherwise noted, including any shortcomings therein, and all efforts have been made to locate the corresponding rights-holders for images reproduced in this book.

y en las olas pequeñas
que van a la playa
unos niños, desnudos,
jugando
con la espuma blanca.
La isla junto al mar
descalza.

— Josefina de la Torre, 'Mediodía' (1934)

Then we will no longer be infants, tossed back and forth by the waves and blown here and there by every wind of teaching [...]. From Him the whole body, joined and held together by every supporting ligament, grows and builds itself up in love, as each part does its work.

— Ephesians 4:14–16

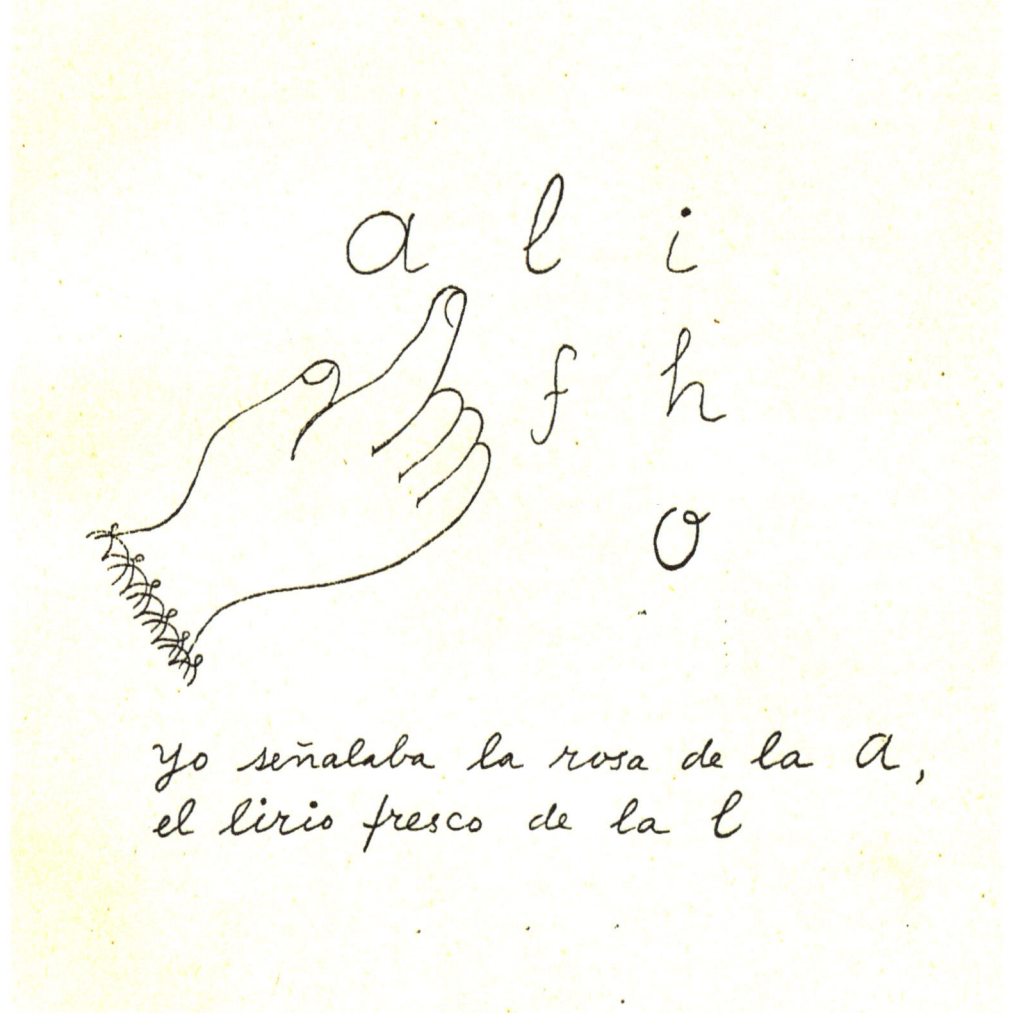

FIG. I.1. A teacher's hand traces out letters on a blackboard in Norah Borges's 1934 illustration for Carmen Conde's poem 'Escuela'. Carmen Conde, *Júbilos: poemas de niños, rosas, animals, máquinas y vientos*, 2nd edn (Murcia: Sudeste, 1934), p. 29. Courtesy of the heirs of Norah Borges.

INTRODUCTION

The Spanish Child as Human Enigma

Entre los atlas y los pupitres, qué firmes y gráciles son las niñas. Se confunden con las líneas azules, con los marecitos como cabelleras de las cartas geográficas.
Cada vez que decían una letra, ondulaba el corro. Yo señalaba la rosa de la *a*, el lirio fresco de la *ele*...
¿De qué isla, de qué árbol, de qué fuente crece este chorro de luceros que son los niños?

[Between the atlas and the desks, how attentive and graceful the girls are. They merge with the blue lines, the little seas like flowing locks of the geographical maps.
Each time they recited a letter, the children's singing circle would whirl. I would point to the rose of an *a,* the budding iris of the *l*...
From what island, from what tree, from what source comes this cascade of shining stars, children?]

Carmen Conde, 'Escuela' (1934)

Opening a collection dedicated to her first child — a girl named María del Mar, stillborn — Carmen Conde's poem 'Escuela' posed a question shared by artists, writers, and scientists of the early twentieth century: who *were* children, and how might society adapt to their intellectual, physical, and personal development?[1] Equating the boundless mysteries of the world's seas with the inner depths of the children before her, Carmen Conde Abellán (1907–96) questioned that which was, and remains, an enigma. In the narrator's tracing of letters on blackboard, one sees, hears, and feels the chalk of the board, the curving grace of the letters, and their sonic representation reverberating from the body of each child. With a blend of fascination, nostalgia, and wonder, these lines form part of a larger collection, *Júbilos: poemas de niños, rosas, animales, máquinas y vientos* [Jubilations: Poems of Children, Roses, Animals, Machines, and Winds] (1934) that drew together remembered sights and sensations of Conde's childhood in Melilla with her first-hand experiences as a committed teacher and pedagogue. Building upon such texts, the present book shows how literature, art, philosophy, and science embraced a secular ideal of early twentieth-century Spanish humanism through the 'figure of the child' and, critically, an interest in the living and vital child, in movement, play, and constant states of change. It asks how and why such intimate examinations and portrayals of childhood held fascination and within what larger sphere of knowledge-building they acted. As I will argue, through representations of children's developing humanity, reformers drew upon children's physical, mental, and spiritual selves to argue for a primary engagement with others and the world.

Júbilos stands as a prime example of collaboration between three female members of a transatlantic avant-garde, with Conde's poems interspersed by simple line drawings by Argentinian artist Norah Borges (1901–98) (Fig. I.1) and a prologue written by Chilean poet Gabriela Mistral (1889–1957). Mistral's introduction described Conde's work as an effort to usher her growing child gently into a harsh world, ensconced in the sounds and sights of childhood.[2] According to Mistral, Conde was a woman whose teachings had yet to be blunted by dry pedagogical theories, whose words possessed the raw power to evoke the extremes of the child's imagination. She stood as the embodiment of that quality most sought in the standard-bearers of a new, modern education, namely an embrace of humanity itself, enacted through empathy, vitality, and direct sensation: 'Españolísima en este aspecto, nos trae enseguida a la lengua el adjetivo que más estimamos en un elogio: el de humana' [Supremely Spanish in this respect, she embodies that adjective we most esteem in an homage: human].[3] Within Conde's 'human' or humane gaze upon the world, the reader encountered the people, children, and adults that made up an intimate mental geography of her childhood, and in turn, an evolving Spain.

With attention to the inner experience of childhood, works such as Conde's brought an aesthetic lens to bear on a transnational, but also particularly national, project of literary and cultural humanism among the avant-garde. From Joaquín Sorolla's (1863–1923) lively painting of his infant daughter *Elena a los cinco meses* [Elena at Five Months] (1895) and his iconic images of children running and playing on the beach, to works such as *Niño con paloma* [Child with Dove] (1901) by Pablo Picasso (1881–1973), the fresh illustrations by Fernando Marco of child and donkey in the beloved *Platero y yo* [Platero and I] of poet Juan Ramón Jiménez (1881–1958), or even private sketches philosopher Miguel de Unamuno y Jugo (1864–1936) made of his own children, societal interest in childhood was aligned with personal and artistic engagement with it. These sources suggest productive tensions between literal and figurative representation, naturalism, and abstraction, contrasts that were amply raised in essays, books, literature, and pedagogical tracts. A canvas by Joaquín Torres García (1874–1949), for instance, a Catalan-Uruguayan teacher, artist, toymaker, and long-time teacher at the experimental Colegio Mont D'Or outside Barcelona (1907–14), sensitively depicts his wife and child (Fig. I.2), serving as a visual complement to the abstract, cutting-edge constructivist children's toys which became key to his larger experimental legacy. As in Norah Borges's delicate drawings of children, their hands, biscuits, games, and curls (Fig. I.1), one finds in a range of both text and image a fascination with children's physical and spiritual integrity, their inscrutability and beckoning humanity.

As *Humanizing Childhood* suggests, for a diverse range of teachers, philosophers, and scientists in early-twentieth century Spain, pedagogy served as a platform for larger, existential arguments about human nature, integrity, and development. Together, these concerns formed what schoolteacher Rafael Verdier (b. 1897) called in 1934 a 'pedagogía de base existencial' [an existentially-founded pedagogy], upon

Fig. I.2. Depictions of domestic intimacy, such as Torres García's of his wife and infant son, served as a counterbalance to quantitative analyses of childhood growth.
Source: Joaquín Torres García, *Manolita y Horacio* (1924), oil on cardboard, 60 × 36.5 cm. Courtesy of the Museo Torres García.

a base of childhood conceived as the core of the self.[4] Diverse voices sought to
formalize through transformed, 'humanized' education new responses to frustrations
expressed in literary works such as Miguel de Unamuno's *Amor y pedagogía* (1902)
and Pío Baroja's *El árbol de la ciencia* (1911). They promoted the enlivening of
education, manifesting in methods based on play, nature study, child art, and open-
air education: various approaches towards developing the child's physical, mental,
and spiritual personhood.[5] The pedagogue and socialist politician Rodolfo Llopis
(1895–1983) described such innovations as a necessary 'humanization' of education
in post-war societies seeking to revolutionize quotidian norms and practices. After
the First World War's 'acceleration' of socio-political change, it was incumbent
upon the school to serve anew the interests of a 'new Humanity': 'Había que
modificarla, transformarla, humanizarla' [It was necessary to modify [the school],
transform it, humanize it].[6]

In this way, reformers' early twentieth-century celebration of the child acted,
for a vanguard of both Catholic and secular reformers, as a stable force within
larger dynamics of instability. Questions of co-education, the hierarchy of the
family and state, and the right of the church to educate and instruct proved divisive
and ultimately unbridgeable questions around which schisms in education policy
developed through the early twentieth century. Yet representations of the child also
reflected larger concerns about the role of education as it related to the shaping not
only of national subjects and liberal citizens, but also of individuals within rapidly
modernizing scientific and philosophical contexts. As this work argues, in accord
with broader tenets of the New Education movement, an early twentieth-century
search for unity found expression across ideological lines in diverse celebrations
of the child as multitudinous, ever-changing, yet radically whole. The living and
indivisible nature of childhood itself came to embody a broader social and scientific
impulse towards the unified, the 'catholic', and the total. Such a discourse took
root via both Krausist and Catholic precedents, with education 'ascribed almost
mystical powers' by early twentieth-century liberal reformers, from regenerationist
work to the Second Republic.[7] Moving towards a transcendent view of children's
developing humanity, this book reads the imagined 'figure of the child' as a source
and generator of such foundational ideas of human value and growth.

Forecast as the 'century of the child', the twentieth century reconfigured
childhood itself.[8] Scholars have looked towards evolutionary, developmental, and
other trends in the natural and human sciences to understand why children, and
childhood as such, became such a central concern to European and indeed global
societies during the late nineteenth and early twentieth centuries. Weaving together
these threads, this work seeks to bring a cultural lens to such preoccupations.[9]
Within a cultural-scientific nexus, it applies a specific lens, that of holistic sciences
and thought, which were introduced as having the potential to infuse needed
vitality into pedagogy. For as intellectuals focused on the child, they sought to
redefine the limits of science itself. They looked to models and language that
could give life to stale and atomistic models, relying on ubiquitous dialectics of the
part and the whole, dispersion and unity, multiplicity and emergence to underpin
descriptions of growth and development.

Thus while artists and poets sought to depict children and their world in ever more sensitive, intimate, and phenomenologically-informed ways, a bevy of experts and pedagogues considered not only *what* children were and how they understood the world, but how best to nurture, educate, and 'humanize' society's youngest members. Moving from a Catholic view of the human towards phenomenological interpretations of growth and integrity, in the words of philosopher Joaquim Xirau (1895–1946), each individual united the 'más alto organismo natural, el cuerpo humano, con la conciencia racional de sí mismo, en la plenitud del espíritu' [highest natural organism, the human body, with rational self-consciousness, in the plenitude of the spirit].[10] Within this new mode of 'antropología filosófica' a creative, holistic, and vital form of education was enacted.[11] Such representations formed part of a transnational network of educational reform, what Thomas Popkewitz has called the 'cosmopolitanism' of early twentieth-century pedagogy, focused on values of universalism and human agency.[12] Against rigid measures of testing, standardization, and quantitative value, against the alleged mechanization of a society, the arguments made by early twentieth-century reformers for a fully-embodied and vital education were critical — and remain all the more so today. Debates relied on the authoritative language of modern science, yet no one discipline could encompass the complexity of life; pedagogy was frequently posed as standing between a science and an art.

Yet education was also *the* problem of a modernizing nation. At the start of the twentieth century, Spain had the lowest rates of school attendance and highest rates of illiteracy in Europe. Spain's Ley Moyano (1857) established the first formal regulation of national education, but frustration about its inefficacies grew amidst regenerationist rhetoric around 1898. Subsequent reforms were driven by a complex network of actors, from the newly-created Ministerio de Instrucción y Bellas Artes (1900) to regional governments and civic organizations.[13] As cities grew, civic organizations such as Madrid's Gota de Leche (1904) sought to address child mortality and urban health through outreach, undertaking local initiatives of childcare, lactation, and maternal education.[14] Efforts were propelled by a heterogeneous array of doctors, eugenicists, sexual reformers, and anarchists, as well as teachers, inspectors, and pedagogical officers who sought interventions in school furniture and architecture, diets and schedules, and the socio-medicalization of children's education.[15]

As a regenerationist project, the health of children and nation were critically connected through open-air schools and excursionist movements. National research institutes and laboratories also professionalized and advanced the nation's international scholarly standing, as reflected in cultural and literary production, with child study forming part of a conscious process of scientific engagement.[16] From 1907, for instance, the Junta para Ampliación de Estudios y Investigación Científica (JAE) began sending promising Spanish teachers and pedagogues to train and study in schools and sites across Europe and further afield. More than a quarter of its total awards fell in fields of education and pedagogy, with grantees visiting schools in the fold of the international New Education movement: what became known as the *Escuela Nueva* in Spanish, *Escola Nova* in Catalan. From

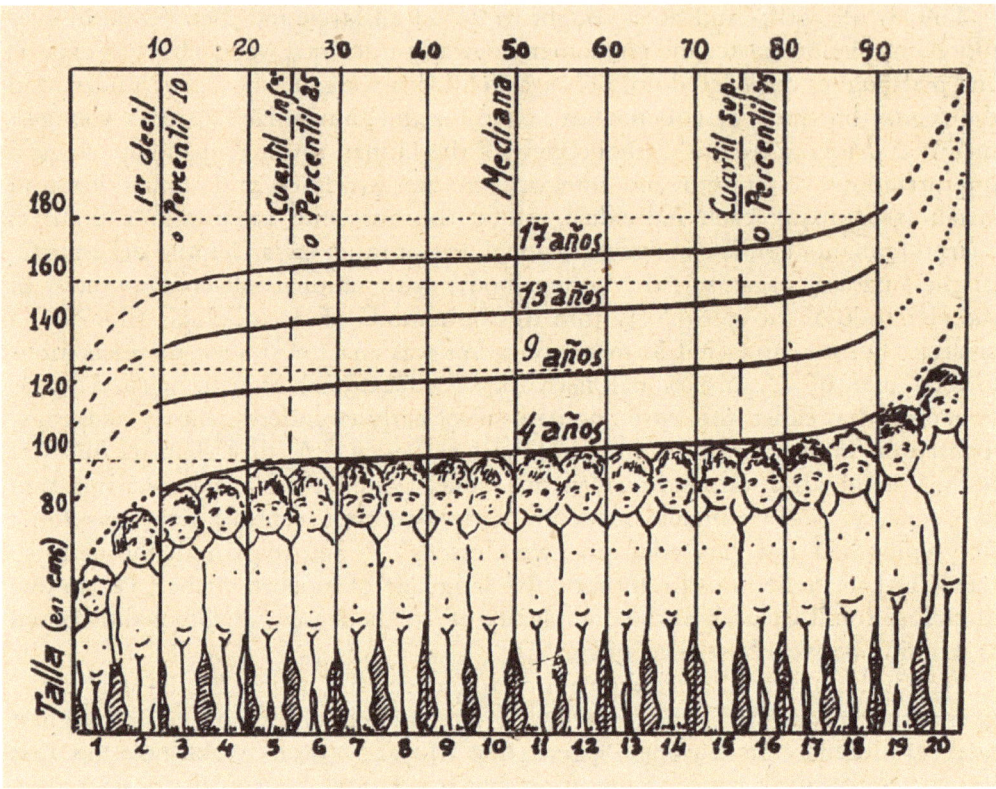

FIG. I.3. A 1936 growth chart visualizing height percentiles at age four.
Source: Rodolfo Tomás y Samper, *La psicometría en la escuela primaria* (Técnica de
paidometría) (Madrid: Editorial Instituto Samper, 1936), p. 112.

1907 to 1923, the JAE funded over 700 Spaniards to observe and participate in the
work of kindergartens, primary schools, universities, and conferences abroad, in
a concerted project of modernization and scientific investment.[17] Based in large
part on the scholarship of those who studied abroad, from the *fin de siècle* until the
mid-twentieth century, countless probes were adapted from international sources to
measure children's health, growth, and development. As along international lines,
childhood began to be rigorously defined and analysed through both quantitative
physical charts and qualitative forms of psychological, intellectual, moral, and
'spiritual' measurement (Figs. I.3 and I.4). Drawing upon temporal scales and trans-
disciplinary fields of analysis, diverse indices marked comparative growth of both
individual children as well as the 'Spanish child'.

In both a cognitive and intellectual sense, thus, child study constituted a
transnational project of knowledge-building in Spain as significant as any other
domain of 'cultural trafficking'.[18] Entire disciplines sprang up that looked to
develop institutions and expertise, from *paidología*, or child study, to *psicometría*,
mental measurement, to *puericultura*, namely the care of the infant and young

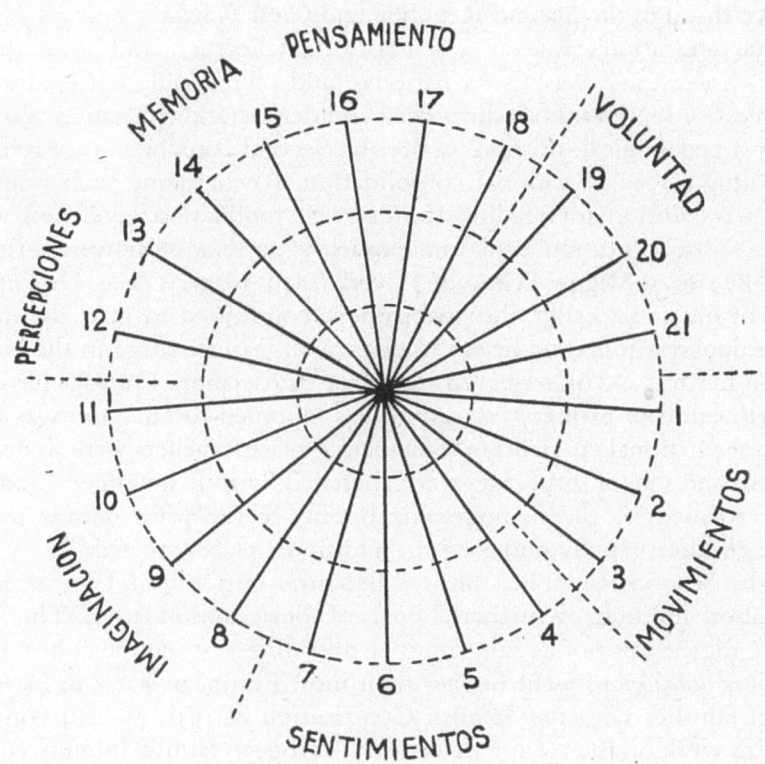

Fig. 52.—Representación gráfica en estrella de un perfil psicológico. (Tipo Lasoursky.)

FIG. I.4. An adapted 1935 personality profile by Russian psychologist Aleksandr Lazursky
(1874–1917), mapping degrees of perception, memory, thought, will, imagination,
emotion, and movement in individual children.
Source: C. Sánchez Freijó, *Paidología e higiene escolar* (Inspección médico escolar)
(Madrid: Editorial Reus, 1935), p. 277.

child.[19] Bridging disciplinary fields, child study was immediately practical. For
one, it constituted a form of disciplinary professionalization through international
engagement, as in the rise and adaptation of intelligence testing. Pedagogues
turned to international models and interdisciplinary collaborations. Works by
leading figures abroad such as Alfred Binet, William James, Henri Bergson, John
Dewey, Sigmund Freud, and Charlotte Bühler were translated and synthesized.
Through this process, a constellation of ideas uniting psychology, the natural and
physical sciences, and philosophy was integrated by a cross-section of Spaniards
active in education, governance, and culture. It was within this context that a rich
literature of phenomenological, scientifically-oriented pedagogical work arose,
with flourishing journals such as the *Revista de Pedagogía* from 1922 and a corps of

teachers — including Conde — who matriculated and trained during the 1920s and would serve through the Second Republic and Civil War.

Alongside education's role as a scientific, intellectual, and social project of renovation, however, it was also a national, and increasingly nationalist, project. Across successive regimes, both dictatorial and democratic, education was a project — literally a pedagogical 'mission' under the Second Republic — of redefinition, with schooling a tool of national consolidation. Recognizing such priorities is a necessary precondition for reading the cultural production generated within its constraints. That education took on explicitly nationalist purposes from 1923, following the rise of Miguel Primo de Rivera (1870–1930), is clear. During the first two years of his dictatorship, the government committed to raise the number of teachers in public schools and began to enact a large-scale surge in the building of new schools in rural and underserved areas. Yet, as Alejandro Quiroga has observed, the nationalization of primary education was 'doomed to fail', and was only ever partial. A 1914 national curriculum remained in place, teachers were underpaid and overworked, and school inspectors were alienated by military supervision. Schools remained crowded, as the demographic booms of the prior decade meant that school-age children rapidly outpaced the additional places created.[20]

Under the Second Republic, meanwhile, rural outreach and the expansion of mass education and literacy furthered goals of social consolidation. The Republic, best known for the force of its campaigns against illiteracy and the cultural visibility of its *misiones pedagógicas*, went further than most European states in its reach into the lives of families with the Spanish Constitution of 1931, as Paul Ginsborg has argued in his work on the twentieth-century European family. It removed Catholic teaching from schools in a zealous separation of church and state and granted the right to equal marriage and divorce. Embracing the 1924 Geneva Declaration of the Rights of the Child, the Constitution affirmed children's rights as individuals, clarified that parents had legal responsibilities towards children and made the state the final safeguard for the sick, elderly, and mothers and children. For the first time, the family itself came under the 'salvaguardia especial', the explicit care, of the state.[21]

Navigating such historical realities, this book recognizes that evolving social realities circumscribed the lives of the children and teachers who animate this study. Indeed, historian of education María del Mar del Pozo Andrés has written of a generation of teachers elected by 'circunstancia', in homage to the towering influence exerted upon them by philosopher José Ortega y Gasset (1883–1955).[22] Educated at Spain's top teacher-training institutes and abroad, educators of Conde's milieu rose to their vocation during a period of rapid professionalization during the Second Republic toward, in many cases, significant educational leadership. Despite gendered limitations, female educators propelled major initiatives, from the early work of Josefa Segovia's Residencia Universitaria Femenina (1914) or María de Maeztu's Residencia de Señoritas (1915) to co-educational projects and school leadership.[23] Figures such as Margarita Comas, Regina Lago, Justa Freire, Concepción Sáiz and others who will appear in this book studied abroad with JAE funding and published original research. They trained in equal numbers as male colleagues at Spain's top institution for teacher training and school inspection, the Escuela de Estudios Superiores de Magisterio, from the late 1910s until the 1930s.[24] Nevertheless, questions of gender, class, and urban/rural geographies indubitably shaped their careers. The social contexts in which protagonists lived, learned, and taught are a critical reminder of the concrete realities behind abstracted discussions of 'el niño' as a neutral subject.

Most broadly, by focusing on humanistic education as a generative force, this book itself constitutes a prehistory of the so-called 'figure of the child' that has in recent years occupied Spanish cultural studies. A current of recovery and re-writing has long been present in literary and cinematic depictions of Spanish childhoods, in which explorations of memory, trauma, and imagination employ the child's interiority as a central frame to interrogate historical memory. Regardless of medium, child protagonists have served time and again as a central lens for examining Civil War and Francoist experiences and post-war trauma. A nexus of childhood, fantasy, and memory is perhaps most famously visible in films from the late Francoist era such as *El espíritu de la colmena* [The Spirit of the Beehive] (dir. Victor Erice, 1973) or *Cría cuervos* [Raise Ravens] (dir. Carlos Saura, 1976), as well as a wide range of twentieth-century films analysed by scholars such as Sarah Wright.[25] Within a literary frame, the works of writers such as Ana María Matute (1925–2014) and notable contemporaries use the structure of childhood to imagine and recover the past. Beyond novels and children's stories, Matute's stories and drawings uncovered from her own childhood have brought her literary works into sharper focus, revealing first-hand the imaginative flights of a child growing up during the Republic and Civil War.[26] Central to each of these representational approaches, among others, is a phenomenologically-attuned vision of childhood. Whether in autobiographical or fictionalized works, both contemporary and retrospective depictions develop from the understanding that a fully embodied childhood is foundational to understanding the world in which one lives, writes, and remembers.

Educating the Whole Child: From Krausism to Totalitarianism

In a 1933 article in *El Sol*, Unamuno observed that the 'culto al niño' [worship of the child] had become society's 'más alto oficio religioso' [highest religious office]. Within a new Republic, the very idea of childhood dominated all else: 'Ahora nos obsesiona el niño en esta España, al parecer renovada. ¿Cómo la sentirán dentro de veinte o más años los que hoy tienen en ella nueve o diez?' [Now we are obsessed with the child, in this apparently renovated Spain of ours. How will those who today are nine or ten years old understand our nation, twenty or more years hence?'.[27] While the official secularization of education made this a politically trenchant observation, it also pointed to his consciousness of the wider cultural transformation of childhood. As Unamuno implored, any cultural investment in this abstract 'child' must also involve a responsibility towards the *almas* [souls] of individual children, from the rural children he saw along roadsides to the thousands of children in a Latin America 'populated' by 'Madre España'. Voices such as Unamuno's filtered national transformation through lenses of childhood and youth, as Leslie Harkema has shown through the frame of adolescence, those periods of energy, struggle, and transformation in which both adult and nation were wrought.[28]

At the base of this turbulence was a uniting fascination with the child as a coherent, enigmatic, and evolving human being. As this book argues, a cross-section of pedagogues sought to develop authentically 'Spanish' pedagogical humanisms that would shape *almas* — variously defined and developed — alongside bodies and minds. While countless systems over time have claimed humanistic ideals, the challenge according to historian of education Alfonso Capitán Díaz was to evaluate how they enacted them. For him, four qualities underpinned pedagogical humanism: first, a development of identity, in interior and reciprocal frames; second, a focus on community, through an openness to the world; third, creativity, the ability to imagine new ideals and practices and to realize them through integral education; and fourth, a sense of historicity, or an awareness of intellectual inheritances and their re-invention in the present. If diverse pedagogical humanisms have all sought 'una forma de ser y de vivir con dignidad' [a way of being and living with dignity], the goal of reading these in a Spanish context is to examine related practices within their critical historical and social milieux.[29]

Most visibly, a consciously new approach to education founded on the interplay of body, mind, and spirit was paradigmatic of Spain's Institución Libre de Enseñanza (ILE), founded on 29 October 1876 by professors dismissed from the Universidad Central de Madrid following their refusal to sign a profession of Catholic faith. While its foundation was decisively secular, its language and rhetoric aligned with the work of a wide swath of reformers concerned with the spiritual and transcendent implications of their educational endeavour.[30] From its start, the ILE built on a philosophy of *krausismo* — after Karl Christian Friedrich Krause (1781–1832) — introduced to Spain by Julián Sanz del Río following travels in Germany in 1843.[31] Reconciling head and heart, metaphysical and divine traditions into a system of 'racionalismo armónico', Spanish Krausism posited the unity of humanity and nature with a transcendent, unknowable spirit. It emphasized the social function of state and community and the interconnectedness of nature and knowledge. God became the uniting principle between nature and spirit, transcending both.

Celebrating individual communion with the world, foundational figures such as Francisco Giner de los Ríos (1839–1915) emphasized liberty of experience and natural contact through their teaching. He and others led summer programmes to beaches and mountains from the late nineteenth century and advanced a humanistic thread of teaching alongside earnest support of scientific modernization and internationalization. The Residencia de Estudiantes (1910) constructed on Madrid's green northern edge, and its associated primary and secondary school, the Instituto-Escuela (1918), took advantage of clear air and open space to join outer to inner formation.[32] Characterizing the ILE's principles as a synthesis of Krausist philosophy and Fröbelian pedagogy, Rosa Bruno-Jofré and Gonzalo Jover have suggested that these influences were 'synthesized in the formula *education of the human being as human*', developing towards a 'transcendent vision of human-hood'.[33] Isabel Pérez-Villanueva has described the environment of the ILE as one of harmonious heterogeneity, marked by the Institution's 'concepción global y unitaria' [global and unitary conception] of the convergence of education and science.[34] The *institucionistas'* work built on Krausist rhetoric rooted in a broader Christian tradition, magnified by a ubiquitous scientific discourse of holistic thought. For the scholar Adolfo Posada (1860–1944), writing in the mid-1920s, a Krausist convergence of unity and spirit allowed one to understand the developing mind, body, and spirit as a unified whole, as in a system which:

> Expresa un todo cuyas partes están y se mantienen encadenadas entre sí, no un conjunto de elementos distintos que coexisten, un agregado fragmentario e incoherente, sino un todo cuyos miembros se penetran y entrelazan íntimamente y se soportan entre sí, y existen el uno en, con y para el otro, y cada uno en, con y para el todo.[35]

> [Expresses a whole whose parts are and remain mutually connected, not a conjunction of different elements that coexist, a fragmentary and incoherent aggregate, but a whole whose members interpenetrate and interlace and intimately support one another, and exist in, with, and for the other, and each one in, with, and for the whole.]

Such was the goal not only of Christian teaching but also of modern science and thought, influenced by neo-Kantian idealism, phenomenology and vitalist impulses. Within the educational field, pedagogues aimed to build the body, mind, and spirit of the child, 'desarrollando todas sus energías, lo mismo las físicas, que las intelectuales y morales' [developing all their energies, physical as well as intellectual and moral].[36]

To this end, reformers across the ideological spectrum promoted integral education in diverse forms. As early as 1864 a Valencian priest had allegedly organized rudimentary mountain colonies for children, as Andrés Manjón (1846–1923) would do in Granada from 1886, while the Krausist educator and art historian Manuel Bartolomé Cossío (1857–1935) initiated a *colonia* in Miraflores de la Sierra, Madrid from 1885. Over the following decades, dozens of regional associations spread the vision of open-air schooling. As cities grew and fears of social degeneration rose, Spain's *colonias escolares* became an early and powerful force in nascent urban efforts towards improving health and welfare, bringing underprivileged children to the seaside or mountains during summer months. Examples included Eugenio B. de Mingo's Jardines de la Infancia, Manuel Tolosa Latour's Inspección Medico-Escolar and its seaside sanatorium in Santander, as well as others supported by local governments in Barcelona, Palma de Mallorca, Santiago, Oviedo, León, Logroño, Valladolid, Badajoz, Málaga, and elsewhere.[37] The international 'active school' movement found explicit expression in *institucionistas* and other New Educational reformers for physical activity and excursions to the urban-cultural attractions of cities as well as the forested or marine environs on their outskirts (Fig. I.5).

In Catalonia, *noucentista* regenerationism joined with neoclassical aesthetic values of light, balance, and harmony within the development of a strong and renovated public school system and leadership in educational thought and reform. Early

FIG. I.5. Children in an open-air school in the hills outside Madrid.
Source: Pedro Roy Herreros, *Planes escolares de la Villa y Corte: parques infantiles,*
excursiones escolares, escuelas al aire libre, colonias escolares y plan económico
(Madrid: Imprenta Municipal, 1929), p. 87.

projects benefited from the support of a nationalist Lliga Regionalista, which
supported the work of pedagogues such as Maria Montessori (1870–1952), who
taught summer schools and established schools in Catalonia from 1915.[38] Barcelona
and Catalonia as a whole soon established themselves at the vanguard of pedagogical
innovation. Significant examples of new school methods and architecture such
as the Escola del Bosc (1914) on Montjuïc and Escola del Mar (1921) in Parque
Guinardó, Barceloneta, encapsulated the reach and ambition of these efforts. Yet
as with linguistic and other national advancement projects, education was often
caught in political crossfire, with drastic centralist restrictions placed on regional
educational organization, funding, and language instruction particularly after the
rise of Primo de Rivera.[39]

Anarchist education constituted a significant precursor in interconnected
conceptions of holism and the 'integral' in mainstream reform education. It was
in Barcelona, for instance, that the rational, 'modern school' movement of integral
education was launched, serving as a beacon for reformers worldwide. Educationalist
Francesc Ferrer i Guardia (1859–1909) opened the Escola Moderna in Barcelona in
1901, seeking from an anarchist framework to promote the physical and mental
health of children from all social classes. Ferrer sought to reconstruct society from
the base up, providing 'rational' education to boys and girls based on a scientific
conception of their physical, artistic, and intellectual development. Followed by
his 1908 establishment of the Lliga Internacional per l'Educació Racional de la

Infância, his work furthered a wave of 'modern schools' the world over. Despite its arguably polar political reception and goals, anarchist education was a key piece in a tradition of integral, or holistic, education in Spain.[40] Drawing on the notion of 'integral' education put forward by Mikhail Bakunin (1814–76) and pedagogical thought from Johann Friedrich Herbart (1776–1841) to Jean-Jacques Rousseau (1712–78), Friedrich Fröbel (1782–1852) to Paul Robin (1837–1912), the Modern School sought to bring out the child's total aesthetic, scientific, rational, and ethical formation through an engagement with questions of moral judgment, justice, and solidarity.

This view of integral education applied not simply to the internal coherence and expansiveness of children's own development, but also to their roles as individuals within a wider social world. Proponents of integral education insisted that schooling should be available *integrally*, to children of all walks of life. As with the 'vitality' and transcendence sought by later educators on phenomenological lines, the principles on which Ferrer and others drew reflected a larger search for meaning and unity, as in anarchists' embrace of spiritualism, a supposed cosmovision of self and universe.[41] Despite common principles of secularism, co-education, and social uplift, Ferrer was largely marginalized or ignored as a model by New Education reformers in Spain, linked to a history of reactionary political violence and a governing fear of radical anarchism. Yet he was celebrated as a martyr beyond Spain after his arrest and execution by the state after the onset of the *Semana Tràgica* in 1909, rapidly becoming internationally among the very most central heroes of rational, reformist, and anarchist education. Catholic and secular alike, Spanish New Education reformers overwhelmingly tended to look outward to the modernity of Western European psychologists and pedagogues or internally and farther back, celebrating Spanish Catholic tradition and Neo-Scholastic antecedents.[42]

In calling for New Educational reforms nationally, educationalists of both conservative and liberal leanings drew upon a Spanish humanistic tradition which was key to their own historiographies of integral education. Leading *institucionista*, New Education pedagogue Lorenzo Luzuriaga (1889–1959) signalled the inherently humanist character of Krausist education when he argued that Spain's turn to new pedagogy had reactivated the 'auténtica tradición hispánica' of Juan Luis Vives (1493–1540), Antonio de Nebrija (1441–1522), and Francisco Suárez (1548–1617).[43] As educators looked to pre-existing Hispanic models, Vives's foundational writings on the structures and social bases of education and his elucidation of the boundaries of mind, soul, and passions in *De anima et vita* (1538) inspired a wave of studies by pedagogues throughout the early twentieth century. Reformers drew on Vives's and others' legacies, articulating the broad social aims and higher ideals of education and its elucidation of a psychological view of perception and learning, synthesizing these works in turn with regenerationist and ILE-driven initiatives.

Chief among Spanish precedents bridging Catholic tradition with 'progressive' pedagogies was the aforementioned Manjón, a priest and law professor who from 1886 operated open-air schools in Granada's Sacromonte (Fig. I.6). Contemporaneous coverage of Manjón's schools documented their focus on the child in his social and

FIG. I.6. A late nineteenth-cenury music class held outdoors at Andrés Manjón's
progressive Catholic school in Granada, a model for subsequent reformers.
Source: 'Escuelas del Ave María en el Camino del Sacro Monte de Granada',
La Ilustración Artística, 18.922 (1899), 555–58 (p. 557).

personal world. His work put forth a universalist message of inclusion of the poor
and marginalized, with many of the schools' pupils drawn from the area's Roma
population. Classes took place largely outdoors and incorporated music, art, and
physical activity in an effort to stimulate not just the mind, but all aspects of the
self. In the words of Manjón, 'Educar es completar hombres' [To educate is to
complete men].[44] For scholar Remedios Sánchez, Manjón's conception of integral
education was not opposed to *institucionista* reforms but rather a flourishing of
it. The Manjonian approach moved from family life to schools as a supportive,
not corrective measure: aligning with, scaffolding, and building upon the child's
development. Relying on an Aristotelian notion of the human as both rational and
animal, *cuerpo y alma,* he sought the development not just of the mind but also of
physical, artistic, scientific, and moral qualities.[45]

Such a convergence facilitated a trinity of educational thought — mind, body,
and spirit — within non-confessional landscapes of reform. Manjón's pedagogy
would be celebrated during the early twentieth century by both liberal and
Catholic reformers, a recuperation that goes some way towards suggesting how
humanistic concerns were inherited and reconfigured in diverse spheres. In both its
fundamental principles and its commemoration through the twentieth century, the
work of Manjón and the Escuelas del Ave María drew on both liberal and national-
Catholic sympathies. During the first two decades of the century, the figure of
Manjón was used to argue for a Spanish precedent in civic initiatives for open,
innovative methods and outdoor school spaces. Under the Second Republic and

during the Francoist era, Manjón's example was used to celebrate Spain's primacy in educational innovation.[46]

Catholic reformers mirrored language and pedagogical bases shared by their New Educational colleagues, through defences of science, modernity, and the vitality of human lives. Figures such as the priest Pedro Poveda Castroverde (1874–1936) continued the work modelled by Manjón, furthering an intellectually progressive Catholic education. Poveda founded a series of schools for children in impoverished communities in the caves of Guadix from 1897. Later, in pamphlets such as the *Ensayo de un proyecto pedagógico para la fundación de una institución católica de enseñanza* (1911), Poveda advocated for scientific, human-centred Catholic educational initiatives. Partnering with Josefa Segovia (1897–1957), fresh from ILE-led training at Madrid's Escuela Superior de Magisterio, he co-founded the Institución Teresiana in 1911 to support young educators and fostered a network of teacher-training centres, culminating in the opening of the Residencia Universitaria Femenina under Segovia's direction in 1914. The first higher-education institution for women in Spain, the Residencia looked to strengthen women's social action through intellectual, pedagogical, and scientific training.[47] Reflecting both Manjonian and *institucionista* influences, Poveda articulated the elevation of life through faith and education. 'Yo quiero, sí, vidas humanas,' he described this ideal, but lives which were also 'vidas de Dios', embodying holiness through human form. Only through such a twinning of humanity and faith could one become 'humano con el humanismo verdad' [human in the true sense of humanism].[48] His pedagogy did not admit a secular humanism, as successive models studied in this book patently would. Yet in its concern for the human root of education, such integrative and integral models built upon the child's developing humanity through holistic frames.

As these examples demonstrate, an early twentieth-century elevation of the 'human' through education was not merely a project of secular or Catholic, liberal or conservative camps. Rather, it was an impulse whose recuperation points towards common questions and contested aspirations. As Capitán Díaz has argued, humanist ideals manifested in two directions: through the *institucionista* movement, leading to the Republican 'escuela única' push for national, standardized, public schools for all, but also through an explicitly 'Christian' or 'social-Catholic' humanism that guided and shaped — in very different ways — the post-war 'escuela nacional católica'.[49] These alignments and disjunctions in both rhetoric and practice matter, possessing the power to shift and nuance histories of science and society. Scholarship on post-war, Francoist education has understandably tended to focus upon its undeniable ruptures, the issues that decisively split and fractured society, and the spread of national-Catholic, authoritarian, patriotic, and centrist practices.

Yet there is also a growing strand of scholarship that reads pedagogical modernity as a shared tradition in which Catholic pedagogues actively sought scientific and pedagogical modernization.[50] Transnational movements and methods visibly influenced the rhetoric and practices of a wide range of educationalists. To a surprising extent, New Educationalists' embrace of transcendent, spiritual notions of children's development were grudgingly approved as an alternative to pure secularism.[51] Social historian Till Kössler, for instance, has shown how Catholic educators during the early twentieth century carried forward scientific interest in child–centred international pedagogical reforms, while historians of education María del Mar del Pozo Andrés and Sjaak Braster have demonstrated a process of reinvention of seemingly progressive principles during early Francoism.[52] After the Civil War, pedagogues denounced New Educational methods born of politically incorrect 'liberalism' as part of an undesirable wave of 'modernismo pedagógico'. Yet, as is briefly explored in Chapter 1, many of these 'modernist' ideas, such as mental 'globalization' and the Decroly method, were celebrated and reclaimed within the very books that denounced their political contexts. Such shifts in the political uses of pedagogical modernism demonstrate the need for a closer reading of the concepts employed by educators, including contested lenses of humanism, holism, universality, and totality.

Radical Wholes: Integrating Holism into Education and Society

Throughout the early twentieth century, notable literary and artistic works used rhetorical frameworks of holism to argue for a new scientific framework. Internationally, 'holistic' education was described as the child of humanism, arising from a yearning for post–First World War unity and manifesting in global movements, whether political (the League of Nations), linguistic (Esperanto), or scientific (Gestalt psychology, post-vitalist biology, and early physical field theory).[53] What each of these movements had in common was an aspiration to a higher, binding notion of universality. How did such images and imaginaries converge and diverge in child study as rhetoric translated into educational practice? What terms were employed to further a view of the child as radically whole? And most critically, as reformers posed rhetorical shifts from science to society, from individual to collective, how did Spain move from a 'catholic' ideal of human development towards an aspiration of universality, indeed totality, of culture and education?

Such a merging of terms has been observed not only in holistic models of education, but also in fundamental scientific concepts across secular and Catholic contexts.[54] Spain's early twentieth century saw a struggle to define the tenets of society. Republicans, Pamela Radcliff has argued, articulated the strongest cultural vision, based upon the 'secularization of public symbols and education' and the 'creation of competing civic rituals, practices and associations' within existing fields.[55] A key point, as this book argues, was the fight to renew science with spiritual vitality through familiar frames, including Spanish humanistic and holistic thought. The essential aspect of human life was the integration of parts within a greater whole, as Catalan pedagogue and philosopher Joan Roura i Parella (1897–1983) suggested from exile in 1940, following a decade of advocating for a Spanish pedagogical framework built upon a humanistic understanding of science. As he wrote, 'Diferenciación e integración del cuerpo, del alma y del espíritu que a su vez se integra en un todo: el hombre. El todo es uno y las partes son a su vez un todo' [Differentiation and integration of the body, the soul and the spirit, which in turn become a whole: man. The whole is one and the parts are, in their turn, whole].[56] Theological and philosophical rhetoric had long built upon the relationship between the part and the whole, but by the 1920s, newly articulated holistic approaches to the natural and physical sciences explicitly sought to bridge the gap between positivist inquiry and human experience.[57] Scientific and religious views suggested a fundamental convergence. South African Monsignor Frederick Charles Kolbe wrote in a Catholic elaboration of holism in 1928, for instance, that 'every human being is a unique *totum* or whole [...]. And the whole is not merely the sum of its parts'.[58] In essence, such a declaration of integral becoming echoed rhetoric put forward by reformist pedagogues looking to absorb and integrate currents of phenomenological theory.

The twentieth-century origins of the term 'holism' have been attributed to Jan Smuts's 1926 *Holism and Evolution*, which suggested that every physical whole involves a total 'field', just as all objects and organisms exist within a total physical and temporal circumstance. The 'holistic-humanist' view went beyond the self, such that, in the words of St Augustine, 'one loving spirit sets another on fire'.[59] For the South African educationalist Theodore J. Haarhoff, a holistic education sought to foster the mind's vitality, for it was only in imagining a 'whole' that 'the mind itself becomes living, instinct with imagination'.[60] Yet the two terms point to radically different readings of society. When Eugenio d'Ors wrote in 1919 of man's 'deseo de ser completo, su sed de totalidad' [desire to be complete, his thirst for totality], an ambivalent scope remained open.[61] In one of the first Spanish uses of 'holism' as a term, the journalist Fabio wrote in 1934 that the term differed from 'totalitarismo' only in its context: 'El totalitarismo de que se habla entre españoles y el holismo difieren en que el holismo es puramente filosófico [...]. El totalitarismo es político-social' [That totalitarianism of which Spaniards speak and holism differ in that holism is purely philosophical [...]. Totalitarianism is socio-political].[62]

This statement began to interrogate the political implications of a formally posed view of both science and society. Could holism become a potentially totalitarian point of view? Could an 'atomistic', liberal individualism prove inherently anarchic, chaotic, in a political sphere? As scholars such as Anne Harrington have explored in Germany's turn from an enveloping intellectual context of Goethean and Gestalt holistic thought towards Nazism and a totalitarian *Volk*, the impulses of a societal search for wholeness led directly from chaos towards order. In Spain, where Orteguian notions of the 'masses' gave way to a fascist state, how did representations of holism align with larger impulses towards the total?[63] Just as the twentieth century saw the rise of the 'new man', regenerationist rhetoric shaped portrayals of the developing child. As this book argues, a convergent scientific and social discourse portrayed children as both whole and constituent parts of a larger, dynamic evolution and cultural accretion.

While Spanish educationalists of this period did not call their positions 'holistic' — they used many interrelated terms such as 'integral', 'global', 'total' — a philosophical concept of integral education and the fullness of the human spirit was rooted in the legacy of Spanish reforms outlined above and advanced by contemporaneous phenomenological and scientific influences. More broadly, a holistic rhetoric of society laid the foundation for its application to educational contexts. This process can be seen, for instance, in notions put forward in 1926 by intellectual Fernando de los Ríos (1879–1949), who argued for a new humanism in society focused on the collective, shifting from 'lo humano individual' towards 'lo humano universal'.[64] In educational terms, the journalist Luis Bello toured Spain in 1926, visiting its many underserved and neglected schools and reporting his findings in a series of columns published serially in *El Sol*. In language that lifts from the part to the whole, Bello advocated an aerial, panoramic view of education through a shared understanding of history and memory. Taking an expansive view of nationhood, he urged support for Spain's schools in all their regional diversity:

> Pero hay otro punto de mira, y lo tenemos nosotros. Es la memoria. Aquí unimos las perspectivas. Visión a un tiempo panorámica y cubista. Visión integral [...]. Visión poética, es decir, perfecta. De esta manera podríamos llegar también a entendernos con las diversas Españas; ir dándolas la vuelta para ver dónde tienen unas con otras su ensamblaje, o ir penetrando en ellas profundamente, para hallar que el fondo es el mismo.[65]

> [But there is another point of view, which we ourselves possess. That is memory. Here we unite our many perspectives. A vision which is both panoramic and cubist. An integral vision [...]. A poetic, that is to say, perfect vision. In such a way might we also come to understand the many Spains; to look inward and see where they fit within the assemblage, to penetrate deeply, only to discover they are the same.]

Bello's panoramic view of a federalist, 'diverse' Spain, viewed 'integrally' and within what he called a 'Cubist' vision of Spain, was akin to declarations in poetry and philosophy, from Ortega's *perspectivismo* to the 'perfección' of earthbound plenitude which Jorge Guillén (1893–1984) signalled in his eponymous poem.[66] Despite intervening political upheavals and regime change, an aspiration towards unity filtered into all levels of discourse in the 1920s and 1930s. Unamuno invoked such an amplified vision at a 1933 conference in Madrid, advocating to an audience including Bergson and Marie Curie that societies must unify 'nuestros puntos de vista' [our points of view]. His words extended Bello's panoramic vision of Spain's schools and regionalisms to a global frame, urging the nation to participate in a universal effort beyond the nation: what he called an 'obra de universalización, que es más que internacionalización'.[67] The scale Unamuno and others evoked was vast, but it was to play out on a national and individual level, in the 'globalization' of education and the humanity of the individual child.

Rehumanizing Childhood: Mind, Body, and Spirit

Through converging strands, the following chapters argue that a cross-section of intellectuals during Spain's Silver Age, its *Edad de Plata*, sought to place the child's humanity at the centre of an all-embracing view of individual and societal development. In so doing, this book takes a consciously trinitarian form to interpret the rise of New Education in Spain, namely through successive frames of mind, body, and spirit. Thus in itself an enterprise in holism, if ever partial in reach, such a multifaceted approach looks towards cultural representations which arose from theoretical convergences before the Spanish Civil War. This introduction has proposed various frames of reference for a holistic view of the child, suggesting ways in which Krausist and Catholic traditions merged with educational modernity. The study to follow seeks to bring out the terms by which the child's humanity was argued. By foregrounding reciprocal relationships between adult and child, child and world, it looks towards shifts in how the child was understood, represented, and educated.

Part I, 'Mind', asks how psychologists, intellectuals, and teachers represented European research on children's mental experience and learning through psychological notions of holistic perception, cognition, creativity, and symbolic understanding. Chapter 1, 'Imagining Infancy: Paidology and a Science of the Mind' considers the reception of Gestalt psychology by pedagogues such as Domingo Barnés, and how such perceptual frames influenced long-forgotten reading strategies and theories. Moving from children's interior world towards verbal projections of it, Chapter 2, 'Pure Poetry: The Child and the Avant-Garde', asks how reform-minded teachers worked with the literary avant-garde to further imaginaries of childhood. Analysing contributions by Conde, Guillén, Federico García Lorca, José Bergamín, Zenobia Camprubí, and others, I consider writings on and about childhood verbality as reflections of ongoing literary renovation. Together, these chapters analyse ways in which avant-garde experimentation and social efforts found common cause.

Part II, 'Body', examines how biological conceptions of child development manifested in both artistic and educational practice. Chapter 3, 'Child and World: Education and the New Biology', introduces a nexus between child and world through physical, tactile, and sensorial interactions. It introduces foreign models of perception and interaction such as the tool-based, circumstantial intelligence Ortega drew out from Gestalt experiments as well as teachers' readings of Jakob von Uexküll's 1909 concept of *Umwelt,* the surrounding world of the organism, and its limits. Building on the corporal and sensorial, Chapter 4, *'Infans Ludens*: Children at the Vanguard of Art and Play', considers how paidological descriptions of haptic ability and tactile learning accorded with representations of the child's world. How did these ideas in turn spur artistic interventions in play, games, and instruction? It shines light on the open-air educational work of three pioneering female pedagogues: the aforementioned Montessori, Rosa Sensat, and Margarita Aranda. In Spain as across Europe, education became both a consciously sensorial practice and a manifestation of larger social and scientific ideas of vitality, interaction, and reciprocity.

Finally, Part III, 'Spirit', asks how philosophical notions of personhood worked to interrogate and break open scientific certainty. Chapter 5, 'Art and the Mind: Childhood and the New *Ingenium*', explores the nexus between psychometric tests, which promised insight into the inner workings of the mind, and the psychology of children's art, asking how visual manifestations both defamiliarized and, in turn, celebrated the child. Through the contributions of artist Ángel Ferrant and writer Manuel Abril, I consider a transcendent counterpart to psychometric studies through the awakening of human imagination. Finally, Chapter 6, 'Early

Plenitude: A Phenomenology of the Child's Spirit', draws out an enduring core of neo-humanist thought within educational theory. This impulse grew from Krausist and *institucionista* roots and extended through the 1940s in publications from major thinkers in exile from post-Civil War Spain. Here, I focus on works by Unamuno, Xirau, and Roura, asking how they theorized an education for life. In closing, I examine a co-existent notion of abiding spirit in poems of childhood in Guillén's *Cántico*, arguing that the child's physical and imaginative being had not only phenomenological but also spiritual depth.

Together, these three parts reconstruct the phenomenological 'world of the child' in early twentieth-century Spanish intellectual thought. This book focuses on select cases in which teachers, scientists, and philosophers used children to enact debates on the role of science in society, seeking a renewal of humanistic thought. Establishing a nexus of art, science, and child study, my concerns are of a primarily philosophical and conceptual nature. They encompass aspects of disunity, instability, and fragmentation, the construction of an integral self over time, and the junctures and crises of ideals of wholeness. As this study moves between scales, from individual children towards larger calls to universality, it is worth recalling the terms in which Gabriela Mistral praised her colleague Carmen Conde in 1934: she was as Spanish as could be, but what was most to admire was that she was *human*, transcending borders: 'humana' in her approach to verse, to words, and to the child. To be human was to fear, to seek sensation, and to connect with others and the surrounding world. Above all, it was to rejoice in the act of living itself. This was a conscious act, drawing from both the avant-garde and the present moment: 'Afirmando el regocijo como principal característica de lo humano' [Affirming joy as the principal characteristic of the human], as a reviewer in 1930 described the transcendence of new children's literature.[68] Gathering around the figure of the child, Spain's heterogeneous avant-gardes in science, literature, and education converged in an effort to define the vital, the universal, and the human.

Notes to the Introduction

1. Carmen Conde, *Júbilos: poemas de niños, rosas, animales, máquinas y vientos*, 2nd edn (Murcia: Sudeste, 1934), p. 8; a version of the poem was earlier published in 'Júbilos (Poema del colegio)', *Meseta*, 1.5 (1928), 2. A pre-eminent voice of twentieth-century Spanish literature, Conde became in 1978 the first woman inducted into the Real Academia Española. *Júbilos*, with its elegiac dedication to 'María del Mar, que se fue a bordo de su nombre' must be read within the context of Conde's longstanding educational work; see Pedro L. Moreno Martínez, 'Carmen Conde y una ilusión: la educación del pueblo', in *Carmen Conde: voluntad creadora (1907–1996)*, ed. by Francisco Javier Díez de Revenga (Murcia: Marcial Pons, 2007), pp. 97–110.

2. Gabriela Mistral, 'Carmen Conde, contadora de la infancia', in Conde, *Júbilos*, pp. 7–13. Mistral's extensive, striking pedagogical writings can be found in her *Pasión de enseñar (Pensamiento pedagógico)* (Valparaíso: Universidad de Valparaíso, 2017). See also Roberta Quance, 'Norah Borges Illustrates Two Spanish Women Poets', in *Crossing Fields in Modern Spanish Culture*, ed. by Federico Bonaddio and Xon De Ros (Oxford: Legenda, 2003), pp. 54–66 (pp. 62–63).

3. Mistral, 'Carmen Conde', p. 10.

4. Rafael Verdier, 'Notas para una pedagogía de base existencial', *Escuelas de España*, 1.2 (1934), 1–10. This discussion is indebted to scholarship on the nineteenth-century transformation of

childhood, particularly Carolyn Steedman, *Strange Dislocations: Childhood and the Idea of Human Interiority, 1780-1930* (Cambridge, MA: Harvard University Press, 1995).

5. See *La construcción de la identidad pedagógica española: entre la Institución Libre de Enseñanza y las Escuelas del Ave María*, ed. by Remedios Sánchez García (Madrid: Editorial Síntesis, 2015), which begins to draw out the counterintuitive convergence of *institucionista* ideas and those of progressive Catholic education.

6. Rodolfo Llopis, *Hacia una escuela más humana* (Madrid: Editorial España, 1933), p. 10.

7. Pamela Beth Radcliff, *From Mobilization to Civil War: The Politics of Polarization in the Spanish City of Gijón, 1900–1937* (Cambridge: Cambridge University Press, 1994), p. 36.

8. Ellen Key, *The Century of the Child* (London: G. P. Putnam's Sons, 1909).

9. See Sally Shuttleworth, *The Mind of the Child: Child Development in Literature, Science and Medicine, 1840–1900* (Oxford: Oxford University Press, 2010), and Andrew F. Jones, *Developmental Fairy Tales: Evolutionary Thinking and Modern Chinese Culture* (Cambridge, MA: Harvard University Press, 2011). Tracking parallel movements in Chinese literature, Jones provides a similarly critical marker of the global fascination with childhood and its vestigial traces in humankind that I read within a Spanish phenomenological thread. On the rise of psycho-pedagogical modernity in Spain, see Miguel Ángel Cerezo Manrique, *Los comienzos de la psicopedagogía en España, 1882–1936* (Madrid: Biblioteca Nueva, 2001).

10. Joaquim Xirau i Palau, *Manuel B. Cossío y la educación en España* (Mexico: El Colegio de México, 1945), pp. 26–27.

11. Joaquim Xirau i Palau, 'La pedagogía y la vida', *Revista de Pedagogía*, 12.133 (1933), 1–6 (p. 4). The renewed urgency of educational humanism is evident in a spate of recent works responding to the rise of technology, defending the liberal arts or elevating creativity; see, for example, Martha Nussbaum's celebration of Rabindranath Tagore's and John Dewey's aesthetic pedagogies in *Not for Profit: Why Democracy Needs the Humanities* (Princeton: Princeton University Press, 2016). I am grateful to Rebecca Gotlieb for sharing her work in educational psychology with me.

12. Thomas S. Popkewitz, *Cosmopolitanism and the Age of School Reform: Science, Education, and Making Society by Making the Child* (London: Routledge, 2008), pp. xiv, 4–5.

13. See above all Alfonso Capitán Díaz, *Breve historia de la educación en España* (Madrid: Alianza Editorial, 2002). A pre-history of Republican reforms can be found in Juan Luis Rubio Mayoral, 'Historia de la educación bajo la idea de las dos Españas (1931–1935)', in *Enseñanza, ciencia e ideología en España (1890–1950)*, ed. by Manuel Castillo Martos and Juan Luis Rubio Mayoral (Seville: Diputación de Sevilla, 2014).

14. Madrid's Institución Municipal de Puericultura was an early seat of maternal and child health; see Raquel Álvarez Peláez, 'La búsqueda de un modelo institucional de protección a la infancia: institutos, guarderías y hogares infantiles: España 1900–1940', in *Salvad al niño: estudios sobre la protección a la infancia en la Europa Mediterránea a comienzos del siglo XX*, ed. by Enrique Perdiguero Gil (Valencia: Publicacions de la Universitat de València, 2004). Advice boomed in books such as César Juarros, *La crianza del hijo* (Madrid: Mundo Latino, 1900). Local institutes and *escuelas de puericultura* published pamphlets on child health and hygiene for mothers; see Belén Jiménez-Alonso and José Carlos Loredo-Narciandi, ' "To Educate Children from Birth": A Genealogical Analysis of Some Practices of Subjectivation in Spanish and French Scientific Childcare (1898–1939)', *History of Education*, 45 (2016), 719–38.

15. Since Philippe Ariès's 1960 *L'Enfant et la vie familiale sous l'ancien régime*, historians have debated when childhood, as imagined and understood, began; see Philippe Ariès, *Centuries of Childhood: A Social History of Family Life*, trans. by Robert Baldick (New York: Vintage Books, 1962). While Ariès depicted a European construction of childhood from the Renaissance onward, nineteenth-century reforms dramatically shifted norms in health, labour, and schooling. On Spanish reforms in childhood health and protection, see José María Borrás Llop, *Historia de la infancia en la España contemporánea (1834–1936)* (Madrid: Ministerio de Trabajo y Asuntos Sociales, 1996), p. 11.

16. On the interplay of science and literature in this period see chiefly Dale J. Pratt, *Signs of Science: Literature, Science, and Spanish Modernity since 1868* (West Lafayette: Purdue University Press, 2001).

17. Archivo de la Junta para Ampliación de Estudios e Investigaciones Científicas (1907–1939),

Residencia de Estudiantes, <http://archivojae.edaddeplata.org/jae_app> [accessed 1 June 2019]; on national impact of such scholarships, see Gabriela Ossenbach and Alejandro Tiana Ferrer, 'La contribución de la Junta para Ampliación de Estudios a la renovación pedagógica en España en el primer tercio del siglo XX', *Boletín de la Institución Libre de Enseñanza*, 63–64 (2006), 97–114.

18. Alison Sinclair, *Trafficking Knowledge in Early Twentieth-century Spain: Centres of Exchange and Cultural Imaginaries* (Woodbridge: Tamesis, 2009). Freud was introduced by Ortega y Gasset in the cultural realm and early discussed in the context of education by José M. Sacristán, 'La teoría psicoanalítica de Freud', *Revista de Pedagogía*, 2.18 (1923), 201–06. On Freud's reception, see Helio Carpintero and Vicenta Mestre, *Freud en España: un capítulo de la historia de la psicología en España* (Valencia: Promolibro, 1984). A concise analysis of the professionalization of mental testing is provided by Annette Mülberger, Mónica Balltondre Pla, and Andrea Graus' 'Aims of Teachers' Psychometry: Intelligence Testing in Barcelona (1920)', *History of Psychology*, 17 (2013), 206–22.

19. Broadly, childhood was divided into a 'primera infancia' up to seven years of age, around the traditional age of reason, and a 'segunda infancia' running through to a child's first signs of puberty: see Borrás Llop, *Historia de la infancia en la España contemporánea (1834–1936)*, p. 21. Development was meticulously charted by psychologists, in works such as Alice Descœudres, *El desarrollo del niño de dos a siete años: investigaciones de psicología experimental*, trans. by Jacobo Orellana Garrido (Madrid: Francisco Beltrán, 1929), and Charlotte Bühler and Hildegard Hetzer, *Tests para la primera infancia: pruebas del desarrollo para el primero al sexto años de vida*, trans. by Alejandro Chleusebairgue and Antonio Calero (Madrid: Editorial Labor, 1933).

20. Alejandro Quiroga, *Making Spaniards: Primo de Rivera and the Nationalization of the Masses, 1923–30* (Basingstoke: Palgrave Macmillan, 2007), pp. 110, 122–27.

21. Paul Ginsborg, *Family Politics: Domestic Life, Devastation and Survival, 1900–1950* (New Haven: Yale University Press, 2014), pp. 229–30; *Constitución de la República Española, 9 de diciembre 1931* ([Madrid]: [s.n.], 1931), <http://www.congreso.es/docu/constituciones/1931/1931_cd.pdf> [accessed 1 August 2018]. See the Geneva Declaration's use in Llopis, *Hacia una escuela más humana*, pp. 13–19. On the larger educational work of the Republic, see Mariano Pérez Galán, *La enseñanza en la Segunda República* (Madrid: Edición Cuadernos para el Diálogo, 1975).

22. María del Mar del Pozo Andrés, *Justa Freire o la pasión de educar: biografía de una maestra atrapada en la historia de España (1896–1965)* (Barcelona: Ediciones Octaedro, 2013), pp. 11–14.

23. Along with discussions of women's education came the topic of sexual education. Explorations of children's sexuality such as José Eleizegui López, *La sexualidad infantil* (Madrid: n.p., 1936) sought to open objective, scientific conversations in the decades between Freud's contributions and their introduction in Spain. On sexual education and sexual reform in Spain, see, for example, Alison Sinclair, *Sex and Society in Early Twentieth-century Spain: Hildegart Rodríguez and the World League for Sexual Reform* (Cardiff: University of Wales Press, 2007), and Richard Cleminson, 'Eugenics by Name or by Nature? The Spanish Anarchist Sex Reform of the 1930s', *History of European Ideas*, 18.5 (1994), 729–40.

24. Antonio Molero Pintado and María del Mar del Pozo Andrés, *Escuela de Estudios Superiores del Magisterio (1909–1932): un precedente histórico en la formación universitaria del profesorado español* (Madrid: Universidad de Alcalá de Henares, 1989), p. 125–39.

25. See Sarah Wright, *The Child in Spanish Cinema* (Manchester: Manchester University Press, 2013), as well as studies such as Fiona Noble, 'The Representation of the Child in Contemporary Spanish Cinema', in *La piel en la palestra: estudios corporales II*, ed. by Alba del Pozo García and Alba Serrano Giménez (Barcelona: Editorial UOC, 2011) and Sarah Thomas, 'Phantom Children: Spectral Presences and the Violent Past in Two Films of Contemporary Spain', in *Espectros: Ghostly Hauntings in Contemporary Transhispanic Narratives*, ed. by Alberto Ribas-Casasayas and Amanda L. Petersen (London: Rowman & Littlefield, 2016), pp. 101–16.

26. Ana María Matute, *Cuentos de infancia*, ed. by Ana María Moix (Barcelona: Ediciones Martínez Roca, 2002). Jo Labanyi has argued for late-dictatorship works' embrace of modernity, glimpsed through child narrators' emergence from trauma and 'haunting'; see 'Memory and Modernity in Democratic Spain: The Difficulty of Coming to Terms with the Spanish Civil War', *Poetics Today*, 28.1 (2007), 89–116.

27. Miguel de Unamuno, 'El niño es el padre del hombre', *El Sol*, 14 August 1932, p. 1.

28. Leslie J. Harkema, *Spanish Modernism and the Poetics of Youth: From Miguel de Unamuno to La Joven Literatura* (Toronto: University of Toronto Press, 2017). These periods are also key to understanding many of the political, sexual, and gender-based implications of education.

29. Alfonso Capitán Díaz, 'Humanismo pedagógico en la España contemporánea', *Revista Española de Pedagogía*, 60.223 (2002), 461–80 (p. 461).

30. On the work of the Institución Libre de Enseñanza and its transnational links through the Junta para Ampliación de Estudios, see: Antonio Jiménez-Landi, *La Institución Libre de Enseñanza y su ambiente*, 4 vols (Madrid: Editorial Complutense, 1996); Antonio Molero Pintado, *La Institución Libre de Enseñanza: un proyecto de reforma pedagógica* (Madrid: Biblioteca Nueva, 2000); and Antonio Viñao Frago, *Escuela para todos: educación y modernidad en la España de siglo XX* (Madrid: Marcial Pons, 2004).

31. The classic early study of Krausist philosophy is Juan López-Morillas, *El krausismo español* (Mexico: Fondo de Cultura Económica, 1956). Since the late Francoist era, this discussion has burgeoned: Elías Díaz, *La filosofía social del krausismo español*, Colección ITS (Madrid: Editorial Cuadernos para el Diálogo, 1973); Antonio Jiménez García, *El krausismo y la Institución Libre de Enseñanza* (Madrid: Cincel, 1985); Elena de Jongh-Rossel, *El krausismo y la generación de 1898* (Valencia: Albatros Hispanófila, 1985); and Gonzalo Capellán de Miguel, *La España armónica: el proyecto del krausismo español para una sociedad en conflicto* (Madrid: Biblioteca Nueva, 2006). Most recently, Christian Rubio's *Krausism and the Spanish Avant-garde: The Impact of Philosophy on National Culture* (Amherst: Cambria Press, 2017) aims to demonstrate a link between Krausist philosophical ideals, aesthetics, and social progressivism.

32. On the genesis of the latter, see Luis Palacios, *Instituto-Escuela: Historia de una renovación educativa* (Madrid: Ministerio de Educación y Ciencia, 1988) and Álvaro Ribagarda Esteban, 'Los orígenes del Instituto-Escuela: los grupos de niños de la Residencia de Estudiantes', in *Ciencia e innovación en las aulas: centenario del Instituto Escuela (1918–1939)*, ed. by Encarnación Martínez Alfaro, Leoncio López-Ocón Cabrera and Gabriela Ossenbach Sauter (Madrid: CSIC, 2018), pp. 47–70.

33. Rosa Bruno-Jofré and Gonzalo Jover, 'The Readings of John Dewey's Work and the Intersection of Catholicism: The Cases of the *Institución Libre de Enseñanza* and the Thesis of Father Alberto Hurtado, S.J. on Dewey', in *The Global Reception of John Dewey's Thought: Multiple Refractions through Time and Space*, ed. by Rosa Bruno-Jofré and Jürgen Schriewer (London: Routledge, 2012), pp. 23–42 (pp. 24, 37).

34. Isabel Pérez-Villanueva Tovar, 'El liberalismo institucionista en la Residencia de Estudiantes', *Studia Historica: Historia Contemporánea*, 8 (1990), 77–88 (p. 83).

35. Adolfo Posada, *Breve historia del krausismo español* (Oviedo: Publicaciones de la Universidad de Oviedo, 1981), p. 38.

36. Manuel Rueda González, *Las colonias escolares y las escuelas al aire libre en su aplicación al mejoramiento de la salud y de la enseñanza primaria* (Palma: Rotger, 1915), pp. 11 and 6.

37. Rueda González, *Las colonias escolares y las escuelas al aire libre*, pp. 6–8. For an introduction to a medicalized view of integral education and national public health reforms through the school system, see Esteban Rodríguez Ocaña, 'Una medicina para la infancia', in *Historia de la infancia*, ed. by José María Borrás Llop, pp. 149–92.

38. As will be discussed in Chapter 4, Montessori's work was critically received and developed in Spain from 1914, sponsored by the Catalan governmental Consell de Pedagogia. Montessori taught international training courses in Barcelona, directed the Mancomunitat's Seminari-Laboratori de Pedagogia (1918–1921), and established a residence in Barcelona from 1918 until the outbreak of Civil War in 1936. See Milagros Sáiz and Dolores Sáiz, 'La estancia de María Montessori en Barcelona: la influencia de su método en la psicopedagogía catalana', *Revista de Historia de la Psicología*, 26.2/3 (2005), pp. 200–12.

39. See the encyclopaedic *Història de les Institucions i del moviment cultural a Catalunya 1900–1936*, ed. by Alexandre Galí, 24 vols (Barcelona: Fundació Alexandre Galí, 1979), II.

40. For a thorough analysis of Spanish anarchism's intellectual and ideological foundations, see José Álvarez Junco, *La ideología política del anarquismo español: 1868–1910* (Madrid: Siglo XXI, 1976), corresponding with the publication of Carolyn Boyd, 'The Anarchists and Education in Spain, 1868–1909', *The Journal of Modern History*, 48.4 (1976), 125–70. Chris Ealham focuses on the urban

impact of these ideas; see *Anarchism and the City: Revolution and Counter-revolution in Barcelona, 1898–1937* (London: Routledge, 2005).

41. On the convergence of anarchist and spiritualist principles, see Gerard Horta, *De la mística a les barricades: introducció a l'espiritisme català del XIX dins el context ocultista europeu* (Barcelona: Proa, 2001), and Mònica Balltondre Pla and Andrea Graus, 'The City of Spirits: Spiritism, Feminism and the Secularization of Urban Spaces', in *Barcelona: An Urban History of Science and Modernity, 1888–1929*, ed. by Oliver Hochadel and Agustí Nieto-Galan (London: Routledge, 2016), pp. 136–57.

42. On the school's pedagogical influences, see Josep González-Agàpito and others, *Tradició i renovació pedagògica: 1898–1939. Història de l'educació: Catalunya, Illes Balears, País Valencià* (Barcelona: Abadia de Montserrat, 2002), pp. 64–65. Unamuno wrote of Ferrer after his execution in vicious terms, before later issuing a mea culpa: Miguel de Unamuno, 'Confesión de culpa', *El Día*, 7 December 1917, p. 1.

43. Lorenzo Luzuriaga, *La educación de nuestro tiempo* (Buenos Aires: Editorial Losada, 1961), p. 41. The work of Vives, in particular, featured in Spain's early twentieth-century pedagogical renaissance as well as Catholic re-interpretations in the post-war years. Major works in this direction include Juan Luis Vives, *Tratado de la enseñanza*, trans. by José Ontañón (Madrid: La Lectura, 1922); Adolfo Bonilla y San Martín, *Luis Vives y la filosofía del renacimiento* (Madrid: L. Rubio, 1929); and Enrique Díaz Jiménez, *Los fundamentos éticos, religiosos y psicológicos de la pedagogía de Luis Vives* (Madrid: n.p., 1929).

44. Andrés Manjón, *Hojas educadoras del Ave-María. (Primer apéndice de las Hojas Coeducadoras). Educar es completar hombres* (Granada: Imprenta-Escuela del Ave María, 1907). See Manjón's writings on education as a process of integral development in his *Escritos socio-pedagógicos: educar enseñando*, ed. by Andrés Palma Valenzuela and José Medina Ocaña (Madrid: Biblioteca Nueva, 2009).

45. Remedios Sánchez García, 'Presentación', in *La construcción de la identidad pedagógica española*, ed. by Sánchez García, pp. 13–16 (p. 13); José Montero Vives, 'Andrés Manjón: discurso leído en la solemne apertura del curso académico 1897–1898 en la Universidad Literaria de Granada', in *La construcción de la identidad pedagógica española*, ed. by Sánchez García, pp. 173–87 (pp. 175–77).

46. 'Escuelas del Ave María en el Camino del Sacro Monte de Granada', *La Ilustración Artística*, 18.922 (1899), 555–58. Among others, see Catalina García Trejo, *Escuelas al aire libre: su organización en el extranjero; la que podría dársele en España; ventajas e inconvenientes del sistema* (Alicante: n.p., 1910); Manuel Rueda González, *Las colonias escolares y las escuelas al aire libre en su aplicación al mejoramiento de la salud y de la enseñanza primaria* (Palma: Rotger, 1915); and Eloy Vaquero Cantillo, *Las escuelas al aire libre atmósfera pura, luz, flores, para los niños* (Córdoba: n.p., 1926). On post-war celebrations of Manjón, see Ezequiel Solana, *Don Andrés Manjón: sus obras y doctrinas pedagógicas* (Madrid: Escuela Española, 1941), and A. Rodríguez Vicente, *Higiene de la edad escolar o paidocultura* (Madrid: CSIC, 1946), p. 503. The UNED Madrid announced in April 2011 that its Centro Andrés Manjón would return to its original name, Centro Francisco Giner de los Ríos; see UNED, 'Cambio de nombre del Centro de Zona *Andrés Manjón*', <http://portal.uned.es/portal/> [accessed 1 May 2018].

47. The Residencia Universitaria Feminina pre-dated the establishment of María de Maeztu's JAE-affiliated Residencia de Señoritas by a year. During that time, it welcomed Victoria Kent, better known for her later feminist organizing, as its first resident. See Consuelo Flecha, 'Alumnas y equipos directivos de la Residencia Teresiana de Madrid', in *La Residencia de Señoritas y otras redes culturales femeninas*, ed. by Josefina Cuesta, María José Turrión, and Rosa María Merino (Madrid: Ediciones Universidad de Salamanca, 2015), pp. 287–311 (p. 294), and a comparative view in Josefina Cuesta, María José Turrión, and Rosa María Merino, 'Dos residencias universitarias femeninas en España, 1914–1915', in *La Residencia de Señoritas y otras redes culturales femeninas*, pp. 11–30.

48. Pedro Poveda, *Itinerario pedagógico*. ed. by Ángeles Galino (Madrid: CSIC, Instituto de Pedagogía, 1964), p. 233, discussed in Presentación Gallegos, 'Humano, con el humanismo verdad', in *Humanismo pedagógico en Pedro Poveda: algunas dimensiones*, ed. by Ángeles Galino Carrillo (Madrid: Narcea, 2000), pp. 15–25 (p. 16).

49. Capitán Díaz, 'Humanismo pedagógico en la España contemporánea', p. 474.

50. Secular institutions such as the ILE, meanwhile, demonstrated notably conservative, elite

characteristics and a reliance on Hispanic, Christian, and classical traditions. See Alison Sinclair, ' "Telling it Like it Was"?: The Residencia de Estudiantes and Its Image', *Bulletin of Spanish Studies*, 81.6 (2004), 739–64.

51. Josefina Álvarez de Cánovas draws on Ramón Ruiz Amado's *El modernismo pedagógico* (Barcelona: Librería Religiosa, 1925) to make her case not for a reborn but an eternal Spain: 'El "modernismo pedagógico" es uno de los errores de la educación nueva que sería funesto para nosotros, españoles. Solo los pueblos niños, los pueblos que no tienen historia, pueden ser partidarios del "modernismo pedagógico" a ultranza' [The 'pedagogical modernism' is one of the errors of new education that would be disastrous for us, Spaniards. Only nations in their infancy, nations without history, can be in favour of an outright 'pedagogical modernism']: Josefina Álvarez de Cánovas, *Psicología pedagógica: estudio del niño español* (Madrid: Espasa-Calpe, 1941), p. 333. On the spiritual grounding of New Education, see her *Psicología pedagógica*, p. 334.

52. María del Mar del Pozo Andrés and J. F. A. Braster, 'The Reinvention of the New Education Movement in the Franco Dictatorship (Spain, 1936–1976)', *Paedagogica Historica*, 42.1–2 (2006), 109–26; Till Kössler, 'Towards a New Understanding of the Child: Catholic Mobilization and Modern Pedagogy in Spain, 1900–1936', *Contemporary European History*, 18.1 (2009), 1–24; and *Kinder der Demokratie: Religiöse Erziehung und urbane Moderne in Spanien, 1890–1936* (Munich: Oldenbourg, 2013), p. 478.

53. Theodore J. Haarhoff, 'The Holistic Attitude in Education', in *Our Changing World-view: Ten Lectures on Recent Movements of Thought in Science, Economics, Education, Literature and Philosophy*, ed. by Jan Christiaan Smuts and others (Johannesburg: University of the Witwatersrand Press, 1932), pp. 103–14 (p. 3).

54. A study of Catholic approaches to unity and totality in science would demand a reading of the Catholic priests and psychologists Manuel Barbado and Francisco Palmés, and abroad, works such as Jacques Maritain's *Integral Humanism* (1936) and the psychological research of Albert Michotte (1881–1965). On this established relationship between Catholicism and psychology, see Sigrid Leyssen and Annette Mülberger, 'Psychology from a Neo-Thomist Perspective: The Louvain-Madrid Connection', in *What's So New about Scholasticism? How Neo-Thomism Helped Shape the Twentieth Century*, ed. by Rajesh Heynickx and Stéphane Symons (Berlin: De Gruyter, 2018), pp. 181–204. On the adoption of Darwinist ideals within Belgian secular and religious pedagogical contexts, see Marc Depaepe, Raf De Bont, and Kristof Dams, 'How Darwinism Has Affected Catholic as well as Non-Catholic Psycho-pedagogical Constructs in Belgium from the 1870s to the 1930s', *Paedagogica Historica*, 48.1 (2012), 51–66.

55. Radcliff, *From Mobilization to Civil War*, p. 197.

56. Joan Roura i Parella, *Educación y ciencia* (Mexico: Fondo de Cultura Económica, 1940), pp. 53–54.

57. According to the Oxford English Dictionary, 'holism' first entered the volume in 1926 as the 'tendency in nature to produce wholes (*i.e.* bodies or organisms) from the ordered grouping of unit structures': see 'holism, n.' in *OED Online*, <http://www.oed.com> [accessed 16 April 2018]. Diverse thinkers from Aristotle to Goethe, Bergson to William James, Rudolf Steiner to John Dewey have been described since as 'holistic' in their philosophical and scientific worldviews.

58. Frederick Charles Kolbe, *A Catholic View of Holism* (London: Macmillan, 1928), p. 48. The idea that a holistic view of development involves a creative process reinforced for this author a 'harmonizing' of principles, from the 'Word' to the 'flesh' (p. 12). For Kolbe, all aspects of matter and organic life — circulation, renewal, digestion — were subsumed by a larger whole, the soul.

59. Jan Christiaan Smuts, *Holism and Evolution* (London: Macmillan, 1926), p. 87.

60. Smuts's colleague Theodore J. Haarhoff wrote of 'Omne vivum e vivo' as an ancient principle which modern educators had only just begun to recapture, see Haarhoff, 'The Holistic Attitude in Education', p. 110.

61. Eugenio d'Ors, *Grandeza y servidumbre de la inteligencia* (Madrid: Revista de Estudiantes, 1919), p. 65.

62. Fabio, '¿Totalitarismo? (Holismo-Tradicionalismo)', *El Siglo Futuro*, 13 November 1934, p. 1.

63. Harrington traces a *fin-de-siècle* search for wholeness in art, science, and philosophy, ruptured by the nationalism of the early 1930s as theories of holism were co-opted to justify political order. While the enemy of wholeness was the machine, the enemy of the *Gestalt* was chaos. The chaos of the 1920s represented an unstoppable 'leveling process', what Harrington calls the 'random rule of untutored masses' — akin, perhaps, to Ortega's 'rebellion of the masses' and his interest in national unity and dispersion: *Reenchanted Science: Holism in German Culture from Wilhelm II to Hitler* (Princeton: Princeton University Press, 1996), p. 104–06; José Ortega y Gasset, *La rebelión de las masas* (Madrid: Revista de Occidente, 1930).

64. Fernando de los Ríos, *El sentido humanista del socialismo* (Madrid: Biblioteca Nueva, 2006), p. 83. The author served in successive roles as Minister of Justice, Education, and State between 1931 and 1933.

65. Luis Bello, *Viaje por las escuelas de España* (Madrid: Magisterio Español, 1926), p. 245.

66. See early views in José Ortega y Gasset, *Meditaciones del Quijote* (Madrid: Publicaciones de la Residencia de Estudiantes, 1914); Jorge Guillén, 'Perfección', in *Cántico*, 4th edn (Buenos Aires: Editorial Sudamericana, 1950), p. 240.

67. Anon., 'Reunión del Comité de Letras y Artes del Instituto de la Sociedad de Naciones', *Residencia*, 4 (1933), pp. 106, 182.

68. Mistral, 'Carmen Conde', p. 10. Joaquín Rodríguez de Cortázar, 'Escaparate de libros: Antoniorrobles: 26 cuentos infantiles. CIAP', *La Gaceta Literaria*, 4.74 (1930), 15.

PART I

Mind

FIG. 1.1. Published two days before the declaration of the Second Spanish Republic in 1931, Cirac's cartoon played on the inscrutability of the Spanish nation.
Source: Eugenio Cirac, 'El enigma', *Acción Gallega: Órgano de la Federación de Sociedades Gallegas de Buenos Aires*, 12 April 1931 [n.p.]. Courtesy of CEINCE, Berlanga de Duero.

CHAPTER 1

Imagining Infancy:
Paidology and a Science of the Mind

¿No sería más discreto confesar paladinamente nuestra ignorancia e inscribir hoy por hoy este fenómeno, como tantos otros, en el capítulo de 'enigmas de la infancia'?

[Would it not be wiser to confess our ignorance here and now and relegate this phenomenon, like so many others, to that chapter known as 'childhood enigmas'?]

Juan Zaragüeta, *El estudio del niño para la cultura nacional* (1919)

A schoolgirl looks towards a classroom map as a stern teacher peers down at her. Pointing at the map, the teacher asks: 'Defíname usted la situación de España' ['Explain Spain's situation'], to which the exasperated girl replies: '¡Por Dios, Don Anacieto! ¿Cómo voy a definirme lo indefinido?' ['Dear God, Don Anacieto! How can I define the undefined?']. To define the undefined, or the indefinable, was not just a problem of the Spanish nation, as this cartoon from 1931 (Fig. 1.1) suggests. Within one enigma lay an array of others. Children were said to be an 'enigma' to those who studied them, just as the world was the child's own 'enigma inmediato'. This indefinable space of childhood was the sphere that philosopher Manuel García Morente (1886–1942) called the 'mundo del niño', a world perceptually and cognitively distinct from that of the adult.[1] It was at this juncture of scientific enquiry and philosophical fascination that a new discipline was born: paidology, the study of the child.[2] Through the work of leading Spanish pedagogue and Republican Minister of Education Domingo Barnés (1879–1940) and his colleagues, I argue that perceptual theories worked alongside phenomenological thought to shape qualitative imaginaries of the world of the child.[3] Amidst rapid scientific development and intellectual synthesis, the child came to reside at the heart of a new human science, one inseparable from national, cultural, and social histories. As this chapter will show, such frames had concrete impacts on reading and learning methods that would outlast the political and social influence of these actors, adapted and integrated into representations of the psychology of the 'Spanish child' even under early Francoism.

Surveying the pedagogical field in 1926, Barnés proclaimed that contemporary education must undergo a 'Copernican' revolution.[4] The metaphor was indeed apt,

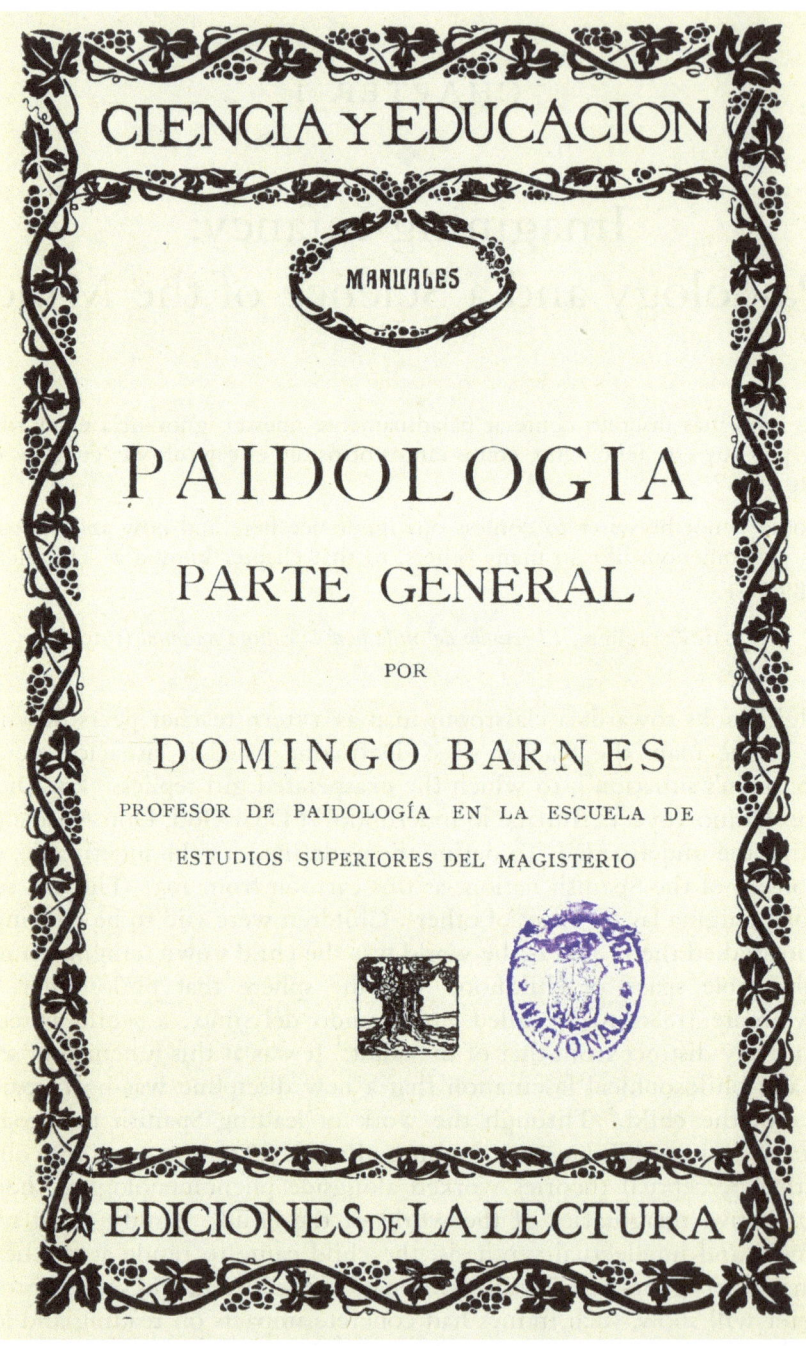

FIG. 1.2. Building on his 1904 doctoral thesis, Barnés' manual *Paidología*
defined the international field of child study in Spain.
Source: Domingo Barnés Salinas, *Paidología: parte general*
(Madrid: La Lectura, [1924]).

bridging the shifting ground of science with a new model of child study. Seeking a comparable scientific realignment, Barnés's generation of educationalists employed the insights of modern science while placing the inner experience of the child, like the Copernican earth, at the centre of modern educational practice. He built on a series of cognitive, intellectual arguments in doing so. A current of holistic thought ran through Spanish calls for a 'new' education, manifest in the psycho-pedagogical realm but reflecting universalist impulses in philosophy and culture. This interpretative nexus arose through terms employed to celebrate children's vitality and integrity. As psychology had evolved from a 'science of the soul' towards a science of the mind, ideas such as the *Geisteswissenschaften* elaborated by Wilhelm Dilthey (1833–1922) from 1883 looked to give equal methodological value to the human sciences.[5] Pedagogy was caught in the rift. Some pedagogues employed a strictly medical, 'quantitative' approach to the child. Others took a middle ground, using advanced technology and novel methods to gain insight into broader human function — as in the intricate drawings of human, including children's, neurons made by Nobel Prize-winning neuroscientist and artist Santiago Ramón y Cajal (1852–1934) — while demonstrating reverence for the formal mysteries of the body.[6] Others started from the 'qualitative', the inner experience of the child.

In a post-Freudian, post-Proustian context, childhood interiority was accepted as both a fundamental and enduring influence upon the adult psyche, as well as a full-bodied phenomenological experience of its own. Psychoanalytic ideas were absorbed by leading psychologists, both before and following the Revista de Occidente's translations of the complete works of Freud from 1922. Yet psychoanalysis was then but one theory among many, and by 1936, the authoritative *Diccionario de Pedagogía* even declared psychoanalysis 'incapable of resolving the essential problems of pedagogy'.[7] In contrast, holistic sciences, particularly Gestalt psychology, had been promoted as combining experimental research with a decidedly humanist, phenomenological perspective. It was for this reason that Gestalt theory was arguably 'more akin to the new Spanish philosophical and cultural needs than those represented by either psychoanalysis or behaviorism', as Spanish historians of psychology have argued, even if its reach was largely limited to educational, philosophical and cultural contexts.[8] Frustrated by what they saw as empirical science's failure to grasp the vitality of life, teachers and intellectuals explored a range of new models that reflected holistic ideals of understanding the child. Within these frameworks, the child was at the base of a longer process of individual and social transformation.[9]

Barnés's work formed part of a broad process of modernization, synthesis, and institutionalization, the rhetorical outlines of which I read through his influential manuals of child-studies. His works *Fuentes para el estudio de la paidología* [Sources for the Study of Paidology] (1917) and *El desenvolvimiento del niño* [Child Development] (1928, 1933) constituted major contributions to the field, from its early consolidation to subsequent evolution. The three editions of his *Paidología* (Fig. 1.2) have been called a product of the 'reconocido fervor paidológico' [notable paidological fervour] that reigned in Spain's early decades of the twentieth century.[10] Barnés also played

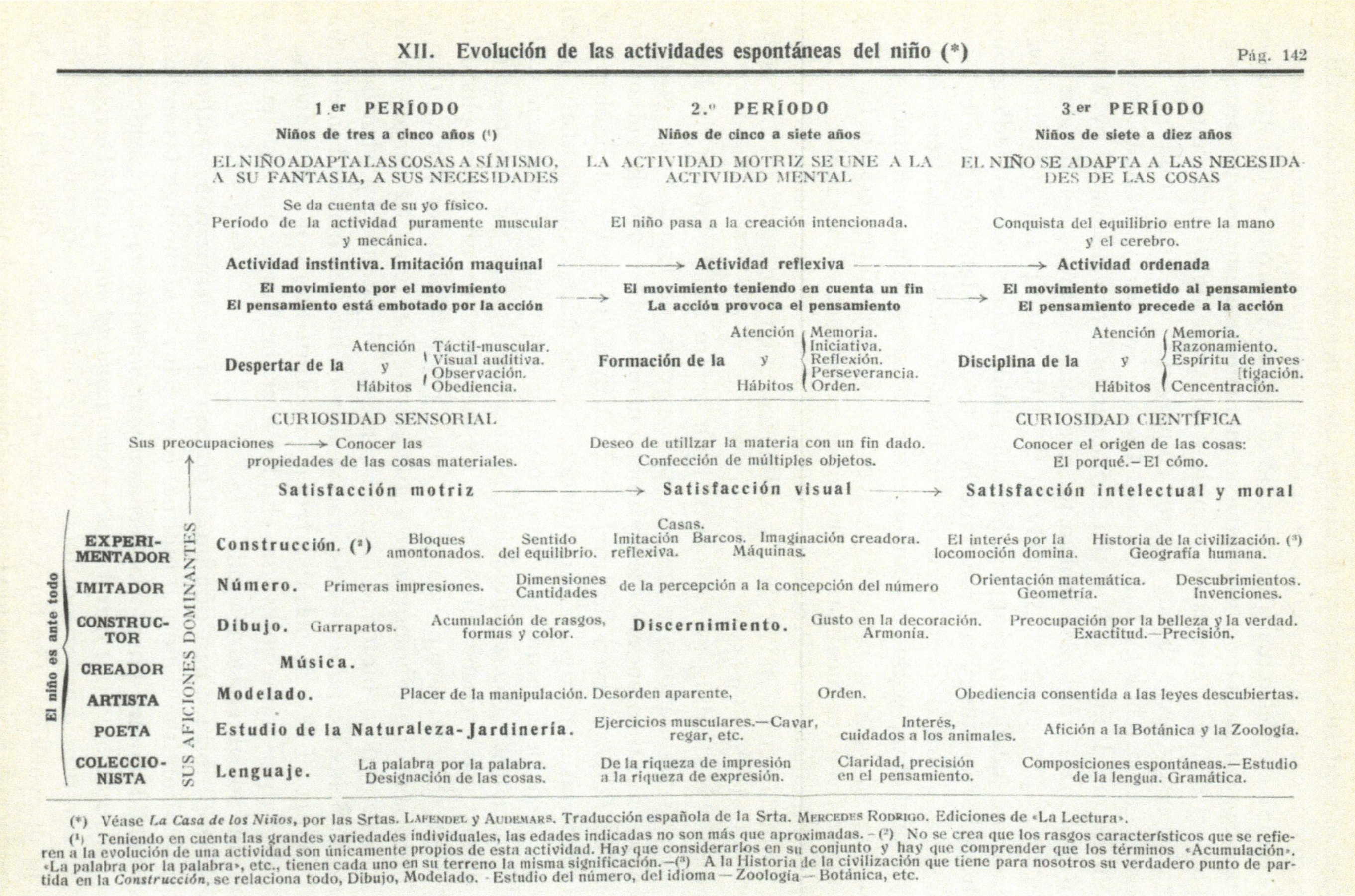

Pág. 142

XII. Evolución de las actividades espontáneas del niño (*)

	1.er PERÍODO Niños de tres a cinco años (¹)	2.º PERÍODO Niños de cinco a siete años	3.er PERÍODO Niños de siete a diez años
	EL NIÑO ADAPTA LAS COSAS A SÍ MISMO, A SU FANTASÍA, A SUS NECESIDADES	LA ACTIVIDAD MOTRIZ SE UNE A LA ACTIVIDAD MENTAL	EL NIÑO SE ADAPTA A LAS NECESIDADES DE LAS COSAS
	Se da cuenta de su yo físico.	El niño pasa a la creación intencionada.	Conquista del equilibrio entre la mano y el cerebro.
	Período de la actividad puramente muscular y mecánica.		
	Actividad instintiva. Imitación maquinal	**Actividad reflexiva**	**Actividad ordenada**
	El movimiento por el movimiento	El movimiento teniendo en cuenta un fin	El movimiento sometido al pensamiento
	El pensamiento está embotado por la acción	La acción provoca el pensamiento	El pensamiento precede a la acción
	Despertar de la Atención y Hábitos { Táctil-muscular. Visual auditiva. Observación. Obediencia.	**Formación de la** Atención y Hábitos { Memoria. Iniciativa. Reflexión. Perseverancia. Orden.	**Disciplina de la** Atención y Hábitos { Memoria. Razonamiento. Espíritu de investigación. Concentración.
	CURIOSIDAD SENSORIAL.		CURIOSIDAD CIENTÍFICA
Sus preocupaciones → Conocer las	propiedades de las cosas materiales.	Deseo de utilizar la materia con un fin dado. Confección de múltiples objetos.	Conocer el origen de las cosas; El porqué.—El cómo.
	Satisfacción motriz →	**Satisfacción visual** →	**Satisfacción intelectual y moral** →
EXPERIMENTADOR			
IMITADOR	**Construcción.** (²) Bloques amontonados. Sentido del equilibrio.	Casas. Imitación reflexiva. Barcos. Máquinas. Imaginación creadora.	El interés por la locomoción domina. Historia de la civilización. (³) Geografía humana.
CONSTRUCTOR	**Número.** Primeras impresiones. Dimensiones Cantidades.	de la percepción a la concepción del número.	Orientación matemática. Geometría. Descubrimientos. Invenciones.
	Dibujo. Garrapatos. Acumulación de rasgos, formas y color.	**Discernimiento.** Gusto en la decoración. Armonía.	Preocupación por la belleza y la verdad. Exactitud.—Precisión.
CREADOR	**Música.**		
ARTISTA	**Modelado.** Placer de la manipulación. Desorden aparente.	Desorden aparente. Orden.	Obediencia consentida a las leyes descubiertas.
POETA	**Estudio de la Naturaleza—Jardinería.** Ejercicios musculares.—Cavar, regar, etc.	Ejercicios musculares.—Cavar, regar, etc. Interés, cuidados a los animales.	Afición a la Botánica y la Zoología.
COLECCIONISTA	**Lenguaje.** La palabra por la palabra. Designación de las cosas.	De la riqueza de impresión a la riqueza de expresión. Claridad, precisión en el pensamiento.	Composiciones espontáneas.—Estudio de la lengua. Gramática.

SUS AFICIONES DOMINANTES ←

El niño es ante todo

(*) Véase La Casa de los Niños, por las Srtas. LAPENDEL y AUDEMARS. Traducción española de la Srta. MERCEDES RODRIGO. Ediciones de «La Lectura».—(¹) Teniendo en cuenta las grandes variedades individuales, las edades indicadas no son más que aproximadas.—(²) No se crea que los rasgos característicos que se refieren a la evolución de una actividad son únicamente propios de esta actividad. Hay que considerarlos en su conjunto y hay que comprender que los términos «Acumulación». «La palabra por la palabra», etc., tienen cada uno en su terreno la misma significación.—(³) A la Historia de la civilización que tiene para nosotros su verdadero punto de partida en la Construcción, se relaciona todo, Dibujo, Modelado. -Estudio del número, del idioma -Zoología -Botánica, etc.

FIG. 13. Domingo Barnés Salinas, *El desenvolvimiento del niño*, 2nd edn (Barcelona: Editorial Labor, 1933), p. 142.

central pedagogical and political roles. He was active in helping to spearhead the first open-air school in Madrid from 1908 until 1918, served as a mentor to notable pedagogues at the Escuela Superior de Magisterio, and during the Second Republic briefly took the helm as Minister of Public Instruction and Fine Arts in 1933. His translations and manuals were published by presses such as La Lectura and Editorial Labor, and advertised and reviewed in reformist pedagogical journals including *La Escuela Moderna,* the *Boletín de la Institución Libre de Enseñanza,* and above all, the *Revista de Pedagogía.*[11] Manuals such as those of Barnés synthesized psychological and theoretical ideas, reconciling decades of research in child studies with new and paradigm-shifting perspectives in the psychological, biological, and physical sciences. Such a process of incorporation and adaptation can be seen, for instance, in Barnés's publication of a chart of children's growth from three to ten years of age, drawing on Mercedes Rodrigo's translation of Swiss psychologists Louise Lafendel and Mina Audemars (Fig. 1.3). In this model, children's mental development passed through clear stages. Early childhood (ages three to five) was a time of fantasy and instinct, in which sensorial and motor concerns are paramount. As children grew (ages five to seven), they passed into a period of visual acuity, in which memories and discernment began to stand out; age seven initiated a period of moral, scientific, and intellectual development.

The characterization in this image of children's early psychological character was clear. They were experimenters, creators, artists, poets, and collectors. Their minds functioned in the most open, flexible manner. New models of reading and writing emerged to serve these tendencies, most notably the concept of 'globalization', first noted by Swiss pedagogue and psychologist Claparède and popularized in the pedagogical methods of Belgian educator Ovide Decroly (1871–1932). Such methods began with the 'global' — concrete, first-hand experience through speech, play, songs, poetry, and drawings — before working back to abstract verbal representations of letters or numbers. Further, active methods of play, projects, art, and music provided an ideal fit for children's developing psyches. Only through handling, playing, experimenting with, and experiencing the world could children comprehend it, through physical engagement and leaps of mental synthesis.[12]

Sound and Symphony: Domingo Barnés and a Gestaltist View of the Mind

As Barnés's colleague Luis de Zulueta (1878–1964) proposed the need for a reversal of perspectives in the inaugural article of the *Revista de Pedagogía* in 1922, educators had to move beyond stale, atomistic views of the child's mind. Calling for a new vision of pedagogy, he adapted Ángel Ganivet's metaphor for the cognitive emergence of an idea: looking out at the sea, one sees the distant form of a boat emerging between horizon and sky. Employing a discourse of visual wholeness and integrity, he suggested that a new, 'modernísima' view was on the horizon. What had been, at first, no more than 'una leve mancha en alguna retina observadora, un punto luminoso en alguna conciencia selecta' [a faint blot on some observing retina, a luminous point in some select consciousness] gradually coalesced into 'un verdadero almacén flotante, sólidamente amarrado a la tierra de las firmes realidades' [a true floating storehouse, solidly moored to the earth of firm realities].[13] According to him (and many others), the pedagogy of the nineteenth century had run its course. Scholars had inherited a belief that the 'ciencias del espíritu' (*Geisteswissenschaften*, broadly translated as 'human sciences') must be studied under the strict criteria of the natural and physical sciences. In this, a false understanding was said to have triumphed, and such was precisely the problem Zulueta identified in Spain. Psychologists could analyse the mind in minute detail, but lose sight of its vitality:

> Descompónese la conciencia, que es, cabalmente, unidad, en sus elementos integrantes, los cuales se estudian aisladamente [...]. Pero, a veces, siéntese que el alma viviente del niño se escurre en silencio entre las manos del operador. La educación no es posible más cuando un espíritu, en su total unidad, actúa sobre otro espíritu, también en su íntegra plenitud.[14]

> [They seek to pry apart consciousness — which is nothing if not unified — into its constituent parts, studying them in isolation [...]. Yet sometimes, one feels that the living soul of the child has been wrung out by the hands of its operator. Education is only possible when one mind, in total unity, acts upon another, both in all-embracing plenitude.]

The reduction of the child's mind to nerves, mechanisms or mass was impossible, Zulueta suggested. Human development was deeper and more profound. That 'vela desplegada en el horizonte' [sail unfurled on the horizon], sailing in 'espacio infinito' [infinite space], was a new pedagogy, one inspired by the fullness and integrity of human life.[15] With the child posed as both a scientific reality and a philosophical possibility, new interpretations were necessary to mediate between qualitative and quantitative approaches.

New educationalists sought to bridge this gap through various psychological and phenomenological perspectives. Beginning with the child's earliest days, Barnés's reading of perceptual theory offers a window onto how early childhood experience was framed. 'Pero ¿cómo serán las primeras percepciones del niño?,' he asked — how does the child first perceive the world?[16] Paidologists such as Barnés sought to explain the elusive 'etapa sensorial o perceptiva con que el niño debuta en la vida' [sensorial or perceptual stage with which the child begins his life].[17] His work centred on ideas of how children receive or construct their earliest sensory impressions. When a newborn opens its eyes for the first time, what does it see? Amidst a haze of input, how does an infant know which elements — faces, lines and boundaries, movements — are significant? In other words, how does the child absorb and integrate sensorial knowledge? Was the world first viewed as a chaotic mosaic of colour and form, 'like the colours upon a painter's palette', as nineteenth-century associationist psychologists were said to have argued?[18] Or was the visible world composed of quantities that could be grasped, conjoined, and dynamically structured? Could this latter perspective open new avenues for suggesting how intuition and insight functioned in the learning process? Much scientific literature turned towards a discourse of structural, unified perception to describe the child's earliest experience of the world. In so doing, paidologists explored the singularity of the child's world.

Paidological literature constituted an interdisciplinary field of research, epistemological and existential in its reach.[19] What was the nature of the child, how did he experience the world, and how did his nascent self endure over time?[20] These questions demonstrated a firm foundation of philosophical thought established in Spain through the work of figures such as Henri Bergson and Max Scheler, and in particular, Ortega y Gasset, Barnés's 'mejor amigo y maestro' [best friend and teacher].[21] Notably, however, Barnés also demonstrated a thorough knowledge of Gestalt psychologist Kurt Koffka's (1886–1941) *Die Grundlagen der psychischen Entwicklung: Eine Einführung in die Kinderpsychologie* [The Growth of the Mind: An Introduction to Child-Psychology] (1921).[22] Koffka's work was one of the most influential examples of a new school of thought. Translated by philosopher José Gaos and published in 1926 as *Bases de la evolución psíquica: introducción a la psicología infantil*, Koffka's work had recently been published by the Revista de Occidente imprint as part of Ortega y Gasset's influential *Biblioteca de Ideas del Siglo XX*. Barnés began to incorporate its findings into his manuals, more frequently than any other single psychologist.

From as early as 1912, Berlin psychologists Koffka, Wolfgang Köhler, Kurt Lewin, and Max Wertheimer had argued that the mind comprehends objects as wholes, not as parts.[23] Drawing on the ideas of Goethe, Ernst Mach, Christian von Ehrenfels, Felix Krueger, and others, these scientists applied concepts such as structure, relationship, quality, and emergence to scientific discourse. Most fundamentally, the Gestaltists suggested that the whole, the *Gestalt*, was greater than — or rather, different from — its constituent parts. Moreover, they saw the mind itself as a vital, functional, living whole, rather than an automaton of parts and pieces. Gestalt theory claimed that all sensations were perceived as total structures, standing out from 'ground' sensations, a model of perception translated into Spanish as a relationship between a 'figura' and its 'fondo'.[24] Numerous critics would introduce and respond to its assertions, demonstrating their understanding of Gestalt psychology as part of an important wave of modern thought with direct implications on teaching and learning.[25] Elements of this model — not least, the very term 'Gestalt' — would shape discussions of cognitive development and perception through much of the twentieth century.[26] While current in pedagogical discourse by the 1930s, the word *holismo* — unlike 'Gestalt' — was not typically used in Spain. Rather, terms such as *estructura, totalidad, globalidad, unidad*, and *conjunto* were frequently employed.[27]

Barnés was one of the first intellectuals in the Spanish educational field to respond to this wave of psychological thought, incorporating brief discussions of its major points in his later paidological works. Ortega y Gasset began to develop its implications for intelligence, creativity, and culture in 'Vitalidad, alma, espíritu' (1925), venturing into the borders and interpenetrations of the mind, the physical body, and the spirit.[28] In turn, Barnés's paidological writings integrated a parallel line of formal rhetoric into explanations of the child's perceptual experiences. From a Gestaltist point of view, first perceptions consisted of forms or structures, in relief from an undifferentiated background. For the Gestalt psychologists, perception was as simple as black and white, form and field, presence and absence. Barnés emphasized how the 'new' psychology defined such contrasts — as a 'fenómeno delimitado y definido, una cualidad, se destaca sobre el fondo ilimitado y poco definido' [delimited and defined phenomena, in relief against a non-limited and little defined background].[29] For example, when the infant sees its mother, Barnés describes a structural difference: 'Que en el hecho de la visión de la madre, hecho en el cual el niño percibe una estructura real y concreta de fondo y de figura, de un fondo neutro sobre el cual se destaca una figura, la madre' [So that in the moment of seeing his mother, a moment in which the child perceives a real, concrete structure of figure and field, of a neutral background against which a figure, the mother, stands out].[30] Barnés explicitly employs Gestaltist language of a neutral 'fondo' and a significant 'figura' to describe a principal paidological imaginary: the child's perceptual reality, as various other pedagogues would similarly do.

Why did this 'new' science of the mind seem to hold such promise? For one, its assertions were radical. The Gestalt movement reacted to the perceived 'crisis' in psychology, which since the late nineteenth century had been criticized as overly mechanistic and atomistic, losing sight of the forest for the trees.[31] Classical psychology focused on isolated mental elements and sensations, rather than taking wholes of function, perception, or movement into account. In contrast, Gestalt psychology held that dynamic structures governed mental development. The Gestalt psychologists posed the mind and its activity as a dynamic totality. Over the course of childhood, they argued, experience did not simply input isolated atoms of knowledge into the mind. Rather, new information continually reconfigured and restructured the whole.

By defending a new model of the developing mind and its function, Gestalt psychology aimed to combine the rigours of methodological science with a humanistic, dynamic, vital perspective. It represented not just a psychological school, but an entire current of holistic thought. It countered prevailing modes of mental analysis which attempted to identify 'atoms' of sensation. As William James described this broader problem as early as 1890, such efforts reduced the mind's 'continuous flow of mental stream' to a 'brickbat plan of construction'.[32] Perception was coherent: it could not be broken down into a chain of elemental sensations. As with Bergson, who described change itself as reality, as 'the very substance of things', consciousness was to be understood as a dynamic whole.[33] Related metaphors of form and structure underlay the conclusions of Gestalt psychology since Max Wertheimer's identification of the so-called 'phi-phenomenon' in 1912. As he showed, humans perceive objects viewed in rapid succession as one continuous whole — as in the viewing of film. According to Koffka, Gestalt theory's great success was to join 'the movement experience, the movement phi, to the psychology of pure simultaneity and of pure succession, the first corresponding to form or shape, the second to rhythm, melody, etc.'.[34]

In both a metaphorical and a psychological sense, this notion of a continuous, total force was central to the way in which paidologists posed the problem of the child's growth and development. The child's dynamism was both an ungraspable entity and the core of a larger phenomenological problem of human existence. Ortega described each generation as a moment of vitality, a 'pulsation' of historical potency:

'cada pulsación tiene una fisonomía peculiar, única; es un latido impermutable en la serie del pulso, como lo es cada nota en el desarrollo de una melodía' [every pulsation has a particular, unique physiognomy; it is the unchangeable beat in a series of pulses, as is every note in the development of a melody].[35]

Precisely such a metaphorical lens of structure, form, and contrast came to be employed in descriptions of visual, auditory, and spatial experiences. Discussing neonatal instincts, Barnés quoted Koffka: 'Una acción instintiva no nos hace la impresión de una serie de sonidos producidos por un niño que oprime en sucesión caprichosa cualesquiera teclas del piano, sino la de una melodía' [An instinctive action does not make the impression of a series of sounds produced by a child who presses piano keys at random, but rather that of a melody].[36] The melody was an example often used in Gestalt arguments as an example of a structure — something that could be transposed to other keys, such that no element was tonally the same, yet was nonetheless recognized as itself. Human behaviour was considered as such a series of harmonic and unified structures, echoing Ortega's suggestion that maturity was nothing more than an integration, rather than a suppression, of childhood. Experience worked upon one, over time, repeating and building upon its earliest melodic harmonies: 'íntegramente, colabora en nuestro ser actual, como en el fin de una melodía actúa su comienzo' [integrally, it shapes our current being, just as the end of a melody re-enacts its beginning].[37] Whether responding directly to Koffka's writings or Ortega's phenomenological descriptions of human development, Barnés's descriptions of the infant's movements were Gestaltist in both influence and portrayal.

Not only were early actions, reactions, and perceptual cues crucial to understanding development, but they also provided one of Barnés's strongest arguments for a structural, indeed Gestaltist, mode of description. Barnés described instincts in the newborn as equivalent to rhythm, melody, or visual form: 'análogos a fenómenos tales como el ritmo, la melodía y la figura' [analogous to such phenomena as rhythm, melody and figure].[38] This was an understanding of movement and reaction which treats the child's body as a dynamic system in which the whole is truly greater than the sum of the parts: a 'curso unitario, una sucesión de movimientos continuada. No una pluralidad de movimientos parciales, sino una totalidad de conducta única, articulada, en la que cada miembro parece determinado por su posición' [a unitary course, a continuous succession of movements. Not a plurality of partial movements, but a totality of unified, articulated behaviour, in which each unit is determined by its position].[39] While seemingly distant from the study of the child, motifs of melody, rhythm, figure, and form were rife in paidological literature. Such terms were used as metaphors for perception, and, as will be seen, were mirrored in diverse reading and learning methods and even the newly modish rhythmic gymnastics.[40]

Joining Barnés in elucidating a new psychological paradigm, contemporaries and protégés offered their own descriptions of structural difference and coherence. For instance, in a 1931 text Rafael Verdier, a teacher from Málaga, explained the critical difference between how the 'old' and the 'new' psychologies understood infant perception. Similarly to Barnés, Verdier's analysis of perception via structures, qualities, figures, and fields followed conventional Gestaltist modes of description. Classical psychology, Verdier explained, understood the neo-natal perceptual field as a 'conjunto amorfo y disperso de sensaciones' [amorphous and scattered mass of sensations], a 'caos primigenio' [primitive chaos] that only successive experiences began to fashion into order. This was the superseded notion of infant vision that Barnés summarized as a 'fondo indiferenciado, caótico, concebido como un mosaico' [undifferentiated, chaotic background, perceived as a mosaic]. In contrast, as Verdier noted, the child's environment constituted for him a 'todo homogéneo' [a homogenous whole].[41]

It was the appearance — or rather, the perception — of outstanding objects that made something significant, both in Gestalt theory and in the newly-opened eyes of the child. Verdier returned to the principles of Gestalt perception to make this point. In inscribing a point (.) on a page, Verdier wrote, one has created a structure — a 'figura' on a 'fondo'. This structure is the relationship between this point and its homogenous background. If we add another point (..), there arises a second relationship, that of a reciprocal one between structures. Adding a third and larger point (...), further relationships follow, including those of relative size. One may conceive of an infinite number of relationships in this way, Verdier wrote, suggesting that such is precisely what happens in the mind of the newborn child, and in all perceptual acts: 'Podemos dividir las cosas totales de nuestro alrededor en dos sectores: uno constituido por la totalidad que *no nos interesa momentáneamente* y otro por uno o varios objetos que en ese mismo momento tiran de nuestro atención' [We can divide the total things around us into two kinds: one constituted by the totality *that does not currently interest us,* and another by the object or various objects that, at this moment, are attracting our attention].[42] It was that common character of *not interesting us* that made one's surroundings psychically as homogenous as a white sheet of paper, or vice versa.

Principles of structural unity had become primary lenses for conveying perception. Verdier envisioned a baby's encounter with an orange from a holistic perspective:

> El niño de modo forzoso debe percibir de golpe el total edificio de la fruta. La naranja, desde el punto de vista psíquico, constituye indestructible síntesis armónica. Y, sin embargo, nada significa si no se halla unida en ciertas relaciones esenciales a las restantes cosas de entorno.[43]

> [The child perceives the total structure of the fruit forcefully, all at once. The orange, from a psychical point of view, constitutes an indestructible, harmonious whole. Nevertheless, it is meaningless if it is not joined up into essential formations with other surrounding objects.]

Beside the Gestaltist echo of a figure and its field, the influence of Ortega's philosophy is undeniable and, indeed, far more explicit than in Barnés's work. Unsurprisingly, Verdier made clear that he considered Ortega the first to connect 'new' scientific ideas to learning and culture.[44] In this passage, Verdier framed the child's vision as a relationship between subject and circumstance; the latter term being inseparable from Ortega's philosophical *oeuvre*. More specifically, it seems

to echo a famous lecture given by Ortega in 1929, less than two years before
Verdier's writing. For Ortega, an orange acted as the key image demonstrating the
impossibility of full, objective knowledge. An observer can only ever glimpse half
of the orange at once and must understand its totality through intuition. As one
only ever views the exterior, or perhaps ever thinner slices of its interior, the full
and total essence of the fruit escapes one: 'A esa intuición inadecuada, pero siempre
perfeccionable, siempre más cerca de ser adecuada, llamamos "experiencia"' [This
inadequate but ever perfectible intuition, always moving closer towards adequacy,
we call 'experience'].[45] Such experience is what the neonate lacks, and what the
child seeks in each successive encounter with the perceptual world. The child
moves from sensation to intuition to experience, towards its own limited outlook
on knowledge of the world.

Tying the child's visual perception to the learning process, Verdier wrote of the
sudden 'golpe' [impact] by which infants grasp formal significance. In the midst
of a larger environment, suddenly a form or boundary becomes clear ('nacen
mágicamente los objetos' [objects are magically born]), forming an indelible
relationship between a child's total perceptual world and the objects within it.[46]
Verdier employs key terms of 'estructura' [structure], 'cualidad' [quality], 'figura'
[figure], and 'fondo' [background] to illustrate the tendency he called one of the
most interesting in modern psychology: the mind's capacity to recognize and form
relationships. In so doing, he incorporated a holistic rhetoric of structure, quality,
and form into his exploration of the child's biological and mental environment.
Further, he did so in a way that bridges visual and auditory descriptions of
sensation. The newborn child's image of its mother, for instance, was understood as
a holistic sensorial totality: 'Si aparece en su campo visual la figura materna, percibe
sobre un fondo de cosas indiferentes un conjunto de notas que se destacan, una bien
trabada melodía de formas, movimientos y actitudes, que el término mamá inscribe'
[If the maternal figure appears in his visual field, he perceives on an indifferent
background a mass of notes that begin to differentiate themselves, a well-woven
melody of shapes, movements, and attitudes, inscribed by the word *mamá*].[47] Word,
sound, and figure act as one meaningful and unified structure in the infant mind.

In particular, faces were represented as constituting not a collection of distinct
features but as an immediate whole — an organically coherent structure. According
to the Gestaltist view, early visual cognition depended on a child's recognition
of relations and structures. The child recognized, for instance, a highly complex
structure — the mother's face — within a few weeks of birth. Her face constituted a
unified whole, namely the definition of a *Gestalt*. Similarly, the first sounds to which
infants responded, according to Koffka, were human voices. Barnés made clear that
the new generation of psychologists saw these as complex structures, engaging
the infant's mind far more immediately than simple stimuli.[48] The coherence of
a face thus became one significant piece of evidence used by Gestaltists to prove
that perception involved the recognition of a whole, not merely a summation
of sensory elements. The Aragonese teacher Teodoro Causí Casaus integrated
Koffka's argument about infants' interest in faces to argue for children's preference

for complex forms over simple shapes and structures. As will be discussed, he used evidence from Gestalt experiments to argue that innovative reading methods known as 'ideo-visual' learning through 'globalization' had concrete scientific grounding. Because the child tended to grasp wholes before parts, he or she understood and incorporated experiential realities, like faces, voices, and words, long before individual letters and numbers. As Causí made clear, what was simple for the child 'no está nunca en lo aislado, sino en la totalidad, en la *estructura uniforme*, sobre la cual puede aparecer *el relieve de una cualidad*, es decir, en lo organizado y en lo vivo' [is never in the isolated, but in the totality, in the uniform structure, on which can appear the relief of a quality, that is to say, on the organized and alive].[49] Koffka argued that the mechanism behind a child's aforementioned recognition of faces had direct implications for all other forms of perception, for instance touch:

> If we wish to reconstruct the phenomenal counterpart of this objective behaviour we must consider the child's state as a whole. Consequently, we ought not to say that the child sees a luminous point; but rather that the child sees a luminous point upon an indifferent background; or, in the case of touch, that pressure is felt upon the hand, otherwise untouched. Generally stated, from an unlimited and ill-defined background there has arisen a limited and somewhat definite phenomenon, a quality.[50]

Developing terms of contrast, Barnés, like the Gestalt psychologists, drew his arguments back to the experience of perception as a structural totality, noting for instance that milk in the child's mouth was an 'estructura' which would provoke precisely such phenomenological reactions of contrasting states.[51] One knows something is hot not because it burns, but because it forms a recognizable structure within a larger whole.

Recurring notions of structure as a dynamic interplay of 'figura' and 'fondo' were applied to rhythm and sound in the psychological literature, just as they had long been understood from a phenomenological perspective. Describing the way in which the mind interprets sound, Koffka sets up a certain rhythmical pattern as follows: '__ . . __ . . __ ', in which the dashes are read as silent and the full stops as beats. The question is, what do we hear between the beats? Koffka was suggesting that silence is just as integral to our total experience as are 'active' sounds. These intervals were equivalent to a visual pattern of figure and field. This phenomenon could be applied more widely to the auditory world, as well as to any sensorial experience:

> Este campo o fondo puede ser 'el silencio' o la mezcla de los rumores de la calle, los cuales, en una ciudad nunca cesan durante el día. Y ahora observemos esto. Cuando abandonamos la ciudad para trasladarnos al campo y nos sentamos a trabajar ante nuestra mesa, podemos ser sorprendidos por un extraño fenómeno, el de que podemos 'oír' el silencio. El fondo auditivo de nuestro trabajo se ha alterado y esta alteración nos sorprende forzosamente.[52]

> [This field or background can be the 'silence' or a mix of sounds from the street, which in a city are unceasing during the day. And now, let us observe something. When we leave the city for the country and sit down at our desk to

work, we are startled by a strange phenomenon: that we can 'hear' the silence. The auditory background of our work has changed, and this change is a forceful surprise.]

Koffka's description of an accustomed white noise or auditory threshold accords with common experience. Indeed, the Gestaltists' work attempted to provide a scientific and theoretical framework for what philosophers and writers had long understood.

Perceptual contrast was a long-recognized psychological phenomenon, including within Spanish writings on perception. Unamuno, for one, had earlier incorporated the concept of 'discernment' into his description of consciousness in *En torno al casticismo* (1895). He noted that those accustomed to sleeping in silence would find themselves awoken by noise. Those used to noise, on the other hand, would be awoken by silence. The contrast between a steady state and a spike is significant: 'de una ruptura de la continuidad en espacio o tiempo' [a rupture in the continuity of space or time]. Environmental discernment, in Unamuno's synthesis, was 'la percepción de una diferencia, y que conocer una cosa es distinguirla de las demás' [the perception of a difference, that to know something is to distinguish it from everything else].[53] Similarly, Ortega would employ such a description of psychological discernment in *Meditaciones del Quijote* (1914). Describing woodland sounds, he characterized these as 'líneas o puntos de sonoridad que destacan por su genuina plenitud y su peculiar brillo sobre una muchedumbre de otros rumores y sones con ellos entretejidos' [lines or points of sonority that stand out for their genuine fullness and particular brightness above a mass of other intertwined noises and sounds].[54] The relationship of a figure to its enveloping field was portrayed as critically intertwined. Outstanding 'points' or 'lines' were given tangible shape and visual form within a profound quality of experiential reality.[55]

What was the impact of these ideas in Spain? How did notions of the child's mind change as new scientific 'revolutions' superseded prior conceptions? From writings on children's perceptual experience during the early 1930s to the Civil War's rupture of educational reform in Spain and beyond, a dialogue began to be established between these early models and a legacy of phenomenological thought through the mid-twentieth century. In 1933, Barnés's former students Juan Jaén and José Peinado published a teachers' manual on paidology, a 1935 review of which called the field a 'new science' and added that it had only recently been added as a subject in the *escuelas normales*, Spain's national teacher-training institutes.[56] These authors acknowledged their debt with a dedication to 'nuestro querido maestro Domingo Barnés' [our dear teacher Domingo Barnés].[57] Their work benefitted from a prolific paidological field in pre-Civil War Spain, with a wealth of newly translated pedagogical and psychological works, from Koffka to Édouard Claparède (1873–1940) to Jean Piaget (1896–1980), on which to consolidate this expertise.

Each of these influences found a place in their portrayals of perception. They, too, made frequent use of synesthetic descriptions of melody and to convey the newborn experience. Following a discussion of the child's development of vision, Jaén and Peinado imagine:

> Del barullo se pasa al sonido, a la sinfonía. Si a un campesino se le pone de pronto en la Puerta del Sol, de Madrid, lo primero que ve es el conjunto, el barullo, y, poco a poco aquel caos se irá ordenando para él y se irá fijando en cada una de las cosas que allí hay.[58]

> [From a din of noise one moves towards sound, symphony. If a peasant suddenly stood in the middle of Madrid's Puerta del Sol, he would first see the totality, the racket; but little by little, that chaos would begin to order and stabilize into each of the things before them.]

As these authors suggest in forcefully synesthetic terms, the uninitiated *campesino* newly arrived in the heart of Madrid finds himself confronted by a wall of new and overwhelming urban stimuli. No less powerful, they suggested, was the newborn's experience of its surrounding world. The *campesino* is as lost in the sensorial world as a newborn: seeking out visual objects, structures, and familiar form to demarcate and structure his worldview.[59] Jaén and Peinado put forward explicitly Gestaltist descriptions of early childhood development that bound touch, spatiality, and vision. Within six to eight months of the child's opening his eyes, they explained, perceptive interests widened and motor coordination began to develop. They wrote of objects in the child's hands as conceptual and physical wholes: 'Estas partes no serán distinguidas hasta mucho más tarde. Al principio, el objeto no es percibido más que en conjunto. Lo primero que percibe el niño son estructuras' [These parts will not be distinguished until much later. At first, the object is only perceived as a whole. The first thing the child perceives are structures].[60] Such rhetoric consciously blurred auditory, visual and other forms of perception, at least in the ways it was popularly explained and communicated to fellow teachers — whether by psychologists such as Koffka or educationalists such as Jaén and Peinado.

Paidological literature used terms of structure, totality, and depth to link the child's biological nature, environment, and phenomenological experience. In these accounts, experience was active, forming representations of the world that were total, vital, and whole. Such a perspective suggests how entwined this mode of 'new psychology' had become with the more profound phenomenological aspects of the child's cognitive development. This rhetoric grew from a larger discourse on how objects are distinguished and interpreted. How could the relationship between the physical, the corporal, and the internal or spiritual be known? These images and imaginaries crossed philosophical and religious lines, gesturing at larger questions of wholeness, totality, and difference. As the Marianist psychologist Pedro Martínez Saralegui, for instance, wrote in the Catholic pedagogical journal *Atenas* in 1931, one must use both quantitative and qualitative — phenomenological — means to understand child development. He described the relationship between child and observer as one of analogy, comparison, and representation. To Martínez, the results gained by observing a child's reactions remained ever a 'signo', a sign, of internal properties unknown and unverifiable:

> Veo llorar a un niño e interpreto que está triste. He aquí un signo o fenómeno exterior del niño, que me indica o asegura la existencia, en aquel mismo

instante, de otro fenómeno individual o personal e interior de ese mismo niño: la tristeza.[61]

[I see a child crying and infer that he is sad. Here is the sign, the exterior phenomenon, given by the child, which indicates and assures me of the momentary existence of a separate, individual, or personal and interior phenomenon common to this same child: that of sadness.]

According to Martínez, knowledge was only possible by imperfect analogy. The interior world remained always inaccessible, but only exterior signs could be compared: between 'los signos que el niño y yo manifestamos exteriormente, no entre el fenómeno físico y psíquico del niño' [the signs that the child and I manifest externally, and not between the physical and psychological phenomena of the child]. Using a mathematical formula ('f:f = e:e') to represent this relationship, his argument sought to bridge the inaccessibility of the mind and soul with logic and structure. In this sense, all gesture was a form of sign, he argued in structural terms.

Through such means, diverse reformers sought to align the realms of experiments and experience. These descriptions continued a post-Proustian discourse on how objects were distinguished and interpreted in the eyes of the child, a question that was key to a deep visualization of mental development. Whether in the child or the philosopher, paidologists of a phenomenological ilk bridged viable 'quantitative' science with 'qualitative' philosophical imaginaries of the child's developing world of perception. Using new modes of holistic scientific discourse, paidologists tapped into longstanding philosophical questions of experience, knowledge, and perception. As has been shown, Barnés was one among various paidologists reading and integrating holistic psychological terms and concepts into his descriptions. Critically, these built on larger impulses of phenomenological thought from Bergson to Ortega, through the scientific authority of German psychology. Together, they suggest the philosophical depth of Spanish paidological thought during the 1920s and early 1930s. Only upon such a basis of rhetoric, image, and imaginary could a more vital, flexible pedagogy be built.

Globalization of the Mind: Reading Holistically from Llorca to Álvarez

Just as psychologists and paidologists came to ask how infants and children saw and processed the world — whether as a whole or a part, suddenly or gradually — so too did philosophers, artists, scholars, teachers, and literary critics interrogate what these concepts meant for intellectual and cultural development. As various theories converged towards a 'holistic' perceptual model of the mind, individual theories gained in stature as part of a larger intellectual wave. According to Ortega's theory of the 'great idea' in human history, paradigm-shifting ideas always arose from a constellation of different notions, independent and individual, which came together to form a greater whole. Employing perspectivist imagery of visual angles and perspective, Ortega suggested that radical, world-changing ideas were accepted as simple, elegant, and *right* precisely because of the multiple points of origin that gave rise to them.[62] Within Spanish pedagogy, such a convergence was claimed in the relationship between holistic theories and a new 'great idea' in educational theory known as 'globalization'. Manifesting in practice as the 'método global' [global method] of learning, a pedagogical notion of globalization relied on the idea that the child primarily perceived the world as a whole (through sensations and concepts), rather than as a conglomeration of individual elements (letters and words). Spanish teacher and pedagogue Juan Comas (1900–79) attributed the child's mental act of recognizing a whole to 'la teoría de la forma, *Gestalttheorie*' [structural theory, Gestalt theory]. School inspector and psychopedagogue C. A. Figuerido, meanwhile, claimed that techniques such as the Decroly method were to pedagogy what the Gestalt movement was to psychology. Upon a concrete structure of comprehension ('global, primario'), the mind developed towards ever more complex abstraction and rational thinking over time.[63]

Within this 'great idea' of holistic perception, a 'globalized' view of the child's mind began to guide reading practices. 'Cuando el niño mira una persona, un objeto, un grabado, un dibujo, ¿percibe el conjunto, una parte, uno o muchos detalles?' [When the child looks at a person, an object, an engraving, a drawing, does he see the whole, a part, one, or many details?], one psychologist asked.[64] The answer to that query — how children perceived the connections between and within objects and ideas — would have concrete effects on educational methods. In a 1921 essay entitled 'The Child's Idea of Part,' the young Piaget claimed that 'sentences are not read and understood in detail, but in one inspection'.[65] Coinciding with Koffka's work on child development, concepts of mental unity entered the Spanish classroom chiefly through the theory of early childhood 'globalization', as elaborated by psychologist and pedagogue Claparède and developed through Decroly's experimental curricular methods.[66] Words were read as visual units rather than collections of letters or sounds. Experience of a word was more significant than an intellectual grasp of it. Each of these theories used spatial terms to understand the child's mind and to design teaching accordingly. Across Europe, globalization was one of the most significant psychopedagogical concepts of the 1920s, with an array of related terms, such as 'esquematismo' [schematism], 'sincretismo' [syncretism], or 'yuxtaposición' [juxtaposition] conveying related psychological concepts.[67]

Surveying the literature on the globalist method of 'ideo-visual' learning in the *Revista de Pedagogía*, Swiss educationalists Robert Dottrens and Emilie Margairaz concluded in 1933 that for the child, sight began not as a collection of isolated parts but as a block, as a unity. Further, this 'visión del conjunto' carried significant implications for teaching. Dottrens and Margairaz used the example of physiognomy and recognition, noting that perception — whether of a face, a picture, or an object — was attained at a glance. The child, they claimed, scanned for totality even when details were not yet fully understood. The concept of globalization was frequently described and explained to teachers in journals such as the *Revista de Pedagogía* and *La Escuela Moderna*, with reports detailing how such theories played out in classrooms abroad and advocating the adoption of similar methods in Spain. One early explanation of reading, adapted from an 1898 textbook of school psychology, described words as a larger mental image or concept ('perro'), which the child must understand from the 'unión íntima' of various sensorial angles: acoustic, muscular, and visual (Fig. 1.4).[68]

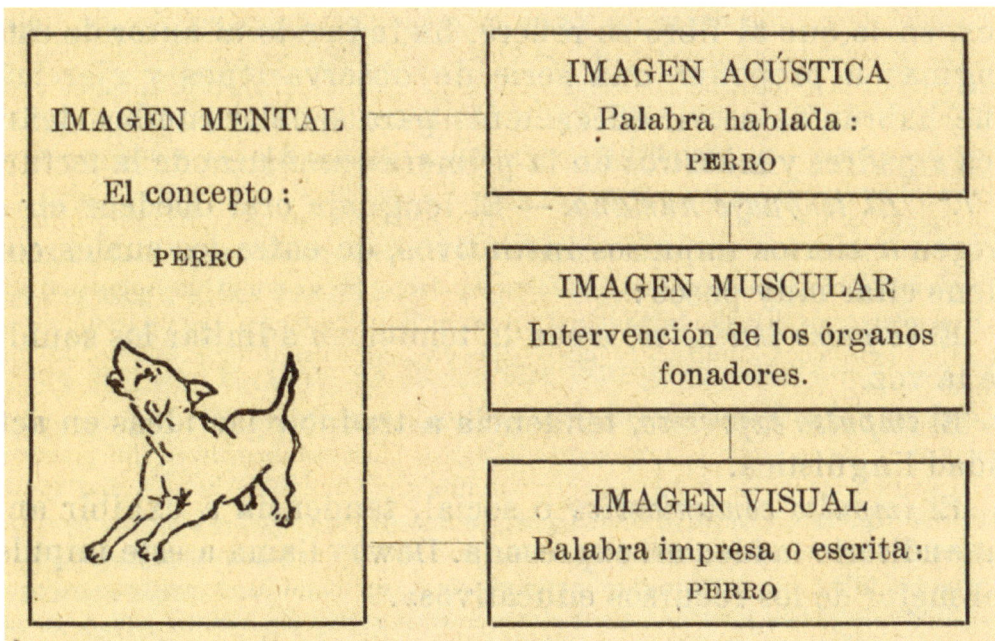

FIG. 1.4. Reading was said to involve a holistic process of synthesis. Here, the concept of a dog is shown as the product of acoustic, muscular and visual input.
Source: Maximiano Flores, 'La enseñanza de la lectura', *La Escuela Moderna*, 34.398 (1924), 802–24 (p. 806).

The pedagogical implications of globalist processing in reading and other forms of primary learning were major. Concepts would be learned before words, words before syllables, syllables before letters, and so on. Reading could not begin simply with the letters of the alphabet, but rather from ideas and experiences themselves. The same principle was seen to hold true universally, for instance in mathematics or music. Children could recognize a melody as a whole, 'de golpe' [at once], rather than as a succession of notes.[69] Equally, before they could read music, they might recognize a song on paper days after it was shown, simply from the shapes on the page.[70] Accounts by Spanish pedagogues suggested that the child sought to grasp the total physiognomy of the word itself: 'la palabra y aún la frase forman un dibujo cuya fisonomía general le atrae mucho más que el dibujo de letras aisladas' [the word and even the sentence form a drawing whose general physiognomy is far more recognizable than isolated letters].[71]

These principles applied to children's recognition of visual and conceptual parts and their greater whole. Pedagogue Ángel Llorca (1866–1942), of the Grupo Escolar Cervantes in Madrid's Cuatro Caminos neighbourhood, created textbooks and classroom methods that drew on globalization theory. He started with listening, speaking, and drawing, such that direct experience preceded reading and writing. Dialogue was a necessary precursor to literacy, providing a radical inversion of traditional learning methods.[72] In a primer for the child's first year at school, Llorca had the teacher begin by reading out descriptive passages from classic or contemporary works such as Ortega's *El Espectador*. He asked his young students to describe who and what each sentence treated, then to imagine and draw the scene from their own perspective.[73] Reviewing this text, school inspector and pedagogue Luis Santullano (1879–1952) wrote that Llorca's work provided an antidote to what Unamuno once called the 'pedagogía del pluscuamperfecto' [pedagogy of the plusquamperfect], namely a pedagogy of mechanized repetition, grammatical analysis, and memorization.[74] Rather, Llorca awoke interest by asking children probing questions about their own lives. In so doing, he suggested in Orteguian terms that children's literacy must be founded on a sound understanding of the 'personajes, animales y cosas' [people, animals, things] that made up their world.[75]

Building on such a vivifying approach, Rafael Verdier and Víctor Argueta's 1935 manual *Ya leo: la lectura y la escritura por el método ideovisual* formalized this practice in a work that would be twice reprinted after the Civil War, in 1945 and 1954. Writing to teachers, Verdier and Argueta noted that the 'ideo-visual' method of learning had been taken up enthusiastically in Spain.[76] They admitted that the first stages could be disheartening. In copying words, the child began writing only in an indecipherable scrawl. But the teacher must not give up, Verdier and Argueta cautioned: 'Dentro de ese garabato irán surgiendo letras, hasta aparecer finalmente la frase clara y limpia' [Within this scribbling will begin to surface letters, until finally the sentence appears, clean and clear].[77] Rather than learning the alphabet and using this as building blocks, children started the reading process with a graspable whole: concepts, speech, activity. In this text, simple elements built up to more complex structures. The idea was to make reading as natural as speaking, tailoring teaching to children's cognitive abilities and growth: 'En su inteligencia se va acumulando silenciosamente este trabajo que, un día, de modo explosivo, hace aparición. Ese día puede afirmarse que el niño lee' [This work accumulates silently in the mind until one day, explosively, it appears. This is the day it can truly be said that the child can read].[78] The evolution of learning was portrayed as a revolution, with one cognitive understanding overtaking the next.

A close link between ideo-visual learning and holistic theories held in both practice and theory. Teodoro Causí's essay 'La globalización de Decroly y la psicología de la estructura', published in the *Revista de Pedagogía* in 1930, testified to what he depicted as a newly unified school of thought. Causí argued that the child's learning could be extrapolated outward to encompass a society-wide scientific framework under development. As with knowledge, the developing child passed through two distinct phases of thought: the global and the analytical. The 'global' perspective began with a 'visión de conjunto' or the whole, while an analytical phase attempted to understand complexity through its elements.[79] He suggested that children's globalist tendencies provided the foundation of their future ability to reason scientifically:

> No hay ciencia sin hipótesis; pero ¿qué es la hipótesis, sino una visión global anticipada para la cual no existe más que lo general, dibujado en sus vagos contornos sobre un fondo de nebulosidades? Cuando queremos saber lo

que es una flor, por ejemplo, no atendemos primero y separadamente a sus cualidades específicas; no analizamos su aroma, sus colores, su forma, sino que nos formamos una representación única, totalizada, de todos sus elementos componentes.[80]

[There is no science without hypothesis, but what is hypothesis but an anticipatory, global vision, of which we have nothing more than a general, vague outline against a background of nebulosities? When we want to know what a flower is, for example, we do not attend first and separately to its specific qualities; we do not analyse its aroma, its colours, its shape, but rather we form a total, unitary representation of all its component elements.]

Causí used theories of child development to argue for a holistic revolution in pedagogy. When children saw the world 'globally', he contended, they constructed hypotheses. The child was a proto-scientist, forming knowledge about the world via constant exploration. Understanding these tendencies, he wrote, could bring about a synthesis of scientific and philosophical thought — helping to reconcile the classic opposition of *ciencia y vida*.

Emphasizing the shared reception of Gestalt theory and *globalización* in Spanish pedagogy, Causí noted that the convergence of such ideas was nothing new. As Ortega had claimed about the appearance of 'great ideas' in history, it was a common phenomenon for disparate minds in faraway places to come up with radically altering, aligned ideas.[81] Such was the case with globalization theory and *Gestalttheorie*, Causí suggested:

El parentesco entre la psicología de la estructura y la concepción de Decroly no puede ser más íntimo. La globalización no es más que lo que [Eduard] Spranger llama un complejo de sentido, una totalidad, una unidad de vida, en la que cada elemento es parte de una estructura en la que cumple su función, en la que vuelca su completa individualidad, mediante la cual realiza su vida.[82]

[The resemblance between Gestalt psychology and Decroly's conception could not be closer. Globalization is little more than what Spranger called a complex of meaning, a totality, a unit of life, in which each element is part of a larger structure in which it carries out its function, from which it draws its individuality, through which it realizes its own life.]

The structure of Gestalt psychology gave globalization theory its power. Despite their different origins, Causí suggested that globalization and Gestalt psychology fit into a wider intellectual discourse in European society. With this argument, Causí began to move within a broader network, from Ortega to Hermann von Keyserling, Bergson and Freud to Edmund Husserl. Causí's interest was not limited to the mind, but rather encompassed life in its totality. Holistic thought relied on one significant idea, namely of the precedence of the whole over the particular. Carried to its extremes, Causí suggested, this 'great idea' of mental totality could change the direction of teaching, from facts to concepts, rote memorization to free play. It allowed pedagogues to abandon broken moulds for new methods, to study the child objectively:

El pedagogo, libre de los prejuicios de la vieja escuela, quedó frente a frente con el niño, cuyo proceso mental siguió; y los psicólogos de la Gestalt acudieron a la observación de la vida animal para sacar conclusiones ciertas acerca del debatido problema de la inteligencia animal. Uno y otros se encontraron ante hechos nuevos, o ante hechos viejos, pero mal interpretados por las brumas del prejuicio; en la presencia de unos seres que mostraban al descubierto procesos idénticos, *mutatis mutandis*, las conclusiones tenían que converger en un punto dado.[83]

[The pedagogue, free of the prejudices of the old school, stood face to face with the child whose mental processes he followed; and the Gestalt psychologists hewed to the observation of animal life in order to draw valid conclusions on disputed questions of animal intelligence. One after another they found themselves before new facts, or before old facts misinterpreted by prejudice; in the presence of beings that openly demonstrated identical processes, *mutatis mutandis*, the conclusions had to converge at a given point.]

But study did not stop at analysis. Following the pedagogy of Decroly and others, Causí sought to turn the Spanish classroom itself into a vital structure built around the individual child's inherent interests and curiosity. If mental images were 'figuras sobre un fondo' in the Gestaltist sense, then it suggested a new context for Ortega's philosophical claim of circumstance, that, for instance, a stone along the road depended upon the earth for its existence.[84] In other words, an object gains its presence only in mutual relationship with its environment. Equally, a person, a child, gains personhood through his or her physical, temporal, and intellectual surroundings. Anything less would deny the dynamism of the individual and the vitality of the surrounding world. This mode of thinking was meant to lend meaning to all the elements which influenced one's being: 'en su excelsa cualidad de ser parte de un todo' [in its sublime quality of being part of a larger whole].[85]

The idea that the mind apprehends forms and complexes as structures primarily, and only secondarily as parts, contradicted the seemingly eternal scientific dogma of induction: that facts could be generalized towards a wider principle. The mind was no longer considered to ascend only from the part to the whole, like a series of tram stops along a route. According to Causí, society's notion of what was 'simple' for the child was mistaken:

La vieja pedagogía, demasiado servil a las palabras, veía lo fácil en lo simple y lo simple en las partes, y veía lo difícil en lo complejo y lo complejo en el todo, y fiel a tan esquemático concepto de las cosas, llevó la desmenuzación y el casuísmo a un grado tan avanzado que las ciencias quedaron reducidas a polvos de conocimiento, con lo que el aprendizaje escolar aumentaba sus dificultades en la misma medida en que se multiplicaban las desarticulaciones.[86]

[The old pedagogy, far too servile to words, saw easiness in simplicity and simplicity in parts, while it saw difficulty in the complex and complexity in the whole. Faithful to such a schematic concept, it led the breakdown and casuism to such a state that the sciences were reduced to mere grains of knowledge. The challenges of education increased as its disarticulations multiplied.]

What was formally 'simple' were single letters, the alphabet, which together build syllables, words, and sentences. These are the elements that compose writing, and which build meaning. Yet parsing language was seen to rupture the totality of comprehension. By breaking knowledge into atomic pieces, or 'desarticulaciones', the greater meaning and function of the subject was lost. The problem was that this method lost sight of conceptual vitality, such that for the child, what was 'easy' was not the letter, but the sentence or phrase endowed with meaning, one which 'posee un sentido y está dotado de una vivencia' [possesses meaning and is enriched by experience].[87] Causí's notion of 'sentido' was more than merely literal. It stood in for layered concepts of life, experience, reality, *razón vital* — everything the 'disarticulated' word lacked.

If the 'old pedagogy' was 'servile' to words, what was the alternative? Whether using grammar to define language or lines to signify the physical world, Causí suggested, one's understanding of reality suffered. Educators must celebrate that which was 'menos geométrico, pero más vivo' [less geometrical, but more alive].[88] To illustrate the vivification of reality in schools, he used the Decrolian model of a word's significance bringing meaning to a phrase (for instamce the connotations of *mamá*), comparing the filling out of a word in the child's mind to a Gestalt taking shape from its background:

> La repugnancia que el niño siente por el elemento suelto, por la letra, por ejemplo, en el aprendizaje de la lectura y de la escritura, pertenece al mismo orden de fenómenos de que nos habla Koffka, de que el niño pequeño no tiene interés por los colores sencillos, sino por los rostros humanos, porque la verdadera sencillez en los fenómenos primitivos no está nunca en lo aislado, sino en la totalidad, en la estructura uniforme, sobre la cual puede aparecer el relieve de una cualidad, es decir, en lo organizado y en lo vivo.[89]

> [The repugnance that the child feels for the solitary element, for the letter, for example, when learning to read and write, belongs to the same order of phenomena of which Koffka writes: that the small child is not interested in simple colours, but rather in human faces, for true simplicity in primitive phenomena is never in the isolated, but in totality, in uniform structure, upon which may appear the relief of a quality, that is to say, in the organized and the alive.]

Organized and alive: this was perhaps the clearest refutation one could make of both mechanistic and 'chaotic' explanations of the world, suggesting that both life and perception were themselves organic and functional structures. Causí's melding of Gestaltist and globalization theories suggested that new arguments could be made for concrete pedagogical changes in the child's environment.

The advent of 'globalization' reading theory in Spain is one marker of the wider political and cultural 'globalization' within society at large. Spain's efforts to internationalize can be seen not only in the scholars sent abroad by the JAE through the early part of the century, but also by the establishment of institutions such as Madrid's Asociación para la Enseñanza Plurilingüe in 1928. The organization was promulgated by intellectual José Castillejo, who from 1918 had collaborated with María de Maeztu in leading the JAE's Instituto-Escuela. The Association's Escuela Internacional Española (Fig. 1.5) was built on the Calle Serrano in the green heights of northerly Chamartín. As Castillejo explained, the school accepted that children possessed a global view of reality prior to language, that they learned

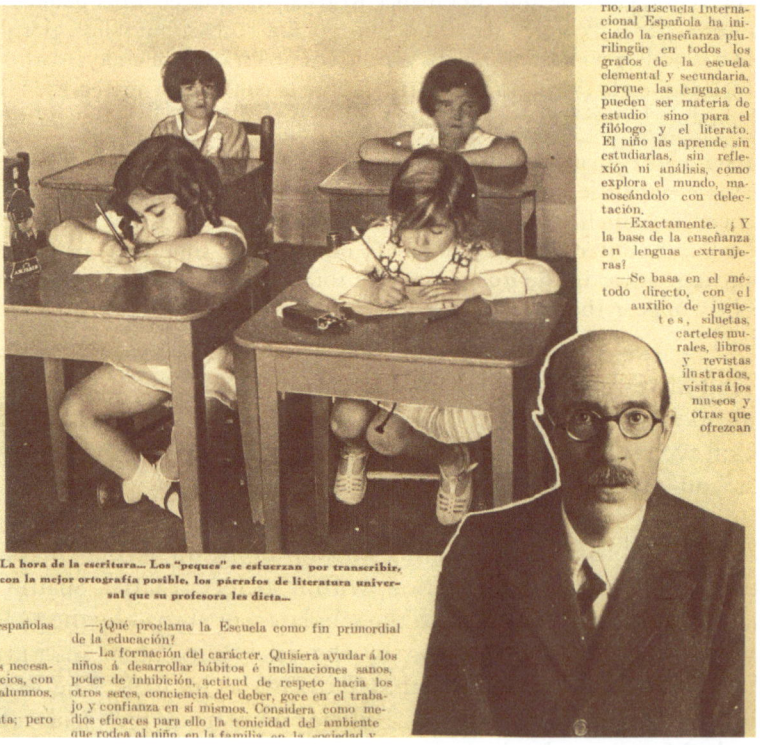

Fig. 1.5. Above, children at the Escuela Internacional Española dance with teacher Joy Blew-Jones; below, José Castillejo drew on theories of language acquisition to encourage learning through stories, music and play.

Source: Juan del Sarto, 'La Escuela Internacional Española', *Crónica*, 11 May 1930, pp. 31–33 (p. 32).

languages more elastically than the adult, and that this talent must be cultivated from a young age. He noted that the child lived in a different verbal and conceptual world, perceiving 'ciertos aspectos y adivina instintivamente ciertas relaciones para las cuales el adulto es ya ciego' [certain aspects and instinctively divining certain relationships to which the adult is blind].[90]

Serving both international students and Spaniards, the school employed a small multinational staff of teachers trained both in Spain as well as Brussels and London. As treasurer Cándido Bolívar y Pieltain described the school's philosophy, it took developmental ages into account, teaching young children about other countries and cultures 'en la forma y con el contenido gradual que cada edad requiere' [in the manner and content each age requires].[91] Teachers employed the 'método directo' in the primary school, relying on toys, silhouettes, murals, illustrated books and magazines, and museum visits to illustrate new concepts. The school followed a plurilingual immersion approach for both the elementary and secondary level because, as Bolívar noted, children learned languages experientially, 'sin reflexión ni análisis, como explora el mundo, manoseándolo con delectación' [without reflection or analysis, just as they explore the world, feeling their way along with delight].[92]

This approach to, literally, hands-on learning was concerned with language itself as a living, tactile entity. Children's learning, whether in Spanish, English, or French, relied upon a vivification of the word through association, image, and experience. Childhood was an age of what Castillejo called 'instinct and abstraction'. It was a fluid time which facilitated activities such as language learning precisely because children could understand verbal inflections of song, poetry, and language *globally* before attempting to break down meaning analytically. They learned by unpacking layers of unmediated sensory experience:

> Para el adulto [las lenguas] son un conjunto de palabras y oraciones, sujeta a normas morfológicas y sintáxicas; pero para el niño son unidades vivientes, de gesto, ritmo y sonidos, encarnadas en las personas que las hablan.[93]

> [For the adult [languages] are a conjunction of words and phrases, subject to morphological norms and syntax; but for the child they are living wholes, of gesture, rhythm, and sound, embodied by the person who speaks them.]

The ringing holism of this statement encompasses physical, rhythmic, and sonic domains, turning lines of language into wholes endowed with synesthetic depth. Children — both boys and girls — educated at Madrid's Escuela Internacional Española were encouraged to exercise their 'imaginación infantil' through drawing, by listening to their professor read from 'literatura universal' and transcribing these stories physically, by their own hand. Like the Institución Libre de Enseñanza, the Escuela Internacional Española emphasized its freedom from religious or political dogma.[94] Yet within a national context guided by Catholic values, morality, and educational structures, the coincidence of these intimately related terms — holism, universalism, totality — mattered. If anything, the new progressive 'wholeness' sought to build on and provide a revised such model for a new age.

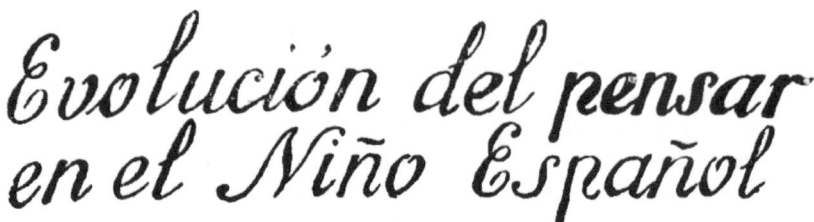

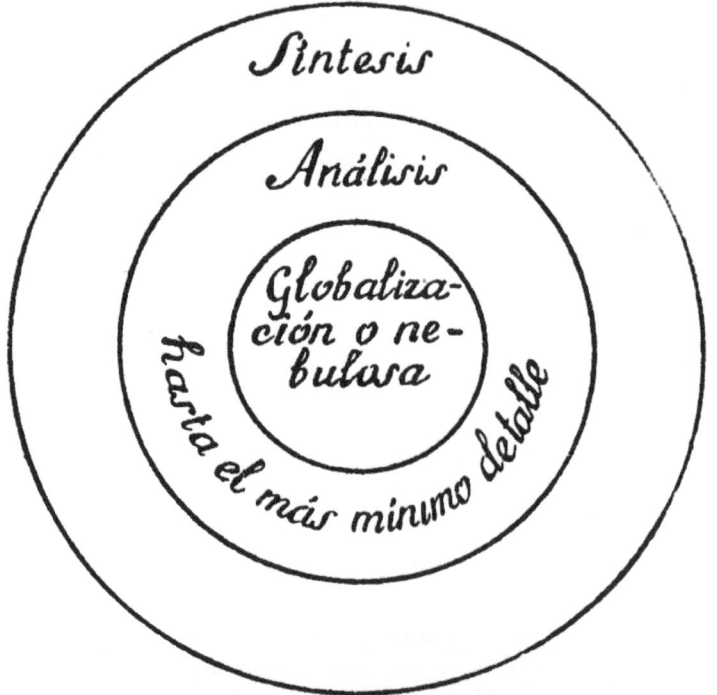

FIG. 1.6. Children's thought was first considered to be 'global', only later developing
toward skills of analysis and synthesis.
Source: Josefina Álvarez de Cánovas, *Pedagogía del párvulo: estudio del niño español*
(Madrid: Espasa-Calpe, 1941), p. 121.

Those embracing a traditional Catholic understanding, meanwhile, had little
need to revise or reject the model as totalitarian representations of society competed
with and ultimately began to replace universalist values through the 1930s. The
international 'método global' was one of many pedagogical concepts popularized
during the Second Republic that carried over into textbooks of reading and child
psychology after the Civil War. On this basis, for instance, Josefina Álvarez de
Cánovas's *Pequeñuelos: la enseñanza de la lectura por el método global* (1943), a reading
primer centred on the lives of two children, Mari-Sol and Pepe-Luís, reached eight
editions by 1958. Álvarez built on research considered established since the 1920s.
Despite explicit patriotic and religious language in her pedagogical explanations,

her works adhered to pre-war and prevailing psychology. To wit, the child perceived wholes before details, 'esto es, que percibe sincrética o globalmente' [that is, syncretically or globally].[95] Children engaged more deeply with the complex than the simple: 'Como el niño se hace con las cosas por esquema, cuanto más complicado sea el esquema, mejor las capta' [Since the child deals with objects through configurations, the more complex one is, the better the child grasps it].[96] Complicated shapes and 'esquemas' were preferable to simple forms: a star preferred over a triangle, a toy over a geometric figure, and the infinite configurations of the human face over a manufactured trinket. Whereas the adult moved from part to whole, the child began with a global vision of the world that became ever more focused. Mental development proceeded in three stages:

> 1. Una visión global, esquemática o sincrética de las cosas,
> 2. Visión analítica hasta el desmenuzamiento
> 3. Visión sintética o de reconstrucción.[97]
>
> [1. A global, schematic or syncretic vision of the world, | 2. An analytical vision, to the point of deconstruction | 3. A synthetic, or reconstructive, vision.]

It was only by inverting the classical method of learning from part to whole that the child's globalist perception could be accommodated. In turn, every lesson should be 'un trocito vivo de la misma vida del niño, una respuesta a sus intereses infantiles' [a living piece of the child's own life, a response to its infantile interests].[98] These interests encompassed the entire living experience of the child. In the globalist method, a holistic emphasis meant moving in concentric circles of knowledge, outward to encompass the entire world of experience (Fig. 1.6).

The lasting influence of globalization theory came to align with psychological explorations of the 'Spanish child', as Álvarez elaborated in her 1943 manual *Pedagogía del párvulo*, where the child's psychological interests and emotions developed outward in growing rings from the self to the family to the nation and God. What she called 'nuestro' [our] psychology was introspective, seeking access to the 'alma', soul, of the child. Despite Álvarez's fierce critique of pre-war Republican and New-Educational policy and methods, it was surprisingly their interest in that same soul of which she grudgingly approved. She quoted the philosopher Manuel García Morente as having described the soul as 'totalitaria'; not a mere sum of homogenous elements but a greater, incommensurable whole. According to Álvarez, for García Morente 'el alma no es *cantidad*, aunque sea esencia, sino *cualidad*; sus elementos no están *sumados*, sino *articulados*' [the soul is not a *quantity*, but essence, *quality*; its elements cannot be *summed* but *articulated*]. Despite the many 'errors' of the 'modernist pedagogy' with which the Gestaltist and globalist positions coincided, including a Rousseauian denial of original sin, at least its proponents embraced a notion of soul: 'si no se acogen a la Filosofía católica, se acogen, por lo menos, a la espiritualista' [if they do not accept Catholic philosophy, at least they accept a spiritualist one].[99] Successive pedagogues did so by seeking objective science that resounded with larger ideas and ideals. For better or worse, these frameworks of 'totality' of self and soul were flexible and multi-purpose, slotting into both secular phenomenological and explicitly national-Catholic frameworks in the years to come.

Perception and its Evolution: Structuring Paidological Knowledge

How can the resonance of globalization theory in Spain, as across Europe, be explained? Above all, it was a central finding of the influential New Education movement and therefore arrived in Spain as part and parcel of early twentieth-century engagement with European pedagogical modernity. In addition, its reception before the Spanish Civil War was a direct result of its convergence with international waves of holistic thought. When teachers such as Causí exposed explicit links between globalization, Gestalt theory, and a phenomenological view of the perceptual world, they linked child study to circulating philosophical currents in Spain. A 'global' view posed the child as an active, synthesizing observer, moving from active infantile perception to a holistic synthesis of letters, objects, and ideas. Within a psychological frame, this was the impulse that would underlie and resound with the pedagogical experimentation and depictions of the child put forward by the teachers, artists, and intellectuals examined in this book.

Pedagogy in a 'global' or Gestaltist frame would continue through the twentieth century, but with an altered character after the Spanish Civil War. Principally, post-war writing on Gestalt psychology moved in two directions. At one end, psychologists represented its findings positively, yet divorced from their pre-war use in reformist pedagogy.[100] At the other, critics argued that its central ideas — whether philosophical or pedagogical — constituted nothing more than re-interpretations of classical Platonist, Aristotelian, or Thomist scholastic thought.[101] Research in Latin America arguably provided a bridge to comparable paidological explorations of the child's phenomenological world, with authors such as Juan B. Soto of Puerto Rico having written key texts on Gestalt and humanistic psychology prior to the Spanish Civil War.[102] The contributions of exiled Spanish and Catalan psychologists and educationalists in Latin America after the Civil War only strengthened this tendency. Chief among these figures were psychiatrist and psychologist Emilio Mira y López (1896–1964), former director of Barcelona's Institut d'Orientació Profesional and key collaborator in the University of Barcelona's Seminari de Pedagogia, and physiologist August Pi i Sunyer (1879–1965), whose 1943 essay 'Biología del todo' [Biology of the Whole] incorporated Gestalt theory into a larger biological idea of functional unity.[103]

International works on perception and phenomenology synthesized this research in new directions. Psychologist Óscar Oñativia in Argentina and Odalmira Maya-goitia Alarcón in Mexico provide particularly good examples of this process and could be considered intellectual heirs to these phenomenological strains of Spanish paidology.[104] Their probing into children's motor and sensorial development owed a great debt to early interpretations of early childhood perception, incorporated in nascent form in the work of Barnés, Verdier, Jaén, Peinado, Causí, and others. These latter authors accomplished two principal achievements in the pre-war period. First, they interpreted and applied complex philosophical ideas to their pedagogical work, incorporating notions such as Ortega's phenomenology into a concrete and useable pedagogy. Second, they recognized the overlap between these concepts and a wave of holistic thought. They attempted to provide crucial balance to purely natural-physical views of the child by introducing models that defended the vitality, unity, and mental dynamism of the developing mind. Spanish paidologists in the 1920s and early 1930s thus began the work of synthesizing theories from various European psychologists, theorists, and educationalists into both intellectual and pragmatic frames, integrating quantitative views of the developing child and — as examined here — qualitative imaginaries of the child's inner world. They attempted to answer through the child's early mental development the larger questions that art, literature, and philosophy would pose about human perceptual experience.

Notes to Chapter 1

1. Eugenio Cirac, 'El enigma', *Acción Gallega: órgano de la Federación de Sociedades Gallegas (Buenos Aires),* 12 April 1931, [n.p.]. Juan Zaragüeta, *El estudio del niño para la cultura nacional* (Bilbao: Bilbaína de Artes Gráficos, 1919), p. 13; Jorge Guillén, 'El infante', in *Cántico*, 4th edn, pp. 374–831 (p. 378). Manuel García Morente, 'El mundo del niño', *Revista de Pedagogía,* 7.74–75 (1928), 49–58, 116–25 (p. 49).

2. The word 'paidology' dates to its first use by an American educationalist, Oscar Chrisman; see *Paidologie: Entwurf zu einer Wissenschaft des Kindes* (Jena: B. Vopelius, 1896). The term rapidly spread across Europe and the United States, appearing in Spain by at least 1904; see Martín Navarro Flores, 'La paidología: su historia y su estado actual', *Boletín de la Institución Libre de Enseñanza*, 28.528–529 (1904), 72–77, 100–05. 'Paidology' remained in use in Spain through the mid-twentieth century, by which time child studies had evolved into new, more specialized fields, such as paediatrics or developmental psychology; see José María Hernández Díaz, 'Introducción', in Domingo Barnés, *Paidología*, ed. by José María Hernández Díaz (Madrid: Biblioteca Nueva, 2008), pp. 17–54 (p. 17). On child study's role in the convergence of cultural and scientific traditions across borders, see Willem Koops and Michael Zuckerman, *Beyond the Century of the Child: Cultural History and Developmental Psychology* (Philadelphia: University of Pennsylvania Press, 2003).

3. See Rosa María Carda Ros and Helio Carpintero Capell, 'Domingo Barnés: Biografía de un educador avanzado', *Boletín de la Institución Libre de Enseñanza*, 12 (1991), pp. 63–74. Barnés studied at the ILE under Giner and Cossío. His work at the *Boletín de la Institución Libre de Enseñanza*, teaching at Madrid's Escuela Superior de Magisterio and the Escuela de Criminología, study tours abroad and prolific publications made him a central figure in paidology. As director of the Museo Pedagógico Nacional in 1927 and Ministro de Instrucción Pública y Bellas Artes in 1933, his career spanned the height of paidological interest in Spain, centring on his publication of *Fuentes para el estudio de la paidología* (Madrid: Imp. de la Revista de Arch., Bibl. y Museos, 1917).

4. Domingo Barnés Salinas, 'Prólogo: Dewey y la filosofía pragmatista', in *La escuela y el niño* (Madrid: Ciudad Lineal, 1926), pp. 9–36, here p. 15. This scientific reckoning in intellectual culture is covered in Pratt, *Signs of Science*. Spain's well-documented — but lesser known — engagement with the theories of Darwin and, later, Einstein, suggest specific ways in which this intellectual expansion took place. See, for instance, *The Reception of Darwinism in the Iberian World: Spain, Spanish America and Brazil*, ed. by Thomas F. Glick, Rosaura Ruiz, and Miguel Angel Puig-Samper (Dordrecht: Kluwer Academic, 2001); and Thomas F. Glick, *Einstein in Spain: Relativity and the Recovery of Science* (Princeton: Princeton University Press, 1988). Ortega was intensely invested in questions of technoscientific modernity, from Galileo to Copernicus to Einstein; see, for example, his 'En torno a Galileo', in *Obras completas* (Madrid: Revista de Occidente, 1964), V, 10–164.

5. Fernando Vidal, *The Sciences of the Soul: The Early Modern Origins of Psychology* (Chicago: University of Chicago Press, 2011). On a *geisteswissenschaftliche* perspective in Spain, see José Ortega y Gasset, 'Guillermo Dilthey y la idea de la vida' (Madrid: Revista de Occidente, 1964), pp. 165–214, as well as Joan Roura i Parella, *Conceptos fundamentales del pensamiento de Dilthey* (Havana: Universidad de La Habana, 1946).

6. On the scientific and artistic legacy of these works, see *The Beautiful Brain: The Drawings of Santiago Ramón y Cajal*, ed. by Larry W. Swanson and others (New York: Abrams, 2017)

7. A 1926 editorial suggested that psychoanalysis was a 'fad', while Barnés himself criticized psychoanalysis for focusing on piecemeal elements while overlooking the mind's total function, see Anon., 'El estudio del niño', *Revista de Pedagogía*, 5.60 (1926), 557–58, and Barnés Salinas, *Paidología*, p. 93; *Diccionario de Pedagogía*, ed. by Sánchez Sarto, I, 432.

8. On Gestalt reception and its limited afterlives in Spain through post-war psychologists such as José Germain Cebrián (1897–1986), see above all Enrique Lafuente Niño, Helio Carpintero Capell, and Alejandra Ferrándiz Lloret, 'The Introduction of Gestalt Psychology in Spain (1923–1936)', in *Psychologie im soziokulturellen Wandel: Kontinuitäten und Diskontinuitäten*, ed. by Siegfried Jaeger and others (Frankfurt am Main: Peter Lang, 1995), pp. 214–20 (p. 219). Carpintero has argued that Ortega's phenomenological thought was essentially 'holista', and understood as such by his contemporaries, including Manuel García Morente; see Helio Carpintero, *Esbozo de una psicología según la razón vital* (Madrid: Real Academia de Ciencias Morales y Políticas, 2000) (p. 41).

9. For a contemporary view of the infant world as phenomenological experience, see Eva M. Simms, *The Child in the World: Embodiment, Time, and Language in Early Childhood* (Detroit: Wayne State University Press, 2008).

10. Hernández Díaz, 'Introducción', p. 44. Early paidological texts include Navarro Flores, 'La paidología'; Rufino Blanco y Sánchez, *Paidología y paidotecnia: breve historia de la paidología* (Madrid: Tip. de la Revista de Archivos, 1912), and Mariano Sáez Morilla, *Introducción al estudio de la paidología y pedagogía moderna* (Pamplona: Imp. Artes Gráficas, 1922).

11. The journal *La Escuela Moderna* (1891–1932) was founded by Pedro de Alcántara García Navarro (1842–1906), sympathetic to the Institución Libre de Enseñanza and Krausist philosophy, and an early importer of Fröbelian methods. The *Boletín de la Institución Libre de Enseñanza* (1877–1936) covered the latest in international pedagogy and the activities of the Institution. The *Revista de Pedagogía* (1922–36), under the guidance of Lorenzo Luzuriaga, closely aligned with the New Education Fellowship, publishing translations of prominent figures such as Montessori and Piaget as well as Spanish pedagogues; for a fuller overview across ideological fields, see Antonio Checa Godoy, *Historia de la prensa pedagógica en España* (Seville: Universidad de Sevilla, 2002).

12. Barnés was an early advocate for the adoption of the new trend for experimental, nature-centred, 'open-air' schools in Spain; see his *Escuelas al aire libre* (Madrid: Ministerio de Instrucción Pública y Bellas Artes, 1909).

13. Luis de Zulueta, 'La vela en el horizonte: una pedagogía más moderna', *Revista de Pedagogía*, 1.1 (1922), 1–5 (pp. 1–2).

14. Ibid. p. 4.

15. Ibid., pp. 4–5.

16. Domingo Barnés, *El desenvolvimiento del niño*, 2nd edn (Barcelona: Editorial Labor, 1933), p. 162.

17. Ibid., p. 127.

18. Kurt Koffka, *The Growth of the Mind: An Introduction to Child-Psychology*, trans. by Robert Morris Ogden (London: Kegan Paul, Trench, Trubner & Co., 1924), p. 132.

19. In its interdisciplinary character, paidology could be considered one possible response to Ortega's criticism of the 'barbarism of specialisation' in *La rebelión de las masas* (1930) and his project to redefine the human sciences. See John T. Graham, *The Social Thought of Ortega y Gasset: A Systematic Synthesis in Postmodernism and Interdisciplinarity* (Columbia: University of Missouri Press, 2001), pp. 423–28.

20. See *Filósofos españoles en la Revista de Pedagogía (1922–1936)*, ed. by Ángel Casado and Juana Sánchez-Gey (Santa Cruz de Tenerife: Ediciones Idea, 2007).

21. Domingo Barnés Salinas, *Ensayos de pedagogía y filosofía* (Madrid: La Lectura, 1921), p. 5. Unamuno took an interest in the evolution of paidology, as evidenced by the presence of Barnés's *Fuentes para el estudio de la Paidología* (1917) in his personal library; see Mario J. Valdés and María Elena Valdés, *An Unamuno Source Book* (Toronto: University of Toronto Press, 1973). Barnés and Ortega were close friends since their years as doctoral students. Their overlapping paths included

Barnés's taking over Ortega's *cátedra* at the Escuela de Estudios Superiores de Magisterio during the latter's influential stay in Germany (1907–10). Ortega's 'Biología y pedagogía' praised Barnés, who in turn dedicated *Ensayos de pedagogía y filosofía* (1921) to Ortega.

22. Kurt Koffka, *Die Grundlagen der psychischen Entwicklung: Eine Einführung in die Kinderpsychologie* (Osterwieck am Harz: Zickfeldt, 1921). The index to Barnés's *El desenvolvimiento del niño* (1928) lists more than twice as many citations to Koffka as to the next psychologist, with eleven citations, outnumbering more recognizable figures such as Claparède (6), Binet (5), Piaget (3), Freud (1), and others. Similarly, Koffka was a significant presence in Barnés's revised *Paidología* (1932). Carda Ros and Carpintero's analysis of *Paidología* (1932) counts citations from 294 authors. Of these, seven authors make up more than a quarter of citations. Koffka is among these, with twenty-one citations, alongside classics of pedagogy: Pestalozzi (47), Rousseau (42), Herbart (29), Claparède (25), and Dewey (24). See Rosa María Carda Ros and Helio Carpintero Capell, 'La Paidología de Domingo Barnés', *Boletín de la Institución Libre de Enseñanza*, 7 (1989), 3–28 (p. 27).

23. On the philosophical roots, psychological and humanistic goals of Gestalt psychology and the post-war fates of its theorists within Germany and in exile, see Mitchell G. Ash, *Gestalt Psychology in German Culture, 1890–1967: Holism and the Quest for Objectivity* (Cambridge: Cambridge University Press, 1995).

24. Kurt Koffka, *Bases de la evolución psíquica: introducción a la psicología infantil* (Madrid: Revista de Occidente, 1926); 'Introducción a la Gestalt-Theorie: la percepción', in *La teoría de la estructura (la psicología novísima)*, ed. by Kurt Koffka, Robert Morris Ogden, and Eugenio Rignano (Madrid: La Lectura, 1928), pp. 9–97 (p. 60). As an editor's footnote in the *Revista de Occidente* summarized Gestalt theory for readers in 1936, 'Situaciones, figuras, estructuras, y no simples colores o sonidos, es lo que percibimos inmediatamente' [Situations, figures, structures, and not simple colours or sounds, are what we perceive immediately]; see Frederik J. Buytendijk, 'Sobre la diferencia esencial entre el animal y el hombre', *Revista de Occidente*, 14.153–54 (1936), 233–59 and 24–53 (p. 236).

25. These authors include Joaquim Xirau, 'La psicología de la forma', *Revista de Pedagogía*, 5.57 (1926), 385–91; Ramiro Ledesma Ramos, 'De la nueva psicologia', *La Gaceta Literaria*, 3.54 (1929), 2, and his 'La Gestalttheorie', *La Gaceta Literaria*, 3.50 (1929), 2; and F. Carmona Nenclares, 'La psicología de la estructura y el mundo del niño', *Revista de Pedagogía*, 11 (1932), 55–66.

26. Piaget's examination of structuralism — from linguistics to mathematics — was based in large part on the Gestalt concept; see Jean Piaget, *El estructuralismo* (Barcelona: Oikos-Tau, 1974). See also the extensive readings done by Maurice Merleau-Ponty on the Gestalt psychologists; Maurice Merleau-Ponty and Jacques Prunair, *Psychologie et pédagogie de l'enfant: cours de Sorbonne, 1949–1952* (Lagrasse: Verdier, 2001).

27. Interest was not limited to liberal contexts: the Jesuit priest and psychologist Ferrán María Palmés would problematize the elusive nature of the term 'Gestalt' in an analysis of that ambiguous 'palabra mágica'; see 'La psicología gestaltista: introducción a su estudio crítico', *Pensamiento*, 1 (1945), 31–61 (p. 35).

28. José Ortega y Gasset, 'Vitalidad, alma, espíritu', in *Obras completas* (Madrid: Revista de Occidente, 1946), VI, 443–82. On this work's exploration of the corporal within a Platonian 'trinity' of mind, body, and spirit, see Nelson R. Orringer, *La filosofía de la corporalidad en Ortega y Gasset* (Pamplona: Servicio de Publicaciones de la Universidad de Navarra, 1999), p. 9.

29. Barnés, *El desenvolvimiento del niño*, p. 162.

30. Barnés, *Paidología*, p. 93.

31. A recent examination of the much-discussed 'crisis' in modern experimental psychology is found in Gary Hatfield, 'Koffka, Köhler, and the "Crisis" in Psychology', *Studies in History and Philosophy of Biological and Biomedical Sciences*, 43.2 (2012), 483–92.

32. William James, *Principles of Psychology* (New York: Henry Holt, 1890), p. 196.

33. Duane P. Schultz and Sydney E. Schultz, *A History of Modern Psychology* (Boston: Cengage Learning, 2007), p. 371, and G. William Barnard, *Living Consciousness: The Metaphysical Vision of Henri Bergson* (Albany: State University of New York Press, 2011), pp. 73–74. Bergson was a critical influence in Spanish thought from the early years of the twentieth century; see, for

example, Unamuno's uptake of Bergson's cinematograph image in *Del sentimiento trágico de la vida*, as quoted in Benjamin Fraser, 'Unamuno and Bergson: Notes on a Shared Methodology', *Modern Language Review,* 102.3 (2007), 753–67 (p. 762).

34. Ash, *Gestalt Psychology in German Culture*, pp. 130–31.
35. José Ortega y Gasset, *El tema de nuestro tiempo*, 12th edn, Colección Austral (Madrid: Espasa-Calpe, 1968), pp. 15–16. After its genesis in the nineteenth century from Auguste Comte to Wilhelm Dilthey, historical analysis of generations peaked twice in the twentieth century: first a 'theoretical and holistic' view during the period 1920–33, the second an empirical one immediately following the Second World War. Ortega y Gasset and German sociologist Karl Mannheim were major voices in the first wave, with Ortega's ideas carried forward by Julián Marías (1949) during the second wave, according to Hans Jaeger, 'Generations in History: Reflections on a Controversial Concept', *History and Theory,* 24.3 (1985), 273–92 (p. 277); Helio Carpintero Capell and Enrique Lafuente, 'El método histórico de las generaciones: el caso de la psicología española', *Revista de Historia de la Psicología,* 28.1 (2007), 67–86).
36. Barnés, *El desenvolvimiento del niño*, p. 57.
37. José Ortega y Gasset, 'La psicología del cascabel', in *El espectador*, 8 vols (Madrid: Calpe, 1921), iii, 173–79 (p. 178).
38. Barnés, *El desenvolvimiento del niño*, p. 127.
39. Ibid, p. 57.
40. Rhythmic games were seen as introducing a harmony between intellectual and corporal activity; see the report on a study visit to Belgium by Jesús Llorca y Radal, 'Los juegos rítmicos en la Escuela', *Anales de la Junta para Ampliación de Estudios e Investigaciones Científicas,* 18.18 (1926), 341–67. Émile Jaques-Dalcroze's (1865–1950) rhythmic gymnastics were considered to be an activity of 'equilibri y d'armonía [*sic*]', incorporated into schools across Spain; for an early initiative by Joan Llongueras, see 'La gimnàstica rítmica i els estudis calistènichs d'E. Jaques Dalcroze a l'Escola Coral de Tarrasa [*sic*]', *La Ilustració Catalana (Feminal),* 36 (1910), 6–8 (p. 8). See also Rogelio Villar, 'Un gran progreso pedagógico: la educación por el ritmo', *La Esfera,* 2.79 (1915), 30, who notes the practice's spread into teachers' colleges by pedagogues such as María Encarnación de la Rigada y Ramón and Anselmo González.
41. Rafael Verdier, *De Uexküll a Decroly* (Málaga: Tipografía Ibérica, [1931]), p. 21; Barnés, *El desenvolvimiento del niño*, p. 164; Verdier, *De Uexküll a Decroly*, p. 22.
42. Verdier, *De Uexküll a Decroly*, pp. 22–23.
43. Ibid., pp. 21–22.
44. Rafael Verdier, 'La pedagogía y la crisis de la psicología experimental', *Revista de Pedagogía,* 5.52 (1926), 152–58 (p. 158); 'Aprendizaje y cultura', *Revista de Pedagogía,* 8.91 (1929) 295–301 (p. 299).
45. José Ortega y Gasset, *¿Qué es filosofía?*, 2nd edn (Madrid: Colección Austral, 1965), p. 136.
46. Verdier, *De Uexküll a Decroly*, p. 22.
47. Ibid, p. 48.
48. Koffka, *The Growth of the Mind*, pp. 133–34; Barnés, *Paidología*, p. 163.
49. Teodoro Causí, 'La globalización de Decroly y la psicología de la estructura', *Revista de Pedagogía,* 9.103 (1930), 293–301 (p. 298, my emphasis).
50. Koffka, *The Growth of the Mind*, p. 131.
51. Barnés, *El desenvolvimiento del niño*, p. 162.
52. Koffka, 'Introducción a la Gestalt-Theorie', pp. 59–60.
53. Miguel de Unamuno, *En torno a casticismo*, (Madrid: Fernando Fé, 1902), p. 98.
54. Ortega y Gasset, *Meditaciones del Quijote*, p. 77.
55. Nelson Orringer links Ortega's idea of 'luminous perception' with the learning process. He suggests that Ortega's own writing and thinking were influenced by voices 'arguing against experimental psychologists who think cognitive development a gradual process in children' rather than a sequence of leaps and bounds. Orringer implicitly evokes the Gestaltist notion of learning as the restructuring of knowledge: 'Not by mindless rote or repetition, but by sudden entry into truth does every act of learning take place'; see 'Luminous Perception in *Meditaciones del Quijote*: Ortega y Gasset's Source', *Revista Canadiense de Estudios Hispánicos,* 2.1 (1977), 1–26 (p. 16).

56. Juan Jaén and José Peinado, *Manual de paidología*, 2nd edn (Madrid: Aguilar, 1935). See Anon., 'Manual de Paidología, por los señores D. Juan Jaén y D. José Peinado, inspectores de Primera Enseñanza', *España Médica*, 27 (1936), 28.

57. Jaén and Peinado, *Manual de Paidología*, n.p. On the authors' impact, see Helio Carpintero Capell, *Historia de la psicología en España* (Madrid: Eudema, 1994), p. 225. Jaén and Peinado were also influenced by cognitive theories subsequent to the Gestalt movement, such as those of Jean Piaget; see Helio Carpintero Capell and Victoria del Barrio, 'La introducción de Piaget en España la figura y obra de Juan Jaén', *Revista de Historia de la Psicología*, 17.3–4 (1996), 186–93; and Helio Carpintero Capell, 'José Peinado y la influencia de Piaget en España', *Revista de Historia de la Psicología*, 18.1–2 (1997), 75–85.

58. Jaén and Peinado, *Manual de Paidología*, p. 135.

59. Even as late as the 1930s, children were often compared to primitive man (and vice versa); thus the significance of a 'humanization' in educational discourse. Ortega, for instance, suggested that 'Gozamos del pintor primitivo como gozamos del alma infantil' [We enjoy primitive painting just as we enjoy children's art]; see Ortega y Gasset, *El tema de nuestro tiempo*, p. 88. Both were understood to see the world from an egocentric point of view and to assume that their own subjective experiences were universally valid.

60. Jaén and Peinado, *Manual de Paidología*, p. 106.

61. Pedro Martínez Saralegui, 'El significado del "test"', *Atenas*, 3.13 (15 October 1931), 15–17.

62. José Ortega y Gasset, *Guillermo Dilthey y la idea de la vida* (Madrid: Revista de Occidente, 1964), pp. 165–214 (p. 168).

63. Trained at Madrid's Escuela Superior de Magisterio and Geneva's Institut Jean-Jacques Rousseau and director of Republican children's homes under the Civil War, Comas is better known for his work as an anthropologist as a Republican exile in Mexico. On globalization and the Gestalt, see Juan Comas, 'Libros: Dottrens (R.) y M. (Emilia): l'apprentissage de la lecture par la Méthode Globale [...]', *Revista de Pedagogía*, 9.105 (1930), 425–27 (p. 425); C. A. Figuerido, 'Psicología y pedagogía', *Revista de Pedagogía*, 13.150 (1934), 263–79 (p. 270). Decroly's explanation of the method can be read in its Spanish translation in Ovide Decroly, 'La función de globalización y su importancia pedagógica', *Revista de Pedagogía*, 2.23 (1923), 401–12.

64. Jean E. Segers, *La percepción visual y la función de globalización en los niños*, trans. by Jacobo Orellana Garrido (Madrid: Espasa-Calpe, 1930), p. 93.

65. Jean Piaget, *The Essential Piaget*, ed. by Howard E. Gruber and J. Jacques Vonèche (London: Routledge & Kegan Paul, 1977), p. 60. The experimenter was Henri Bergson.

66. A concise summary is given in Francine Dubreucq, 'Jean-Ovide Decroly (1871–1932)', *Prospects: The Quarterly Review of Comparative Education*, 23.1–2 (1993), 249–75.

67. Segers noted that the term 'sincretisme' drew from Ernst Renan's 1848 *L'Avenir de la science*, which saw 'la primera edad del espíritu humano', passing through three stages: first a general (syncretic) view of the whole, secondly an analytical view of the parts, and finally its synthetic re-composition; see Segers, *La percepción visual*, pp. 95–96. See these terms' usage in, for example, Regina Lago de Comas, 'El realismo intelectual y la aparición de la perspectiva', *Revista de Pedagogía*, 9.105 (1930), 391–98 (pp. 391–92).

68. Maximiano Flores, 'La enseñanza de la lectura', *La Escuela Moderna*, 34.398 (1924), 802–24 (p. 806). Flores drew on Thomas F. G. Dexter and Alfred H. Garlick's early classic *Psychology in the Schoolroom* (London: Longmans, Green & Company, 1898), a physiological approach to learning that helped lay the groundwork for active methods.

69. Verdier, *De Uexküll a Decroly*, p. 21.

70. Roberto Dottrens and Emilia Margairaz, 'Método global de lectura: sus fundamentos psicológicos', *La Escuela Moderna*, 44.496 (1933), 40–48 (pp. 41–43).

71. Lago de Comas, 'El realismo intelectual y la aparición de la perspectiva', p. 425.

72. See discussion of Vives's critical precedent for individual development and cultural transmission, influential for both secular and confessional education, in Concepción Cárceles Laborde, *Humanismo y educación en España: 1450–1650* (Pamplona: Ediciones Universidad de Navarra, 1993), pp. 184–86.

73. Ángel Llorca, *El primer año de lenguaje* (Madrid: n.p., 1923), p. 50.

74. Luís Santullano, 'La enseñanza del idioma', *El Imparcial*, 1 May 1923, p. 4.

75. Llorca, *El primer año de lenguaje*, p. 28.

76. Rafael Verdier and Víctor Argueta, *Ya leo: la lectura y la escritura por el método ideovisual* (Málaga: 'La Española', 1935), p. 5.

77. Ibid., p. 6.

78. Ibid.

79. Causí, 'La globalización de Decroly y la psicología de la estructura', p. 295.

80. Ibid., p. 294.

81. Ibid., p. 293; Ortega y Gasset, 'Guillermo Dilthey y la idea de la vida', p. 169.

82. Causí, 'La globalización y la psicología de la estructura', p. 298. He refers to psychologist Eduard Spranger (1882–1963), German philosopher and psychologist concerned with education and personality types, former student of Wilhelm Dilthey and strong proponent of the cultural sciences or *Geisteswissenschaften*. Spranger's writings called for greater spiritual meaning in the experimental and holistic turn in psychology, particularly in his *Psicología de la edad juvenil*, trans. by José Gaos (Madrid: Revista de Occidente, 1929).

83. Causí, 'La globalización de Decroly y la psicología de la estructura', p. 300.

84. Ibid., p. 297.

85. Ibid.

86. Ibid., p. 294.

87. Ibid., p. 295.

88. Ibid.

89. Ibid., p. 298.

90. José Castillejo, 'La enseñanza plurilingüe', *La Escuela Moderna*, 53 (1931), 86–88; José Castillejo, '¿Malgastamos la niñez de nuestros hijos?', *El Sol*, 29 September 1932, p. 1.

91. Juan del Sarto, 'La Escuela Internacional Española', *Crónica*, 11 May 1930, pp. 31–33.

92. Ibid., p. 32.

93. Castillejo, '¿Malgastamos la niñez de nuestros hijos?', p. 1.

94. Sarto, 'La Escuela Internacional Española', p. 29. According to Bolívar y Pieltain, the school rejected all political and religious controversies, respected all beliefs, obeyed the laws of the land, and admitted students indiscriminate of sex or nationality. It drew its curriculum from both Spanish and international sources and considered religion a matter to be taught by families, not schools: Sarto, 'La Escuela Internacional Española', p. 33.

95. Josefina Álvarez de Cánovas, *Pequeñuelos: la enseñanza de la lectura por el método global (el libro en que aprendió a leer Mari-Sol)*, 6th edn (Madrid: n.p., [1943]), p. 9.

96. Ibid.

97. Ibid.

98. Ibid., p. 10.

99. Josefina Álvarez de Cánovas, *Pedagogía del párvulo: estudio del niño español* (Madrid: Espasa-Calpe, 1943), p. 121; and *Psicología pedagógica: estudio del niño español*, p. 334. In addition to syntheses of research in the field of developmental psychology, the latter volume includes hagiographical writing on Vives and Huarte de San Juan and robust rebuttals of the 'errors' of New Education; see pp. 330–45.

100. José Germain, *Kurt Koffka 1886–1941* (Madrid: s.n, 1945).

101. Manuel Barbado, 'Antecedentes escolásticos de la "Gestaltpsychologie"', *Revista de Filosofía*, 1.2–3 (1942), 371–76; Palmés, 'La psicología gestaltista', p. 60. This reaction mirrors two related trends during the early Francoist era, including the revival of Baroque, Counter-Reformation, and particularly Jesuit educational methods as an alternate form of Catholic modernity, as argued in Till Kössler, 'Education and the Baroque in Early Francoism', *Bulletin of Spanish Studies*, 91.5 (2014), 673–96.

102. Principally Juan B. Soto, *Las leyes mecanicistas del aprendizaje y la nueva psicología alemana (Gestalttheorie): estudio de psicología comparada* (Madrid: Espasa-Calpe, 1933).

103. See Emilio Mira y López, *Psicología evolutiva del niño y el adolescente*, 2nd edn (Buenos Aires: El Ateneo, 1944). Mira hosted notable European psychologists in Barcelona, including Gestalt psychologist Wolfgang Köhler in 1927 (Chapter 3) as well as Gestaltist and psychoanalyst Werner

Wolff from 1933 to 1936; see Angel C. Moreu Calvo, 'Presència d'un psicòleg exiliat: Werner Wolff a Barcelona (1933–1936)', *Educació i Història: Revista d'Història de l'Educació,* 9–10 (2006–07), 270–83. See also August Pi i Sunyer, 'La biología del todo', in *La unidad funcional,* 2 vols (Mexico: Compañía General Editora, 1944), I, 129–69 (p. 179).

104. Oñativia's major works treat perception and its role in education: *Percepción y acción* (Buenos Aires: Universidad de Buenos Aires, Facultad de Filosofía y Letras, 1951); *Dimensiones de la percepción* (Tucumán: Universidad Nacional de Tucumán, 1963); and *Método integral para la enseñanza de la lecto-escritura inicial* (Buenos Aires: Editorial Humanitas, 1967). Mayagoitia focused on sensorial and spatial tests of intelligence: *El análisis del mundo circundante por el niño, con referencia especial al niño anormal* (Mexico: Secretaría de Educación Pública, 1950).

FIG. 2.1. 'Encarnita' immersed in a book, as captured by Spanish photographer Rúa.
Source: Manuel Abril, *Los niños en el arte y en la fotografía*
(Madrid: M. Aguilar, 1936), p. 83.

CHAPTER 2

Pure Poetry:
The Child and the Avant-Garde

[E]l niño debe empezar a leer la poesía primera, la poesía infantil, la que, como él, contiene los balbuceos retóricos, los temblores líricos de una estrella recién creada.

[The child should begin by reading the first poetry, children's poetry, which, like him, has the rhetorical stirrings and lyrical trembling of a newly-formed star.]

Carmen Conde, *Por la escuela renovada* (1931)

In 1931, Carmen Conde published a book, *Por la escuela renovada* [Toward the New School], that made a case for various aspects of reform education. Chief among these new priorities was an inculcation of lyricism in the classroom. Conde had recently finished her teacher training (1927–30) at the Escuela Normal de Murcia and the Escuela Normal de Maestras de Albacete. In 1931, she founded the Universidad Popular de Cartagena with her husband, Antonio Oliver Belmás (1903–68), which was the beginning of several years of intense social engagement in the pedagogical initiatives underway in the new Republic. Conde was, in addition to her educational leadership, a prolific poet and essayist of childhood, who, as has been noted, would be recognized as one of the preeminent figures of post-war Spanish literature over the course of the twentieth century. In this collection of short essays, Conde argued for the importance of incorporating art and literature into primary education. Poetry served to 'perfeccionar y afinar al niño' [perfect and refine the child], yet little formal thought or research had gone into how educators used it. '¿Existe una teoría pedagógica sobre Poesía?' [Is there a pedagogical theory of poetry?], she asked.[1] As experts embarked on all possible lines of research into the child's physical and mental development, Conde sought to emphasize children's lyrical, creative, poetic needs. By enveloping childhood under the aegis of a new pedagogical aesthetics, a generation of teachers, poets, and artists shared a conception of the child as muse, receptor, and poet par excellence.

What Conde sought to draw out was an immersion in poetic sensibility rather than 'dry' theories, 'al tratado íntimo del alma poética, que tan hermoso bien puede reportar a la infancia' [the intimate treatment of the poetic soul, which can bring such gifts to childhood]. Poetry could only be approached lyrically, thus opening up a rich new 'continent' of sensorial experience, one which departed from practical, objective teachings in mathematics, geography, or grammar to go deeper into spirit and expression: 'Para el niño y la niña que aún orientan su universo entre las vigilantes altezas de los mapas, hay que hacer selecciones de gusto irrefutablemente lírico, si se quiere enseñar la Poesía' [For the boy and girl who still orient their universe between the watchful majesties of charted lands, one must choose irrefutably lyrical pieces, if you want to teach Poetry]. Arguing for poetry's place in intellectual development, Conde suggested that teachers could use it to 'reach' the child more deeply. Her argument was twofold: that the study and performance of poetry gave children a unique insight into the culture in which they lived and that that surrounding culture was itself 'returning to childhood' through its art:

> El niño nacido en la edad del cubismo, ¿podrá apreciar el sentido puramente pictórico, solemnemente geométrico del cuadro cubista? ¿Podrá percibir las minuciosas infantilizaciones del poema presente? En realidad, el arte moderno tiende a una aspiración eterna: volver a la infancia.[2]

> [The child born in the age of Cubism, will he know how to appreciate the purely pictorial, solemnly geometrical character of the Cubist painting? Will he notice the minute infantilizations of the present poem? In fact, modern art tends towards an eternal aspiration: a return to childhood.]

Reaching from Cubist artists to her own poetic circles, Conde suggested that early twentieth-century art revolved around a search for that which defined childhood. She drew on the verse of poets Jorge Guillén and Juan Ramón Jiménez to make her case:

> Si comparamos el Arte con el Día, por lo luminoso y perenne, recordemos dos versos que no morirán nunca: 'Es un día parado en su mediodía', dice Jorge Guillén meditando en la luz; 'Es un día que vuelve a la aurora', dice Juan Ramón Jiménez, el poeta de todos los meridianos. Cabe en esta afirmación suya un calor romántico que encuadra perfectamente nuestra indagación de la teoría poética escolar: el Arte vuelve a su aurora.[3]

> [If we compare Art with the Day, equally luminous and perennial, let us remember two immortal verses: 'It is a day held at its meridian,' writes Jorge Guillén meditating on the light; 'It is a day that returns to the dawn,' says Juan Ramón Jiménez, the poet of all meridians. There is in Jiménez's affirmation a romantic warmth that perfectly suits our investigation of a theory of scholastic poetry: Art returns to its aurora.]

Conde's 'theory of educational poetry' made the case that art was returning steadily to its own dawn, towards an innate childhood at its heart. Its 'meridian', the present moment, the lived instant, represented the ongoing presence of childhood in each life. But what role might this 'aurora' of modern art play in education? As art turned towards the elemental, Conde suggested that a trembling, immediate poetry of experience was at hand. To connect this poetry to children, as she did in her own writing and first-hand instruction (Fig. 2.3), was the task of the teacher.

FIG. 2.2. Poetic sensibility was seen as central to the 'new' education in a new Republic. Source: Carmen Conde, *Por la escuela renovada* (Valencia: Cuadernos de Cultura, 1931), cover.

Taking Conde's challenge as a starting point, this chapter moves from intellectuals' fascination with the child's mind towards the close links that writers such as Conde forged in the field of pedagogy. Avant-garde artists and writers sought to examine the integration of word and reality. They adopted circulating images of childhood as support for their approaches to language, imagination, and metaphor. Considering works by Conde, Jiménez, Guillén, José Bergamín (1895–1983), Zenobia Camprubí Aymar (1887–1956), Arturo Serrano Plaja (1909–78) and others, this chapter demonstrates how poets of Spain's Silver Age absorbed and reimagined theories of the developing mind in poetry written for, about, and by children. How did notions of poetic invention stimulate avant-garde writings on childhood perception, genius, and imaginative development?

Spanish writers and critics pointedly recognized the close connection between literature and the development of the imagination. This was so most acutely in the years following the founding by dramatist Jacinto Benavente (1866–1954) of a short-lived children's theatre in Madrid, the Teatro de los Niños (1909–10), which put on productions of classic Spanish works.[4] As the educator Antonio Linares mused in 1921, remembering this earlier venture, children's theatre created a bridge between adult and child. Linares suggested that theatre was a critical aspect of modern education. Like literature, theatre went to the children's level, entering their small, yet infinite world. It was in this 'reino de maravilla' [kingdom of marvels] where inanimate things came alive, where 'todo vive y habla y donde a veces dialogan acerca de lo divino y de lo humano el muñeco de trapo asomado a un balcón y la primera estrella que palpita en el cielo' [where everything lives and speaks, where the ragdoll on the balcony and the first star flickering in the night sky set to discussing the human and the divine].[5] In theatre, barriers were torn down between human and non-human, high-brow and low-brow. Watching a play, he pointed out, the child absorbed larger lessons about the world through interaction (what he called a 'lección de cosas') while laughing at a marionette or puppet on stage.[6] To reach children's minds and spirits was teachers' greatest challenge: 'No hay nada tan fácil ni tan difícil; nada tan sencillo ni tan complejo' [There is nothing so easy nor so difficult, so simple nor so complex], Linares claimed, connecting teacher and artist in shared efforts to understand and stimulate the imagination.[7]

In addition to adapting theatrical works, well-known poets and artists published frequent works directed at and 'for' children. The foremost example of this activity was Jiménez's beloved *Platero y yo*, first published in 1914, which brought an intimate tenderness to childhood and to people, places, and sensations past. As is well-documented, *Platero y yo* found a ready audience both through commercial positioning and clear, evocative prose, as did the works and collaborations of numerous other members of the artistic and literary avant-garde. His was a prose marketed for children but originally written for, and indeed reaching, a far wider audience. As Jiménez explained, La Lectura press had suggested publishing selections in its juvenile series. It was by no means incidental that the first edition, then, began with a pointed warning, what he called an 'Advertencia a los hombres que lean este libro para niños' [Warning to adults who read this children's book].[8] Works for children should embody the best, the most poetic, forms of poetry.

FIG. 2.3. Conde with students at the Escuela Nacional de Párvulos, El Retén, in 1934.
Courtesy of the Legado Carmen Conde, Patronato Carmen Conde-Antonio Oliver,
Cartagena.

A swell of works by Spanish poets and artists consolidated an avant-garde interest in childhood as both theme and aesthetic. Tying together visual and verbal depictions of childhood in a work edited and introduced by Jiménez, the painter Benjamín Palencia in 1923 published a collection entitled *Niños* consisting of simple line drawings. The following year, Ramón Gómez de la Serna (1888–1963) published three children's books illustrated by the Uruguayan artist and noted *vibracionista* Rafael Barradas (1890–1929). Connecting one of the most infamous figures of the Madrid avant-garde with a central hub of Barcelona's artistic scene, such a collaboration suggests the fluidity between children's literature and the avant-garde.[9] Indeed, the stories were treated as both children's literature and as art. Reviewing Gómez de la Serna's works for children, a contemporaneous reviewer and schoolteacher, Pablo de Andrés Cobós, praised the author for a 'crystalline' style even as he wrote cynically of his dip into children's entertainment:

> El siglo del niño y el siglo de la escuela; el niño y la escuela preocupación de los grandes políticos, de los más altos filósofos, de los más prestigiosos escritores. He aquí que Ramón, el pontífice de la nueva literatura, escribe cuentos para niños. Buenos cuentos infantiles. ¿Se nos permitirá declarar que nos gustan más que cualquiera de las otras producciones del autor [...]? Estos cuentos hacen gozar a los niños sin violencia ninguna. Pero no seré yo quien pida a Ramón que se dedique a la literatura infantil; sé que no le queda tiempo.[10]

> [The century of the child and the century of the school; the child and the school are the preoccupation of all the great politicians, the highest philosophers, the most prestigious writers. So it is that Ramón, the pontiff of new literature, writes children's stories. Good children's stories. May we declare that we like them more than any of the author's other productions [...]? Children will undoubtedly enjoy these stories without any duress. But it will not be I who asks Ramón to dedicate himself to children's literature; I know he hasn't the time.]

In the author's view, Gómez de la Serna was riding a faddish wave of child-centred pedagogy — yet with a natural grace and admirable result. Childhood was already at the centre of social, political, and intellectual life. Authors were merely responding to the world that they found, contributing to the concerns and images of an age.

The work of theorizing and shaping children's representations in literature was not just a rhetorical task of authors, however, but also one that could be practically enacted, in the classroom or on the stage. While some works, notably Jiménez's *Platero y yo*, Federico García Lorca's 'Canciones para niños' (1921–24), or Rafael Alberti's 'Nanas' (1924), traversed the child-adult literary boundary with ease, others' inclusions in the disputed category of 'children's literature' proves more surprising. Children's anthologies, in particular, sought inclusions from leading intellectuals of the literary *vanguardia* as a marker of pedagogical and cultural modernity. Madrid schoolteacher Ángel Llorca, for instance, incorporated works by Golden Age and contemporaneous poets and philosophers into his reading primers. He advised teachers to read to children in their first year of school simple passages by figures including Luis de Góngora, Azorín, Benito Pérez Galdós, Jiménez, or

Ortega, then to probe them on the images and ideas contained therein — all this before children had actually learned to read.[11]

Similarly, illustrated books of verse for children, such as José Luis Sánchez Trincado and Rafael Olivares Figueroa's edited volume *Poesía infantil recitable* (Fig. 2.4), featured poems by the Spanish avant-garde, with the editors thanking notable 'poet friends' and including affectionate dedications to the children thereof. In this anthology of poetry for children, Olivares (1893–1972) included a poem dedicated to Guillén's firstborn, 'Teresita Guillén, graciosa como un cuento de hadas' [Teresita Guillén, amusing as a fairy tale] and another to her brother, young Claudio Guillén.[12] In a 1932 anthology of Jiménez's poems 'for' children edited by his wife Zenobia Camprubí Aymar (1887–1956), she included an entire prose sketch by Jiménez recalling Teresa's mischievous mock fright at his long beard and her attempts to corral Claudio into sneaking up on the illustrious poet: '"Vamoz a azuztar a Juan Ramooónnn..."' ['Let's scare Juan Ramooónnn...'], scrambling over chairs, running through doors and over windows, before nestling in the refuge of his 'smiling' black beard. In addition to such memories, the anthology is a rich fount for unpacking the *poesía pura* of childhood. As Camprubí assured, it was enough that children 'se tome del sentimiento profundo' [imbibe the deep sentiment] of poetry, hear its running water, sense the colour of the light and the fragrance of the trees — the precise meanings of which neither the child, the adult, nor the poet himself could ever truly understand.[13]

Like Olivares and Jiménez, poets furthered this form of internal dedication, playfully directing works towards the children who inspired them. Lorca (1898–1936) would dedicate poems, including several in his collection *Canciones*, to real children, from his younger sister Isabel to the children of Guillén or Pedro Salinas (1891–1951). The poem 'El lagarto está llorando' [The Lizard is Crying], for instance, begins with a dedication 'To mademoiselle Teresita Guillén playing her six-note piano'.[14] Rafael Alberti (1902–99) dedicated the 'Nanas' of his 1924 *Marinero en tierra* [Sailor on Dry Land] to his cousin, Milagro Díaz de Cevallos, while Carmen Conde's whimsical 1929 poem 'Oda a Gato Félix' [Ode to Felix the Cat] was dedicated to Salinas's nine-year-old daughter, known as Solita, whose spirit Conde sought perhaps to capture and inspire: 'A Soledad Salinas, poeta, en su Madrid florido de lápices de colores' [To Soledad Salinas, the poet, in her flowery, coloured-pencil Madrid].[15] These dedications were not solely odes among friends; most of Conde's 'Poemas de niños' and other poems in *Júbilos* bore the names of real children, either those she had taught or classmates and friends from childhood. In contrast to the abstract *niño* or *niña* of poetry inspired by a ballad or folk tradition, the children Conde depicts are contemporaries with concrete name and form: Freja, Javiva, Salvadora García, María Vega, Alberto Candelas, Carmen Morillas, Lucía Jiménez, Emilia Rubí Montoya. Their personhood is honoured in verse, their lives and individuality drawn with care and affection.

In producing works 'for' children, Lorca, Alberti, Gómez de la Serna, Conde, and others joined a wide field of adult pioneers in the field of children's literature, including Manuel Abril (1884–1943), Salvador Bartolozzi (1882–1950), Magda

FIG. 2.4. Paidologists and amateur poets sought to define Spanish poetry for children, drawing on a range of well-loved classical and avant-garde authors.
Source: *Poesía infantil recitable*, ed. José Luis Sánchez Trincado and Rafael Olivares Figueroa (Madrid: Aguilar, [1934]), cover.

Donato (pseudonym of Eva Nelken, 1898–1966), 'Elena Fortún' (Encarnación Aragoneses Urquijo, 1898–1952), and Antoniorrobles (Antonio Robles Soler, 1895–1983).[16] Publishers such as La Lectura, in the case of Jiménez's *Platero y yo*, or Saturnino Calleja engaged prominent artists and writers to publish story after story for children, alongside textbooks and manuals of childrearing and pedagogy.[17] In its style, engagement with aesthetic trends and global corpus of cultural production for children has itself been considered an 'avant-garde' in its own right.[18] In the ephemeral market, almost all major newspapers also took on rotating stories or sections for children, such as Magda Donato's comic short stories in *El Imparcial* through the early 1920s, often illustrated by her spouse Bartolozzi, or with dedicated magazines created especially for the children's market, such as *Pinocho* (Saturnino Calleja, 1925–31) or *Macaco* (Rivadeneyra, 1928–30). Works for and about children had both an established artistic grounding and commercial viability. They sparkle with exclamations, jokes, and vibrant illustrations, often centred on the misadventures of a bourgeois young boy or girl, in line with a modernist visual aesthetic shared by a network of illustrators and writers. These works formed an inseparable counterpart to a wider avant-garde project of cultural enlivenment.

Collaborators and contributors moved from the page to the stage to film, often linked by marriage, friendship, or shared intellectual circles. Gómez de la Serna, Bartolozzi, Abril, and Bergamín, for instance, were all regulars at the Café Pombo, coming into close and frequent contact. María Teresa León (1903–88)'s book for children, *Rosa-Fría, patinadora de la luna* [Rosa-Fría, Moon Skater] (1934) was illustrated by her husband, Rafael Alberti.[19] Author Concha Méndez (1898–1986), too, through her professional involvement in children's theatre, crossed genres with ease. As Pilar Nieva-de la Paz recounts, after Méndez's marriage to Manuel Altolaguirre (1905–59) the couple moved to London, where she spent days in the British Museum reading the latest works in children's theatre and completing her own play, *El carbón y la rosa* (1935), published in Madrid by the couple's own press.[20]

Such avant-garde works for children were taken seriously enough to be subjected to criticism. Reviewing Antoniorrobles's collection *26 cuentos infantiles* in 1930, the literary critic Joaquín Rodríguez de Cortázar interpreted its aesthetics in terms of contemporaneous literary trends. His stories were short narrations, compact and streamlined: 'sintéticas, tectónicas, reducidas a una línea pura según los cánones de las más actual estética' [synthetic, tectonic, reduced to a pure line according to the most recent aesthetic norms].[21] In Antoniorrobles's intuitive approach, the author was said to have drawn from a deeper philosophical well: 'La orientación del libro — de los libros — es francamente real. Fenomenológica. De hoy' [The orientation of this book, of all his books, is frankly real. Phenomenological. Contemporary'].[22] Above all, the review cut to the heart of what made childhood a subject of such fascination:

> Obra de infancia y de vanguardia a la vez, responde a la época en que el cine nos da imágenes puras del movimiento; bichos que se mueven, globitos que se mueven, pajarillos y aire y olas y campanas. Quiere Robles que la literatura infantil sea toda ritmo, movimiento puro, danza nueva, estilización de la ligereza y la alegría de vivir. Reduciendo la vida a su forma arquitectónica. Afirmando el regocijo como principal característica de lo humano.[23]

[A work of childhood and the avant-garde at once, it responds to an age in which the cinema gives us pure images of movement: animated bugs and balloons, birds and air and waves and bells. Robles wants children's literature to be all rhythm, pure movement, modern dance, the stylization of a lightness, and joy in living. Reducing life to its architectonic form. Affirming joy as the principal characteristic of the human.]

Centring on descriptions of movement, joy, and humanity, Rodríguez's review suggests perhaps more about circulating aesthetic and moral concerns than it does about Antoniorrobles's short stories. When this reviewer signalled that a work could be a work of 'childhood and the avant-garde at once', he drew an equivalence between these two states. As with Conde's concern for the poetic sensibility of children 'born in the age of Cubism', their shared aesthetics celebrated a culture of total movement: balls, birds, air, waves, bells, of rhythm, form, dance, vitality, and life itself. All of these qualities came to a head in one clear affirmation: to be human was to rejoice. As this chapter suggests, literature on, about, and for children shared a sense of rejoicing in contact, movement, and engagement with the world. In various and varied ways, authors used experiments with language, form, and genre to seek Conde's 'return' to childhood.

The Advent of the Word: Lorca, Alberti, and the Roots of Language

Language was at the heart of this project, and children's acquisition of language mirrored poetic experimentation. Speaking at Madrid's Residencia de Señoritas in May 1930, prominent writer José Bergamín, founder of the intellectually rigorous, avant-garde Catholic journal *Cruz y Raya,* read out a quasi-satirical ode to illiteracy. Exploring the child's transformation from pre-verbal to verbal, pre-literate to literate, the address was couched as a playful benediction upon this first stage of linguistic purity, in which the illiterate were the children — the spiritual children — of the world. 'Todos los niños, mientras lo son, son analfabetos' [All children, as long as they are such, are illiterate] he proclaimed.[24] Children, as beings not yet touched by reason and rationality, existed in an 'immaculate' state of grace:

No es que no pueda conocer el mundo, sino que lo conoce puramente: de un modo espiritual exclusivo, y no literal o letrado o literaturizado todavía. La razón del niño es una razón puramente espiritual: poética. El niño piensa solamente en imágenes como, según Goethe, hace la poesía: y piensa imaginativamente, sin duda, aun antes de vocalizar su pensamiento.[25]

[It is not that [children] do not know the world, but that they know it purely: spiritually, not yet in a literal or literate or literaturized way. The child's reason is purely spiritual: that is, poetic. The child thinks only in images as, Goethe suggests, poetry does: such thought comes imaginatively, without doubt, even before it is vocalized.]

A theoretical connection between childhood and a blessed, romantic isolation pre-dated the Spanish avant-garde, as Bergamín suggested in referring to Goethe. Yet it was by theorizing Spain's twentieth-century poetic practice that poets and intellectuals sought to draw out and reinforce the childlike aspects of their own production. Bergamín's assertion that the child thought in images was, on the one hand, a social critique of the ongoing democratization of knowledge in Spanish society. As Sandy Holguín has discussed, his address sought no such social crusade to educate that illiterate third of Spanish society.[26] It celebrated a state of blessed, pre-Enlightenment grace. But in his simultaneous romanticizing of the child's pre-verbal access to images and imaginaries, Bergamín also spoke to a larger avant-garde adoption of children as poetic referents and pre-verbal muses. If children thought visually, then their very essence was aligned with a goal of 'pure' poetry — to represent the essence of the thing, whether by metaphor, juxtaposition, or the elimination of the extraneous.

Pitting 'literate' culture against a larger 'spiritual' culture, Bergamín hinted at the limits of language upon which numerous poets of the *Edad de Plata*, from Alberti to Lorca, would focus. The beginnings of verbal experience and the arrival of knowledge ruptured the child's egocentric play with the world. Language, they supposed, flattened and deadened reality. Only children, Bergamín argued, retained the rich, imaginative purity of another world. Poetry offered a chance of capturing that essential world. Poets, like children, sought an intrinsic 'play' with language:

> Si el niño juega porque es niño o es niño porque juega, pensar es para el niño, jugar: poner en juego, graciosamente, las imágenes de su pensamiento: las cosas; poner, que es lo que hacen los niños, todas las cosas en juego. La razón de ser niño el niño, es este, su estado de juego: la razón de estado de la infancia, como de todo estado poético o de pura racionalidad, es el juego.[27]

> [Whether the child plays because he is a child or is a child because he plays, thinking becomes playing: to put into play, gracefully, the images of his thought: namely, things; to put, as all children do, all things into play. The reason that a child is a child is *this*, this state of play: the reason for childhood, like all poetic or purely rational states, is play itself.]

The imagined child was as close to a wholly poetic being as possible. With his own recursive plays on words, Bergamín made clear that the act of play was inextricably linked to the child's very nature. The abstract child here was little more than a melange of word, image, and sensation, suspended in a state of playful shifts and evolutions. The idea of a primary, sensorial, pre-verbal essence in childhood drew from larger scientific roots and had much to do with contemporaneous theories of play and development. It also highlighted the pre-linguistic aspects of childhood. In children's earliest days, psychologists such as Bergamín's contemporary Emilio Mira y López agreed that they existed in a pre-verbal universe, in which perceptual activity constituted an entire world. After involuntary instincts — from the bucal (sucking, smiling) to the internal (digesting, excreting) — the child's developing visual perception was its first, primary, most active sense. More globally, awareness of the world was direct and primary, with no interference between experience and consciousness.[28] Early childhood was considered to constitute the purest state of interaction between body and world. Direct experience was at the heart of the new pedagogy because it allowed contact with the things themselves. Through poetry, it was suggested, the linguistic relationship between self and world was at its most essential.

The word, from the child's earliest days, served as a measure of maturation and mental development as well as the growing humanity, for better or worse, of the child. Writing soon after Bergamín's address, in 1931, teacher and paidologist Rafael Verdier explored the mechanisms of this verbal shift in a work on the child's cognitive development of language. How do infants recognize their mothers before they have the language to encompass her? What relation does a name hold to one's intrinsic experience of perceiving that object? Verdier noted that, for instance, there could indeed be a conceptual structure which signified *mamá*, based on the primary, total maternal *Gestalt* in the child's visual field. But the synthetic concept of 'mother' evolved over time. It became ever subtler, coming to signify not just any woman, but this one woman, whose facial structure and visual form joined with successive experiences of warmth, nurture, sound, smell, and interaction. The concept was built up by experience as well as by the accumulation of similar but subtly contrasting ideas: 'father', or '*his* mother'. In this way, idea and word worked in mutual evolution; 'se condicionan y corrigen' [they condition and modulate one another] in a process of assimilation and alteration.[29]

An inextricable link between language and childhood mental development was not merely a theoretical or poetic conceit. Bringing together idea and word, and viewing these within children's developing verbal expression, poets sought to isolate, celebrate, and find their own inspiration in the primary openness of the child's mind. A poem from Pedro Salinas's early work *Presagios* (1923), 'La niña llama a su padre "Tatá, dadá"', sets the tone for these questions. Here, children's earliest grasps at language were elastic and expansive. A young girl calls her father 'tatá, dadá'. She calls her mother 'tatá, dadá'. She calls everything before her 'tatá, dadá', from her food to the landscape beyond the train window. Thinking her child entirely hopeless at learning words and names, the girl's mother exclaims:

> 'Todo lo confunde' dijo su madre.
> Y era verdad. Porque cuando yo la oía
> Decir 'Tatá, dadá',
> Veía la bola del mundo
> Rodar, rodar,
> El mundo todo una bola
> Y en ella papá, mamá,
> El mar, las montañas, todo
> Hecho una bola, confusa;
> El mundo 'Tatá, dadá'.[30]

['She's mixing everything up,' her mother said. | And it was true. Because when I heard her | Say 'Tatá, dadá', | I saw the globe | Spinning, spinning, | The world was a ball | And in it papa, mama, | The sea, the mountains, | everything a blurry ball; | The world 'Tatá, dadá'.]

In the eyes of the child, Salinas suggested, the world was an all-encompassing perceptual and emotional whole. Accordingly, the language children used reflected this global vision. Key was the child's transition from sensation to memory, imagination to symbolic production. Were children's representations more vivid, concrete, or unadulterated than those of adults? What could be learned about differing modes of perception by focusing on the child's mind?

For poets such as Salinas or Guillén, the child was the clearest argument for wonder and possibility in poetic creation, giving direct and unmediated access to the world. Guillén, whom Conde cited along with Jiménez as a prime example of the nexus between childhood and poetry, once sought to pinpoint Luis de Góngora's source of inspiration. He mused that such genius arose from a childlike simplicity of style. Like Lorca and others of his 'generation', what he considered great in Góngora's verse was its pure regard for the spirit of things, its 'gracia pueril' [childlike grace], a gift made visible only to children and to poets with the capacity to appreciate it: 'Gongorino esplendor, visible para los niños y para ciertos poetas cuyo gusto, pese a la adulta complejidad, rememora una fuente aniñada' [Gongorine splendour, visible to children and to certain poets whose taste, despite adult complexities, draws from a childlike source].[31] Simplicity versus complexity — this was the standard argument for privileging the child's view of the world and elevating poetry as the essential art of childhood. It was at this moment when children's literature was at once beginning to flourish and in which the 'world of the child' had become a common trope, yet also one in which artists argued paradoxically that there was no dividing line to be drawn between good literature for children and for adults. Children benefitted from clear, engaging verse and prose, just as the vibrancy of childhood was essential to a modern, vital poetry.

Connecting children's 'literature' to poetic theory, the genre of the *nanas* suggests how the avant-garde sought to connect verbal development to aesthetic goals. This folkloric enterprise drew from the most primary form of literature: song and verse, which joined studies of rhythm, form, and folklore to the study of the child. Lorca's 1928 conference, 'Las nanas infantiles', at the Residencia de Estudiantes described the qualities that made lullabies and nursery rhymes — like so many other aspects of culture, such as old songs or sweets — such a telling marker of a people's character, history, fears, and desires. On the outskirts of Granada, Lorca recalled, he had heard a local woman singing to her child. It was only then that it struck him how incredibly sad the Spanish lullaby could be. Without the slightest hint of personal melancholy, this young mother was nonetheless passing on to her child Spain's 'melodías de más acentuada tristeza' [most acutely sad melodies].[32] With their songs, the mothers of Spain served to 'teñir el primer sueño de sus niños' [tinge their children's first dreams] with tones and rhythms qualitatively different from those of any other land or nation. Sensing the living tradition that she embodied, Lorca declared that he had, ever since this encounter, been actively collecting lullabies from all the various regions of Spain, seeking to understand how they differed from one another and what insight they gave into the 'mapa melódico de España' [melodic map of Spain], its interpenetrations of history, culture, and blood.[33]

Lorca's profound connection between childhood and these deep expressions of land and culture — the 'natal' in 'nation' — suggests one reason that the Spanish avant-garde saw in childhood a key project. For the decisive aspects of a melody, Lorca noted, were by no means its formal or factual qualities — whether it was written in the seventeenth century or followed a certain rhythmical form — but rather whether it had the emotional power to evoke an entire imaginative landscape, to bring a vivid world to life before the 'ojos recién cuajados del niño' [child's recently-focused vision].[34] The power of word, rhythm, and emotion worked through song to shape the child's developing visual sensibility. In Lorca's depiction, *nanas* could be brutal in their stark evocation of desolation, loneliness, danger, and fear. But the child, Lorca argued, possessed a total faith that imbibed and was sustained by these rhythms and lines, 'Muy lejos de nosotros, el niño posee íntegra la fe creadora' [Unlike us, the child maintains his creative faith intact], Lorca noted, with the child equipped to understand in some way beyond intellect the emotional charge behind the *nanas*: 'Comprende, mejor que nosotros, la clave inefable de la sustancia poética' [He understands, better than we, the ineffable key of poetic substance].[35]

Lorca wrote verses that vastly enlarged the world and reduced the child to a minuscule and powerless size, or that did the opposite, reducing the scale of reference to foreground the child and its mother in a protective cocoon of nurturing scale, evoking an imaginative dyad of mother and child against the world:

> A la nana, niño mío,
> a la nanita y haremos
> en el campo una chocita
> y en ella nos meteremos.[36]

[With the lullaby, my child, | with a lullaby we'll build | a little hut in the country | and hide ourselves away.]

In reading the children of Lorca's verses, Christopher Maurer has described them as a conscious reconciliation of past and present, an 'act of poetic faith' equal to that demanded by poetry of both poet and reader. Bringing qualities of imagination and expression together, Lorca's lecture demonstrated a fascination with the ways in which lullabies provide a first experience of poetic transportation:

> A la nana, nana, nana
> A la nanita de aquel
> Que llevó el caballo al agua
> Y le dejó sin beber...[37]

[The lullaby, lullaby, lullaby | Little lullaby of the one | Who led the horse to water | Then away without a sip...]

The pure lyric beauty of this phrase, Lorca noted, gave way to the world of dreams. A nameless, faceless 'aquel', leading a horse to water, stimulated fascination and anguish: 'Nunca el niño los verá de frente' [The child will never see them face to face]. One must always imagine within a dark 'penumbra' the hidden qualities of that roughly outlined scene. In such a way Lorca imagined children's mental process: they see a figure in profile. Based on limited visual cues, they begin to fill out a profile from all angles, imagining and creating the scene, thus becoming the creative author of their own internal realities:

El niño reconoce al personaje y, según su experiencia visual, que siempre es más de la que suponemos, perfila su figura. Está obligado a ser un espectador y un creador al mismo tiempo, ¡y qué creador maravilloso! Un creador que posee un sentido poético de primer orden.[38]

[The child recognizes the character and, according to his own visual experience, which is always greater than we think, he sketches its outlines. He is obligated to be both spectator and creator at once, and what a marvellous creator! A creator who possesses a first-rate sense of poetry.]

It was precisely this quality of being both a visual spectator and a spontaneous generator of imagery and detail that makes Lorca's take on the *nanas* a necessary precedent to understanding the avant-garde's wider fascination with the child.

Lorca's interest in the *nanas* was shared by Rafael Alberti, who linked the songs to a Spanish literary tradition and sought to connect them to his larger poetic project. In an address on Lope de Vega's influence on contemporary poetry delivered in Havana in April 1935, Alberti quoted a verse of Lope's that echoed the aesthetic he sought to capture:

> Íbase la niña,
> noche de San Juan
> a coger los aires
> al fresco del mar.[39]

[The girl went out, | on St John's Eve, | to take the | fresh sea air.]

Noting the grace of Lope's language, Alberti suggested that this lightness accorded with the present season, the spring air outside, 'llena de cantos, de canciones' [filled with singing and song], a lightness he found equally in spring and popular song. He recited a verse Lope had written for his son Carlos Félix, collected in his *Pastores de Belén*, in which the poet pleads with the angels of Bethlehem to hold still the towering palm trees above, to let the child sleep through the battering winds.[40] In making a case for Lope's poetic influence upon the evolution of contemporary Spanish verse, Alberti suggested that the poet drew on the tradition of rural mothers rocking their children to sleep with melodies, rhythmic and lulling like the monotonous swaying of boats. Diverse but equally present across Spain's regions, from 'Asturias hasta Cádiz, desde Extremadura hasta Valencia', these lullabies persisted and evolved from Lope and Gil Vicente to the poets of his present day.[41]

As Alberti employed these verses, they were entirely removed from space and time. Like all ballads and popular songs, they were meant to be sung, passed on, and to evolve. They were the thread which connected Lope to the poets of his age, transmitted from mother to child, and which shaped Spanish verse and culture to the present. These *nanas* continued in new forms, taken up by the most eminent of Spanish poets and writers. Alberti recalled seeing Miguel de Unamuno one day, pulling from his pocket like a schoolboy a *nana* dedicated to his first grandchild, Miguel Quiroga. The poet had written, he quoted:

> La media luna es una cuna
> ¿y quién la briza?

Y el niño de la media luna
¿qué sueños riza?
La media luna es una cuna
¿y quién la mece?
Y el niño de la media luna
¿Para quién crece?
La media luna es una cuna
va a luna nueva.
Y al niño de la media luna,
¿quién me lo lleva?[42]

[The crescent moon is a cradle, | And who rocks it? | And the child of the crescent moon | What dreams sway it? | The crescent moon is a cradle, | And who swings it? | And the child of the crescent moon | For whom does he grow? | The crescent moon is a cradle | That becomes the new moon. | And the child of the crescent moon, | Who will bring him to me?]

Drawing a direct line in theme and intent from Lope de Vega and Gil Vicente to Unamuno — while acknowledging the rootedness of this verse in the folkloric song of women across the ages — Alberti made a claim for the centrality of *nanas* to a Spanish poetics.

Both Lorca and Alberti connected childhood imagination to avant-garde experimentation with language. Lorca's works had the images, colours, and drama of childhood imagination at their heart, with various of his theatrical works drawing on his own interest in puppets and marionettes. This interest in puppetry is said to have dated back to the arrival in Fuente Vaqueros of a travelling puppet theatre during his own childhood; the dramatics of the *guiñol*, along with the music and folklore he heard from nannies and maids, underlay much of his subsequent poetic and dramatic production.[43] One of his first works of theatre was the playful *La niña que riega la albahaca y el príncipe preguntón* [The Girl Who Waters the Basil and a Most Inquisitive Prince] (1923), performed at home at Epiphany for his twelve-year-old sister Isabelita and young friends. He worked with Manuel de Falla on the music, with songs performed by Isabel and Laurita de los Ríos Giner, with puppets designed by the artists Manuel Ángeles Ortiz and Hermenegildo Lanz.[44] Later, as director of La Barraca theatre company and a contributor to works of popular theatre during the Second Republic, Lorca made the language and aesthetics of childhood central to his pedagogical mission. In 1935, for instance, in one among many artistic-theatrical collaborations, he would correspond with sculptor Ángel Ferrant about the latter's marionette designs for his *Retablillo de don Cristóbal* [Don Cristóbal's Puppet Play].[45]

In a comparable conjunction of childhood aesthetics and dramatic production, in 1925 Alberti began writing a work of children's theatre he called *La pájara pinta,* based on a popular children's refrain: 'Estaba la pájara pinta | sentada en el verde limón' [The colourful bird was | perched on the green lemon tree].[46] The work, incomplete, debuted at the Salle Gaveau in Paris in 1932 and in Seville and Madrid that same year, with music by Oscar Esplá and Federico Elizalde. In Madrid, the play was put on by students of the Instituto-Escuela to celebrate the opening of a new building, performed at the Jardines del Campo de Moro before an audience that included Niceto Alcalá Zamora, then President of the Republic, and Manuel Azaña.[47] The play became the theatrical centrepiece of the new building's celebratory inauguration, directed by teacher Jimena Menéndez Pidal and overseen by school director María de Maeztu. In keeping with the boldness of Alberti's work, the new building was described as a symbol of 'la moderna pedagogía', with its clean lines, windows, and open spaces.[48]

In this celebratory modern setting, Alberti's play demonstrated the tight linkage between children's theatre, poetic experimentation, and the development of language through imitation and play. Embracing both familiar children's rhymes and popular song and a flexible, shifting, associative, onomatopoeic language, the prologue begins with the Pájara Pinta seated on a branch of a lemon tree, with the dozen characters of the play assembled around her. A smartly dressed rooster explains the plot, according to Alberti's stage direction:

> ¡Pío — pío
> pío — pío!
> ¡Verdo — lari — lari — rio,
> rio — rio!
> ¡Kikirikiiii!
> ¡Ladón
> landera
> deralón
> dinera,
> nederlín
> nedirlón
> nedirlera
> ronda, rondalín, randul,
> faró, faralay,
> guiri, guirigay,
> bul!
> [...]
> ¡Uuuh,
> ru,
> bi,
> buuu!
> ¡Dilí
> dilo direvi dilí!
> ¡Dalá
> dalo darevi dalá!
> ¡Uuuh,
> ru,
> bi,
> buuu![49]

In three pages of linguistic play, an extended 'monologue' from the Pipirigallo, Alberti's work recalls the playful linguistic experimentation of the European avant-garde, bringing to mind everything from Hugo Ball's Dadaist poem 'Karawane' (1916) to, that same year, James Joyce's melding of sounds and words in the mind of the child Stephen Dedalus.[50] By putting non-language in the mouths of children, Alberti's play both drew from, exaggerated and expanded upon childhood pre-verbality through the pushing forward and deconstruction of language.

Shared engagements with linguistic and visual play through poetry, puppetry, and theatre served as a marker of the close linkage between children's perceived linguistic flexibility, their development into independent and articulate actors, and the pure sense of joy and playfulness inherent in poetry, theatre, and play. What role did these works have in the development of a voice for each child, or for Spain's poetic tradition as a whole? As Alberti noted in his 1935 address on Lope de Vega, in the poet's theatrical work in the new world, the theatre acted to open its doors to the masses of the city, where the illiterate and the literate came together on equal terms. New forms of performance paved the way for 'new democracies'.[51] It is no stretch to suggest that Alberti, who followed his address on Lope by reciting the nonsensical text of *La pájara pinta*, saw in children's play with words and characters a direct engagement between poetic experimentation, young voices, and the development of a democratic culture in Spain.

Cultural interest in children's lyric development was not restricted to a poetic circle, but was also communicated in print to a wide range of teachers. The following year, in 1936, the editors of the journal *Escuelas de España* invited Luis Cernuda to contribute a piece on poetry and education, noting that it was their 'fervent desire' to orient Spanish teachers towards the latest movements in contemporary culture.[52] Writing for an audience of educational reformers, Cernuda furthered the link between early childhood education and poetic fluidity. Paraphrasing a 'French critic', Cernuda described poetry as a mysterious current or fluid which could be freely received and transmitted.[53] As with electrical currents, some materials were better conductors than others. Children were the ideal conductors of poetry, he noted, an ability and, in some cases, a particular gift that should be identified and nurtured. Teachers who wished to awaken a love of poetry in their pupils, Cernuda wrote, must pay attention to a few key points: 'a la percepción, al contagio del lirismo, forma de la poesía moderna, individual y al mismo tiempo universal efusión del poeta ante el mundo' [to perception, the contagion of lyricism, modern poetic form, an individual yet simultaneously universal effusion of the poet before the world].[54]

As each of these poets — Salinas, Lorca, Alberti, Cernuda — made clear, a tight connection was forged between childhood and avant-garde literature. On the ground, it was teachers themselves (often in close communication with, or identifying as, poets and artists) who sought to cement that connection. They did so in diverse ways, through the development of school libraries, school presses, theatrical plays, or the incorporation of literature in the classroom, but also through publications and advocacy. Whether in Conde's suggestion of a return to childhood within art itself, Bergamín's assertion of childhood as a state of blessed illiteracy, or Lorca's and Alberti's arguments on the primacy of the *nana* to Spanish literature as a whole, the poetic word was never far removed from the act of learning.

Word and World: Alicita Venturino and the Childhood Fount of Poetry

What was 'poetry for children', a reviewer of a new children's anthology asked in 1935? While the concept of 'poetry' was relatively clear, no one had yet provided a satisfactory answer to the question of what exactly constituted *children's* poetry: 'poesía infantil para los niños'.[55] In the introduction to the reviewed work, *Poesía infantil recitable* (1934) collected by Venezuelan teacher Rafael Olivares Figueroa (1893–1972) and school inspector José Luis Sánchez Trincado (1901–1950), the editors set out to theorize a new form of *poesía pura* for the children of Spain. Their introduction examined what made poetry stimulating for children, celebrating these qualities in verse. The anthology collected new poems of young poets alongside classics of Spanish literature and anonymous folk ballads. Together, the authors framed what children's own innate poetic sensibilities could offer to vanguard literature:

> Llamamos infantil a una poesía, no porque sea accesible de repente a los niños, sino porque esté impregnada de esencias infantiles, y a veces, solo por su acento, por su gracia, por su ingenuidad, por su leve sabor de cosa primitiva, porque no se trata de descifrar la poesía, sino de sentirla.[56]

> [We call this children's poetry not because it is instantly accessible to children, but rather because it is saturated with childlike essences, and at times is inflected with a certain grace and naivety, a mild flavour of the primitive; because we should not attempt to decipher poetry, but to feel it.]

Here, 'children's poetry' came closer to Jiménez's notion of *poesía pura*: verse stripped down to its essentials, its 'esencias infantiles'. Children need not decipher the symbols that encoded the adult world, but recognize them and sense them.

In the wake of this publication, Olivares delivered an address to the Academia de Ciencias, Bellas Letras y Nobles Artes de Córdoba in which he attempted to understand what constituted children's poetic genius. In doing so, he blurred the lines between children's production and the nature of poetry itself. Why were children the originators and ideal recipients of poetry, he asked? The answer had to do with a specific form of genius, one shared by all children but — as with the talent of poets and artists — arising prodigiously only in rare cases. Closely reading and celebrating her work as an entrée into theories of poetry, he introduced the writings of a nine-year-old Chilean-Salvadoran child by the name of Alicita Venturino Lardé. Alicita was the daughter of Salvadorian poet and natural scientist Alicia Lardé de Venturino and Chilean sociologist Agustín Venturino Sotomayor. She accompanied her parents on a lecture tour of Europe coinciding with Olivares's paidological publications (1934–36), during which she allegedly recited poems and was introduced by figures including Joaquim Xirau in Barcelona.[57] Through her work, Olivares sought to defend the receptive and imaginative qualities of childhood and make a case for all children's poetic exceptionality.

While Olivares amply reprinted her verse, the content and quality of the works themselves are of lesser analytical significance here. Rather, the reception of Venturino's verse epitomizes the close links forged between a celebration of childhood imagination, *naïveté*, and the possibilities and limits of children's natural abilities. Through notions of natural and poetic genius, a celebratory representation of childhood showed its inherent inseparability from psychological and pseudo-scientific diagnostics. Alicita's works aligned with an animist channelling of the world through the eyes of a child. Her works surveyed the 'wide clinic of the world,' he wrote, transfiguring it into clear and perceptive insights on her surroundings and the imagined world beyond.[58] The dynamism of childhood, Olivares argued in the case of young Alicita, lent fluidity to these works: 'Llegó el adulto a su meta de cristalización, mientras, proteico, el niño se transfigura en un mar de aspectos y matices' [The adult has reached peak crystallization, while, protean, the child is transfigured into a sea of aspects and nuances].[59] The child accessed not simply *another* reality, but one uniquely oriented towards lyric expression.

In both their curiosity for 'scientific order' and their ability to 'understand' art, children combined sensorial and rational approaches to the world. In a description of children as 'buenos conductores de fluido poético' [ideal fluid-conductors of poetry], Olivares presented this quality as one of mutual feedback between perception and curiosity. Venturino's poetry served as an intermediary between the imaginary and the concrete, 'un Coloquio entre el Alma-niña y el Mundo' [a meeting of the child's soul and the world]. In her collection *La naturaleza y yo*, Olivares exclaimed that Venturino could spin a 'spider's web' to ensnare the world, that she could evoke her world from its skies down to its rocks. Across the extensive selection of poems, Venturino was constantly anthropomorphizing her objects of reflection, seeking to elevate them to their full stature, in his words, 'humanizada y magnífica'.[60] From the sea to animals, rocks and sky, her eye surveyed all with equanimity. Her work demonstrated, for Olivares, not intellectual representation but a primitivist translation of totemic realities into verse. In what could be an analogy for how adult poets from Juan Ramón Jiménez to Josefina de la Torre Millares (1907–2002) to Jorge Guillén portrayed the child — as a metaphorical island, an impenetrable mystery, an enigma — Venturino's poem 'Isla' [Island] defamiliarized islands as strange masses rising up from the sea:

> ¿Cómo puede ser este fenómeno
> que te levantes de entre las aguas?...
> ¡Ah, es que la naturaleza te ha formado así![61]

[How can it be, this phenomenon | That has you rising up above the seas? | Ah, nature has made you that way!]

In its glowing metaphors and personification of the natural world, Venturino's verse can be read as an inspiration for poets seeking to celebrate an aesthetics of childhood, while being itself a product shaped by that surrounding fascination.

For Olivares, Alicita Venturino's poetry represented all that was notable and praiseworthy in *poesía pura*. Her verse consisted of a stripped-down play of metaphors which recalled the sort of lullaby and folklore-tinged works found in Alberti's *Marinero en tierra* (1924) or Lorca's *Romancero gitano* (1928). Poems such as Venturino's 'Las gaviotas' [The Gulls] recall poetic precedents:

> Las gaviotas vuelan sobre el mar.
> Con sus alas tan grandes
> se van a las rocas, y hacen su nido
> muy bien tejido...
> y, cuando cae la tarde, todas las gaviotas
> se reúnen en vuelo...
> y, cuando la noche llega,
> se duermen en silencio...[62]

[The gulls fly over the sea. | With their great big wings | they fly to the rocks, and weave | their nests well... | and, when evening falls, the gulls | reunite in flight... | and, when the night comes, | they sleep in silence...]

Given that Alicita's parents were prominent South American intellectuals in contact with Spain's leading lights, she was almost certainly raised on a nurturing diet of modernist poetry, from Jiménez and Mistral to Rabindranath Tagore (1861–1941). The echo of poets such as Antonio Machado (1875–1939), who sought in his verse to ground a view of the 'eterno humano' within world and landscape and wrote lovingly and extensively on childhood images and memories, comes through in her verse. His expressions of a 'laughing sea' and soaring doves from his 'XLIV' [El casco roído y verdoso] of *Soledades* [Solitudes] (1903): 'La gaviota palpita en el aire dormido, y al lento | volar soñoliento, se aleja y se pierde en la bruma el sol' [The gull trembles in the still air, and in its slow | drowsy flight, is lost in the haze of the sun], in particular, echo through this poem.[63]

Pedagogues' elevation of child-poets suggests a circularity within the field. They praised and sought to imbibe the spirit of children's poetry, even as those verses brought the reader back to their models and sources. Poems such as Lorca's 'Caracola' [Seashell] of *Canciones* (1921–24), dedicated to young Natalia Jiménez Cossío, overflow with a comparable sense of childlike wonder:

> Me han traído una caracola.
>
> Dentro le canta
> Un mar de mapa.
> Mi corazón
> Se llena de agua
> Con pececillos
> De sombra y plata.
>
> Me han traído una caracola.[64]

[They brought me a shell. | Inside sings | A map's ocean. | My heart | Fills with water | And little fish | Of shadows and silver. | They brought me a shell.]

One finds similar reflections in fragments such as Alicita's 'La barca' [The Boat], which rather than adult reflection and synthesis begins from simple visual observation:

> La barca pescadora
> está flotando sobre el mar.
> Es la hora de la pesca.

Los pescadores
tienden las redes al mar.
Y al sacarlas, vienen dentro
un sin fin de pececitos
de todos colores,
que brillan con el sol...[65]

[The fishing boat | is floating on the sea. | It's fishing hour. | The fishermen
| cast their nets to the sea. | As they pull them out | a multitude of little fish
| appear gleaming in the sun...]

Venturino was one of various child-muses celebrated by the avant-garde, both
those they knew personally and others who rose to some public prominence. For
Olivares, Venturino was the exceptional representation of 'poetic invention' in
the child. She was also a 'superdotada', blessed with seemingly effortless ability to
record and order her world.

If genius is that which 'defies analysis', then paidologists and artists saw a particular form of unquantifiable genius in children's symbolic production.[66] Yet
Olivares distinguished 'superdotados' like Alicita, whose growth should be furthered, from 'niños precoces', prodigies whose talent was sudden, hobbling, and
destructive.[67] In this, he drew from a wider personal and societal fascination with
giftedness and genius, as evidenced by a survey of child prodigies he had earlier
published in the *Heraldo de Madrid* (Fig. 2.5). These children appear as cosmopolitan
madrileños: cultured, well-off, and highly educated. Four of the seven were girls
or young women; all evidenced skill in some aspect of the arts or performance.
All were for him representatives of the larger phenomenon of the 'niño precoz'
[precocious child].[68] According to Olivares, 'precocious' children had remarkable
abilities in intellectual fields, mathematics, reading, drawing, or other forms
of performance, but their skills were not a true, communicative intellectual
discourse.[69] Olivares's analysis suggested critical distinctions in verbal performance
and access within the boundaries of 'normality'. While children's innate access to
poetic fluency was an aspect of fascination, it was also an entry point for defining
interventions outside the bounds of 'normal' development. Noting that Alicita's
childhood promise was not a sign of precocity but of cultivation, Olivares argued
that the genius exhibited by young Alicita could, in principle, be found in any child.
He cited work on gifted children by Claparède, Piaget, Dewey, Roger Cousinet,
and, in particular, American psychologist Lewis Terman to suggest that *superdotados*
were more frequent in families of good means. Their ability was, therefore, less a
result of nature than of nurture.[70] Building upon Terman's conclusions, Olivares
advocated for a larger process of 'genicultura', in which teachers could aid children's
intellectual flourishing across all walks of life, regardless of family means.

Alicita's poetry, while of limited literary significance in its own right, formed
part of a rich discussion of genius and talent within the Spanish and Latin American
avant-garde that reflected back not only on aesthetic but social and political
priorities. It illustrates how imaginative liberation from conventionality — of both
verse and upbringing — was sought even as pedagogues drew upon new quantitative,
descriptive, and diagnostic metrics.[71] As with Bergamín's 'blessing on the illiterate',

UNA INFORMACIÓN TODAS LAS NOCHES

REPORTAJE DE RAFAEL N. OLIVARES

Unos cuantos niños precoces madrileños

FOTOGRAFÍAS HERALDO DE MADRID

Manolito Camacho
(Foto Moreno.)

Blanquita R. Cardona
(Foto Marí.)

Manolita Martín
(Foto Mateo.)

Conchita Rodríguez
(Foto Marí.)

Alfredito Hurtado (Pitusín)
(Foto Lagos.)

Matildita Ferrández

FIG. 2.5. Rafael Olivares Figueroa, study of child prodigies in *El Heraldo de Madrid* (1931).
Source: Rafael Olivares Figueroa, "Unos cuantos niños precoces madrileños",
El Heraldo de Madrid, 18 April 1931, p. 14.

the development of language could be both an obstacle to direct sensorial experience and an elemental mode of grasping the totality of the surrounding world. Drawing together linguistic primacy, socialization, and development, Olivares and fellow educators sought to describe through poetry how children's linguistic abilities were cultivated and understood. Here, the perceptual and the imaginative collided. Across Spain, in Europe, and through Salinas's entire invocation of the 'world "tatá, dadá"', research on globalized thinking and the acquisition of language bolstered the interest of philosophers, artists, and intellectuals in symbolic understanding and invention. This nexus could be observed not only in poetry and art, as will be explored in Chapter 5, but also in child study and psychometrics. From Olivares's study of young Alicita's poetry to avant-garde poets' use of the child-figure in verse, intellectuals engaged in the political action of education reform alongside literarily grounded attempts to understand the child's symbolic integration of reality.

The New Moon of Childhood: Camprubí, Tagore, and Poetic Synthesis

In a 1934 article lauding Juan Ramón Jiménez's literary and spiritual connection with children, the critic José Luis Sánchez Trincado spoke of poetry as something sacred, made and destined for the hands of children. Children were the 'fieles' [faithful] of poetry, for whom the poet, in a state of inspiration, conceived 'versos primitivos, humanos, primarios, esenciales, unos, simples' [primitive, human, primary, essential, singular, simple verses]. Wherever children went, in all the classrooms of the nation, in the libraries of the Republican *misiones pedagógicas*, alongside the works of Lope de Vega and Tirso de Molina, Machado and Alberti: anywhere such classics of literature could be found, Jiménez's works would follow. Beyond the possibility of literal analysis, he suggested, his works possessed a simplicity that connected across the years: children understood them as 'suya, esto es, pura' [theirs, that is, pure].[72] Whence this intimate connection between 'their' literature and the poetic project of the Spanish avant-garde?

One suggestion comes from the particular models in which poets and artists were steeped and which they actively adopted and embraced. In 1915, Zenobia Camprubí, a young writer and translator and Jiménez's soon-to-be spouse, published what became a wildly popular edition of Tagore's poems for children, *La luna nueva (poemas de niños)* [The Crescent Moon: Poems for Children]. Tagore, a Bengali poet and recipient of the 1913 Nobel Prize for Literature celebrated by W. B. Yeats, Ezra Pound, and others, had a major influence on global writings on childhood as well as inspiring educators through his experimental model school in India. In the reception of the Camprubí-Jiménez translations, one finds a marked convergence of childhood imaginaries and literary experimentation, but also, as Gayle Rogers has argued, a textbook case of modernist translation, revealing not only influence but also the 'fissures, gaps, ambivalences and breaks' in the process.[73] These complexities were the case not only interlinguistically and transnationally, but within Spain itself as the Tagore translations were received, incorporated, and set within a larger tradition of romantic poetic depictions, odes, and celebrations of childhood. Alongside major, ubiquitous works such as Juan Ramón Jiménez's *Platero y yo* in the Spanish classroom, the Tagore translations inspired authors of a new generation who not only found concrete inspiration in Tagore's own pedagogical initiatives, but responded to his imaginaries of childhood through new approaches to verse and experimentation.[74]

The bilingual Camprubí began the project of translating *The Crescent Moon* with Jiménez two years before their marriage. She was deeply engaged in literary production, having published in North American journals throughout her youth.[75] The couple collaborated closely over the coming decade. As has been shown through their correspondence and manuscripts, Jiménez was heavily invested in the translation process.[76] Camprubí would send Jiménez her most accurate Spanish translations of the English text, which he would rework towards a unified rhythm, diction, and voice in line with his own verse. Through these works, Camprubí took on significant professional standing within the growing field of children's literature, while Jiménez made the works central to his own poetic project.[77] While translating and popularizing Tagore's work in the Spanish-speaking world, Camprubí defined the aesthetic project in which she and Jiménez were engaged. In a translator's note to her publication of Tagore's 1919 *Morada de paz (Shantiniketan)*, a collection of essays which relate his establishment of a humanistic, experimental school in India, Camprubí included a foreword that defended the work's renewed artistic and spiritual value in its Spanish incarnation:

> (NINGUNA obra, y menos si es traducción, puede tener, mientras su autor viva, sino un valor transitorio. En cada nueva edición, este libro se ha de ir desnudando más, maestro de sí mismo, hasta llegar a su expresión permanente.) Madrid, 1919.[78]

> [(NO work, and far less if it is a translation, can have, while its author lives, anything but a transitory value. In each new edition, this book must become further denuded, mastering itself, in order to arrive at its permanent expression.) Madrid, 1919.]

As thoughts and verse moved from Bengali to English, English to Spanish, rather than losing their essence the works began to find it, she suggested. In each edition, 'desnudando' in the language of *poesía pura*, the work found new resonances and new readers.

Camprubí's translation of *La luna nueva* was published a year after Jiménez's *Platero y yo*, selling 9,000 copies over three printings that first year. These translations set off a frenzy in Spain and Latin America, with twenty-one further works and thousands of copies, legal and pirated, appearing until 1922. During this period Tagore even accepted the couple's invitation to visit Spain at the end of a longer tour. Plans proceeded for a ten-day Spanish visit for April of 1921, hosted by Camprubí and Jiménez, Gregorio Marañón, and others, meant to culminate in a grand celebration of Tagore's work at the Residencia with readings by the Jiménez's, the young teacher Jimena Menéndez Pidal (1901–90), and various students. Ultimately, however, Tagore cut the tour short and the trip was cancelled.[79] Taken together with the weight of Camprubí and Jiménez's inter-lingual and intra-lingual translations, Tagore's verse influenced a generation of poets who embraced the child as a source of inspiration. The translations, for instance, furthered the use of a common phrase in child studies in Spain, the 'world of the child'. A poem of Tagore's entitled, in its English translation, 'Baby's World' became 'El mundo del niño' in Camprubí's rendering. This phrase, the 'mundo del niño', was commonly used to indicate the irreconcilable gap between infantile and adult perception and experience of the world, as in Manuel García Morente's 1928 article of the same title.[80] Tagore's text — included here in a second Spanish draft, further edited and refined by Jiménez — gives a sense of an imaginative universe which relied on vivid, living imagery:

> Quisiera yo poder hallar un rinconcito de paz en el mismo corazón del mundo de mi niño. Sé que en él tiene estrellas que le hablan, y un cielo que baja hasta su cara para divertirlo con sus nubes tontas y con sus arcoíris. Allí, esas cosas que parece no dicen nada y que no se mueven, llegan, arrastrándose, hasta su ventana, y le cuentan cuentos y le ofrecen bandejas llenas de juguetes de vivos colores.
>
> Quisiera yo poder andar ese camino que va por el pensamiento de mi niño, salirme de todos sus confines, llegar adonde no sé que mensajeros llevan y traen mensajes sin razón, por reinos de reyes sin historia; adonde la Razón remonta, como cometas, leyes; adonde liberta a las acciones de sus cadenas la Verdad.[81]

> [I wish to find a little corner of peace in the very heart of my child's world. I know there are stars that speak to him and a sky that reaches down to amuse him with silly clouds and rainbows. Things that seem mute and immobile come tiptoeing to his window, telling tales and offering up an array of colourful toys.
>
> How I would like to walk the path that leads through my child's mind, to break free of all confines, to arrive where messengers dash between the kingdoms of kings without history; where Reason flies laws like kites; where Truth frees actions from their chains.]

Stars that speak, a sky that turns its face to the clouds: these visions evoke a world of rich, colourful tales and dreams. Such images and ideas had a marked resonance with poets around the world, including, through Camprubí and Jiménez, in Spain during the coming decade, both in its echoes of renovation and liberation and in distillations and maturations of Tagore's imagery.

These works established a precedent for the connection of poetry and childhood within the pedagogical avant-garde in Spain, with figures such as Ortega, Ramón Pérez de Ayala, and Lorenzo Luzuriaga lauding their pedagogical significance.[82] Pérez de Ayala celebrated Tagore's embrace of the universe, including its celebratory 'amor de los niños' and 'amor humano'.[83] Ortega, in a series of three articles, claimed that these works cut to the essence of the poetic imagination. With attention to the desires of Tagore's children and objects, the texts in their Spanish translations promoted the vital and the imaginative: 'No hay sino anhelos, señora; lo demás no existe, por lo menos no existe vitalmente' [There is nothing but yearning, *señora*; the rest does not exist, at least not vitally]. Tagore, like all 'great spirits', innately understood how to listen to the child within, 'el niño en nosotros'.[84] Luzuriaga, meanwhile, lauded Tagore as an author who suggested that literature could bring practical, revolutionary change within the field of education. Surveying the great humanists of history, from Plato to Tolstoy, he suggested that the work of writing great poetry was inextricably aligned with that 'otra labor de creación y configuración espiritual' [other labour of creation and spiritual development], that of educating the next generation.[85]

By idealizing childhood, poets sought to elevate it to its full potential — to humanize and spiritualize children's sensibilities and future actions. As Luzuriaga noted, Tagore's influence was not limited to verse. In 1901, he had founded a revolutionary school at Shantiniketin, West Bengal, which promoted a holistic view of learning through academic, physical, and spiritual development. While based on the Hindu tradition of the ashram, Luzuriaga describes the school as a melange of international New Education principles and those established in Spain's own *escuelas al aire libre* and Krausist, *institucionista* innovations. The tenets of Tagore's school included a rural location, secluded yet close enough to a train station to benefit urban children, and a curriculum based around creativity and collective self-governance: music, song, writing, farming, exercise, prayer, and discussion. The connection between lyrical, poetic heights and practical reality was Tagore's strength, according to Luzuriaga: he not only inspired an enlivened imagination and spiritual depth in his readers, but he also put these ideals into practice. Within Tagore's teachings, the imagination flourished and, through artistic, physical, poetic, and spiritual practice, the innate humanity of each child was recognized.

In Tagore's accounts of his Indian school, one can understand why Luzuriaga and Ortega would find qualities to praise. Whether in its 1917 English account or Camprubí's 1917 Spanish translation, the school's philosophy accorded closely with the excursionist and experiential ethos of the Institución Libre de Enseñanza and schools following the New Education model of attention to bodily practice and individual development, with a focus on inner life and the fostering of imagination from teacher to child. Describing the work of one young teacher, Tagore wrote that his strength consisted in conversing with children with feeling and interest, walking them into the forest as spring trees blossomed to read Shakespeare or Browning, and allowing them to cultivate a fascination with life in its totality, 'shimmering in the leaves, tingling in the roots of the grass under the earth'.[86] The teacher privileged these first-hand encounters, never reducing a work's complexity but rather allowing its content to work alongside their own innate curiosity for the world:

> He knew that it was not at all necessary for the boys to understand literally and accurately, but that their minds should be roused, and in this he was always successful. He was not like other teachers, a mere vehicle of text-books. He made his teaching personal, he himself was the source of it, and therefore it was made of life-stuff easily assimilable by living human nature [...] He had the power to see ideas before him, as he could see his friends, with all the distinctness of form and subtlety of life.[87]

Bringing together mental life, sensation, and physical contact between child, peers, and world, Tagore's delineation of a new ideal of pedagogy both accorded with and inspired the neo-humanist, vanguard Spanish pedagogical reformers described throughout this book. As intellectuals held up Tagore's school as a model of *institucionista* values and incorporated his poetry into the Hispanic canon, Camprubí's successful translations of Tagore introduced new poetic images of education as a way of accessing the child's world.

A line of humanist and New Educational educators and poets alike sought to capture his vision of 'living human nature' in all its forms. To find and embody a teaching that drew from the teacher's spirit, and awakened the mind of the child, was their goal. Their texts, meanwhile, drew the focus not only to the child at their heart, but also to the adult intermediary: the writer, mother, father, observer, apart and watchful, separate from the child's world. One of Tagore's most famous poems, 'On the seashore...' from *Gitanjali*, was first translated by André Gide into French in 1913.[88] It begins, in its English rendering:

> On the seashore of endless worlds children meet. The infinite sky is motionless overhead and the restless water is boisterous. On the seashore of endless worlds the children meet with shouts and dances. They build their houses with sand, and they play with empty shells [...]. Pearlfishers dive for pearls, merchants sail in their ships, while children gather pebbles and scatter them again. [...] The sea surges up with laughter, and pale gleams the smile of the seabeach. Death-dealing waves sing meaningless ballads to the children, even like a mother while rocking her baby's cradle. The sea plays with children, and smiles the sea-beach.[89]

Juxtaposed with images such as that on the cover of this book, namely one of Sorolla's many depictions of children playing at the edge of the sea, one senses at first glance the shared shouts and splashes of children. In its concealed violence, cyclical images, and 'death-dealing' waves, it foretells the thematic — if not stylistic — elements of certain works by Jorge Guillén, including poems such as 'Niño' or 'Playa (Niños)' of *Cántico* (1928) (Fig. 2.6), the latter illustrated by a child-like sketch of waves and a deified sun in a chapter of *Poesía infantil recitable* dedicated to the sea, the forest, and the mountains. Guillén's poem begins:

> Este sol de la arena
> guía manos de niños:
> las manos que a las conchas
> salven de los peligros.
> Conchas bajo la arena
> tienden hacia los niños:
> niños que ya hacia el sol...[90]

> [This sun of sand | guides children's hands: | hands that save | seashells from danger. | Shells under the sand | reach towards children: | children towards the sun...]

The scene of the beach is, in the parenthetical 'niño' of the title, equated with the being of the child. The sun radiates life into the moving legs, hands, and fingers below, collecting round shells that echo the sun above. Yet this state of childhood

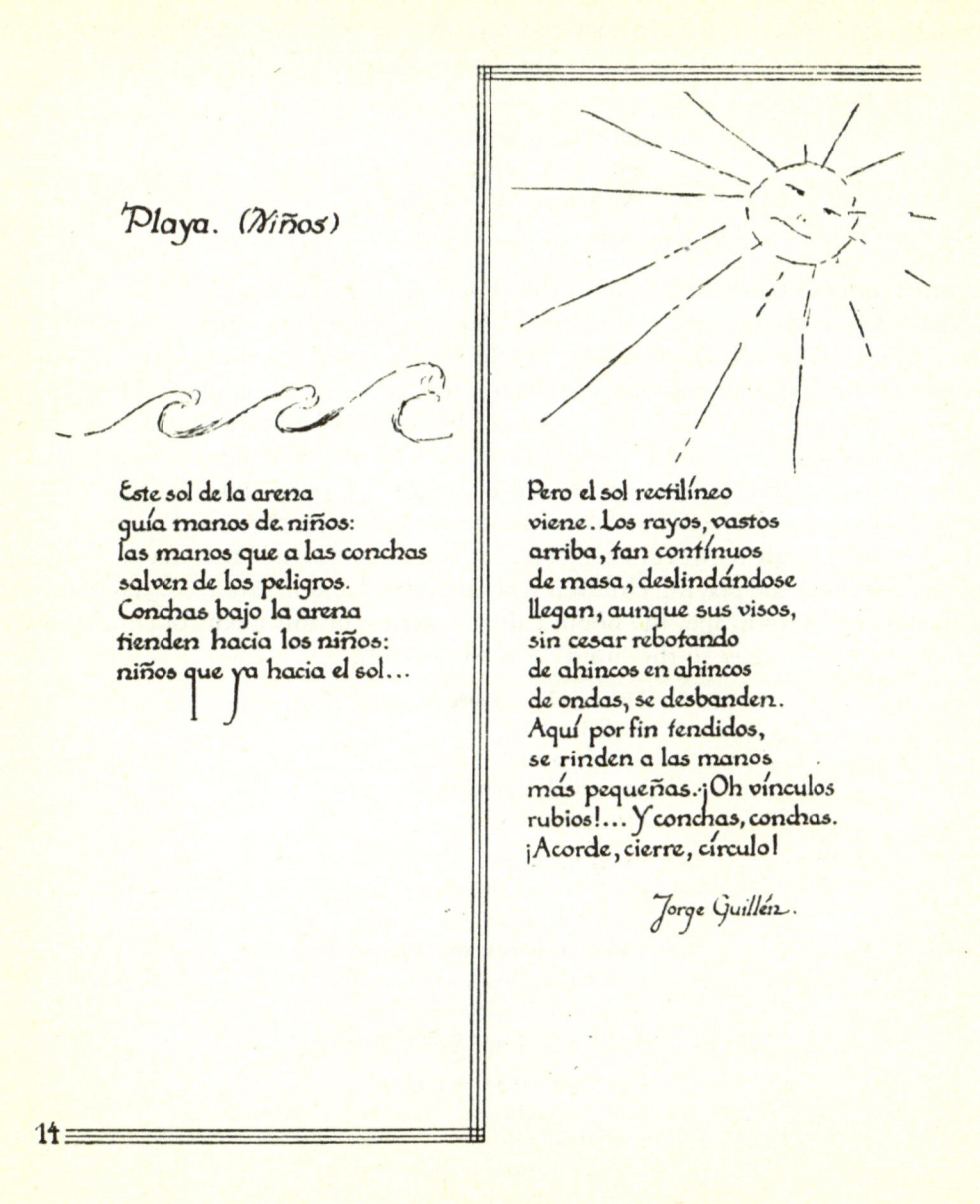

Playa. (Niños)

Este sol de la arena
guía manos de niños:
las manos que a las conchas
salven de los peligros.
Conchas bajo la arena
tienden hacia los niños:
niños que ya hacia el sol...

Pero el sol rectilíneo
viene. Los rayos, vastos
arriba, tan contínuos
de masa, deslindándose
llegan, aunque sus visos,
sin cesar rebotando
de ahincos en ahincos
de ondas, se desbanden.
Aquí por fin tendidos,
se rinden a las manos
más pequeñas. ¡Oh vínculos
rubios!... Y conchas, conchas.
¡Acorde, cierre, círculo!

Jorge Guillén.

FIG. 2.6. Jorge Guillén's 'Playa (Niños)' illustrated for children.
Source: *Poesía infantil recitable*, ed. by José Luís Sánchez Trincado and
Rafael Olivares Figueroa (Madrid: Aguilar, [1934]), p. 14.

is not without terror. The child saves a shell from 'danger', while the sun is a menacing presence: it is 'rectilíneo', its rays are 'vastos', 'continuos', and beat down 'sin cesar'. Yet together, its waves are the same 'cántico' of praise that binds the *oeuvre* in its totality:

> ¡Oh vínculos
> rubios!...Y conchas, conchas.
> ¡Acorde, cierre, círculo![91]

[Oh blond | bonds! And shells, shells. | Accord, enclose, circle!]

From Tagore to Guillén, images of the child's vital presence within enduring land-scapes crossed disciplinary and temporal bounds. Alongside artistic representations such as Sorolla's paintings of children at the sea, running, splashing, diving, 'On the Seashore' recalls poetic responses to the liminal quality of the adult-child boundary. The epigraph to this book, a fragment of Josefina de la Torre's poem 'Mediodía' [Midday], depicts in simple, evocative verse a scene of children playing at the edge of the sea. Her seaside scene, unlike Tagore's moons and suns that smile or speak, shuns metaphor and animism to show children, rather, as they are seen by the watching adult or world itself. Here it is not the sea nor the waves which are personified, but the playing children who are reified and naturalized. In contrast to Tagore's living landscape, the poem paints a picture of this nexus of child and sea, a distilled *mise en scène* in the mind's eye. She writes:

> Llueve el sol sobre la arena
> mojada,
> y en la orilla,
> hay muchas piedrecitas menudas
> brillantes.
>
> En el horizonte,
> corta el mar una cinta de roca
> jugosa de agua.
> Pasan las barcas que vienen de pesca
> y, al pasar, dejan
> un brillo de plata nervioso
> de los peces que traen en el fondo.
>
> Hay muchas velas blancas,
> junto al cielo
> más allá.
> Donde miran los ojos
> y en las olas pequeñas
> que van a la playa
> unos niños, desnudos,
> jugando
> con la espuma blanca.
> La isla junto al mar
> descalza.[92]

[The sun rains down upon the wet | sand, | and on the shore | are many small, glimmering | pebbles. | On the horizon, | a ribbon of rock spurting water | cuts the sea. | The boats come in from fishing | and, as they pass, leave | a glint of nervous silver | from the fish they carry behind them. | Many white sails | merge with the sky | beyond. | Where the eyes gaze | and in the small waves | that lap the beach | a few children, naked, | playing | in the white froth. | Barefoot | island by the sea.]

Short sentences, with significance and grammar displaced from line to line, set up a scene that appears to have been composed of notes. A first-hand visual perspective moves from near to far. The poet shifts in scale from vast to minute, from sun to pebble, horizon to rock, boat to child. Static form and physical, bodily movement come together, bringing vibrancy to stillness. Within this seascape, the children become a visual and thematic focus. From an indistinct group on the shore, each child remains separate, whole, divided by the waves and water and froth. Barefoot, vertical, cutting the horizon as surely as the rock behind, each of them becomes an island, whole, naturalized, integrated into its landscape. These imaginaries had resonance, emerging again and again in works that celebrated a form of purity and primacy of engagement: light, air, breath, sun, and salt.[93] With Camprubí describing translation itself as a 'purifying', distilling process, such echoes and reflections spoke to an essential childhood beyond borders of time and space.

Through a studied enthusiasm for works such as Tagore's *La luna nueva*, inter-pretations of the child-poetry-nexus continued through a generation of teachers and intellectuals. Its terms undoubtedly shaped, for instance, the depiction of childhood put forward by young writer Arturo Serrano Plaja.[94] Twenty-three years old in 1932 and a founder of the avant-garde journal *Revista Nueva*, Serrano's writings suggest this close relationship between the Spanish avant-garde and the poetic muse of childhood. Alongside writings in *El Sol,* in which he published an article on the spiritual links he saw between Tagore and Jiménez, Serrano was a prolific contributor to numerous avant-garde journals, working with figures including Alberti, Guillén, Maruja Mallo (1902–95), and María Zambrano (1904–91). Serrano depicted an intellectual affinity between Tagore's India and his own Spain — two dry, southern peninsulas, steeped in mysticism and folklore — that paralleled the lyrical affinity he saw uniting Tagore and the Juan Ramón Jiménez of *Platero y yo*. From the moon over Moguer to the eastern landscapes of India, Serrano waxed lyrically, the child rode the donkey Platero through infinite space, illuminated by the light of Tagore's crescent moon. In a cosmic transition from east to west, Serrano imagined a brief moment in time and a point in space where these two trajectories might touch, a 'púnto-tránsito' within the act of literary translation.[95] Visible in this convergence was not simply the meaning conveyed across language, but also 'intellectual proximity': an assimilation of one voice into another. Serrano was chiefly interested in what this spiritual, poetic intersection meant on the level of understanding the world of the child. In Tagore's children, he observed an overarching 'anhelo, un ansia de infinito' [yearning, an anxiety for the infinite]:

> Mirad, mirad este niño: contempladle bien: absorto en su infantil navegación, abismado también en su silencio [...]. ¿No es, acaso, este niño toda

una raza? ¿No late en sus venas todo el misterio del nirvana hindú, estoicamente brahmánico?

Esa es su vida y esa es su fuerza: una quietud absorta en lo indecible.[96]

[Observe this child; contemplate him well: absorbed in his infantile navigation, plunged into his own silence [...]. Is not the child, perhaps, a race of his own? Do not the great mysteries of Hindu nirvana, stoic Brahmanism, beat in his veins?

That is his life and this is its force: a quietude immersed in the unsayable.]

A sense of common wonder and contemplation, Serrano argued, was common to all children, whether in India or Spain. Children constituted an exceptional, borderless 'race' of their own, with their own behaviour, culture, and form of being, in a world beyond language.

What Serrano found in the imagined child echoed the sense of cosmic possibility inherent in his larger depiction of modern literature. In 1931, he published a series of verses melding childhood imagery and avant-garde prose which began to illuminate cultural imaginaries of this children's realm. Entitled '¿Por dónde se escapa el Sudeste? (poema de niños y poesía)' [Whence escapes the Southeast? (poem of children and poetry)] in the Murcian avant-garde journal *Sudeste*, in this piece Serrano began to make the case for a post-geographical, universal or cosmic, formulation of childhood, between authors and spaces, within the vastness of the imagination. The 'southeast' of the imagination thus became unanchored from the compass. It was with this piece that he began to synthesize the lyricism of Jiménez's *Platero y yo* with contemporary, vanguard referents.[97] Through Serrano's quasi-surrealist lens, childhood is pre-verbal and unspoken, beyond the adult confines of speech and reason. He poses that silent, unspoken 'anhelo' as an essential condition of childhood:

Lo inabsoluto, lo que nadie puede alcanzar, lo que es nada, estremeciendo la sonrisa incólume de un cielo enjaulado en meridianos: desmodelando las antiguas picardías ingenuas de un campo sin flores — ¡ y Sol de vacaciones! ¡ Ah! —

★ ★ ★

Exactamente inmaculados, el Norte, el Sur, el Este y el Oeste. ¿Por qué parte del mundo — del mapa-mundo — andará el sudeste? ¿En cual de los dos redondeles llorará su incógnita desgracia? ¡Si siquiera hubiese un cartel que asaltase nuestra vista con un: Polo Sudeste!

★ ★ ★

Mas sin embargo su piadosa luz impúber debe alumbrar un buen polo: sin Frío [sic] ni calor que absorber — desintegrándolos — el Norte y el Sur.

★ ★ ★

Pero ¿por qué su obstinación inexpugnable en ocultarse? ¿Cuáles sus profundos motivos para no aparecer? Ni tú ni yo — ni este, ni ese, ni aquel — habríamos de decir nada, y entonces ¿a qué esforzarse en desaparecer embarcado en el silencio *sud* de su misterio? Pero no, no quiere — no permite — que se sepa; nadie lo sabe. Ni Búfalo Bill, ni nunca persona alguna llegó hasta allí. Tan solo Tomás Mix consiguió aproximarse llegando hasta el Oeste.

★ ★ ★

Lo que es casi seguro, es que Caperucita Roja y el Gato Félix, han hecho su aparición mundial en aquel crítico punto. De allí que los ríos no tienen afluentes ni las montañas cordilleras; de allí que las estrellas son estrellas y las flores y no angiospermas o gimnospermas; que el Sol lo es sin necesidad de convertirse a un mismo tiempo, en el centro de nuestro sistema planetario. De allí, que sin saber por qué no existen la geografía ni la gramática.[98]

— — —

[The inabsolute, the unreachable, that which is nothing, shudders the unscathed smile of a sky encaged in meridians: demolishing the old crafty naivety of a flowerless field — and, oh Sun of vacations! Ah!

★ ★ ★

Precise and immaculate, the North, the South, the East, and the West. But from what part of the world — that *mappa mundi* — comes the Southeast? In which of the two hemispheres cries its disguised disgrace? If only there were a sign to point the way: the Southeast Pole! Its virtuous, prepubescent light must illuminate a good pole nonetheless: one with neither cold nor heat to absorb — and disintegrate — the North and the South.

★ ★ ★

Whence its inexpugnable, stubborn hiddenness? What are its deep motives for not appearing? Neither you nor I — nor he nor him or them — would say a word. So why insist on disappearing *south* into the silence of its own mystery? No, it does not want — nor permit — us, nor anybody, to know anything more. No one, not even Buffalo Bill, has visited. Only Tom Mix managed to get close, out West.

★ ★ ★

What is almost certain is that Little Red Riding Hood and Felix the Cat made their global debut at this critical junction. There, where the rivers have no tributaries nor the mountains foothills; where the stars are stars, where flowers are not angiosperms nor gymnosperms but simply flowers; where the Sun is the Sun, without also needing to be the centre of our solar system. There, where geography and grammar are unheard of.]

Drawing on fairy tales and cartoons, cinema and Westerns, from Little Red Riding Hood to Felix the Cat, Buffalo Bill to the cowboy film star Tom Mix, Serrano situates the reader in an infantile world beyond orientation and rationality. From north to south, east to west, one searches for a fantastical 'southeast' which is nowhere to be found. That place which nobody can reach is the child's world of fantasy and image. This was a vaulted appeal to the imagination, beyond the banal enclosures of a world bound by meridians and Latinate rationality. The heroes of this world, like Caperucita Roja or Gato Félix, come from a world where rivers need not flow from a source; flowers need not be categorized scientifically, nor must the sun stand statically at the centre of the planetary universe. The journal, *Sudeste*, and this imagined region becomes in Serrano's telling synonymous with the world of childhood. Such descriptions echoed through avant-garde poetry inspired by or read in the shadow of Tagorean images of childhood. These built on fantastical views of the imaginative, non-translatable world of the child, but also sought a distilled, quiet view of its essential state.

Tagore's works, in Camprubí's translations, encapsulated a sense of wonder which has been argued to have influenced the consolidation of an avant-garde aesthetic. Jordi Mas López has suggested as much for a leading circle of Catalan writers and artists, noting the marked influence of Tagore on poets and artists such as Joan Salvat-Papasseit (1894–1924), Joaquín Torres Garcia, and Rafael Barradas. The world of childhood was seen by these artists as a 'reserve of spiritual purity' on which they drew and took inspiration, including through various concrete involvements with schools and a longstanding interest in children's drawings (Chapter 5).[99] In his poem 'El record d'una "fuga" de Bach" (1919), Salvat-Papasseit upheld childhood in terms as mystical as those imagined by Tagore, a world glimpsed only in prophetic visions and the child's own imagination. In a personification that brings to mind Tagore's 'speaking moon', the sea and sky, sun, moon, and stars of countless rhymes and poems because living characters whether in the mind or in literary, theatrical, and artistic form. Salvat-Papasseit writes:

> He vist més: — Que l'infant de bolquers
> esguardava rient una estrella
> Però cap llibre no parla del somrís de l'infant
>
> I heus aquí que vaig dir-los   una cosa vulgar :
>
> — L'estel hexagonal de colors en el Circ enclou totes les síntesis del món.[100]
>
> [I've seen more: — The child in nappies | looked up laughing at a star |But no book speaks of the smile of the child | And here's what I told them something common: | — The hexagonal, coloured star of the Circus includes all the syntheses in the world.]

Salvat-Papasseit portrayed the child as standing beyond reason, at the centre of its own world. Smiling, the child held a star, a radiating hexagon of light. That world itself constituted a cosmic synthesis, an amalgam of the world's colours, shapes, and forms. As with Tagore's and Serrano's cosmic invocation, no aspect of this image, its 'Circus' of colour and energy and movement, could be encapsulated by books, expertise, or rationality: 'no ho sabria comprendre' [he couldn't comprehend it], Salvat-Papasseit writes of an 'antiquarian' observer of this world. The creative energy embedded in this brief verse recalls Serrano's claim that neither science nor geography could locate the elusive 'southeast' of childhood imagination, while integrating childhood into a wider synthesis of art, literature, and culture.

Equally, the notion of childhood synthesis before and through language returns one to Conde's notion that the 'continent' of poetry could not be taught rationally but must rather be approached by intuition and sensation.[101] Drawing from a fount of rich images and the child-world put forward by Tagore, via Camprubí and Jiménez, and the successive incorporation into literature of imaginaries of the child's world, the operative word in Salvat-Papasseit's poem is 'synthesis'. It was this total view, the child's global grasp of the world even before language, that formed the imaginative — and poetic — world of the child. What role did the child play across each of these poems, studies, and renderings? How did the figure of the child both represent the aesthetic goals of early twentieth-century avant-gardes while engaging teachers, poets, and paidologists in a shared lyrical and social project?

When Conde wrote of poetry's crucial role in the classroom, she argued that art itself was returning to its dawn, to the childhood core whence it sprang. Whether in poems for and about children, or in the plays and verses of canonical figures such as Lorca, Alberti, or Guillén, intellectuals did not stop at the creation of literature of and for the child. Like teacher and paidologist Olivares Figueroa in his celebration of Alicita Venturino, they engaged with and were concretely inspired by real children. They sought to promote and nurture what they saw as the essential, inherent quality of childhood: direct access to the heart of things, a sensorial and emotional access to the world. Even as the realities of words and rationality began to impose themselves upon the developing mind, children were celebrated by poets and artists alike for the freshness of their prose, the radiant colour of their imaginings and their all-embracing perspective on the world. For an avant-garde seeking cultural renovation, children's development of language altered and re-created anew the very shapes and forms of the imagination.

Notes to Chapter 2

1. Carmen Conde, *Por la escuela renovada* (Valencia: Cuadernos de Cultura, 1931), p. 48. Conde would next return to these themes in the hands-on, instructional work *La composición literaria infantil (Escuela primaria)* (Barcelona: Publicaciones Mujeres Libres, 1937).
2. Conde, *Por la escuela renovada*, p. 48.
3. Ibid.
4. On Benavente's efforts and his production of works by Ramón del Valle-Inclán and others, see Juan Cervera, *Historia crítica del teatro infantil español* (Madrid: Editora Nacional, 1982), in the *Biblioteca Virtual Miguel de Cervantes*, <http://www.cervantesvirtual.com/obra-visor/historia-critica-del-teatro-infantil-espanol--0/html> [accessed 10 January 2019].
5. Antonio G. de Linares, 'Del cuento al teatro, pasando por el guiñol', *La Esfera*, 8.379 (1921), 18.
6. Ibid. The 'lecciones de cosas' was a popular genre of schoolbook from the late nineteenth century. Building on Pestalozzi's work, the model helped children learn by discussion of images and texts around specific themes, from railways to the seasons. The lessons involved a variety of skills: reading, drawing, examining images, and answering questions. Pedro de Alcántara García, *Educación intuitiva y lecciones de cosas* (Madrid: Gras y Compañía, 1881) and Ángel Llorca, *Más lecciones de cosas* (Girona: Dalmau Carles & Compañía, 1912) are examples of this evolving genre.
7. Ibid. This remains the central problem of children's literature. As a contemporary critic put the problem of childhood aesthetics, children's literature must transcend thematic concerns: 'ser puro y primario, sin ser pueril; [exigir] una desnudez poética' [to be pure and primary, without being puerile, [to demand] poetic nakedness]. See María Jesús Ruiz, 'Vieja tradición oral y nueva pedagogía: el teatro infantil de Alejandro Casona', in *La palabra y la memoria*, ed. by Pedro Cerrillo (Cuenca: Universidad de Castilla-La Mancha, 2008), p. 124.
8. Juan Ramón Jiménez, *Platero y yo: elegía andaluza* (Madrid: La Lectura, 1914). Despite his intended adult audience, he agreed: 'Este breve libro [...] estaba escrito para... ¡qué se yo para quién!... para quien escribimos los poetas líricos... Ahora que va a los niños, no le quito ni le pongo una coma. ¡Qué bien!' [This little book [...] was written for... who knows for whom! For whomever lyric poets write. Now that it is going to children, I won't add or remove a comma. All the better!] (p. 4).

9. Benjamín Palencia, *Niños* (Madrid: Índice, 1923). Gómez de la Serna's children's stories, namely the books *El bazar más suntuoso del mundo, El marquesito en el circo* and *Por los tejados*, along with his 1909 *Cuento de Calleja: drama para los niños*, are collected in his *Cuentos para niños* (Madrid: Clan, 2004).

10. Pablo de Andrés Cobós, 'Bibliotecas Infantiles: *En el Bazar más suntuoso del mundo* [por] Ramón Gómez de la Serna', *Escuelas de España*, 1.1 (1929), 126.

11. Llorca, *El primer año de lenguaje*.

12. *Poesía infantil recitable*, ed. by José Luis Sánchez Trincado and Rafael Olivares Figueroa (Madrid: M. Aguilar, [1934]), p. 23. The editors exchanged numerous letters with the senior Guillén, updating him on the publication of their anthology and corresponding after their respective exiles and departures from Spain after 1936. See Madrid, Biblioteca Nacional, Arch.JG, boxes 88/34, 150/33, 71/37. Guillén's replies seem to have been sporadic at best.

13. Juan Ramón Jiménez, *Poesía en prosa y verso (1902–1932), escogida para los niños* [1932], ed. by Zenobia Camprubí (Madrid: Alianza, 1984), p. 53 and n.p. ('Prologuillo al niño y al hombre').

14. Federico García Lorca, 'El lagarto está llorando', in *Obras completas* (Madrid: Aguilar, 1969), p. 373.

15. Rafael Alberti, *Marinero en tierra* (Buenos Aires: Editorial Losada, 1998); Carmen Conde, 'Oda al gato Félix', *La Gaceta Literaria*, 3.56 (1929), 2. Soledad (Solita) Salinas de Marichal later became a literary scholar in her own right; see among other works her *El mundo poético de Rafael Alberti* (Madrid: Publicaciones de la Residencia de Estudiantes, 2004).

16. For a succinct overview of the field, see Marisa Fernández López, 'Children's Literature Research in Spain', *Children's Literature Association Quarterly*, 27.4 (2002), 221–25. For an excellent catalogue of works that followed, see Ana Pelegrín, María Victoria Sotomayor, and Alberto Urdiales, *Pequeña memoria recobrada: libros infantiles del exilio del 39* (Madrid: Ministerio de Educación, Cultura y Deporte, 2008), pp. 187–288. The pioneer in documenting Spanish children's literature was the academic, author, and folklorist Carmen Bravo-Villasante, whose *Historia de la literatura infantil española* (Madrid: Doncel, 1972) led the field; her work is carried on today by CEPLI, the Centro de Estudios de Promoción de la Lectura y Literatura Infantil at the Universidad de Castilla-La Mancha. On Bartolozzi's energetic illustrations and production see Raquel Pelta, 'Salvador Bartolozzi: un ilustrador para una infancia moderna', *Boletín de la Institución Libre de Enseñanza*, 42–43 (2001), 189–97. On Antoniorrobles as the epitome of 'new art', see Rodríguez de Cortázar, 'Escaparate de libros', p. 15, and Herminio Almendros, 'Libros: Antoniorrobles: Veintiséis cuentos en orden alfabético', *Revista de Pedagogía*, 9.101 (1930), 236–37.

17. See Anastasio Martínez Navarro and others, *La Editorial Calleja: un agente de modernización educativa en la Restauración* (Madrid: UNED, 2002).

18. On the aesthetics of production for children see *Century of the Child: Growing by Design, 1900–2000*, ed. by Juliet Kinchin and Aidan O'Connor (New York: Museum of Modern Art, 2012).

19. María Teresa León, *Rosa-Fría, patinadora de la luna* (Madrid: Ediciones de la Torre, 1990).

20. Pilar Nieva-de la Paz, 'Concha Méndez y Manuel Altolaguirre: la memoria de una vocación teatral', *Anales de la Literatura Española Contemporánea*, 38.3 (2013), 257–83 (p. 272).

21. Rodríguez de Cortázar, 'Escaparate de libros', p. 15.

22. Ibid.

23. Ibid.

24. José Bergamín Gutiérrez, 'La decadencia del analfabetismo', *Cruz y Raya*, 1 (1933), 61–94 (p. 63).

25. Ibid., p. 64. Bergamín's *La decadencia del analfabetismo* would return to currency in published form in 1961, published in the revamped *Renuevos de Cruz y Raya*, taking up where the progressive Catholic journal *Cruz y Raya* had left off before the Civil War.

26. Sandy Holguín, *Creating Spaniards: Culture and National Identity in Republican Spain* (Madison: University of Wisconsin Press, 2002), pp. 157–58, 146.

27. Bergamín Gutiérrez, 'La decadencia del analfabetismo', p. 64.

28. Mira y López, *Psicología evolutiva del niño*, p. 66. This notion is akin to the phenomenological concept of a pre-reflexive consciousness, developed from Sartre to Husserl to Merleau-Ponty,

in which awareness develops before one's apprehension of it. See Shaun Gallagher and Dan Zahavi, 'Phenomenological Approaches to Self-consciousness', in *The Stanford Encyclopedia of Philosophy*, ed. by Edward N. Zalta (2016), <http://plato.stanford.edu/archives/win2010/entries/self-consciousness-phenomenological/> [accessed 1 May 2018].

29. Verdier, *De Uexküll a Decroly*, p. 48.

30. *Poesía infantil recitable*, ed. by Sánchez Trincado and Olivares Figueroa, p. 102.

31. Jorge Guillén, 'Cinco florinatas', *España*, 9.354 (1923), 8–9 (p. 8).

32. Federico García Lorca, 'Las nanas infantiles', in *Obras completas*, pp. 91–108 (p. 93).

33. Ibid., p. 108.

34. Ibid., p. 93.

35. Ibid., p. 101.

36. Ibid.

37. Christopher Maurer, 'Prologue', in *Collected Poems* (New York: Farrar, Straus & Giroux, 2002), pp. xi–lxiv (p. l); Lorca, 'Las nanas infantiles', p. 100.

38. Lorca, 'Las nanas infantiles', p. 100.

39. Rafael Alberti, *Lope de Vega y la poesía contemporánea seguido de* La pájara pinta, ed. by Robert Marrast (Paris: Centre de Recherches de l'Institut d'Études Hispaniques, 1964), p. 3.

40. Ibid., pp. 4 and 14.

41. Ibid., pp. 15–16.

42. Ibid., p. 18.

43. Ana Gómez Torres, 'La carnavalización del teatro: los títeres y la ruptura del canon dramático', in *Analecta malacitana: Revista de la Sección de Filología de la Facultad de Filosofía y Letras*, 17.2 (1994), 313–22.

44. Nelson R. Orringer, *Lorca in Tune with Falla: Literary and Musical Interludes* (Toronto: University of Toronto Press, 2014), pp. 7–8; Javier Huerta Calvo, 'Cervantes y Lorca: La Barraca', *Don Galán: Revista de Investigación Teatral*, 5 (2014), 1–20 (p. 11).

45. The Republic's *misiones pedagógicas* all had a *teatro guiñol*, a popular show of puppetry that reached audiences of adults and children daily across Spain; see Luis Sáenz de la Calzada, *'La Barraca', teatro universitario* (Madrid: Revista de Occidente, 1976), p. 151; Federico García Lorca, *Canciones, 1921–1924*, ed. by Mario Hernández (Madrid: Alianza, 1982), p. 165.

46. For a full account of Alberti's development of the *Pájara*, its importance as a frustrated project for him during the 1920s, and its recuperation within musicology, see Eladio Mateos and Ismael Ramos, 'Alberti en el teatro de las vanguardias: vida y fortuna de La pájara pinta', *Papeles del Festival de Música Española de Cádiz*, 1 (2005), 61–81.

47. Robert Marrast, 'Prólogo', in Alberti, *Lope de Vega*, pp. 11, 15.

48. Anon., 'El nuevo edificio del Instituto-Escuela, destinado a centralizar todas las secciones del Preparatorio, que suman más de un millar de alumnos', *Crónica*, 10 July 1932, p. 9.

49. Alberti, *Lope de Vega*, pp. 41–43.

50. Hugo Ball, 'Karawane', Academy of American Poets, <https://www.poets.org/poetsorg/poem/karawane> [accessed 1 December 2018]; and James Joyce, *A Portrait of the Artist as a Young Man* (New York: B. W. Huebsch, 1922), p. 1.

51. Alberti, *Lope de Vega*, p. 19.

52. Luis Cernuda, 'Unas palabras sobre la poesía actual española', *Escuelas de España*, 3.29 (1936), 221–24 (p. 221).

53. See, in the following, Rafael Olivares Figueroa's 1933 claim for the child as 'fluid conductor' of poetry par excellence. Both pedagogue and poet seem to be making reference to an image of poetic reception used by Henri Brémond in a 1925 address: 'Nous nous offrons à ces vibrations fugitives, si exquises d'ailleurs que soient leurs caresses, non pour goûter le plaisir qu'elles donnent, mais pour recevoir le fluide mystérieux qu'elles transmettent: simples conducteurs [...] qui doivent leur sonorité même et leur splendeur éphémère au courant qui les traverse' [We offer ourselves up to these fugitive vibrations, their exquisite caresses, not to taste the pleasure they offer but to receive the mysterious fluid they transmit: simple conductors [...] who owe their sonority and ephemeral splendor to the current that courses through them]; 'La poésie pure', Académie Française (1925), <http://www.academie-francaise.fr/la-poesie-pure> [accessed 19 June 2018].

54. Cernuda, 'Unas palabras sobre la poesía actual española', p. 223.

55. Anon., '*Poesía infantil recitable.* — José Luis Sánchez Trincado y R. Olivares Figueroa. — Aguilar. — Madrid', *Escuelas de España*, 2.13 (1935), 42–43.

56. *Poesía infantil recitable*, ed. by Sánchez Trincado and Olivares Figueroa, p. ix.

57. Rafael Olivares Figueroa, 'La invención poética en el niño', *Boletín de la Academia de Ciencias, Bellas Letras y Nobles Artes de Córdoba*, 14.45 (1935), 149–69. On the Venturinos' Spanish visit, see Anon., 'Visita de dos ilustres personalidades americanas', *ABC*, 27 March 1935, p. 27, and Anon., 'Vida docente: Visita de dos intelectuales chilenos', *La Vanguardia*, 18 April 1936, p. 9.

58. Olivares himself had a larger interest in paidology; in a brief 1933 book he had set out to understand every aspect of child development: physical, mental, physiological, sexual, and otherwise. A pedagogue by training and a poet and journalist in practice, Olivares surveyed the educational and psychiatric fields as they intersected in the child, citing scholars from Koffka to Melanie Klein, Marañón to 'Haveloc Hellis' [*sic*]; see *El estudio del niño y sus aplicaciones* (Madrid: Cuadernos de Cultura, 1933), p. 19. After the outbreak of the Spanish Civil War, Olivares returned to Venezuela, where he continued to publish diverse poetry anthologies for children and maintained a sporadic correspondence with, among others, Jorge Guillén.

59. Olivares, 'La invención poética en el niño', p. 155.

60. Ibid., pp. 153, 151.

61. Ibid., p. 162.

62. Ibid., pp. 155–56.

63. Antonio Machado, 'XLIV' [El casco roído y verdoso], in *Soledades. Galerías. Otros poemas*, ed. by Geoffrey Ribbans (Madrid: Cátedra, 1983), pp. 149–50. Much of Machado's early poetry, including poems such as 'Sueño infantil' and 'Renacimiento', foreground the luminous, clear light of childhood read through Guillén in Chapter 6, a remembered light which projects, dreamlike and nostalgic, towards the present. On reading Machado's verse through the lens of land and place see Xon de Ros, *The Poetry of Antonio Machado: Changing the Landscape* (Oxford: Oxford University Press, 2015).

64. Lorca, *Obras completas*, p. 372.

65. Olivares Figueroa, 'La invención poética en el niño', p. 166.

66. Penelope Murray, *Genius: The History of an Idea* (Oxford: Blackwell, 1989), p. 1.

67. See his definitions of these categories in Olivares Figueroa, *El estudio del niño*, pp. 35–37.

68. Rafael Olivares Figueroa, 'Unos cuantos niños precoces madrileños', *El Heraldo de Madrid*, 18 April 1931, p. 14.

69. Olivares Figueroa, *El estudio del niño*, p. 36. He cited the young Spanish pianist Pepito Arriola (1895–1954), a child whose prodigy had allegedly burned out by adolescence. Other 'precoces' might be prone to criminality, and each constituted 'un enfermo, cuya maravillosa aptitud le suele ser fatal' [an ill person, whose marvellous aptitude is usually fatal]: ibid., p. 36. The case of Arriola's prodigious talent was studied in Charles Richet, 'Des limites de l'incrédulité', *Annales des Sciences Psychiques*, 18.7–8 (1908), 97–101.

70. Lewis M. Terman, *Genetic Studies of Genius: Mental and Physical Traits of a Thousand Gifted Children*, 4 vols (Stanford: Stanford University Press, 1925–47), I.

71. On the debate around giftedness and cultivation across classes, see, for example, César Madariaga, 'La selección corporativa de los "superdotados"', *El Imparcial*, 22 February 1928, p. 1, and Antonio Linares Maza, 'Diagnóstico de niños anormales y superdotados', *Revista de Pedagogía*, 10.117–18 (1931), 412–17, 56–64.

72. José Luis Sánchez Trincado, 'Juan Ramón Jiménez y los niños' in *Pasión del arte nuevo* (Caracas: Grupo "Viernes", 1940), pp. 29–32.

73. Gayle Rogers, 'Translation', in *A New Vocabulary for Global Modernism*, ed. by Eric Hayot and Rebecca Walkowitz (New York: Columbia University Press, 2016), pp. 248–62 (p. 254).

74. Most accounts follow the rapt attention detailed in Antonio Benaiges y Nogués, 'Los niños ante *Platero y yo*', *Escuelas de España*, 3.29 (1936), 315–16, but for a more critical view in a leading Catholic journal, see teacher Alf Iniesta's argument, supported by quotations from Tagore and from aforementioned Catholic literary scholar Henri Brémond, that an appreciation of beauty and lyricism only came with maturity. His students allegedly clamoured for *Peter Pan* over

Platero y yo: children's psyches first found them seeking 'palpitating', 'living', 'complex' myths and stories. See Alf Iniesta, 'La lírica y los niños', *Atenas*, 4.28 (1933), 226–27.

75. In addition to significant time spent in the United States, the young Zenobia contributed various stories to American magazines, from the children's publication *St. Nicholas* in 1902 to a piece on Joaquín Sorolla's studio in *The Craftsman* in 1910; see Antonio Campoamor González, *Juan Ramón Jiménez y Zenobia Camprubí: años españoles (1881–1936)* (Seville: Universidad Internacional de Andalucía, 2014), pp. 435–36.

76. Howard Young, 'The Invention of an Andalusian Tagore', *Comparative Literature*, 47.1 (1995), 42–52 (p. 44). The Tagore translations may be a rare instance in which the male partner played a larger role than is recognized by the official authorship. The contributions of Jiménez were, however, already assumed by critics. Readings of *La luna nueva*, despite Camprubí's sole authorship, take his presence as a given: 'el hálito de Juan Ramón aporta nuevos quilates al valor total de traducción' [the breath of Juan Ramón adds new sheen to the total value of the translation]: Arturo Serrano Plaja, 'Juan Ramon Tagore', *El Sol*, 21 February 1932, 2. The title of this piece ('Juan Ramon-Tagore') isolates the two authors of interest.

77. R. Neill Johnson, 'Juan Ramón Jiménez, Rabindranath Tagore, and "La Poesía Desnuda"', *Modern Language Review*, 60.4 (1965), 534–46, and Young, 'The Invention of an Andalusian Tagore', p. 45. Jiménez rejected intimations that his verse was derivative of Tagore. To the contrary, he insisted that he himself had given Tagore's work the rhythms, structures, and accents that made it beloved in Spanish. He had created an 'Andalusian Tagore', not the other way around: Francisco Garfías, 'Rabindranath Tagore en español', in Rabindranath Tagore, *Recuerdos* (1983), pp. 9–17 (p. 11).

78. Rabindranath Tagore and W. W. Pearson, *Morada de paz (Shantiniketan)*, trans. by Zenobia Camprubí de Jiménez (Madrid: Fortanet, 1919), n.p.

79. Young, 'The Invention of an Andalusian Tagore', p. 43; Garfías, 'Rabindranath Tagore en español', p. 15.

80. Young, 'The Invention of an Andalusian Tagore', pp. 50–51; García Morente, 'El mundo del niño'.

81. See drafts of Camprubí and Jiménez's translations reproduced in Young, 'The Invention of an Andalusian Tagore', p. 51.

82. Pérez de Ayala seems to have been the first Spanish writer to translate fragments of Tagore, from *Gitanjali*, published in 1913 in *La Tribuna* and surely known to Camprubí during her reading of the work that year; see Pérez de Ayala's translation of Canto 60, 'On the Seashore of Endless Worlds Children Meet', in Agustín Coletes Blanco, 'Un apunte sobre la fortuna de Tagore en España', *Archivum*, 48–49 (1998), 171–73.

83. Ramón Pérez de Ayala, *El país del futuro: mis viajes a los Estados Unidos (1913–1914 y 1919–1920)* (Madrid: Biblioteca Nueva, 1959); Coletes Blanco, 'Un apunte sobre la fortuna de Tagore en España', pp. 170, 173.

84. José Ortega y Gasset, 'Un poeta indo (II)', *El Sol*, 3 February 1918, p. 5.

85. Lorenzo Luzuriaga, 'La escuela de Rabindranath Tagore: "Morada de Paz": (Shantiniketan)', *El Sol*, 21 July 1919, p. 12.

86. Rabindranath Tagore, 'Introduction', in Rabindranath Tagore and W. W. Pearson, *Shantiniketan: The Bolpur School of Rabindranath Tagore* (London: Macmillan, 1917), pp. 1–7 (p. 6). For Camprubí's translation see Tagore, 'Prólogo' in Tagore and Pearson, *Morada de paz (Shantiniketan)*, p. 28.

87. Tagore and Pearson, *Shantiniketan: The Bolpur School of Rabindranath Tagore*, pp. 6–7.

88. Johnson, 'Juan Ramón Jiménez, Rabindranath Tagore, and "La Poesía Desnuda"', p. 535.

89. Rabindranath Tagore, *Gitanjali: Facsimile of the Original Manuscript* (Calcutta: Sahitya Samsad, 2011), p. 173.

90. *Poesía infantil recitable*, ed. by Sánchez Trincado and Olivares Figueroa, p. 14.

91. Ibid.

92. Josefina de la Torre, 'Mediodía', in *Poesía infantil recitable*, ed. by Sánchez Trincado and Olivares Figueroa, p. 7.

93. On visual reverberations see Lily Litvak, *A la playa: el mar como el tema de la modernidad en la pintura española de 1870–1936* (Madrid: Fundación Cultural Mapfre Vida, 2001).

94. As a student at the University of Madrid, Serrano founded the short-lived journal *Revista Nueva,* meant to represent the young voice of the avant-garde. Over the next half-decade, he would collaborate in the establishment of several culturally significant journals, including *Hoja Literaria* and *Hora de España* in wartime Valencia. He was tightly integrated both in Spain's literary as well as progressive, left-wing politics, including as a secretary and speaker at the II Congreso Internacional de Escritores para la Defensa de la Cultura in 1937. During the Civil War he co-directed the theatre of the *misiones pedagógicas,* fought and was wounded, and went into exile in 1939; see Francisco Caudet, *Las cenizas del fénix: la cultura española en los años 30* (Madrid: Ediciones de la Torre, 1993), pp. 211–13.

95. Serrano Plaja, 'Juan Ramon-Tagore', p. 2. Serrano gave Juan Ramón credit for this spiritual meeting of minds; the Tagore translations were considered inseparable from the poet's *oeuvre.*

96. Ibid.

97. José Ramón López García, *Vanguardia, revolución y exilio: la poesía de Arturo Serrano Plaja* (Valencia: Pre-Textos, 2008), p. 28.

98. Arturo Serrano Plaja, '¿Por dónde se escapa el Sudeste? (poema de niños y poesía)', *Sudeste,* 4 (1931), 8.

99. Jordi Mas López, *Josep Maria Junoy i Joan Salvat-Papasseit: dues aproximacions a l'haiku* (Barcelona: Publicacions de l'Abadia de Montserrat, 2004), p. 204.

100. Joan Salvat-Papasseit, *Poésies complètes,* ed. by Joaquim Molas, 3rd edn (Barcelona: Editorial Ariel, 1981), p. 20. English translation adapted from Joan Salvat-Papasseit, *Selected Poems,* ed. and trans. by Dominic Keown and Tom Owen (Oxford: The Anglo-Catalan Society, 1982), pp. 24–25.

101. Conde, *Por la escuela renovada,* p. 49.

PART II

Body

CHAPTER 3

Child and World:
Education and the New Biology

El *ahora* del niño es una imposición orgánica, vital; el *devenir* es en el hombre el
imperativo de su misión histórica.

[The child's *now* is an organic, vital imposition; *becoming* is the imperative of
man's historical mission.]

Teodoro Causí, *Bosquejo de una teoría biológica del juego infantil* (1924)

Advocating a new science — and one with vital significance — an intellectual
vanguard of Spanish teachers during the 1920s sought to redefine pedagogy
through attention to the biological bases of education. They celebrated what
was often referred to as the 'new' biology and the 'new' sciences, namely holistic
approaches that countered seemingly cold and overly rationalist, positivist methods
of empirical analysis. In doing so, they read and responded to diverse theories put
forward inside and outside of Spain, from August Pi i Sunyer's functional unity to
José Ortega y Gasset's interest in Gestalt research on the 'intelligence of chimpanzees', to German biologist Jakob von Uexküll's notion of unique perceptual
worlds for every organism. Crossing fields, Ortega's project of a 'ciencia del hombre'
sought to develop an 'anthropology' of modern life, interrogating man's animal
and intellectual selves.[1] In turn, the 'science of the child' — paidology — made a
comparable effort for the youngest members of society. Teachers integrated these
ideas into practice. This chapter opens a view into how educators promoted active
learning upon a theoretical base of the biological nature of childhood. Through
theories taken up by both teachers and intellectuals during the 1920s and early
1930s, an ideal of vitality was harnessed to goals of pedagogical evolution. Here,
two strands of thought converged: a natural-scientific drive to analyse, diagnose,
and strengthen the developing body; and a phenomenological view of mutuality
between child and world within an individual ecosystem of experience.

The body of the child was a crucial aspect of New Education, a balanced third
within an integral trinity of mental and spiritual development. But how should the
child be understood within his or her larger environment? As numerous teachers
argued, children must be conceptualized as living, participating members of a larger
system. Among a mass of notes for a book project, 'La educación vivida' [Lived
Education], pedagogue Ángel Llorca reflected on his time as director of Madrid's

Grupo Escolar Cervantes (1918–26) and the school's subsequent development through 1933. Collected in the school's archives at the Fundación Ángel Llorca in Madrid, Llorca's descriptions of the school's methods, schedules, practices, and philosophy are one among many examples of how theory moved into practice. His notes moved from the larger organism: the rooted, localized school, to the dynamic, evolving individuals which composed it. These were students and teachers, in mutual interaction with each another and with the world around them:

> La escuela es fundamentalmente los niños y el maestro.
> Niños y maestros viven en un determinado lugar.
> Vivir es actuar en relación con la tierra que se pisa y con todos los que con nosotros la pisaran, con el aire que nos envuelve y con todo lo que más allá del aire vemos o que sin verlo nos influencia, y con todas aquellas tierras, personas, y cosas de las cuales nos llegan noticias.
> Ese es el qué.
> El cómo y el cuánto es cosa de los niños y del maestro.[2]

> [The school is fundamentally children and a teacher.
> Children and teachers live in a certain place.
> To live is to act in relation to the earth on which one treads and with all those who tread it with us, with the air that envelops us and with all that we see beyond the air — or that we cannot see, but by which we are influenced; and with all those lands, people and things of whom we hear news.
> This is the 'what'.
> The 'how' and the 'how much' are a matter for the children and the teacher.]

What was at issue in contemporary education, according to Llorca, were not the particular subjects taught nor their methodology, but the experience of learning within a complex and interconnected world. This was the 'cómo' and the 'cuánto' — the enactment of theory with real children, teachers, and classrooms. As reformers such as Llorca made clear, education had tangible roots and branches that intertwined with the world in which one lived.

How did such a holistic, new 'biological' view of the child, encompassing not just physical growth and vitality but also environmental perception and cognition, influence the terms by which educators understood children's development? Did all children begin with the same primary needs, gradually developing a biological *Weltanschauung* based on environment and influence? Or were they endowed with critical, individual properties which could be accessed to determine their personality 'type' and professional orientation? Seeking insight into unquantifiable stages of transformation, pedagogues addressed problems of inheritance versus environment, nature versus nurture.[3] Institutions such as the Centros de Orientación Profesional in Madrid (led by Gonzalo Rodríguez Lafora, 1886–1971) and Barcelona (by Mira y López) aimed for objective knowledge by designing new metrics and interventions. Others sought to use psychometric tests to match children with appropriate careers, seeking 'una profesión a la medida del muchacho' [a profession tailored to the boy], on the assumption that future aptitude could be objectively measured and tailored: 'que en profesión como en ropa, el secreto está en que sea a la medida' [in professions as in clothes, the secret is in the fit].[4] The idea behind this latter, tailored approach was to find the environment which best suited the child's unique structure and tendencies, rather than mould an individual towards a predetermined end. Whether Taylorist, eugenicist, or simply scientific, research on children's natures and tendencies offered codified insights into the mysterious process of development, overlapping with the efforts of reformers and local governments to make concrete interventions in health, hygiene, and social conditions.[5] These concerns transcended political and religious divides, with Michael Richards calling eugenics in Spain a 'highly protean scientific and social category' lacking clear allegiances between liberal and traditionalist Catholic positions. Debates on psychology and psychiatry, and their eugenic consequences, were 'modern, sophisticated and eclectic' in their importation and discussion.[6] Such an intermingling of positions within the realm of scientific thought reinforces the dual and flexible constructions of holism, in the body as in the mind. If the child was a biological whole within a larger society, what were the implications of such a view? To what degree could teaching and learning shape the future course of the child's development? What were its limits?

Rhetorical constructions of the child's biological place in society were longstanding. Building on Herbert Spencer's 1860 notion of the 'society [as] an organism' and incorporating Adolphe Ferrière's biogenetic laws of education, one teacher in 1929 compared the entire institution of the school to an 'embryo', self-regulating and cyclical, dynamic and reproductive in its functions. Just as children were seen to recapitulate the evolution of society as a whole, their development was an organic process that could be analysed with contemporary tools.[7] Amidst these invocations of the importance of 'biogenetic' view of growth, discussions began to explore the role of the external world of circumstance and environment in children's lives, rather than purely biological analyses of the body. They looked to differentiate the child's essential self, its *ser,* from its evolving and current state of being, its *estar.* These were ideas passed down through readings of a series of new scientists in the 1920s. As philosopher Manuel García Morente synthesized current research in his 1928 essay 'El mundo del niño', children were, like all living creatures, bounded and shaped by their environments:

> El animal y su mundo se condicionan mutuamente. El animal se define por su mundo; como a su vez el mundo viene determinado por la estructura del animal que en él vive. Para cada animal hay, pues, un mundo perfectamente adecuado, y ambos, el animal y su mundo, encajan y coinciden como los dos lados de una misma cosa.[8]

> [The animal and its world are mutually conditioned. The animal defines itself through its world, as in turn the world is determined by the structure of the animals living in it. For every animal there is a perfectly suited world, and both, the animal and its world, enclose and coincide with one another like two faces of the same object.]

In García Morente's telling, the child's world was a perfect fit of organism and ecology. Whether grown or small, humans were neither omnipotent rulers of the environment nor existentially threatened by it. All were participating members of a relational, dynamic system. External and internal realities were intimately bound in a holistic totality. It was upon this basis that educators under the sway of philosophers and cultural influencers such as Ortega and García Morente looked towards theory that was both embracing of change but ultimately aware of the limits of science in understanding the human condition.

A holistic perspective on education came to stand for a variety of arguments that countered purely analytical views of body or mind. In the realm of biology, reformers sought to depict the body as a functional system within a larger whole. They did so upon a base of Spanish precedents. Leading work was early laid out by Catalan physiologist August Pi i Sunyer, whose writings on 'functional unity' from 1917 built towards more explicit, interdisciplinary discussions of biological holism after the Civil War. His research on human physiology explored the dynamic, systemic nature of growth. Could the child be studied as an organism like any other? How might development affect its essentiality, its self as a 'complete whole'?[9] He would integrate this discussion of the possibilities of unified biological being into an evolved, richer historical and intellectual conception of scientific holism, what he called 'la biología del todo', the biology of the whole.[10] More broadly, the close conflation of science and philosophy in Pi i Sunyer's writings, alongside the conceptions of humanistic medicine sought by scientists such as Roberto Nóvoa Santos (1885–1933), indicates the significance of epistemological debates on the body within Spanish intellectual history. These speak to the ways in which Spanish scientists and intellectuals were both contributing to and situating themselves within larger dialogues on the body, self, and mind.[11]

Teachers sought to bridge the psychical, the biological, and the vital in their analyses, with teacher Rafael Verdier suggesting in 1926 that the beginnings of an authentic 'pedagogía española' could be latent in this project.[12] As will be explored through his writings in this chapter, the problem was a conflicted notion of the child's being. For many educators, a purely quantitative, mechanical reading of development — what they saw coming from the medical sciences — neglected a fuller view of life. By reducing existence to a set of physiological, chemical reactions, children's vitality risked being lost. As these voices argued for a transition from positivist science towards an emergent perspective of dynamic systems, they anchored a defence of the developing child. Learning was not a quantifiable result of mechanism or causality, but a process of dynamic growth over time. For this reason, teachers writing about biological change made ample connections between the growth of the body and a broader sociological view of complex systems. If the medical meaning of the term 'crisis', a critical turning point in the body's condition, was commonly linked to ideas of regeneration and modernization in *fin-de-siècle* Spain, so too was this societal analogy applied to the child in new ways over the coming years. In 1928, Víctor Mercante, an Argentinian educationalist contributing to the *Revista de Pedagogía*, described children's growth across key developmental stages as a zigzagging, divergent correlation between 'physical and intellectual crises', all interacting within one functional system.[13]

Such characterizations of education as a biological system echoed through writings on infantile growth and development. If education was a process of responding to dynamic growth, it must be as agile, flexible, and dynamic as children themselves. Verdier agreed. Childhood should be understood as a process whose 'índole biológica huye a toda medida, desborda todas las barreras' [biological nature evades all measurement and overflows all constraints]. He described growth not as a gradual evolution, but a series of shocks: 'a saltos bruscos, a modo de explosiones' [in sudden jumps, like explosions].[14] Both of these teachers portrayed organic and biological changes in the child's body as subject to the exigencies of time, environment, and physical laws. In turn, the child's biological growth, particularly at its points of 'crisis' in physical development, was continually equated to wider historical, political, sociological, or scientific crises in Spain and the modern world.[15] Discussions of biological holism, not necessarily neatly aligned by categories or allegiances, indicated priorities and fault lines in society. Chiefly, these fell between those who saw scientific research as a necessary technical tool of sorting and diagnosis and those who fought to study these empirical principles deeply and flexibly, while defining the practical limits of their influence.

The Child and the Chimpanzee: Ortega on Play, Action, and Intelligence

In a 1921 volume of pedagogical essays, *Biología y pedagogía*, Ortega began to explore what lessons a new generation of educationalists should take from the rapidly expanding domain of biological research. This latter area was defined at its broadest and most liberal in his work, as it arguably is in this chapter: he drew from a heterogeneous array of topics — evolution, primitivism, myth, desire, emotion, endocrinology, Uexküllian biology, Gestalt psychology — to make wider arguments about the place of education in society. To understand a life, he said, whether human or animal, one must 'hacer antes el inventario de los objetos que integran su medio propio o, como yo prefiero decir, su paisaje' [first inventory the objects that make up its environment, or, as I prefer to say, its landscape]. Just as the objects of one's world constituted its landscape, the surrounding society was key to understanding the shifting terrain of education. But more than a socio-political view of pedagogy — a topic which he had amply explored over the prior decade — Ortega opened a wider discourse among Spanish teachers on a 'new' biology of engagement, circumstance, and relationality.[16] These were ideas developed explicitly in *Biología y pedagogía*, but which he would continue to promote through new, complementary sources over the coming years and which in turn impacted those interested in the limits of science and society. What defined unique situations of learning, and indeed intelligence, were the moments in which a mind was confronted with novel situations. How did the mind form links of significance between key elements? What distinguished instinct from intelligence? And how could reformers use these lessons to champion new methods and a new system entirely?

These were questions Ortega worked through explicitly in his introduction to Spain of a Gestalt view of intelligence, namely through the work of the German psychologist Wolfgang Köhler (1887–1967). 'En territorio español — en las islas Canarias, en Tenerife,' Köhler began his 1927 lecture in Barcelona.[17] He had been invited by Emilio Mira y López's Institut Psicotècnic to give a series of four lectures on his by-then famous chimpanzee experiments, testing ingenuity and intelligence through a series of interactions with tools and objects. These experiments had indeed taken place on Spanish soil, when Köhler was director of the Prussian Academy of Sciences's anthropoid research station in Tenerife for some six years (1913–19). Opening his first address, Köhler remarked that he could easily fill his lecture with amusing stories about his primates. Instead, his reach was greater: intelligence, invention, understanding; the relationship between physical and psychic worlds; the phenomenological basis of perception; and what these concepts meant for learning and practice. A prominent Jesuit psychologist in attendance at the Barcelona presentation, Ferrán María Palmés, later recalled that the presentation was delivered in 'correcto castellano' [good Spanish] and that Köhler even showed a brief film of his work with the chimpanzees.[18]

Addressing teachers, psychologists, and the public, Köhler stressed the impact of his findings on the field of education. He described the sight of a sea of blank faces in a university lecture hall. He might explain a concept once, twice, to his students, with no response. On the third or fourth time, suddenly, a few faces lit up. Somehow, the concept had become clear:

> Algo ha sucedido en su alma, como una reacción química entre las proposiciones, mediante lo cual adquiere cada una un sentido en relación con las demás y todas ellas en relación con el todo. Así, la serie de proposiciones se transforma en una totalidad orgánica.[19]

> [Something has happened in their minds, like a chemical reaction between elements, through which each element acquires a new character in relation to every other, as well as in relation to the whole. Thus, the series of elements is transformed into an organic totality.]

This was the sense of totality of which the Gestalt psychologists spoke. Learning was not simply perceptual, but transformational. Whether in a university hall or in a primary school, Köhler pointed out, learning happened when leaps of intellectual activity took place. Therefore it was necessary to cultivate children's activities such that these leaps could occur spontaneously, creating 'un juego de adquisición de *materiales* nuevos' [an interplay in the acquisition of new *materials*].[20] While Köhler was by no means the first to advocate play as a way of recognizing relationships, the Gestalt depiction of insight made explicit its philosophical and psychological role in such a dynamic conception of education.

Soon after Köhler's visit to Barcelona, Ortega attended his 1927 address to the Sociedad de Cursos y Conferencias at the Residencia de Estudiantes in Madrid. Ortega's resulting article in *El Sol*, 'La inteligencia de los chimpancés', defended a notion of intelligence based on action and interaction at a time when the very concept of intelligence — and its measurement — was under construction.[21] In Köhler's words, an intelligent being was one who could 'reconocer la estructura de la situación, las posibilidades que contiene y concebir inmediatamente la forma del rodeo adecuado' [recognize the structure of a situation, the possibilities it contains, and immediately conceive of an appropriate route to solving it].[22] Köhler showed that intelligence resulted from the ability to engineer a novel solution rather than to enact rote responses. It was the ability to respond to one's given environment and change the totality of its significance.

As Ortega and teachers around him would suggest, these were the qualities that must be inculcated in the very structures of education. Köhler had moved to Tenerife in 1913 to undertake what Ortega called the 'operación infantil' [childish operation] of scientific experimentation. Köhler's experiments had important applications not just for the test subject of the chimpanzee, but also for the definition of 'intelligence' in child and man. 'Pocas veces una pura investigación psicológica ha producido impresión tan honda y fulminante como el examen de la inteligencia de los chimpancés de Wolfgang Köhler' [Rarely has purely psychological research produced such a profound and immediate impression as Wolfgang Köhler's chimpanzee experiments], wrote Ortega.[23] Köhler's chimpanzees went beyond instinct towards acts of insight and intelligence. For example, when the animal sat in a cage with a bunch of bananas hanging high above, the instinctual action was to jump up and try to grab them. Moving a box across the cage and clambering upon it to reach the bananas, on the other hand, demonstrated a more complex awareness of spatial relations, means, ends, and solutions. This was a sequence of steps, both in the behaviour of chimpanzees and in turn of society's youngest members turning towards human intelligence, that would be examined in successive articles in the Spanish press over the coming years (Fig. 3.1). Specifically, Ortega described one chimpanzee reaching the fruit through the adoption of a stick as tool:

> ¿No ha habido aquí una creación inteligente? El cajón ha adquirido un *nuevo* carácter. Antes era para el mono un objeto habitual, sobre el cual los otros chimpancés se sentaban; ahora es miembro de una relación ideal, y no meramente visual: es medio o instrumento para alcanzar la fruta [...]. El animal parece haber *entendido* el nexo ideal que se establece entre un objeto y una finalidad, merced al cual el objeto se convierte en *medio para* otra cosa.[24]

> [Have we not witnessed an intelligent creation? The box has acquired a *new* character. Previously it was a habitual object for the monkey, on which the other chimpanzees would sit; now it is part of an ideal relationship, and not merely a visual one: it has become a means or an instrument to reach the fruit [...]. The animal seems to have *understood* the ideal nexus established between an object and a result, through which the object is converted into a *means for* something else.]

Köhler's findings suggested to scientists and pedagogues alike that intelligent action began with the establishment of relationships between self, object, and the world. Whether in the chimpanzee, the child, or the adult, Köhler held intelligence to be that which created a sudden change in one's recognition of relations between things, what contemporaneous psychologist Jean Piaget would later develop as a 'reorganización repentina del campo perceptivo' [sudden reorganization of the perceptual field].[25] This shift was what Ortega referred to when he suggested that intelligence was the realization of relations. An intelligent being, as Ortega defined

FIG. 3.1. Described in the Spanish press as a continuation of psychologist Wolfgang
Köhler's work, experiments undertaken in Suchum, Georgia (USSR) in the 1930s
replicated the scenario. Here, a chimpanzee contemplates a bunch of hanging cherries
before using a series of tools to reach it.
Source: Anon., 'La inteligencia de los monos: nuevos ensayos en el parque
experimental de Suchum', *Mundo Gráfico* (1932), 8–9 (p. 8).

it, acted upon relationships. In doing so, he mentally shifted the significance of these surrounding things, suddenly able to 'percib[ir] el cambio de papel, de "sentido" de las cosas integrantes' [perceives the changing role or 'sense' of the component parts].[26] These realizations happened in an instant: a cognitive switch flipped, and the world took on a new *Gestalt*.

Ortega's writings on Gestalt psycho-biological research thus moved from a redefinition of intelligence towards an examination of science itself. In his discussion of Köhler, Ortega claimed that science was linked to childhood: 'Un hombre de ciencia es un poco niño toda su vida' [A man of science remains in some sense a child all his life]. In turn, investigation could only be conducted with a childlike spirit, and progress would be impossible if scientists did not maintain 'un lujo de infantilidad' [the luxury of infantilism].[27] Such was a common way of explaining and elevating childhood. As contemporaries noted in 1922, Ortega's view of the *biology* of pedagogy emphasized how education could harness those most compelling, animating capacities of emotion, fantasy, and energy in the child, particularly those that reflected the innate scientific qualities of growth and development. Children were little more than small scientists and vice versa, as Swiss pedagogue Édouard Claparède allegedly noted: wise men were 'niños grandes', sharing a curiosity for the roots of things, a love of play, and a 'visión ingenua' of the world.[28] Ultimately, Ortega argued that the child and the scientist shared a tendency to configure the world through hypotheses and experimentation. They learned by recognizing and acting on a network of relations, binding together relevant facts or objects, and thereby accessing new knowledge about their surroundings. By bringing child-like vitality into a potentially mechanistic and rationalistic discipline, Ortega created a new *razón vital* for scientific experimentation. Ultimately, Ortega summarized Köhler's findings simply: how well does a subject respond to a new situation?

What Ortega found noteworthy about Köhler's lecture, however, were not his scientific findings per se but the audience's reaction. According to Ortega, Madrid's 'gente de letras y gente de mundo' [people of letters and well-travelled people] found the lecture interesting 'pero un poco ingenua' [somewhat naive].[29] How could such a reaction be squared against Ortega's evident fascination with Köhler's research, one might well ask? Ortega explained that it was not unusual for adults, once they understood a radical concept, to find it eminently straightforward. The best discoveries were the ones that all walks of life could understand, which uncovered fundamental truths about the world: 'Hay en la ciencia un fondo de ingenuidad, más aún, de puerilidad, que contrasta con la "listeza" del buen madrileño' [There is in science itself a foundation of naivety, even childishness, that contrasts with the "savvy" of the good *madrileño*].[30] The experimentation which led to the child-scientist's conclusions suggested a form of play with the world, a continual probing and questioning which allowed a new idea to emerge. Historian of science Thomas Kuhn has spoken of the 'thought-experiments' that scientists use to replace broken paradigms.[31] Leading to such shifts, in Ortega's portrayal, was a vast discrepancy between the solitary, imaginative vision of the world which one constructs internally and the facts which surround one. Science was the process of drawing these together and finding where they overlapped. By seeking the space of truth between 'hechos' and 'realidad', it attempted to decipher the 'jeroglífico' of the unknown.[32] These disconnected stages of understanding proved equally true for the scientific process. It was difficult to conceive of the beliefs, or paradigms, one had discarded — the flatness of the earth, the constancy of time and space.

These ideas were not limited to the insights that Ortega drew from Köhler's chimpanzees, but rather were circulating within the field of psycho-pedagogical research. Piaget, who started his career as a biologist and whose work on children's cognitive development began to be published by colleagues in Spain during the 1920s and 1930s, famously argued that a child's stages of mental development were separate and non-communicative.[33] For instance, a child of nine years could not fathom having ever believed that a piece of clay weighed more in one shape than another. Later, the principles of conservation of mass had become so integrated into the child's understanding of the world that his or her own former beliefs, illogical cognitive precursors, no longer fit into their worldview.[34] This was the process that children undertook to understand the 'laws' and 'causes' of the world, as psychologists from Köhler to Claparède to Piaget argued — and as Ortega's interest in child-science analogies suggests. This process of transformation was continual. In a 1926 piece published in the *Revista de Pedagogía*, Piaget suggested that the notion that the child learned by doing, akin to a scientist, was already passé. What must still be understood, and enacted in practice, was the psychology behind the child's need to reach, touch, and engage. Children conducted experiments all day long, but according to Piaget, their minds were like two superimposed 'capas geológicas', one verbal, one motor. The verbal was akin to simple explanation: a superficial acceptance of laws, concepts, and results. What they must cultivate was that deeper terrain, the motor level, which integrated all those experiences and sensations they concretely possessed and were steadily acquiring. Learning resulted from the active contradiction of these two planes.[35]

This, indeed, was the basis of the active school. Considerations of the nature of intelligence and, in turn, what distinguished the human development of the child relationship formed part of a wider reckoning with the relationship between education and scientific modernization. Children's abilities to engage with objects, to use signs and tools, and to revise their views of the world were central to new theories. Commentators' rhetoric drew from contemporaneous anxieties about a changing technical and industrial framework, while foreshadowing the ways in which such a framing would continue to be used to discuss the importance of agility, adaptability, and dynamic development for a complex, globalized world. Through his discussion of animal, child, and 'scientific' experimentation, Ortega suggested that it was not a set of skills or knowledge that constituted intelligence, but rather an ability to recognize relations in the world in order to act upon them. As he summarized, 'La inteligencia es, pues, la percatación de relaciones entre las cosas; es ver a éstas como miembros de una estructura en la cual cada una tiene su papel, su "sentido"' [Intelligence is the recognition of relationships between things; it is seeing these as part of a structure in which each one has its role, its 'meaning'].[36]

Relating intelligence to an individual's capacity to recognize relationships allowed for both a defined and broad definition of intelligence. Novel solutions could be found through the infinite relationships formed by the self and every element of one's circumstance. For the child, whose early activity consisted of reflexive, instinctual reactions — from crying to feeding — it was the voluntary, creative acts which elicited wonder.[37] In Köhler's experiments, intelligent behaviour not only surpassed but even contradicted the instinctual act. Discovering, for example, that in order to get a banana through a complex set-up of boxes and cages, the chimpanzee must first push the banana away in order to reach it proved the most difficult task of all for Köhler's chimpanzees. It meant an active engagement in one's changing environment and over one's instincts, 'haciéndose cargo de las circunstancias' [taking charge of one's circumstances], as Ortega wrote.[38] Köhler's Tenerife experiments, as read and understood by philosophers and educators, had far-reaching implications beyond the realm of psychology.

In closing his essay, Ortega invited the reader to meditate on one final question. Why was it more challenging for the chimpanzee to *remove* a box, when that simple move would solve a problem, than to add another box or tool to the current configuration? Ortega suggested that it was more difficult to imagine an entirely new structure or situation than it was to alter it slightly, to add a new but ineffective element to that which was already present. It took more effort for one to think, literally, outside the box. Ultimately, this was precisely the problem faced not just by Köhler's chimpanzees, but educators and society as a whole. Europe could not conceive of a solution radical enough to achieve the progress it needed: 'Pero tenemos mucho pasado, mucha supervivencia arcaica, muchos cajones que quitar' [But we have a great deal of past, many archaic legacies and boxes to remove].[39]

New biological and psychological theories suggested radical ways of re-thinking the developmental process. These were posed not as minor textbook revisions, but as the creation of an entirely new canon. Many of these methods had long roots, from the Socratic method on towards the pedagogical innovations of Rousseau, Johann Heinrich Pestalozzi, Friedrich Fröbel, and others. Indeed, modern reformers consciously embraced the historical precedents of their work, celebrating precursors, examining their legacies, and marking their anniversaries with publications and tributes.[40] But across Europe, the aim of the New Education movement was to lay aside stale models. It sought to embrace, rather, an avant-garde conception of the future, one that accepted development as unknown, unsteady, and ever in flux. Reformers sought to create new spaces and new models, from open-air and active schools to free play and learning by inquiry, which prepared children not for given scenarios, but for precisely such new and novel situations. Inner experience was impossible to ascertain in another, particularly in children; children were as foreign to adults as Köhler's chimpanzees. Childhood had been considered a time when genetic inheritance and instinct governed, in which an inheritance of 'organic memory' endowed children with ancestral knowledge.[41] Yet pedagogy, to serve the future, must be designed for a changing era, in which no individual inherited an understanding of the world but rather acquired the tools to approach it in a novel manner. Educationalists sought to find new solutions to old problems. Such efforts worked not just to remove, as Ortega had written, the 'cajones' standing in the way, but to provide children with the tools they needed to erect an entirely new edifice.

The *Umwelt* of the Child: Uexküll, Verdier, and a New Spanish Pedagogy

Just as Ortega sought to redefine the humanities and human sciences, so too could a primary school teacher set out to revise what 'science' and 'culture' meant for learning and development. As school director Rafael Verdier of Málaga wrote in the *Revista de Pedagogía* in 1929, education must be both lived and experienced: 'Todo acto de aprendizaje ha de ser vivido' [all learning must be lived], while pedagogy itself must become the 'centro de gravedad de todo proceso cultural' [the gravitational centre of all cultural processes].[42] Verdier's writings from the 1920s and early 1930s delved explicitly into questions of this environmental relationship between child and world, providing a case study for the synthesis of new scientific and philosophical ideals in service of a 'modern' pedagogy, and indeed, an authentic 'Spanish pedagogy'.[43] According to Verdier, the roots of this effort in Spain were nascent but unfulfilled. Scientists as illustrious as Santiago Ramón y Cajal, August Pi i Sunyer, Ramon Turró i Darder and Gregorio Marañón, he wrote, had had the 'brilliant' idea of creating a national 'Instituto de Pedagogía', but their effort never came to fruition.[44] Seeing a gap, Verdier suggested a window for innovation in which educators could apply a new phenomenological view of development to the Spanish child. As the remainder of this chapter will argue, his writings on the biological nature of growth and development integrated Ortega's thought on intelligence and culture. Through his lens, teachers' enthusiasm for active methods might be read anew.

Verdier is almost entirely unknown outside the pages of old pedagogical reviews, footnotes, and regional museums, and like most of the pre-war educators and paidologists here discussed, his name is absent from encyclopaedic sources such as the Real Academia de la Historia's 2011 *Diccionario Biográfico Español*. A primary school teacher and school director in Málaga, he worked in the pedagogical circle of the Institución Libre de Enseñanza, through which he attended and reported on centralized training courses.[45] But he also developed his ideas theoretically through contributions to the reformist journals *Revista de Pedagogía* and *Escuelas de España*, as well as publishing two monographs: *De Uexküll a Decroly* (1931), on the biological turn in pedagogy, and with Víctor Argueta, a children's reading primer, *Ya leo* (1935), employing an 'ideo-visual' method of conceptual learning. He was a firm supporter of the Second Republic and its educational ambitions. In February 1936, his name appeared below those of Lorca, Alberti, and others in a statement adhering to the Frente Popular. Verdier remained in Spain after the end of the Civil War, teaching and writing, largely on pedagogical subjects such as handwriting and manual dexterity as well as children's stories during the 1960s and 1970s.[46] In his only pre-war pedagogical monograph, *De Uexküll a Decroly*, Verdier set out to study the biological and environmental influences which shape the child's world, arguing for their interconnected centrality. How could circulating biological approaches to perception and cognition — from insects to birds, chimpanzees to babies — change society's understanding of learning and development? Jakob von Uexküll's *Umwelt und Innenwelt der Tiere* [The Surrounding and Inner Worlds of Animals] (1909) and *Bausteine zu einer biologischen Weltanschauung: gesammelte Aufsätze* [Elements of a Biological Worldview: Collected Essays] had, in recent years, proposed a theory of life based on a perceptual view of the world. Uexküll's argument was that every life-form, from mussels to children to adults, possessed a different physiology which informed the sensory information it received and transmitted. This biological structure conditioned how the organism understood and interacted with the world. With Uexküll's *Bausteine* published in Spain by the Revista de Occidente as *Ideas para una concepción biológica del mundo* (1922), Ortega introduced his work as an encapsulation of the 'new spirit' of twentieth-century thought.[47]

Reading Verdier's reception of Uexküll, one finds that the idea of a 'mundo del niño' was more than simply rhetorical. In *De Uexküll a Decroly*, Verdier demonstrated a conception of the child as a holistic unity, encompassing a self shaped by its biological nature, its relations with the world, and larger transcendental self of spirit, character, and personality. These representations were spread across five chapters: the 'mundo circundante' in biological and human life; the 'mundo del niño'; the 'alma del niño'; and, finally, two chapters covering the application of these concepts in education, both at home and school. In this effort, Verdier transparently aligned with influential voices importing the new biology. Ortega elaborated an Uexküllian view of vital circumstance in his essay 'El medio vital' of 1921, in which he criticized the idea that children's environments could be equated to those of adults, that they were 'sumergidos en el mismo medio que nosotros' [submerged in the same medium as us]. According to Ortega, who expanded on these ideas in a series of articles including 'El Quijote en la escuela' [Don Quixote in the School] and 'La vida infantil' [The Life of the Child], childhood was not 'una etapa enfermiza, defectuosa' [a sickly, defective stage] of life, but rather the manifestation of a distinct biological structure and corresponding outlook.[48] Philosopher Manuel García Morente likewise developed an Uexküllian view of perception in his 1928 essay on the world of the child: 'No es, pues, tan absurda, señor, la idea de los múltiples mundos, esta idea de que cada viviente tiene su mundo propio. Y no solo no es absurda, sino que yo la creo verdadera' [This idea of multiple worlds, sir, is not so absurd, this idea that every living being has its own world. And not only is it not absurd, but I believe it is true].[49] The imaginative 'world of the child' was argued in a philosophical frame to have literal biological roots and implications.

If the child's world differed from that of the adult, Verdier sought to understand these differences and situate them practically for educators. How and when did the child's understanding of the world evolve towards that of the adult? What distinguished humans from all other animals? Did there exist an extra-biological quotient of imagination and interaction in human development, in other words, of culture? These questions were the crux of his reliance on Uexküllian thought for a pedagogy of experience. The world, he wrote, appeared at first glance the same to all its inhabitants. If we all descended the same staircase and looked upon the same objects, it would be reasonable to assume that we were all experiencing the same patterns of meaning. And yet these surroundings were not equal in each of our gazes: 'no significan lo mismo para todos' [they do not mean the same for everyone]. An element of experience and social signification was necessary: a hammer, for instance, was instantly recognizable by most as a tool with a specific purpose. To the uninitiated mind, or to a 'savage tribe', the hammer would be nothing more than an object, 'carente de significación, algo muerto, desarticulado' [lacking in meaning and significance, dead, disarticulated].[50] As Verdier suggested, children went through a process of meaning-making in each gesture they learned, each word they spoke, and every image they drew.

Recalling the teacher Teodoro Causí's reference to the dangers of the 'dis-articulated' word in support of unified arguments for globalization and Gestalt theories (Chapter 1), Verdier's understanding of articulation made the case for new practices of education.[51] Teachers of the New Education movement were convinced that children had to touch, experience, and interact with the world of objects in order to know a word or a concept. This argument also began to break into a much larger discourse on the semiotic nature of words and objects, and how children unpack the 'code' of communicative life through the symbolic nature of writing, drawing, or mathematical and scientific activity. All of these practices raised questions of how the child — or any living being — made cognitive sense of its environment, responded to it, and developed within it. In Uexküll's telling, it was the inextricable relationship between the part and the whole that endowed the unity of the organism. One could not conceive of a species in terms of elements for any modification altered the whole, altering its relationship to its world.[52] Outdated conceptions of scientific units and relationships could not encompass the functional system that Uexküll proposed. He argued that the contemporary view of nature drew from a theory of chaos, a purely physical–chemical but only partial understanding:

> Dieses Chaos bildet die allgemeine ungeformte Außenwelt, in der alle Organismen leben. Jeder Organismus tritt aber gemäß seiner Bauart nur mit einem sehr kleinen Teil der Außenwelt in Beziehung. Jedes einzelne Lebewesen schafft sich durch diese Beziehungen eine ihm allein eigentümliche Umwelt, in der sich sein Leben abspielt.[53]

> [This chaos forms the general and diffuse external world in which all organisms live. But every organism, in accordance with its structure, enters into relationship with only a very small part of this total world. Every living being, through these relationships, creates a surrounding world, unique and individual, in which its life plays out.]

From chaos to order, there was a structural basis to Uexküll's claims. Nature did not simply choose the fittest or best adapted organisms to survive, as in a Darwinist view; rather, each organism grew in relationship to the chosen world most suited to its biological form.

Verdier early picked up on Uexküll's Darwinist critique in order to distinguish the novelty of Uexküll's thought. Whereas Darwinism would claim that bats evolved a system of radio-location because it allowed them to function in dark environments, 'la nueva biología' claimed the reverse: that bats sought out caves because such an environment suited their perceptual abilities. The organs of one animal would be fatal to another. A spider with a human eye would see only an 'iconographic' image of a fly, 'su figura total recortada sobre un fondo' [its outline in silhouette against a background], he wrote in a Gestaltist echo. The spider would not recognize the fly as a source of sustenance in this new world: 'En el mundo de la araña la mosca no es nuestra mosca' [In the spider's world, a fly is not the same fly as in our world].[54] The biological structure of the organism limited and controlled what information it received, as well as how it viewed and perceived the world. For instance, the human eye, Uexküll suggested, processed only a limited range of light waves, while the human ear was deaf to the vast majority of sounds. Humans possessed only the senses they need to interact within their own surrounding world, as seen in the child's more limited range of relations. An animal's struggle for survival played out within its own 'condiciones de existencia' — less a Darwinist struggle for existence than a coexistence of multiple and distinct functional worlds, as Uexküll argued:

> Nur ausnahmsweise treten die Organismen in direkten Wettbewerb untereinander. Der Hauptsache nach hat ein jedes Lebewesen das Bestreben, einen anderen Teil der Außenwelt zu organisieren, den es zu seiner Umwelt umschafft. Diese Wechselwirkungen zwischen Tier und Umwelt stellen dem Biologen die subtilsten und geistvollsten Aufgaben.[55]

> [Only exceptionally do organisms enter into direct opposition to one another. Fundamentally, every being aspires to organize another part of the external world, integrating it into its surrounding world. These reciprocal actions between animal and world present the biologist with the most subtle and spiritual questions.]

Uexküll's definition of a contingent new biology implied a concern with the internal and interrelated systems which governed the individual's relationship to the world. In all living beings, Uexküll made clear that scientists should not limit themselves to investigating the specific details of form and anatomy, but should rather consider and study the organism as a whole. Organs were necessary for the body's functioning, just as individual mechanical parts were necessary for a machine. Yet unlike a machine, the living organism possessed the self-generating capacity to create and foster its own organs, beginning from a simple cell and culminating in the complex form of the body. This endowed the living body with vital properties which could not be encompassed by a purely physical, mechanical conception.[56]

Uexküll's biological view of growth privileged, instead, the idea of a dynamic system. It refused to accept the governing mechanist notion of the body. Through the latter part of the nineteenth century, an explanation for reflexes and reactions had been that of the 'reflex arc', entailing a process connecting a receptor organ, through mediators in the nerves, to the muscular entity which would mechanically perform the action.[57] What Uexküll and others were moving towards was an idea of a dynamic physiological regulation. The myriad functions of the body — from temperature fluctuation, to digestion, to growth — were reactions seeking a changing equilibrium with the environment. Such a movement took into account a dynamic process of change and development over time: 'Das wesentliche am Tier ist nicht seine Form, sondern die Umformung, nicht die Struktur, sondern der Lebensprozess "Das Tier ist ein bloßes Geschehnis"' [The essential aspect of the animal is not its form, but its transformation; not its structure, but its vital processes. '*The animal is pure process*'], as Uexküll had written.[58] His theory focused on relationships of transformation, posing development as progressive within the individual and across society. Following the continuities of thought and memory put forward by William James and being read alongside Bergson's notions of duration and re-creation, such a cyclical view of the body made sense. It both allowed an essential, individual core to develop, while allowing room for constant and continual change in the growth and evolution of the self.

Like Ortega and Verdier, the prominent Catalan physiologist August Pi i Sunyer was an early Spanish proponent of Uexküll's thought, citing the latter's work as early as 1917 and incorporating it into his own view of human growth. As Pi i Sunyer wrote in a 1921 essay on the 'constitution of the individual' across its lifespan, this ever-shifting development resulted from the ancestral inheritance of the species as well as the life of the individual:

> Línea viviente, equilibrio móvil, conflicto entre lo que fue y lo que es y de lo cual resulta lo que será. En la intersección de las influencias que nos vienen de nuestros antepasados y las influencias actuales, se encuentra la individualidad: masa más o menos considerable de materia viviente, sujeta a la acción del medio y que goza, al mismo tiempo, de una cierta independencia porque constituye un todo, una unidad en la que se coordinan las funciones y que puede responder de manera adecuada a las circunstancias de origen externo y también interno.[59]

> [Living line, moving equilibrium, conflict between what was and what is and what results from what will be. At the intersection of influences drawn from our ancestors and our present, individuality can be found: a more or less considerable mass of living material, subject to the workings of the environment but which benefits from, at the same time, a certain independence because it constitutes a whole, a unity, in which functions are aligned and equipped to respond adequately to internal and external circumstances.]

Individuality was inscribed in a moving line from past to future. Pi i Sunyer's idea of the organism as equilibrium, both internal and temporal, was not far removed from a philosophy of the developing child. Childhood, as the shifting early stages of the body, was in turn central to an idea of functional unity. Educationalists made this connection between internal unity and dynamic circumstances fluidly in pedagogical arguments. Verdier, for instance, called childhood 'elástico': 'una vida de puro dinamismo' [a life of pure dynamism].[60] Childhood was the time in which growth processes were in greatest flux, in which development from stage to stage was most irregular. It was this dynamism that biologists, paidologists, and teachers found worth studying.

As a teacher-philosopher, Verdier connected the dots between biological life-worlds and the perceptual life-world of the child, seeking to draw relationships of meaning not just on the page but in the classroom. Verdier's book was praised by a fellow teacher in a review for bringing the theory of education back into the hands of educators. He bridged theory and teaching, described by a colleague as the pedagogical 'hijo espiritual' [spiritual son] of Ortega.[61] Just as evident as his work, however, was a wholehearted fascination with the ways in which environmental engagement shaped development. His portrayal of the child's 'mundo circundante' attempted to provide no less than a sweeping theory of knowledge couched in the current terms of biological thought. While Uexküll led a new wave of fundamental biology, this reviewer suggested, Verdier incorporated these ideas seamlessly into a philosophy of education in which:

> Cada animal tiene su mundo, tiene su repertorio de cosas entre las cuales vive. El hombre tiene también su mundo específico. Las cosas adoptan ante nosotros una arquitectura determinada. Pero la arquitectura de nuestro mundo no es la misma que la del mundo infantil.[62]

> [Every animal has its world, its repertory of things among which it lives. Man too has his particular world. Objects adopt before us a certain architecture. But the architecture of our world is not the same as that of the child's world.]

For these educators, the idea of a child's world was not just a manner of speaking. It had direct roots in a wider form of holistic biological thought, hence Verdier's tying these ideas of perceptual worlds to a larger body of research. There was a coherent sense to all one perceived and experienced. Every element in sight was a spur to play and exploration, interaction and socialization. Verdier portrayed these relationships as an endlessly expanding web, with the 'human world' as a world 'poblado de relaciones infinitas, fijamente establecidas unas, otras posibles' [filled with infinite relations, some clearly established, others possible]. It was *possibilities* of relationship that connected spaces between people and that formed a larger relational web: 'lo que hace que el mundo de cada personaje humano constituya algo característico y peculiar' [which makes each person's world something characteristic and individual].[63] The 'relaciones infinitas' invoked by Verdier formed a world in which every person constructed relationships of meaning from the things around them.

Ultimately, by defending Uexküll's perceptual worlds, Verdier propagated one specific pedagogical intervention in the Spanish classroom: the so-called 'Decroly Plan', based on the 'centres of interest' pioneered by the pedagogue Ovide Decroly (1871–1932) at his Hermitage School in Brussels from 1907 and one of the most popular outlets for the melding of biological thought and new education.[64] Decroly's method posited that children's learning should be based on thematic groupings around their developmental needs. Key was the idea that children responded to that which they vitally required from their environment. A lesson plan might be built around food, transport, the sea, or any other number of intimate, graspable, lived concepts. As pedagogue José (Josep) Mallart y Cutó (1897–1989) depicted in a book on active learning in 1935, for instance, a class focused on ideas such as 'navigation' and 'fish' could be held at the seaside, thus making these ideas lived and real in children's physical, everyday experiences (Fig. 3.2).

FIG. 3.2. Children learning about the sea during an open-air class on the beach.
Source: José Mallart y Cutó, *La educación activa*, 4th edn
(Barcelona: Editorial Labor, 1935), plate 4.

Commentary in the Spanish pedagogical press explored the uses and implications of the Decroly Plan — and a range of related methods — in both teaching and theory. Advocates of a Decrolian model in the classroom, including María Luisa Navarro, Teodoro Causí, Rodolfo Llopis, Jacobo Orellano Garrido, Rodolfo Tomás y Samper, and others, began to incorporate the theories of 'centres of interest' into their promotions of the *escuela nueva* from the late 1910s to the 1930s. The Decroly model of experience, projects, and concentrations around thematic topics was widely discussed in newspapers such as *El Sol*, *El Imparcial*, and *La Libertad*, among others, and was widely incorporated into classroom publications.[65]

Decroly's centres of interests were incorporated into classroom practice not only through individual efforts by motivated teachers such as Mallart, but also in more structured ways via books that continued to be printed and reprinted during the early Francoist era. One educator, José Xandri Pich, published a series of classroom textbooks following the Decroly method in Spain from the mid-1920s (Fig. 3.3).[66] His brightly illustrated books focused on aspects of children's lives in the classroom and out, with chapters modelled on commonly experienced concepts such as 'what surrounds us', 'bodies', 'nature', or 'man', with sub-sections treating individual examples of these phenomena or terms.[67] Topics were designed to lead children into study through their own bodies and the world around them. These texts relied on a globalist notion of the child's mind, beginning with the reality of ideas and concepts before introducing the symbolic form of word and letter. Lessons combined images, text, and activities with questions about the day's topic into one

FIG. 3.3. Textbooks such as this popular series structured learning around thematic 'centres of interest' known to the child. Source: José Xandri Pich, *La vida en la escuela: primer grado. Primer año de estudios* (Madrid: Yagüe, [1927]), cover.

cohesive whole, with the curriculum moving in widening, overlapping circles, called 'concentraciones' — through which students grasped ever more advanced and complex ideas. What this theory, and the entire *escuela nueva*, rested on was a biological notion of the child's needs and experiences.

Active theories of education resonated with pedagogues who sought to integrate larger philosophical ideas into both the 'new' science and a 'new' education. Whether in Verdier, Ortega, or Bergson, human development was said to depend on constantly interacting organic systems and was thus continually creative and 're-creative'.[68] Yet one finds a degree of caution as to the reach of science into education, even when biological theories formed the motivating base of a new view of pedagogy. Voices such as Verdier's insisted that a scientific approach to pedagogy must not fall victim to the same one-dimensionality that had occasioned the alleged 'crisis' of the sciences in the late nineteenth and early twentieth centuries. By celebrating a biological viewpoint they sought to open up to a wider conception of meaning and experience in which the child was biologically driven, psychologically complex, and spiritually whole.

Transcending Biology: Learning, Culture, and the New Education

How far could a biologically-based science of pedagogy go? In a short article from 1929, 'Aprendizaje y cultura', directed at fellow teachers, Verdier asked how a widened, plastic notion of intelligence, drawing on experience, sensation, and vitality, could reform the pedagogical sciences in Spain. It interrogated closely associated concepts: was knowledge equivalent to culture? Was learning a gradual process of receiving knowledge, or an active process of individual development? What role did the biological self play in mediating between knowledge and culture? How could these insights inform pedagogical practice? In line with discussions of 'new art' and 'new schools', this teacher was concerned with the role of the 'new' sciences in human society. Ultimately, these theories stood for something larger: he argued for a rebellion from strict specialization and a defence of an integral notion of human development.

Winning an annual prize from the *Revista de Pedagogía*, Verdier's article synthesized the more troubling discrepancies seen as circulating between biological, psychological, and spiritual views of the child. While a biological conception of the child was necessary to understand growth and learning, it was also clear that education must transcend biology. According to Verdier, such was the problem with most current theories, which remained stuck in an overly mechanistic or analytical mode of thinking. The governing work of behavioural psychologists including Edward Lee Thorndike, John B. Watson, B. F. Skinner, and Ivan Pavlov were seen to fall short in this respect as they drew general conclusions based on mice, cats, and other lower mammals, working within an overly narrow definition of biology. For Verdier, their results may have been scientifically accurate, but their frameworks were restrictive when considering the richness of human behaviour. As such, their conclusions about learning would be insufficient for organisms on a higher level — namely humans, those beings of most 'organic and psychical complication'.[69]

While a scientist could prove that an animal was 'learning' by its ability to perform tasks in progressively shorter intervals of time, such knowledge represented solely one 'functional and quantitative perspective' upon a large whole. For Verdier, behaviourists limited themselves to the animal's particular nervous structure without considering the wider cultural, sociological, historical, and psychological structures that played a role in its development:

> Acepta [el conductista] que cada reacción viene inmediatamente impuesta por una vía nerviosa determinada. Por tanto, cada organismo solo es apto para aquellas reacciones que son posibles, dada su contextura somática. Se llega así a un determinismo riguroso, dentro de cuyos moldes estrechos la acción educadora pierde la mayor parte de [su] eficacia.[70]

> [The [behaviourist] accepts that every reaction is the direct result of a determined nervous path. Therefore, each organism is only able to elicit those reactions possible for its somatic structure. We arrive in this way at a rigorous determinism within whose narrow confines the act of education itself loses most of its benefit.]

Where the behavioural psychologist saw input, output, and reaction, Verdier saw a system whose potential was limited by its structure. The empirical perspective simply could not represent the phenomenon of learning in all its complexity: 'en toda su plenitud, en todo su sentido y trascendencia' [in all its plenitude, in all its meaning and transcendence].[71] If every reaction was pre-determined and limited to a network of neuronal associations, then what was the point of education? How could new and synthetic networks be formed in order to bring about a more complex and generative form of learning? Terms such as *vivencia*, *sentido*, and *trascendencia* functioned as Verdier's key terms of opposition to a strictly mechanistic view of learning. These terms may have been nebulous or open to interpretation, but taken together they represented a studied rejection of limited or strict conceptions of life.[72]

Ultimately, Verdier argued that portrayals of humans as pure organism must never govern practical theories of learning. This claim stood for an ideal of a broad, philosophically-minded science, of knowledge that demanded *vivencia* in order to reach transcendence. Verdier, like Ortega, saw Western culture as standing on the brink of a new way of understanding disciplines, claiming that 'la luz auroral de nuevas corrientes de cultura' [the dawning light of new cultural currents] was becoming ever brighter.[73] One promising example of convergence, he suggested, was that of *Gestalttheorie*, or 'la teoría de la figura'. He looked to Köhler's Tenerife experiments on chimpanzees, in particular, as an example of learning as a synthetic, unified process, in which the biological and the psychical were intimately, inseparably bound. Köhler had observed a correlation between intelligence and manual activity in his simian subjects, concluding that action, in its 'pure dynamic character', was crucially linked to intelligent discovery.[74]

For this reason, Verdier argued that teachers must recognize the role played by spatial and conceptual relations in the child's mind. The process of learning, he argued, was not just the formation of a mental image or the strengthening of an association, but a complex interaction between subject and environment. He described an experiment in which hens were trained to feed from a light blue container, placed next to a dark blue vessel. When the light blue container was substituted with an even darker blue container, the hen rejected the new one in order to try its luck with the formerly rejected, now *relatively* lighter one. What this showed, Verdier suggested, was that in decision-making the animal was structurally aware of relationships between objects, of their structural difference, and not just of the things themselves: they took greater notice of the comparative relationships existing between two objects than purely sensational data of the colour itself.[75] Speaking to an audience of teachers, Verdier suggested that there was a level of reality and sense that the subject constructed from accumulated experience. Given a multitude of comparative and complementary relationships, an individual's understanding was not mechanistic but rather evolving and dynamic. Above all, it was suggested, learning was iterative and regenerative. It was not the drilling and filling of a hole, but rather the modification of an organic whole, a process which:

> modifica profundamente lo más íntimo del organismo animal, algo que aun cuando no añada nuevos órganos, otorga una mayor permeabilidad a las vías nerviosas creando nuevas y ricas asociaciones interneuronales, que de modo indudable han de repercutir sobre la total actividad intelectual. Así se llega a una concepción plástica de la inteligencia.[76]

> [modifies profoundly the most intimate aspects of the animal organism, which even when it does not build up new organs, grants a greater permeability to its nervous channels, creating rich new inter-neuronal associations which cannot help but have an impact on the organism's intellectual activity as a whole. Thus a plastic conception of intelligence is reached.]

Verdier's notion of a 'plastic' conception of intelligence was crucial to a potentially widened approach to education. Was it possible to re-define intelligence even as it was being codified within a broader culture of quantification and modernization?

Verdier's reference to the plasticity of intelligence, especially when read beside theories of the 'multiplicity of intelligences' and differing psychological orientations and forms of thinking in children — as described by psychologists such as Mira y López as early as 1927 — suggested that a widened conception of intelligence was idealized, even during a golden age of psychometric tests, experiments, and diagnoses.[77] Such an analysis of intelligence sought a broader influence on human development and culture. While a biological *ser* was essential to thinking about human development and education, as Ortega had earlier argued, there was a crucial difference between purely biological intelligence and a larger, integral intelligence, both in the individual and in a wider culture.[78] More than specialized expertise in any one skill set or discipline, Verdier argued that intelligence refracted across all of human society:

> No es, pues, más culto el hombre que sabe más, ni tampoco aquél cuya existencia haya adquirido mayor prolongación en el tiempo. Solo podrá llamarse culto el que por razón de un mayor número de vivencias se haya capacitado para responder de modo inmediato y armónico a las situaciones nuevas de carácter mental, sentimental o activo [...]. Saber y cultura pierden así toda inmediata correlatividad.[79]

[The man who knows more is not more educated, nor is he whose existence has lasted longest in time. Only he whose many experiences have enabled him to respond in an immediate, harmonious way to new mental, emotional, or physical situations can truly be called educated [...]. In this way, knowledge and culture lose all direct correlation.]

The single most important factor for education, he argued, was experience, which equipped the educand to respond to futurity, to the unexpected. If the pedagogical viewpoint were limited solely to biological reactions, human culture would suffer, becoming 'inelástico y desconsolador' [rigid and dispiriting].[80] The most learned would be those with the most highly developed technical skills and physical ability. Yet skills, training, and knowledge paled beside values of creativity, agility, and spontaneity. A biological view of life, he suggested, had not (yet) triumphed.

Rather, experience was at the heart of learning, and life itself must be at the heart of any philosophy of education. According to the New Education, educators must reject a piecemeal approach either to the mind or to learning, rather reaching for a holistic view. They must encompass 'lo subjetivo y lo real, lo biológico y lo psíquico, lo mecánico y lo químico, en síntesis global. Porque el espíritu humano está fatigado de análisis' [the subjective and the real, the biological and the psychical, the mechanical and the chemical, in a global synthesis: because the human spirit is tired of analysis].[81] From such a perspective, the individual could be neither purely biological nor purely intellectual. Both qualities must combine with a notion of spirit, encompassing emotion, personality, and experience. Broadening a *Spanish* pedagogical notion of intelligence, therefore, meant separating human knowledge from human culture and learning from education. Doing so brought together the phenomenological ideas of Ortega, the living unity of organisms conveyed by physiologists such as Pi i Sunyer, and the new biology and new psychology translated and imported and read by an audience of teachers.

Such a separation accorded individuals an amplified frame of action and a new radius of experience. It meant not memorizing a set of dates, facts, and figures, but focusing upon modes of thinking and feeling. Practically, an educational ideal of *vivencia* formed the core of methods such as Decroly's centres of interest as well as related models such as the German *Erlebnisschule* or 'experiential school', one model among many held up by Spanish pedagogues.[82] Verdier praised the New School movement for attempting to re-evaluate the relationship between knowledge and intelligence and cited the *Erlebnisschule*, along with the Decroly Plan and other models of active learning, as methods which would awake true learning through biological engagement. For Verdier, the *vivencia* was what was left after all analysis was done. Experience transformed quantitative analyses into qualitative understandings. Finally, he hinted at a much wider concern among teachers of the early twentieth century, that is, the role of testing in a broader understanding of ability and value. While psychometric measures were becoming ubiquitous, Verdier suggested that evaluation should be kept to a proper scope and orbit.[83] This was a plea that rigid definitions of intelligence not define the child. The sentiment echoed through the New Education movement, which aimed to see the school not as 'una fábrica de *embotellar* conocimientos' [a factory for *bottling* knowledge], but rather for cultivating it.[84]

Defences of the physical, mental, and spiritual responsibilities of educators were features of authoritative works on pedagogy during the Second Republic. In the *Diccionario de Pedagogía* (1936), a two-volume, encyclopaedic work, one particular entry explores the relationship between 'Biología y pedagogía', echoing Ortega's 1921 publication of the same name. These two concepts were critically linked. As the entry notes, man 'como unidad físico-psíquica' was inevitably limited by his physical body.[85] Environmental and internal factors were critical, but ultimately, education should tend towards a 'liberación' from the *merely* biological. More to the point, the methods employed by biological study must not be extended to the larger ethical, cultural, or intellectual aspects of education — all those qualities that distinguished humans from other organisms. Education was not a purely empirical enterprise. While biological needs dominated the first months of life, these authors challenged the view that 'el recién nacido no es más que "un pequeño animal"' [the newborn is little more than a 'small animal'], arguing instead for a humanist view of human development.[86] While hygienicist and medical views of the child's body were critical, these diminished in comparative importance as the child's psychical life became ever more complex. It was upon this interplay of biology and the psyche that pedagogues should focus, the entry suggested. For this reason, any attempts to create a 'biological ethics' of pedagogy, the authors argued, would be in vain. For the aim of pedagogy — and this was the crux of the issue — was to form a sound individual in all respects: 'físico-psíquico-unitario'.[87] Pedagogy that was conscious of its relationship with the human sciences, a pedagogy that had 'ambiciones intelectuales', must avoid too close a reliance on biological method. Neither a purely divine conception of man was helpful, nor a purely biological one: 'Una psicología meramente naturalista o biológica sería monstruosa' [A merely naturalist or biological psychology would be monstrous].[88]

This was a marked declaration of intellectual humanism within modern pedagogy. New educationalists sought an elusive balance between the biological and the spiritual. Teachers such as Verdier recognized and drew attention to competing impulses within pedagogy, which held up science as a panacea for understanding the child. Drawing on an alternate line of circulating holistic approaches in the 'new' psychology and biology of education, they looked to construct a bridge between the body's physical unity and the equally important shaping of mind and spirit. Across a psycho-biological field of experimentation, from Tenerife to Barcelona, and the psycho-pedagogical field from Geneva to Brussels to Madrid, an educational notion of *vivencia* was posed as the spiritual and physical engagement with one's own lived world. While basing his claims on experimental work, Verdier and other humanistic advocates in the field of New Education recognized the limits of empiricism and actively sought to counter them in their classroom engagements. Drawing on a wave of holistic thought represented by the Gestaltists, Uexküll, and others, an intellectually-oriented vanguard of educators from Ortega to Verdier argued that hermetic interpretations of biological and physical research must not govern education. Rather, society must remain alert to the cultural, sociological, and historical factors that shaped individual development, and as the following chapter will suggest, draw these into the classroom through active and sensorial games, stories, myth, dialogue, and the arts. Combining intense interest in these 'new' sciences with an unmistakable critique of purely quantitative and empirical views of the body, a humanistic perspective articulated by intellectuals and teachers alike sought to delineate the limits and promises of modern pedagogy.

Notes to Chapter 3

1. José Lasaga, 'El mono fantástico (Notas sobre la "ciencia del hombre" de Ortega)', *Revista de Occidente*, 384 (2013), 5–22 (p. 8).
2. Ángel Llorca, 'Notas educativas escritas en 1942 para el proyecto de libro *La educación vivida*', Document 34, Archivo Digital 'Los viejos papeles' (Madrid: Fundación Ángel Llorca, 1890–1933), <http://www.fundacionangelllorca.org/materiales/archivo-digital-viejos-papeles> [accessed 1 September 2018]. On Llorca's critical place in the educational landscape, see María del Mar del Pozo Andrés, 'Ángel Llorca: un maestro entre la Institución Libre de Enseñanza y la escuela nueva (1866–1942)', *Historia de la Educación*, 6 (1987), 229–48.
3. See, for example, Antonio de Zulueta, 'Herencia y ambiente', *Revista de Pedagogía*, 6.69 (1927), 420–26; Enrique Suñer Ordóñez, *Herencia y educación* (Madrid: n.p., 1932); and Margarita Comas, 'L'herència i el medi en l'educació', *Revista de Psicologia y Pedagogia*, 1.4 (1933), 422–30.
4. Juarros, *Educación física y moral del niño*, p. 42. Juarros refers to the early scientific management theories known as 'Taylorism', suggesting that such principles applied prudently could aid the child's intellectual and material development. In contrast to vitalist depictions of the individual and social body he used explicitly mechanistic terms in his depiction of education, writing that 'autonomía' did not imply 'aislamiento' [isolation], as each individual part of a machine carries out a crucial and interconnected role. On Taylorism in Spain, including Mira y López's involvement, see Mauro F. Guillén, *Models of Management: Work, Authority, and Organization in a Comparative Perspective* (Chicago: University of Chicago Press, 1994), pp. 159–60.
5. José Eleizegui López, *Biología de la edad escolar* (Madrid: [Saez Hermanos], 1929), p. 7. See also Margarita Comas, 'Algunos problemas biológicos', *Revista de Pedagogía*, 12 (1933), 211–17. On the historiography of hygienic reform in Spain, see, for instance, *Historia de la infancia*, ed. by José María Borrás Llop, which focuses almost exclusively on social conditions, including mortality, literacy, child labour, and delinquency.
6. Michael Richards, 'Spanish Psychiatry c. 1900–1945: Constitutional Theory, Eugenics, and the Nation', *Bulletin of Spanish Studies*, 81.6 (2004), 823–48 (p. 823).
7. Herbert Spencer, *The Principles of Sociology*, 3 vols (New York: D. Appleton, 1897), I; Adolphe Ferrière, *La ley biogenética y la escuela activa*, trans. by Lorenzo Luzuriaga (Madrid: Publicaciones de la Revista de Pedagogía, 1928). On Hispanic comparisons of school as organism see Vicente López, 'La escuela, embrión social', *Revista de Pedagogía*, 8.89 (1929), 208–14 (pp. 209–10). Ferrière suggested that education must rely on biological interests, understanding the child as transitioning from primitive to civilized. This transition had four phases: sensory (early childhood), imitation (later childhood), intuition (adolescence), and reason (youth and maturity). On applications to the New Education Fellowship, see Daniel Hameline, 'Adolphe Ferrière (1879–1960)', *Prospects: The Quarterly Review of Comparative Education*, 33.1–2 (2000), 373–401.
8. Manuel García Morente, 'El mundo del niño', in *Obras completas, 1906–1936*, 4 vols (Barcelona: Anthropos, 1996), I, 217–33 (p. 219).
9. August Pi i Sunyer, *Classics of Biology*, trans. by Charles M. Stern (London: Sir Isaac Pitman & Sons, 1955), pp. 316–19. See also August Pi i Sunyer, Jesús M. Bellido, and Pedro Nubiola, *La doctrina de las secreciones internas*, 2nd edn (Barcelona: Instituto Bioquímico 'Hermes', 1919).
10. Pi i Sunyer, *La unidad funcional*, I, 129–69. In a 1955 anthology, Pi i Sunyer would publish works by Spanish philosophers Ortega y Gasset, García Morente, Xirau, and Unamuno and scientists such as Ramón y Cajal and Turró, alongside intellectuals from Aristotle, Descartes, and St Augustine to Erwin Schrödinger, Ivan Pavlov, Freud, and Bergson.

11. Nóvoa Santos's works would make a fitting complement to a larger study of early biological and medical holisms. See, for example, Roberto Nóvoa Santos: *El problema del mundo interior* ([Santiago de Compostela]: s.n., 1920); *Physis y psyquis: fragmentos para una doctrina genética y energética del espíritu* (Santiago de Compostela: El Eco de Santiago, 1922); and *Cuerpo y espíritu: fragmentos para una doctrina genética y energética del espíritu* (Madrid: Compañía Ibero-Americana de Publicaciones, [1930]).

12. Verdier, 'La pedagogía y la crisis', p. 158.

13. Víctor Mercante, 'Correlación inversa de las crisis físicas e intelectuales', *Revista de Pedagogía*, 7.80 (1928), 362–68 (p. 362).

14. Verdier, *De Uexküll a Decroly*, pp. 27–28.

15. Ibid. This was a crisis famously named by Nicolas Kostyleff; see Kostyleff, *La crisis de la psicología experimental*, ed. by Domingo Barnés (Madrid: Daniel Jorro, 1922). This rhetoric of crisis across the sciences had a clear convergence with Ortega's thought, as explicated in a series of lectures at the University of Madrid in 1933, published in 1942; see Ortega y Gasset, 'En torno a Galileo'.

16. José Ortega y Gasset, 'El medio vital', in *El espectador*, III, 168–73 (p. 192). See also José Ortega y Gasset, *Personas, obras, cosas* (Madrid: Renacimiento, 1916), particularly his discussion of social pedagogy from Plato to Pestalozzi to Paul Natorp (pp. 227–31) and the ethical values of not just a social but a *socialist* pedagogy responding to a two-tiered system of rich and poor, educated and uneducated, human and sub-human. The creation of a just public education system was the work of a true democracy (p. 233).

17. Wolfgang Köhler, 'El problema de la psicología de la forma', *Anales de la Sección de Orientación Profesional de la Escuela de Trabajo [Barcelona]*, 3.3 (1930), 57–103 (p. 57).

18. Palmés, 'La psicología gestaltista', p. 33. In 1922 Palmés had visited Köhler, Koffka, and Wertheimer at the University of Berlin, the seat of Gestalt psychology, during a study tour of laboratories of experimental psychology, as he later recounted to the Spanish public; see Ferrán María Palmés, 'Hacia la psicología experimental: impresiones de un viaje de estudios', *Ibérica*, 475 (1923), 267–71. For more on Palmés's psychological work within a Catholic institution, see Alicia Peralta Serrano, 'El Padre Ferrán Ma. Palmés y el laboratorio de psicología experimental del Colegio Máximo San Ignacio de Sarriá de Barcelona', *Revista de Historia de la Psicología*, 15.3–4 (1994), 461–75.

19. Köhler, 'El problema de la psicología de la forma', p. 64.

20. Ibid., pp. 64–65.

21. José Ortega y Gasset, 'La inteligencia de los chimpancés', *El Sol*, 23 April 1927, p. 3. See notice of the lecture in, among others, Anon., 'El profesor Kohler [*sic*]', *La Época*, 6 April 1927, p. 4.

22. Köhler, 'El problema de la psicología de la forma', p. 58.

23. Ortega y Gasset, 'La inteligencia de los chimpancés', p. 3.

24. Ibid.

25. Piaget, *El estructuralismo*, p. 71.

26. Ortega y Gasset, 'La inteligencia de los chimpancés', p. 3.

27. Ibid. Barnés had earlier made a similar claim about the child's scientific nature, seeking to discover 'que late insaciable en toda su actitud inquisitiva, y en su complicación creciente llega hasta el concreto espíritu de indagación del científico' [what beats insatiably behind all his inquisitive attitude, which in its increasing complexity attains the scientist's concrete spirit of investigation]: Domingo Barnés Salinas, 'La función biológica de la infancia', *Boletín de la Institución Libre de Enseñanza*, 46.743 (1922), 41–51 (p. 39).

28. Barnés Salinas, 'La función biológica de la infancia', p. 43. Such a comparison was longstanding. One of the first Spanish paidological texts, Manuel Tolosa Latour's *El niño: apuntes científicos* (Madrid: s.n., 1880), p. 144, held to a romantic notion of the innocent child for whom father and teacher must act as 'popularizadores de la ciencia'. In 1918, psychiatrist César Juarros argued that the child's natural curiosity was at the root of a scientific mind, that it 'trae consigo la siembra del hábito de la investigación científica' [brings with it the seed of habit of scientific research]: *Educación física y moral del niño en la familia como preparación de su futuro desenvolvimiento integral* (Madrid: Imprenta Artística, Sáez Hermanos, 1918), p. 42.

29. Ortega, 'La inteligencia de los chimpancés', p. 3.

30. Ibid.

31. Thomas S. Kuhn, *The Structure of Scientific Revolutions* (Chicago: University of Chicago Press, 1970), p. 88.

32. Ortega y Gasset, 'En torno a Galileo', p. 16.

33. While Domingo Barnés and Juan Comas were the first to translate Piaget, his chief interlocutors in Spain during the 1920s and 1930s were arguably Mercedes Rodrigo (1891–1982) and Père (Pedro) Rosselló (1897–1970). Rodrigo was Spain's first female doctor of psychology, Piaget's classmate at Geneva's Institut Jean-Jacques Rousseau, and author of significant 1923 adaptations of psychometric tests with Rosselló. At the time of Ortega's writing, she was pedagogical director at Lafora's Instituto Médico-Pedagógico in Carabanchel, Madrid. Rosselló epitomizes the internationalism of Spanish reform pedagogy: in 1927 he became a lecturer in Geneva, collaborating with Piaget, Claparède, and Pierre Bovet from 1929 to turn the International Bureau of Education into the world's first inter-governmental institution of education. See Fania Herrero, 'Mercedes Rodrigo (1891–1982), la primera psicóloga española', *Revista de Psicología General y Aplicada,* 56.2 (2003), 139–48, and for an early collaboration with Piaget, see Jean Piaget and Pedro Rosselló, 'Note sur les types de description d'images chez l'enfant', *Archives de Psychologie,* 18.3–4 (1922), 209–10.

34. Jean Piaget, *The Child and Reality: Problems of Genetic Psychology,* trans. by Arnold Rosin (New York: Viking Press, 1974), p. 6.

35. Jean Piaget, 'El nacimiento de la inteligencia en el niño', *Revista de Pedagogía,* 5.60 (1926), 529–36 (pp. 534–36).

36. Ortega y Gasset, 'La inteligencia de los chimpancés', p. 3.

37. Bergson described intelligence and instinct as two complementary and interpenetrating qualities which maintained a crucial distance: 'what is instinctive in instinct being opposite to what is intelligent in intelligence': *Creative Evolution,* trans. by Arthur Mitchell (London: Macmillan, 1911), p. 11.

38. Ortega y Gasset, 'La inteligencia de los chimpancés', p. 3.

39. Ibid.

40. For instance, see historian Rafael Altamira's marking of the centenary of Pestalozzi's death by chronicling the creation of a circulating library and championing his values, including humanism, thought and action, personal development, and social justice; see Rafael Altamira, Luis de Zulueta, and Alfredo Jara Urbano, *Pestalozzi en Albacete* (Albacete: Imprenta de Sebastián Ruíz, 1932).

41. On this alleged inheritance, see Laura Otis, *Organic Memory: History and the Body in the Late Nineteenth and Early Twentieth Centuries* (Lincoln: University of Nebraska Press, 1994).

42. Verdier, 'Aprendizaje y cultura', pp. 298–99.

43. Verdier, 'La pedagogía y la crisis', p. 158.

44. Ibid. This was a project which would only be realized in 1941, if merely in name, when an Instituto de Pedagogía was created under the Consejo Superior de Investigaciones Científicas (CSIC), populated by the resources of the ILE's former Museo Nacional de Pedagogía.

45. Emilio Ortega Berenguer, 'El problema educativo en la Segunda República', *Jábega,* 24 (1978), 29–32 (p. 32).

46. On involvement with the Frente Popular see Hilario Jiménez Gómez, *Alberti y García Lorca: la difícil compañía* (Madrid: Renacimiento, 2014), p. 242. Verdier's post-war works include *La enseñanza de la ortografía en la escuela primaria* (Madrid: Diana, Artes Graficas, 1963) and *Zurdera y destreza* (Málaga: Instituto de Cultura, 1969).

47. For Spanish reception, see Jakob von Uexküll, *Ideas para una concepción biológica del mundo,* trans. by R. M. Tenreiro (Madrid: Calpe, 1922), p. 5.

48. Ortega y Gasset, 'El medio vital', in *El espectador,* III, 168–72.

49. García Morente, 'El mundo del niño' p. 51.

50. Verdier, *De Uexküll a Decroly,* pp. 9–10.

51. See Chapter 1, and specifically Causí, 'La globalización de Decroly y la psicología de la estructura', p. 294.

52. Jakob von Uexküll, *Bausteine zu einer biologischen Weltanschauung: gesammelte Aufsätze,* ed. by Felix Gross (Munich: Bruckmann, 1913), p. 20.

53. Ibid., pp. 20–21.

54. Verdier, *De Uexküll a Decroly*, pp. 12–13.
55. Uexküll, *Bausteine zu einer biologischen Weltanschauung*, p. 21.
56. Uexküll, *Ideas para una concepción biológica del mundo*, p. 9.
57. Ibid., p. 13.
58. Uexküll, *Bausteine zu einer biologischen Weltanschauung*, p. 29.
59. August Pi i Sunyer, *Dispersa y conjunta (ensayos)* (Caracas: C.A. Artes Gráficas, 1945), p. 115.
60. Verdier, *De Uexküll a Decroly*, p. 27.
61. David Bayón, 'Libros: *De Uexküll a Decroly*', *Escuelas de España*, 3.4 (1931), 95–97 (p. 97).
62. Ibid., p. 95.
63. Verdier, *De Uexküll a Decroly*, p. 23.
64. Notices of Decroly and his method appeared in the press as early as 1918, in vehicles such as the *Boletín de la Institución Libre de Enseñanza*; see Juan Mainer Baqué, *La forja de un campo profesional: pedagogía y didáctica de las ciencias sociales en España, 1900–1970* (Madrid: CSIC, 2009), p. 748. Works on the Decroly classroom in Spain exploded in the years following; see, for example, Ángel Rodríguez Mata, 'La escuela de Decroly y el método activo', *Revista de Pedagogía*, 1.3 (1922), 86–89; L. Dalhem, *El método Decroly aplicado a la escuela* ([Madrid]: La Lectura, 1924); Florentino Rodríguez y Rodríguez, 'El método Decroly', *Anales de la Junta para Ampliación de Estudios e Investigaciones Científicas*, 18.16 (1925), 295–319; Rodolfo Llopis, *La pedagogía de Decroly* (Madrid: La Lectura, 1927); Antonio Ballesteros y Usano, *El método Decroly* (Madrid: Publicaciones de la Revista de Pedagogía, 1928); Gérard Boon, *Aplicación del método Decroly a la enseñanza primaria y la instrucción obligatoria*, trans. by Rodolfo Tomás y Samper (Madrid: Francisco Beltrán, 1926); Anna Rubiés, *Aplicación del método Decroly a la enseñanza primaria* (Madrid: Publicaciones de la Revista de Pedagogía, 1929); and Clotilde Guillén de Rezzano, *Los centros de interés en la escuela* (Madrid: Publicaciones de la Revista de Pedagogía, 1929).
65. Within the *Hemeroteca Digital* of the Biblioteca Nacional de España, Decroly is cited more than five hundred times during the period 1918–36. Admittedly, a good number of these instances were sports results from the Colegio Decroly's matches within a Madrid children's league. Founded by Ladislao Palenzuela in northern Chamberí, the school under Decroly's name operated from 1927 (and continues today).
66. See, for instance, José Xandri Pich, *Niñerías: primer libro de lectura y lenguaje: grado preparatorio* (Madrid: [s.n.], 1943). Xandri Pich, newly graduated from the Escuela de Estudios Superiores de Magisterio and appointed to direct Madrid's *escuelas graduadas*, had received the first of numerous *becas* from the JAE in 1921 to study primary schools in France, Belgium, and Switzerland, experiences from which his expertise draws; see Teresa Marín Eced, *Innovadores de la educación en España: becados de la Junta para Ampliación de Estudios* ([Ciudad Real]: Universidad de Castilla-La Mancha, 1991), p. 354.
67. José Xandri Pich, *Concentraciones: cuarto y quinto grado o grado medio de la escuela primaria*, I: Letras (Madrid: Tipografía Yagües, 1932), p. 11.
68. Simplistically, this was Bergson's suggestion in *L'Évolution créatrice* (1907) about human consciousness: that it is as eternally creative and regenerative as the universe. Unamuno too delighted in the linguistic play of this word: '¡Hermosa palabra ésta de re-crear! El vocablo re-creación, aplicado al juego, lleva en sus entrañas la doctrina toda de Schiller sobre el Arte, re-creación de la creación' [Lovely word, this re-creation! The word re-creation, applied to play, carries in its innermost being Schiller's entire doctrine of art, the re-creation of creation]: *En torno al casticismo*, p. 40.
69. Verdier, 'Aprendizaje y cultura', p. 296.
70. Ibid.
71. Ibid., p. 297.
72. See in this context the discussion of spirit in Part III.
73. Verdier, 'Aprendizaje y cultura', p. 297.
74. Ibid., p. 298.
75. Ibid. In similar terms, Ortega's early aesthetic writings described the 'misticismo' [mysticism] inherent in vision: when one sees a swath of a faded colour, it is simultaneously imbued with all the layers and resonances of its former richness, as time enlarges and expands one's present moment of perceptual experience; see Ortega y Gasset, *Meditaciones del Quijote*, p. 82.

76. Verdier, 'Aprendizaje y cultura', p. 298.

77. Emilio Mira y López, 'Pruebas para la determinación de los tipos de inteligencia en los niños', *Archivos de Neurobiología, Psicología, Fisiología, Histología, Neurología y Psiquiatría*, 7.1 (1927), 3–37 (p. 3).

78. José Ortega y Gasset, 'El ser no es individuo biológico', in *Personas, obras, cosas*, pp. 217–20 (p. 217).

79. Verdier, 'Aprendizaje y cultura', p. 300.

80. Ibid., p. 299.

81. Rafael Verdier, 'Filosofía y educación', *Escuelas de España*, 2.1 (1930), 33–53 (pp. 40–41).

82. The *Arbeitsschule* or *escuela del trabajo*, such as that of German pedagogue Gustav Wyneken, brought together young people from wealthy as well as modest backgrounds within a 'free community', seeking to level social classes and inequality of birth; see Anon., *La Escuela de Wickersdorf* (Madrid: La Lectura, 1926). The social-pedagogical aims of the *Arbeitsschule* were arguably antithetical to the fascist resonances with which it could be read today. See, for example, José Mallart y Cutó, *Escuelas-asilos de artes y oficios para niños pobres, huérfanos y abandonados: su organización práctica y útil* (Madrid: Imprenta de la Ciudad Lineal, 1926), *La escuela del trabajo* (Madrid: Revista de Pedagogía, 1928), and *Colonias de educación* (Madrid: Revista de Pedagogía, 1931).

83. Verdier, 'Aprendizaje y cultura', p. 301.

84. José Mallart y Cutó, *La educación activa*, 4th edn (Barcelona: Editorial Labor, 1935), p. 98.

85. 'Biología y Pedagogía', in *Diccionario de pedagogía*, ed. by Sánchez Sarto, I, 432.

86. Ibid.

87. Ibid.

88. Ibid., pp. 433–34.

CHAPTER 4

Infans Ludens:
Children at the Vanguard of Play

La razón de ser niño el niño, es este, su estado de juego.
[The child's *raison d'être* is this, his state of play.]

José Bergamín, 'La decadencia del analfabetismo' (1933)

Early twentieth-century representations of children's play were founded on declarations of their very being, as the above epigraph by José Bergamín suggests. Reflections upon children's needs and behaviours went hand-in-hand with observations of their spatial and sensorial development. As did colleagues abroad, Spanish pedagogues studied play, reflexes, and behavioural changes in efforts to adapt education to children's perceptual and biological experience. Never before had medical, psycho-biological conceptions of the child's body been so central to educational theory and practice. Building upon new theories of perception, teachers looked to structure the classroom around active contact between child and environment. From early movements in the cradle to boisterous games in the schoolyard, from Fröbelian blocks to Montessori objects, learning was a process of contact and engagement. Studies of children's sensorial primacy, in turn, drew from representations of the child as other. Whether tracking eye movements in response to stimulation or drawing up charts marking children's abilities to grasp or select objects, early developmental psychologists worked to ascertain how children moved from an early egotism towards full engagement in the adult world. These efforts connected to larger conceptions of society. As the philosopher Julián Izquierdo Ortega wrote in 1935 in an analogy of the human struggle for knowledge, 'El niño aprende cómo son las cosas tanteando, ensayando, luchando con ellas, asimilándoselas' [the child learns about things by touching, probing, struggling with them, assimilating them].[1] Through an active process of growth and engagement with the world, the child represented the very core of humanization.

This process of sensorial integration was what the novelist Benjamín Jarnés called, in a 1928 fictional narration of a child's walk to school, a 'teoría de contactos' of perceptual experience.[2] This chapter examines precisely such a discourse of contact through play, first theoretically and then via representative examples of practice. It begins with the extensive play theory explored both in Spain and beyond, enacted in open-air and active school methods. As a frame for re-evaluating these practices, it analyses the essayistic contributions of teacher Teodoro Causí and philosopher Manuel García Morente. Teacher and philosopher alike looked towards a conception of play that was not purely medical or utilitarian, but existential: of play as an innate reflection of the child's essential being. From here I consider the sensorial bases on which play was centred: from Jarnés's narration of a 'contact theory' of development towards a paidological grounding that argued in favour of touch and haptic play. In concluding, the chapter examines three paradigmatic case studies of sensorial pedagogies in Spain, namely those of the aforementioned Maria Montessori, Catalan pioneer Rosa Sensat i Vilà (1873–1961), and lesser-known educator Margarita Aranda Baciero in Madrid.[3] From 1914 until 1936, across varying frames and scales, each of these women led schools which prioritized the child's physical exploration of objects, sensations, and the natural world. Together, such cases suggest converging lines of pedagogical engagement around the child's physical body and tactile sensibility.

Above all, sensorial education gestured at larger humanist concerns about the role of the individual in society. Increasingly, a perceived division between artistic and technical education loomed. Defining the human senses and their 'education' or cultivation in 1936, the authoritative *Diccionario de pedagogía* attributed society's recent interest in sensorial education to the rise of the Machine Age. It argued that individual sensorial attenuation was a paradoxical consequence of the steady mechanization of life. For the Machine Age, even as it became highly technical, demanded increased attention and a finer differentiation of the senses — and this, indeed, was what the self-directed aspects of sensorial, play-based, and art education were seen to provide.[4] As Jarnés's 1928 'teoría de contactos' suggested within a literary frame, the base of children's integration in the world was direct and dynamic contact with objects and environment. Through play, active learning, and pedagogies of sensorial engagement, the line from primitive, natural, and integrated experience to scientific, attuned modern method was drawn.

The Pluriverse of the Child: Play from Causí to García Morente

As the poet Jorge Guillén wrote in 1923, there was no reason, no 'por qué' behind laughter: it simply *was*.[5] In the same vein, paidologists explored the nature of childhood through biological and sociological theories of play, moving toward a recognition of these theories' inherent limits.[6] Play, as the Aragonese schoolteacher Teodoro Causí wrote, radiated spontaneously from the child, 'como toda vitalidad orgánica emerge del fondo de un protoplasma' [as all organic vitality emerges from the depths of a protoplasm].[7] While its purpose remained unclear, theorists considered play an essential factor in the development of the child and indeed humanity as a whole. Focusing upon Causí's treatise on the biological science of play, this section analyses some of the major considerations concerning child's play, including those put forward by Manuel García Morente, whose exploration of the alleged 'world of the child' anchors this book.[8] As with Guillén's laughter above, García Morente suggested that a discourse of 'purpose' was meaningless: play simply *was.* This argument lay at the heart of the biological understanding of pedagogy. As García Morente argued, play existed because children were growing beings. Play was most essentially a reflection of the child's total phenomenological experience, what he called not the *universe*, but the imaginative *pluriverse* of the child.

This was a revision of prevailing views of play as having quantifiable and concrete ends. Chief among these was physical and mental training. Through the late nineteenth and early twentieth centuries, paidologists had undertaken a studied revival of play. Pedagogues such as Granadan priest and teacher Andrés Manjón advocated play above all other pursuits: 'de 0 a 5 años, el juego es la única asignatura; de 5 a 10 años, la asignatura más importante; de 10 a 15, necesaria, y de 15 en adelante conveniente' [from 0 to 5 years, play is the only subject; from 5 to 10 years, the most important subject; from 10 to 15, necessary, and from 15 onwards, advisable].[9] Others treated play in a more utilitarian manner, as tools for which to better understand reaction and result. The civil planner and inventor Arturo Soria y Mata (1844–1920), for instance, claimed that games functioned as 'pequeños talentómetros' [little talentometers], posing play as a way to measure infantile genius and future professional aptitude.[10] Early twentieth-century educators drew on the work of international scholars such as the German psychologist Karl Groos (1861–1946), whose monograph *Die Spiele der Tiere* [The Play of Animals] (1896) argued that play served clear evolutionary, preparatory functions for the organism, and, as extrapolated, for the child.

By Spain's *fin de siècle,* an ideal of vitality, health, and exploration had become both medicalized and nationally apropos. From 1900 paidologists such as César Juarros (1879–1942) and José Eleizegui López (1879–1956) wrote 'medical-pedagogical' guides for teachers and parents, drawing on the theories of Groos and others to instruct on ideal educational games to help their children learn. Moving these theories of development into the classroom, the teacher Ricardo Rubio noted that Spain's schools suffered from a lack of formalized play: 'Y es que nuestros niños no saben jugar. Aprenden algunas cosas: a leer, a escribir, "se saben" la Gramática; pero nadie se ha preocupado de dirigir y fomentar la enseñanza del juego' [For our children do not know how to play. They learn certain things: to read, to write, grammar; but nobody has bothered to direct and promote the teaching of play]. This larger effort of encouraging playtime came bundled with regenerationist rhetoric. Rubio, for instance, suggested in line with post-1898 declarations that the vital energy of the Spanish 'raza' was depleted. Rather than succumb to *abulia,* vigorous activity must be undertaken in schools as both a preventative measure and a cure. Play allegedly stimulated children's natural energy stores and invigorated exhausted bodies; animated the imagination and awakened the dormant mind; and brought moral 'salvation' through exercise and the open air.[11]

Such logic proved a driving force in the introduction of play-based methods in Spain. Lorenzo Luzuriaga, founder of the *Revista de Pedagogía*, used precisely such reasoning to argue in 1918 that current educational thought demanded a solid biological foundation. He concluded that research on energy, vitality, and play should act as a spur to action in the national educational field: 'ya que nuestra raza parece actualmente hallarse desprovista de esa cantidad mínima de biología, de energía vital' [given that our race now seems to be devoid of that minimal amount of biology, of vital energies]. In order to understand the effects of education, Luzuriaga surmised, one must study children as thoroughly as we do plants or any other organisms. What were their natures? What were their laws of inheritance and diversity? How did they develop? What threats prejudiced their growth — anxiety, fear, pain, or even excessive mental strain? And what interventions could counteract these forces? Principally, Luzuriaga concluded, the world of education had come to realize that the necessary treatment and preventative was play: 'el juego, que es uno de los mejores y más armoniosos medios de desarrollar las capacidades' [play, which is one of the best and most harmonious means of developing capabilities].[12]

Play defined the biological nature of childhood, but in ways that arguably went beyond pure function. If every organ was defined by its function, what role did childhood play in the development of human life? This was a question taken up by *institucionista* figures such as Luzuriaga and Barnés, among others, through not only physiological but also increasingly existential lenses. Only by understanding childhood as a unique phase of life, with its own temporality, stages, and values, could play be valued as a 'continua y fecunda experiencia' [a continuous, rich experience]. This abstract entity of 'childhood' was to be answerable not to social, religious, or ethical concerns nor to the 'artificial' pedagogical ideals of the educator, but only to the biological necessities of the individual child.[13] Building upon Ortega's 'Biología y pedagogía', readings of Uexküll's biology, and Claparède's psychology, Barnés followed convention in describing play as an initial unregulated discharge of excess energy, working as a 'prototype' of spontaneous activity for later life. Yet over time, he suggested, play took on a new character, ever more organized, intelligent, and coordinated, as human personality took shape: 'el niño, jugando e imitando, va desplegando, ensayando y tomando posesión de su personalidad indecisa, fragmentaria e instintiva primeramente, cada vez más precisa, unitaria y consciente después' [the child, playing and imitating, displaying, testing, and taking possession of his indeterminate personality, initially fragmentary and based on instinct, but becoming ever more precise, unified, and aware]. This view of child's play held to the contention that play, whatever its biological roots, promoted the social and imaginative individual and human development of the child.[14]

Paidologists employed a range of biological arguments to bring scientific validity to play-centred methods of learning. They celebrated early twentieth-century models such as open-air schools, heliotherapy, nature lessons, and the German *Arbeitsschule*, which in varying ways drew upon physical and sensorial activity, work, and play to strengthen body and mind. They also introduced active or 'functional' methods of education by New-Educational pedagogues such as José Mallart y Cutó. Mallart had spent the academic year 1915–16 in Geneva and was one of the most frequent visitors from Spain over the coming decade.

Mallart's on-the-ground studies at the Institut Jean-Jacques Rousseau, like those of many other visitors, radically influenced his advocacy. In both image and text, he promoted methods that incorporated physical activity, outdoors exploration,

FIG. 4.1. Children playing in Madrid's Parque del Oeste during the early 1930s.
Source: José Mallart y Cutó, *La educación activa*, 4th edn (Barcelona: Editorial
Labor, 1935), p. 91.

manual work, and play into the course of the school day. His numerous publications
on the movement are richly illustrated with images of European model schools and
Spanish schoolchildren at play, in fields, in forests, classrooms, and parks, as in the
image above from Madrid's Parque del Oeste during the 1930s (Fig. 4.1). According
to Mallart, education took place in primarily a biological sphere, 'biológica en su
más ancho sentido' [biological in the broadest sense], and had to focus chiefly on
'el campo de la vida' [the terrain of life], lived and experienced first-hand. Like
a tree on a mountainside, whose roots sought sustenance and whose branches
stretched towards sunlight, children's growth was built upon the constraints of their
environments: 'Desde el principio de nuestra existencia tenemos que adaptarnos
constantemente a las situaciones que nos impone el medio físico [...]. Todo tiende
a la vida, al desenvolvimiento de nuestra organización, a la expansión de nuestra
personalidad' [From the beginning of our existence we have to adapt constantly to
the situations imposed by the physical environment [...]. Everything tends to life, to
the development of our organization, to the expansion of our personality].[15] Whether
in work or in play, Mallart later wrote, the child was *biologically* predisposed towards
an expansion of the self through the sensorial: 'adelantando la mano para tentar
superficies, contornos, etc., o empujando para ver si puede ponerlos en movimiento'
[moving the hand forward to touch surfaces, contours, etc., or pushing to see if he
can set them in motion].[16]

It was this accepted fact of play's biological centrality in education that motivated
a sweeping treatise by teacher and school director Teodoro Causí, namely his

Bosquejo de una teoría biológica del juego infantil [Outline of a Biological Theory of Child's Play] published in 1924. Only since a post-Enlightenment recognition of man's value, Causí noted, could the meaning of childhood be fully explored. In turn, it was only by studying the child that a fuller understanding of humanity itself could be reached. Surveying influential works on play from Groos to Frederik J. J. Buytendijk (1887–1974), Causí considered the logical extensions of various theories of play.[17] Was play a genetic, atavistic holdover from an ancestral need, as Haeckel's biogenetic law would have it? Was it a form of training for future activity, as Groos suggested, which the developing child undertook spontaneously as preparation for life? Was it a form of bodily rest — a rejuvenation of energy — amidst exhaustive growth? Or was it meant to expel excess energy, helping to regulate the child's equilibrium? All these theories were explored in depth, but Causí's purpose was ultimately philosophical. He sought to put aside a purely utilitarian view and embrace an instrumentalist uncertainty, accepting that one could never truly explain the underlying roots of play. Play was at the heart of what it meant to be a child, and thus must be of central concern to educationalists and others alike. But it would remain inscrutable. The question of play, he suggested, was the very 'problema del niño, la expresión de su vitalidad, el centro de gravedad de toda la biología de la infancia' [problem of the child, the expression of his vitality, the gravitational centre of all biology of childhood.][18]

Causí connected child development to the process of scientific change. In making an argument for the essential nature of play, Causí cited and paraphrased Uexküll's *Bausteine zu einer biologischen Weltanschauung* in its 1922 Spanish translation, suggesting that life was not an adaptation to one's environment, but rather a selection of those elements which had a vital significance for the organism. Contrasting Uexküll with Darwin on selection and adaptation, Causí sought an overarching theory of play in the light of this 'new' biology of the 1920s. Specifically, he posited a new biological conception of play, thus engaging critically with shifting interpretations of theory and knowledge. It would be hard to find a neater paraphrase of Kuhn's subsequent notion of seismic shifts in scientific paradigms than this one put forward by Causí:

> Para que una teoría que pretende explicar un grupo determinado de hechos pueda sea aceptada, es preciso que no manifieste contradicción alguna con el sistema de idea de que forma parte, pues admitida la realidad científica del sistema, la interpretación de un grupo de hechos aislados no puede estar en oposición con los principios en que el sistema se basa, a menos que todo el edificio de la ciencia se resquebraje y amenace con un total derrumbamiento.[19]

> [For a theory that seeks to explain a particular set of facts to be accepted, it must not contravene any aspects of the idea-system of which it forms part. Once the scientific reality of a system is accepted, the interpretation of a set of isolated facts cannot stand in opposition to the principles on which the system is based, or the entire scientific edifice will crack and threaten total collapse.]

Causí's moment of scientific collapse was, prospectively, the crisis of which Kuhn famously wrote: the point at which a new theory rises to replace an old paradigm. For Causí, play was a prime example of science's potential for radical change. If theory held that play was a necessary stimulus for the healthy development of bodily organs (as had been argued), then the discovery that organs could develop perfectly well without play should bring that theory crashing down. Most fundamentally, he suggested, play could not be explained teleologically. A human's being and nature should not be considered a *result* of play. Rather, play simply happened; it was as inherent to a child's being as breathing. Causí relied on metaphors that connected play to natural laws:

> El movimiento de la Tierra sobre su eje nos proporciona la seguridad de una aurora, preludio del mediodía; pero ni el planeta se mueve para despertar de su sueño a los seres que en él viven, ni el amanecer tiene por objeto llegar a la hora del mediodía. El mediodía llegará [...] como el niño llegará a la madurez.[20]

> [The turning of the Earth on its axis gives us the security of a dawn, the prelude to midday; but the planet does not move in order to wake living beings from dreams, nor does the sunrise take noontime as its goal. High noon comes [...] as surely as the child arrives at maturity.]

For Causí play was a natural phenomenon, as regular and demonstrable as organic growth or physical reactions. His argument rested on its very biological normalcy. Nothing in the child's environment held meaning if it could not be turned into a vehicle for play. For that reason, play must be incorporated into culture itself: 'a hacer del juego, que para el niño es un fin en sí mismo, el medio educativo por excelencia, el vehículo de la cultura' [of transforming play, which is for the child an end in itself, into the educational medium par excellence, a vehicle of culture].[21]

Ultimately, Causí disputed the view that play served primarily as preparation for future development. A rabbit must not have 'conejeado' for *x* amount of time in order to become a *conejo*, nor a *gallina* have 'gallineado' to become a hen.[22] Play was an expression of growth and vitality which must become an instrument of culture. Child's play should not simply be tolerated alongside more 'intellectual' work. Rather, the work of humanizing the child meant adapting education to the child's natural mode of expression, and vice versa:

> Si el niño ha de humanizarse en la escuela, si cada día ha de incorporar a su ser substancia ideal de hombre hecho, solo podrá conseguirse a condición de que la pedagogía infantilice sus procedimientos, a condición de que su arte arranque del subsuelo de la vida del niño, donde el juego extiende sus raíces.[23]

> [If the child is to humanize himself at school, if each day he is to incorporate into his being the ideal substance of the grown man, pedagogy must infantilize its methods, it must draw from the substratum of the life of the child, where play extends its roots.]

Play was an end in itself, not a means 'for' something. It must be accepted as part of the child's natural function, around which smart and effective models of education would pivot. This humanization was at the core of both the new biology and a new theory of play. In order for the child to actively cultivate his or her own 'humanization', the educator must build a system that allowed for openness, experimentation, and physical contact with the world.

Whereas Causí, a teacher, explored the biological bases of play to argue for its scientific and cultural centrality, the philosopher García Morente made play central to a two-part series of articles he wrote in 1928, 'El mundo del niño', an exploration of the child's phenomenological nature. Centring on play, he suggested that the child viewed reality *not* as one fixed world, but as an instantaneous succession of worlds — all internally real and valid. Play both allowed this multiplicity and gave evidence to it, in the shifts and elisions of characters, realities, and contexts that children fluidly entertained. In this respect, García Morente's description of the child's world(s) owed a clear debt to the work of John Dewey. Translated by Barnés in 1926 as *La escuela y el niño*, Dewey's *The Child and the Curriculum* (1902) considered education through the child's eyes. Their world, Dewey posited, was 'a total and growing experience'.[24] Yet it was also a fluid and unstable totality, characterized by rapid transformations between state and attention:

> The child's life is an integral, a total one. He passes quickly and readily from one topic to another, as from one spot to another, but is not conscious of transition or break. There is no conscious isolation, hardly conscious distinction. The things that occupy him are held together by the unity of the personal and social interests which his life carries along. Whatever is uppermost in his mind constitutes to him, for the time being, the whole universe. That universe is fluid and fluent; its contents dissolve and re-form with amazing rapidity. But, after all, it is the child's own world. It has the unity and completeness of his own life.[25]

Throughout children's development, they were never conscious of ruptures in thought, only of the passing moment. With the entire world a total experience, traditional curricula 'fractionized' that mental fluidity: arithmetic divided it, geography abstracted it, grammar fractured it. As García Morente presented it, the life of a child was a continual alternation between states of work — these early moments of rupture — and play. The world of the child was one of constant variety, change, and transformation. Childhood was a time of 'tanteos, ensayos y pruebas' [trial and error, experimentation, and tests] before the straight course of professional adult life began. All of this 'disorientation' could be summed up by the concept of play, which he called childhood itself. In contrast to adulthood's emphasis on action and accomplishment, childhood was a time of pure being: 'la infancia es forzosamente la edad del ser siendo' [childhood is indubitably the age of the being's being].[26]

What was that state of play, for García Morente? Like Causí, he considered various theories of biological utility, but discarded these as inessential, irrelevant, and inconsequential to the essence of childhood. Failing to account for the rich 'psychological interiority' that play entailed, purely biological explanations of play proved insufficient. Rather than asking, as most pedagogues and medical doctors had done, 'que ventajas, consecuencias, efectos, etc., produce el juego?' [what advantages, consequences, effects, etc. does play produce?], García Morente suggested that one must dig deeper and inquire, rather, about the essential matter at hand: 'qué es el juego?' [what is play?]. According to him, play demonstrated an internal coherence within the child's world. This vision of play was not disconnected or random, a mere matter of chance or spontaneity, of mechanical reflexes or of the passing fancies of ideas. Rather, he described play as unified and meaningful: 'una actividad ordenada, reglada, reducida a un sistema, subordinada a una finalidad; es, en suma, una actividad que tiene un sentido, que es inteligible' [an ordered activity, regulated, reduced to a system, subordinated to an end; it is, in sum, an activity that has sense, that is intelligible]. Like an internally regulated system, the child's movements had their own logic. Likewise, the child's thoughts were not vague, capricious occurrences, but rather formed a coherent stucture within the child's mind. Play was a meaningful activity, possessing its own finality.[27] But its purpose remained indefinable.

Ultimately, García Morente suggested that the purpose of play was both circular and fundamental: as much as one searched for causes and intentions, there was nothing more than play itself. The player's actions were wholly oriented towards the act, creating 'un mundo cerrado y perfecto en sí' [a self-enclosed and perfect world].[28] In early childhood, in that purest form of play between self and world, he argued, one does not play to win, but simply to play. The child acted, not *para algo,* but simply *por jugar:*

> La niña, con su muñeca en brazos, la mece, le canta, le habla, le regaña, le pega, la consuela. Todos estos actos y pensamientos de la niña son perfectamente claros, inteligibles; están llenos de sentido; tienen una finalidad diáfana. Y, sin embargo, ¿para qué los hace y los piensa la niña? Para nada, por nada, porque sí, por jugar.[29]

> [The girl who cradles a doll rocks it, sings to it, speaks to it, scolds it, hits it, consoles it. All these acts and thoughts on the child's part are perfectly clear and intelligible. They have meaning and possess a clear finality. Yet, to what end does the girl do and think all this? For no reason, and because of no reason, but simply to play.]

Critics, he suggested, argued that play was frivolous falsehood or fantasy, while 'real' work was serious, anchored in reality, and dealt with verifiable ends and means. Such a dichotomy was false. For the child, all play was serious. Play constituted the most basic, 'primordial' form of life, indeed the most 'fecund', 'productive', and 'vital' activity possible.[30] What distinguished this productive work of play from true 'work', then, was its role within a dynamic system. It encompassed an endless series of moments in the child's conscious life, functioning and changing organically. Rather than simply 'playing', or playing 'a' game, he noted that children play 'games'. This plural was essential, as children moved continuously from one activity, one schema, to another. The constant evolution and fluctuation of play was as natural as physical change or biological growth. Just as the games changed across the seasons, so children transformed from one moment to the next. They imposed infinite and constantly-shifting variations of meaning upon words, toys, dolls, and all surrounding objects. Play was the act of imbuing meaning: giving 'un conjunto de cosas una serie indefinida de sentidos unívocos' [a group of things an unlimited number of unique meanings].[31]

Play overlay a philosophical problem of perception and recognition between mind, body, and world. As García Morente made clear, adults saw and understood chairs, tables, seats, books in one way; they had a fixed signification. For the child, these objects could transform completely, in being and essence, from moment to moment. Objects for the child were empty units of signification. This was why he ultimately claimed it impossible to speak of any one 'world of the child' (despite his own titular use of the phrase). The world of the child was many worlds, indeed infinite worlds: 'El mundo del juego — el mundo del niño — no es, pues, un mundo, sino muchos mundos, todos los mundos que al jugador se le ocurra evocar' [The world of play — the world of the child — is not, in the end, a world, but many worlds, as many worlds as the player thinks to evoke].[32] The child organized and re-organized its world in every moment. Following Dewey, García Morente proposed a notion of the child's mind based on total and radical shifts in state. Every conscious act served to restructure perceptions in a certain way; yet these same perceptions could be instantaneously substituted by new, equally valid ones. This was the essential contrast between 'universe' and 'pluriverse':

> El mundo del adulto es un *universo*, una unidad coherente, total, cuyas partes permanecen idénticas a sí mismas, con un sentido unívoco y constante, mientras que el mundo del niño es plural, no constituye un universo, sino un — por decirlo así — pluriverso, una pluralidad de mundos en inestable y efímera formación.[33]

> [The world of the adult is a *universe,* a coherent unity, total, whose parts remain identical to themselves, with a univocal and constant meaning, while the world of the child is plural; it does not constitute a universe, but rather — let's say — a pluriverse, a plurality of worlds in unstable and ephemeral formation.]

External realities imprinted themselves in a 'centripetal' manner upon the adult, becoming the base of rationality and objectivity, scientific and otherwise. Meanwhile the child's reality functioned in 'centrifugal' form, moving from inward to outward: the child transformed external reality into whatever he thought, felt, or desired. Rather than converging within the expansive limits of the adult *yo*, the child's fleeting worlds were 'irradiado por el yo' [irradiated by the self].[34]

Portrayals of children's perception and learning infiltrated all aspects of child studies during the first third of the twentieth century. A play-based reading of education solidified over this period, characterized by the incorporation of the influential work of pedagogues and psychologists, with interest in Spain signalled by events such as a well-received lecture on children's play by leading German developmental psychologist Charlotte Bühler at the Residencia de Estudiantes in 1933.[35] These discussions built on an essential dispute between the implications of various biological ideas of play: should play be understood as a means to an end, or an expression of the child's very nature? As has been seen, the teacher Causí argued, ultimately, for the latter; play was an expression of culture that must move reciprocally between child and society. García Morente nuanced this reading, via Dewey, to suggest that only play, understood in the most playful terms, could characterize the fluidity of the child's phenomenological world. Together, these works provide an essential counterpoint to medicalized claims that attempted to attribute pure reason and biological finality to play. These discussions, while never settled as such, made clear the significance of not only the — largely accepted — importance of play within modern education, but also differing modes of understanding its roots, purpose, and larger role in the 'humanization' of the child.

From Foreigner to *Flâneur*: A Sensorial Map of the Child's World

— ¡Sol, balón de fuego, arrojado al aire por los niños!
[— Sun, ball of fire, thrown into the air by children!]
Benjamín Jarnés, 'Un niño descalzo' (1928)

In a fragment published from his novel *El convidado de papel* [The Paper Guest] (1928), Benjamín Jarnés (1888–1949) conjured a barefoot boy named Adolfo whose walk to school was an overpowering experience of the senses. A descendent of an ancient 'savage' race from a time 'free of chronology' and made of 'metaphor', Adolfo and his contemporaries had lost their cosmic abilities and were now bound by the limits of their skin. Children like Adolfo were sensitively, precisely tuned sensorial receptors of the world around them. As Jarnés narrated, 'Sobre un ancho teclado de losas bruñidas, incrustadas entre ralas cenefas verdes, tañen los pies del niño una rara sinfonía' [Upon a wide keyboard of polished stones, inset between thin bands of green, a strange symphony peals from the child's footsteps], thereby incorporating a synesthetic portrayal of colour, texture, sensation and music in one brief narration that was, in compact literary form, an effective constellation of larger notions about the child's sensorial integration.[36] As Michel de Certeau has described, the process of auto-consolidation in the world was as much a separation from the mother's body, playing out of the experience of loss and recapture, presence and absence, proximity and distance, as it was the engagement of the body as a physical, independent whole. This practice of moving closer and further apart, making contact, and losing it again was at the base of that spatial coming-to-know of one's environment, whether that be a city or any extra-corporal context: 'To practice space is thus to repeat the joyful and silent experience of childhood; it is, in a place, *to be other and to move toward the other*'.[37] Within a frame of contact and return, Jarnés's and others' descriptions of the child's successive processes of sensorial integration looked towards modes of pre-rational sensorial perception as both a form of inward expansion and the incorporation of the outside world.

Reading Jarnés's portrayal of Adolfo's walk, a path he knew intimately and could trace by touch and feel, indicates the significance of sensory cues as a marker of early childhood nature and ability. As Adolfo walks, the stones beneath his feet burn. His steps take on the rhythm of a dance, a 'primitive' dance of fire. He knows every step of the way by muscle memory and sensorial integration: the crunching, rustling plants, the sparkling minerals of the pavement, the stark forms that cast shadows across his path. He continues his walk:

> El niño brinca por el teclado ardiente; aquieta un instante los pies en los guijarros menudos; se deja cosquillear por las cenefas verdes; hunde los dedos en la hierba sedosa, muelle; siente crujir bajo sus plantas fragmentos de teja convexa; desciende lentamente por la segunda rampa, y respira, al fin, acogido al triángulo de sombra. El niño llega al colegio después de rendir homenaje a un dios milenario y de aprender una ardua lección de sensibilidad.[38]

> [The boy hops along the burning keyboard; rests his feet a moment on tiny pebbles; lets himself be tickled by green bands; buries his fingers in the silky, pleasing grass; feels the crunching beneath him of fragments of convex tile;

slowly descends by the second ramp, and breathes, at last, within a cool triangle
of shade. The boy arrives at school having paid homage to a millenary god,
through an arduous lesson in sensibility.]

In contrast to the geometrical forms of this landscape, whether 'square', 'round',
or 'convex', the boy is all organic form. His path is guided by an innate sensorial
knowledge: which plants sting and which caress, how plants smell and move along
his route. He could trace this route by its various gradations: 'trazar un pintoresco
mapa de deleites epidérmicos' [trace a picturesque map of epidermal delights], an
imaginary, physical landscape he describes as ridged with deep canals, rough hills,
tough outer shells, and undulating veins. From the moment the child leaves home,
he devotes himself to the pleasure of sensorial contact: 'entrega plenamente su carne
a esta rica gama de cálidos contactos' [gives himself over to this rich range of warm
contacts]. He jumps, bounds, making 'bellas parábolas' [beautiful parabolas] over
the glinting stones. His walk through the world is limited to contact, a 'panorama
sensitivo' [sensorial panorama] of the world.[39]

This quality of touch was the building block of what Jarnés called in this passage
a 'pentágrama', which I read as the five senses of the child's mental and physical
development. Indeed, his descriptions extend across this sensorial panorama,
though with a clear primacy given to the haptic. Yet, in the narration, this primary
state of sensation cannot last indefinitely. As Jarnés's Adolfo moves from outside to
inside, the reader begins to see how a primary experience of the world gives way to
reason and knowledge. At school, the boy pulls out a book on agriculture. Inside
are stories of growing seeds, flying pollen, and entangled roots. He reads about a
plant he knows well: saffron, which he has glimpsed every day on his walks. But
he also encounters a term he doesn't know:

> — Criptógamas... Criptógamas...
> El niño no conoce las criptógamas. Cuando ve llegar al maestro, se le acerca
> y le pregunta.
> — ¿Qué son criptógamas?[40]

> ['Cryptogams... cryptogams...'
> The boy does not know cryptogams. When he sees the teacher arriving, he
> approaches him to ask:
> 'What are cryptogams?']

Moving from exterior to interior, towards new forms of processing the world,
Adolfo's early base of contact and sensation is contrasted with the development of
rational intellect. In Jarnés's representation of Adolfo's literary recapitulation of
human development, the child moves from 'primitive' towards rational and intellectual ability. The parallels to biogenetic law are clear, whether evoking early
nineteenth-century biological ideas of ontogeny recapitulating phylogeny — individual development mirroring the progress of ancestors — or Herbert Spencer's
application of such ideas to teaching, whence 'education shall be a repetition of
civilization in little'.[41] Building on a core of foundational texts that explored biological progress, reformers sought to ground their teaching in contact and sensation
during children's most sensitively-attuned years of reception and integration.

Jarnés's Adolfo was but one instance of a larger discussion of 'humanization' through contact with the world. From birth, the child was portrayed as moving from foreignness to familiarity, enclosure to engagement. Seeking to understand these points of contact, the Madrid paidologist Francisco Santamaría Esquerdó (1866–1925) in 1918 had described the child as, in essence, a *flâneur* within his own sensorial world. Infants learned their surroundings through intimate experience and physical contact by legs, hands, and fingers:

> Aquel niño que está en la cuna horas y horas palpándose las piernas y las manos, y mirándolas y volviéndolas a mirar, recuerda al extranjero que pasa el día dando vueltas por las calles, fijándose en las esquinas y detiéndose ante los edificios. Los dos, aunque parece que nada hacen, están haciendo mucho, están tanteando y tomando notas de sensaciones táctiles, musculares y visuales que luego les han de permitir decir con la rapidez de una intuición: en tal parte del cuerpo me han tocado, o por tal parte de la población debo andar ahora.[42]

> [The child lying in his cot for hours and hours, feeling his legs and hands, looking at them again and again, evokes the foreigner who spends his days wandering the streets, stopping at street corners and pausing before buildings. Both, while they do not appear to be doing anything, are doing very much indeed: they are feeling their way and taking note of tactile, muscular, and visual sensations that will allow them to say with the rapidity of intuition: I have been touched on this part of my body, or it is through this part of the city I should now walk.]

Mingling physical and geographical space with sensorial awareness, Santamaría expressed a deep appreciation for the complexity of the relationship between child and environment, self and world: tactile, muscular, and visual clues worked together in a unified process of sensorial integration. Just as a traveller notes the details of everyday life in a foreign city, walking the streets to engrave the city in memory, precisely so does the child learn his surroundings. Like Adolfo's mental map of his sensorial landscape, this imagined child probes, touches, moves, and responds to objects such that they form an indelible, intuitive, and functional mental whole. Santamaría thereby accorded these imagined infants physical agency, taking charge of their circumstances through actions, decisions, and engagements, and setting in motion a feedback loop of action and reaction, cause and effect, touch and sensation.

Such descriptions echoed through paidological discourse on the child. Whether comparing children to foreigners, explorers, animals, or 'primitives', paidologists employed countless ways of suggesting the 'otherness' of children's primary experience within a world of foreign sensory stimulation. As paidologist César Juarros wrote in 1918, play was a delight common to all infants, whose 'pleasure' in sensation could be observed anthropologically: 'A los bebés les encanta oír repiquetear sobre la mesa, silbar, mirar colores' [Babies love to hear clattering on the table, whistles, to look at colours].[43] The following year, the Basque priest, philosopher, and psychologist Juan Zaragüeta Bengoechea (1883–1974) used the image of the child encountering the sensations of the world as 'un viajero que abordara por vez primera ver regiones totalmente desconocidas' [a traveller who embarks for the first time in regions entirely unknown], thus appearing to adults as an unsuspecting 'encantador turista' [charming tourist].[44] The connection of primary sensation to, alternately, qualities such as innocence, the foreign or the underdeveloped proved a common thread that opened up rhetorical spaces for subsequent development and entry into a supposedly rational adult civilization. The paidologists Jaén and Peinado, in their 1935 manual of paidology, similarly described the newborn as a wide-eyed and disoriented peasant, encountering the world as a *campesino* would emerge from the metro to face the dizzying chaos of Madrid's Puerta del Sol.[45] In each of these varied descriptions of the child's earliest days, he or she enacted a form of contact with a foreign world.

These terms of sensorial exploration were critical to thinking through children's early development, for the boundaries of the self were formed in successive encounters in space. Like a traveller to whom all foreign measurements are unknown, paidologists considered the child to lack useful concepts to quantify or mediate the relationship between early self and the world. Zaragüeta described this problem as a disjunction between the child's direct experience and recognition of that external, measurable world:

> Cuando realizamos un viaje por países completamente exóticos, por grandes que sean las novedades que cautiven nuestra atención, dos cosas permanecen siempre idénticas en nuestra personalidad: la conciencia de nuestro propio cuerpo y la unidad de medida que aplicamos a los objetos exteriores. Ya sea que recorramos el Oriente ya el Occidente, el Septentrión como el Mediodía, en todas partes reconocemos nuestro cuerpo como propio y medimos las cosas con las mismas unidades de longitud, superficie y volumen [...].
>
> Pero cuando un niño inicia el viaje de la vida, ¿sabe lo que es una dimensión, una distancia, un movimiento; tiene una idea clara de su cuerpo como distinto del mundo exterior?[46]

> [When we make a journey through new and exotic lands, however great the novelties that capture our attention, two things remain unchanged in ourselves: the consciousness of our own body and the unity of measurement that we apply to external objects. Whether traversing the East or the West, the North or the South, everywhere we recognize our own body as our own and we measure objects with the same units of length, area, and volume [...].
>
> But when the child begins the journey of life, does he know what a dimension, a distance, a movement is? Does he have a clear idea of his body as distinct from the external world?]

Like Zaragüeta, successive psychologists in Spain and abroad sought to understand how the child establishes the boundaries between self and other, and between objects in space. That the child must undergo a process of spatial apprehension was central to pedagogy since at least the mid-nineteenth century, when German pedagogue Friedrich Fröbel (1782–1852) introduced building blocks and spheres designed to aid children's spatial and numerical development and started the global kindergarten movement.[47] From resulting pedagogies based around objects, as in the work of Fröbel or Montessori, to emerging concepts of psychoanalytic object relations, intentional explorations of physicality shaped developmental theory. Jean Piaget, while more famous for his mid-century constructivist psychological work, conducted experiments on children's spatial apprehension as early as the mid-1920s in research that reached Spanish pedagogues through New Education forums and JAE-funded visits to Geneva's Institut Jean-Jacques Rousseau. Exploring 'schemes of action', Piaget and Bärbel Inhelder argued that intelligence developed through sensory-motor interactions. Stimuli must fit or correspond to an internal structure in order for the child to recognize them as such. Grasping was an example of precisely such a schema: objects that could not be grasped did not enter into the baby's knowable world. Intelligence was not added from outside but rather developed in relation to intrinsic yet evolving structures of body and mind.[48]

Pedagogues' and psychologists' use of spatial and sensorial cues differed according to author, period, and goal, but many centred on play because it united spatial and physical awareness into a broader psycho-spiritual integration. In a medical essay taking a phenomenological approach, Zaragüeta wrote of a new 'psicología biológica' that should unite the mental and the physical. An individual's consciousness of spatial, physical reality relied upon the fundamental problem of recognizing oneself and others in space:

> Este organismo que llamo mío — y ello no sin motivo en atención a la íntima sensibilidad que de él tengo en las llamadas *cenestesia* y *cinestesia* — me es casi totalmente inconsciente en el orden de la sensibilidad externa: aparte de la posibilidad superficial, fragmentaria y episódica de palparme a mí mismo, de verme a mí mismo, o de oírme a mí mismo, la casi totalidad permanente de mi cuerpo resulta impermeable a mi conciencia; ¡mucho más podemos saber, por esta vía, del cuerpo ajeno que del cuerpo propio![49]

> [This organism I call my own — due in no small part to the intimate sense I gain from the so-called *cenesthesia* and *kinesthesia* — is almost completely unconscious to me when it comes to external sensibility: aside from a superficial, fragmentary, and episodic possibility of feeling myself, seeing myself, or hearing myself, almost the permanent totality of my body is imperceptible to my own consciousness; we can know much more about a foreign body, in this way, than our own!]

Physical sensation was depicted as a contingent and limited quality, limited by one's spatial surroundings at any given moment. Only through movement and touch did one come to know the circumferences of one's own reality. Through the formation of images, ideas, and ultimately the development of concepts of past, present and future, one amplified the 'horizons' of consciousness. Sensorial awareness of one's surroundings made way for a spectral imagination of 'los objetos ausentes, los pasados y los del porvenir' [absent objects, past ones, and those to come], a notion with both 'affective' and 'cognitive' qualities.[50]

Equally, paidologists discussed ways to develop children's senses of form, colour, size, and space through posed interactions with objects, starting from the understanding that children had little notion of objective measurement. Towards the end of their pedagogical studies in Madrid in 1923, the young Catalan philosopher Joan Roura i Parella and *madrileño* educator Felipe Panizo Gambón published a pamphlet which explored, among other notions seen as key for teachers, the fact that children lacked a concept of distance: 'quieren alcanzar la luna con los manos' [they want to reach the moon with their hands].[51] First grasping for an object just outside the cot, children gradually learned to calibrate sensory and manual activity. Roura and Panizo recommended setting children exercises in visual perspective, gradually working up to longer distances, while increasing complexity through geometrical and nature-based images, or gradually, the observation of objects and images in museums. They accepted that sensation and perception functioned differently across various senses and described what they called embodied 'motor' or 'muscular' images, in which the imagination was stimulated by that which one has touched, such as a drawing whose lines one's fingers have traced.[52]

Psychological theories provided further reasons for promoting play-based pedagogy, including Gestaltist theories about the unity of the senses and tactile interaction with the surrounding world. Significant for Spanish paidologists, for instance, was the work of Gestalt psychologist David Katz (1884–1953), particularly his 1925 study of haptic perception, of knowledge gained through physical contact, *Der Aufbau der Tastwelt* [The World of Touch]. The book was translated by Manuel García Morente and published by Ortega's Revista de Occidente press in 1930.[53] Katz's text constituted a philosophically-oriented entry into the unified 'world of touch.' He melded research in visual, auditory, and other sensory activities to argue for the epistemological primacy of the tactile sensation.

According to Katz, society's orientation towards sight and hearing as higher senses was mistaken. Touch held a greater role in our understanding of the world than any other sense: 'Nichts überzeugt uns so sehr von ihrer Existenz wie auch von der Realität unseres eigenes Leibes wie die, manchmal vom Schmerz nuancierten, Zusammenstöße, die zwischen dem Leib und seiner Umgebung erfolgen' [Nothing convinces us as much of its existence and of the reality of our own body as the clashes, often painful, that occur between the body and its environment]. Especially for the developing child, he wrote, the mind and the hand worked as a coordinated unity. Touch allowed one to penetrate more deeply than sight, which stayed on the outer, visible surface of objects.[54]

The hand was a Gestalt of its own, functioning as a sensorial *'tastende Einheit'*, a tactile unity, within a larger perceptual whole. Katz defended haptic primacy, in part, in linguistic terms. He related the terms involving the hand to their metaphorical incarnations, as well as Latin and Greek roots. To these, García Morente added the Spanish terms for each German word: *Griff* ('mano'), *begreifen* ('concebir, comprender'), *Begriff* ('concepto'), and so on. Reminiscent of Unamuno's playing with roots and variants to tease out a matter of larger signification, linguistic arguments for the primacy of touch furthered in pedagogical contexts the close connections between language and physicality, as well as the stark reality of constant physical collisions between body and environment.[55]

Such a reciprocal relationship between self and surroundings suggests the centrality of holistic sensorial awareness within a new education based on interaction and activity. From Gestaltist concepts of sensorial experience to psychoanalytic theories and consideration of object relations, the intellectual development of the child's mind over time built upon a base of first-hand sensorial experience. In subsequent years, psychologist Emilio Mira y López would expand greatly upon these psychoanalytic and Gestaltist foundations in discussing the child's earliest development through movement, touch, and objects. He synthesized contemporary thought in his discussion of *Aktionsdinge*, a term coined by Uexküll to refer to all the objects within an organism's *Umwelt* upon which it might act. Accordingly, Mira argued, one could authoritatively claim that objects existed selectively and sensationally for children: 'los objetos del mundo exterior van a ser aislados y explorados por el niño, *solamente en la medida* en que sirven para satisfacer una *tendencia a la acción*' [the objects of the exterior world will be isolated and explored by the child, *only to the extent* to which they serve to satisfy a *tendency towards action*].[56] This call to action, touch, and play went hand in hand with the burgeoning of toys and educational materials designed specifically to suit the child's interests and abilities.

For alongside specially designed classroom materials and furniture, Spain saw a niche of experimental, avant-garde toys that arose through and with child-centred and active learning principles. A wealth of photographs of Republican-era classrooms held by the Associació de Mestres Rosa Sensat, for instance, show children undertaking various physical activities: sorting objects, both natural and manmade, by shape or colour or form; playing with manufactured cards of ink blots or images; weaving; constructing; farming; and other hands-on tasks that aimed to connect them with the world and make them active participants in it. Notable in the realm of toys and constructivist methods were the wooden block figures produced by the aforementioned Joaquín Torres García in Barcelona, whose 'juguetes transformables' could be handled, taken apart, constructed, and re-combined at will. Torres García's toys complemented a range of synthetic, experimental projects by artists such as Ángel Ferrant, whose series of paper games, his *arsintes* of 1933, allowed children to piece together geometric or organic shapes to create human forms in all shapes and ranges of activity. More broadly, an entire commercial industry of educational products burgeoned. From a base of books, companies such as Espasa-Calpe branched out to educational materials for classrooms, including looms, construction sets, balls for counting, and anatomical models of the human body.[57] Behind such developments in both form and content lay not only a commercial and social interest, but a practical and theoretically grounded notion of the educational importance of the child's sensorial, experiential 'pentagram' of physical engagement, in Jarnés's evocative term.

Air, Sea and Mountains: Learning with Montessori, Sensat, and Aranda

> ¡Niño [...] ¡grita que eres la montaña! y el sol te posará en la cima.
> ¡Grita que eres el sol!, y el cielo se ensanchará para ti.
> ¡Grita que eres la vida!, y el universo, que espera tu grito de posesión, se quedará dormido de luz, oyéndote.

> [Child [...] Cry you are the mountain! and the sun will place you on top.
> Cry you are the sun! and the sky will expand for you.
> Cry you are life! and the universe, which awaits your call of possession, shall remain suspended in light, listening to you.]

> Carmen Conde, 'El indeciso', in *Júbilos* (1934)

Explorations of children's sensorial development went hand in hand with a celebration of open-air, natural, physical practices. Alongside the schools of Italian pedagogue Maria Montessori, invited to introduce her 'scientific' pedagogy in Catalonia from 1915, a range of local initiatives introduced a range of sensorial, nature-centred modes of teaching and learning. Tackling social problems through equal physical engagement, Montessori schools began working with children from a range of backgrounds between three and four years of age, when they could both explore freely and integrate new impressions into their widening worldviews. Acknowledging Montessori's centrality to the story of sensorial education in Spain while looking to integrate her work within a wider picture of initiatives and experiments, the following section introduces Montessori's arrival in Barcelona alongside the contributions of two other reformers. These are, namely, leading pedagogue Rosa Sensat, who directed the girls' section at Barcelona's Escola de Bosc, and local teacher Margarita Aranda, who founded a semi-urban *colonia escolar* in Madrid's Ciudad Lineal in the early 1930s. Three tiers of interaction, namely the global standing of Montessori, Sensat's local, institutionalized work, and the filtering of these principles by individual teachers such as Aranda, offers a widened view of educational holisms in practice.

Montessori's work in Catalonia demonstrates that her structured, play-centred methods found a firm base of support among reform educationalists eager to adopt the latest, scientifically-sound methods and principles from abroad. Considering the rapid global spread of Montessori education, it was perhaps only a matter of time before Spanish cities established model Montessori schools of their own. But equally, Spain — Catalonia, in particular — became a central presence in the development of Montessori's own career. Spanish was among the first languages into which her Italian works were translated, often even before French, as the editors of the *Revista de Pedagogía* proudly emphasized in introductions of her work.[58] Having made a name for herself through her work in educational renovation, Maria Montessori was invited to Barcelona by the Catalan Consell de Pedagogia in 1913, thanks to the advocacy of educator Joan [Juan] Palau Vera and politician Eladi Homs, under the aegis of the Lliga Regionalista of Enric Prat de la Riba.[59] As an early enthusiast, Palau Vera was first granted the chance to open a small-scale Montessori classroom in 1913, travelling to Rome and soon sending a small group of teachers to train at her first international course in 1914. Montessori's involvement in Catalonia was extensive. Her collaborator Anna Maccheroni arrived to start training courses in Barcelona from 1915, opening the nursery- and primary-level Escola Montessori in 1916. Montessori followed that year, and by 1918 had accepted the directorship of the newly established Laboratori i Seminari de Pedagogia under the Mancomunitat de Catalunya's Institut d'Estudis Catalans, which she would direct until 1921. Amidst political upheavals and the rise of Mussolini in Italy and Primo de Rivera in Spain, Montessori herself maintained a home in Barcelona from 1918 until the outbreak of the Spanish Civil War in 1936.[60]

Designed to accommodate boys and girls from all walks of life, the Montessori method considered play the child's immediate reality. Taking an 'anthropological' and assuredly 'scientific' approach to development, Montessori suggested that children would develop naturally, according to their biological capacity, provided that their environment included appropriate material and emotional support.[61] Montessori had begun practicing at what she called a 'casa dei bambini' in a working-class district of Rome from 1906, where she made famous a method of sensory learning translated into Spanish as 'lecciones de cosas', lessons based around a certain theme or object.[62] But it was not only physical 'cosas' that she had children handle. While traditional schooling started from a foundation of words and numbers, Montessori schools placed an emphasis on direct contact, such that each lesson corresponded to an 'experiment'.[63] Classrooms employed all manner of objects, such as cylinders, cubes, and strips of painted wood, used to practice tactile sensation and to learn to count, measure, and distinguish colours in early arithmetical and geometric play.[64] The method also strengthened the body through various kinds of physical activity: 'muscular' exercises to aid physiological development, 'free' gymnastics such as marches, tag, and songs, 'educational' gymnastics that included gardening and cultivation of plants and animals, and 'respiratory' gymnastics, focusing on breathing and the formation of speech habits.[65]

These exercises may read today as regimented, but they were designed in the service of idealistic values of play and individual exploration towards knowledge. According to Montessori, the 'education of the senses' must assume the 'greatest importance', with the goal of pedagogy being not to measure (though hers was patently a 'scientific pedagogy' with significant quantitative support), but to educate the child's senses.[66] Tasks included sorting and ordering cubes by size; arranging silks in colour gradations; performing tasks blindfolded in order to identify objects haptically; arranging bowls of water by temperature, describing smells or tastes; handling wooden blocks in the shapes of letters, or playing 'games of silence', in which children focused on silence in order to accentuate normally inaudible sounds, from the ticking of a clock to the tip-toe of a classmate.[67] Montessori's perceptual exercises encouraged nuanced and analytical acts of differentiation, comparison, and synthesis between objects, qualities, and degrees.

In the years before the establishment of the first *casa del niño* (or *casa dels nens* in Catalan) in Spain, Montessori's method was described in the Hispanic press as a revolution of play sweeping the world, from Rome to New York, in 'Inglaterra, en Méjico, en la India, en China, en Corea, en Honolulú'.[68] Reformers had long criticized the state of Spain's system of primary education, despite the influence of positive and progressive but increasingly 'antiquated' precedents such as Fröbel's *Kindergarten* model. Prominent reformers advocated the incorporation of Montessori methods in Spanish schools, including in 1915 tracts by pedagogues Leonor Serrano and Ezequiel Solana.[69] Besides Serrano's and Solana's explications of the method, Palau Vera's translation of Montessori's *L'autoeducazione nelle scuole elementari* (1916) sought to justify and elaborate the overarching principles of the method. These included the development of character, intelligence, and emotion; the role of sensorial and temporal cues in the growth of intelligence; and above all, the principle of liberty through guided play and self-governance.[70] Yet the method's freedom was also frequently considered its weakness. As Barnés reported, criticism of Montessori's teachings came from those who considered play an inappropriate vehicle for development: 'la que más parece preocupar al público es la inmoralidad de una educación en la cual el placer ocupa un lugar tan considerable' [what seems to worry the public most is the immorality of an education in which pleasure plays such an important role].[71] By reformist educators, however, the Montessori model was hailed as a socially conscious movement that understood the poor as educable. They were 'golfos', children marginalized and left behind by society, not because of their inherent biology or constitution but because of a lack of education and resources in their social environment.[72] With sensorial education and individual attention to children's development, society as a whole would benefit.

Within a year of the first Montessori schools being founded in Barcelona, some thirteen further schools had been established in the rest of Catalonia, the heart of the movement. By 1936, the Sociedad Montessori de Barcelona reported that a further twenty-two had sprung up in Catalonia and twenty-four throughout the rest of Spain.[73] However, the Mancomunitat withdrew its support of Montessori herself and her team of academic collaborators in 1921 and the Laboratori i Seminari de Pedagogia was closed, for reasons which Sáiz and Sáiz relate to an official lack of productivity and perceived inefficiencies. In addition, Montessori's continual refusal to take a partisan stance would surely play a role in the restrictions placed by both regional and central governments. In 1924, following the rise of Primo de Rivera, reforms to the Institut d'Estudis Catalans led to the closure of the principal Montessori school.[74] Responding to these measures of control, parents banded together to support alternatives practicing Montessori methods such as the Mutua Escola Blanquerna, directed by historian and pedagogue Alexandre Galí (1886–1969). As new nurseries and primary schools were established in subsequent years, many chose to adopt Montessori models.[75] Regardless of the official rupture, the 1920s remained a rich period of pedagogical translation and publication with the consolidation and growth of a community of reform-minded teachers across the country. Texts and manuals on the Montessori method and abutting models were published throughout the dictatorship, with methods fitting into a larger framework of modernization and psycho-pedagogical research.[76] In addition to her influence upon collaborators and fellow educators in Catalonia and across Spain, Montessori's legacy bolstered existing and subsequent efforts furthered by local practitioners of open-air and sensorial education.

The most well-known of these efforts within Spanish pedagogical history, that of Barcelona's Rosa Sensat, fits under the wider umbrella of the 'open-air school' movement early pioneered by Barcelona's Escola del Bosc (1914) and Escola del Mar (1922).[77] Like Barnés and others, Sensat had observed and learned from Europe's vanguard schools first-hand through tours and conferences, and sought to implement the best of their teachings in Barcelona. Through journeys to international educational events and a 1912 grant from the JAE to visit schools in Belgium, Switzerland, and Germany, she observed closely the growing European interest in 'open air schools', such as those made famous by Berlin-Charlottenburg's Waldschule from 1905 and the active practices being explored at Geneva's Institut Jean-Jacques Rousseau and its Maison des Petites. In order to address problems of health among children in the city, Barcelona opened similar 'forest schools' from 1914, including the Escola del Bosc de Montjuïc, at which Sensat began putting her pedagogical ideas into practice.[78] Its success would quickly give rise to various open-air schools and colonies around the city, including the spectacularly situated 1922 Escola del Mar, with a grand school building on the Barceloneta beach.

At the Escola del Bosc, Sensat served as director of the girls' programme from the school's opening in 1914 until her departure to lead the Milà i Fontanals school group in 1930. Her diary entries from the Escola del Bosc were meticulously handwritten after each class, giving extensive insight into the daily lives and practices of her pupils, their expeditions and activities in the forests and hills around Barcelona, and the wonderment of their teacher. She wrote, just days after the school's opening on 8 May:

> Miércoles, 20 mayo, 1914. [...] Han tenido fisiología. Hemos hablado de las regiones [del] cuerpo humano, y de la cabeza, asiento de los principales órganos de los sentidos. Luego escritura sobre lo mismo. Después, en el descanso, cantos y marchas. Quisiera enseñarles a bailar la sardana [...]. La lectura comentada la hacemos al aire libre debajo de unos pinos hermosísimos, que embalsaman el aire de agradables perfumes. Se oye el canto del ruiseñor. Los primeros días, una mariposa que paraba, una caracola encontrado entre la arena, distraían la atención y teníamos que suspender el trabajo para ocuparnos de lo que la naturaleza nos ofrecía; pero ya el hábito va adquiriendo su imperio y la lectura se va haciendo con toda regularidad e interés.[79]

> [Wednesday, 20 May, 1914. [...] Today was physiology. We spoke about [the] human body, and the head, seat of the organs that regulate our senses. Then we wrote about it. During the break, songs and marching. I would like to teach them to dance the *sardana* [...]. We discussed our reading in the open air, below pines from which the most fragrant perfume wafted. A nightingale was singing. During the first days, when a butterfly landed or a seashell was discovered in the sand, these distracted us and we had to pause our work to attend to these offerings of nature; but now habit has taken over, and the readings are done with utmost regularity and interest.]

FIG. 4.2. Rosa Sensat looking on as her pupils sort natural specimens at the Escola del Bosc, *c.* 1910s. Source: Historical Archive of the Biblioteca Rosa Sensat.

Immersing one in the sights and sounds of school life, her diary entries reveal several notable qualities that characterized her work at the Escola del Bosc. There was the focus on the education of girls alongside movement towards co-education, for instance. While she led a girls' section, the school brought together girls and boys in overlapping circles of play and study, with attention to the body, movement, and above all a close study of nature in all its guises (Fig. 4.2). Secondly, this was an education attuned to place and time, as in children's drawing of neighbourhood and world maps or learning regional dances and songs. It was interactive and reciprocal, with pupils discussing stories or readings in conversation with their teacher. And finally, this mode of learning was flexible yet pedagogically focused. Ideals of open and independently-driven exploration allowed children's discoveries to guide their learning, yet there was a clearly set goal and rationale to each lesson, hour, and day.

Lessons drew on the immediate forms of nature, asking students to apply these to writing, drawing, counting, and science. Study of the natural world was not separated from life, but rather offered a profound form of engagement with it. Sensat's own narrations of the classroom are imaginatively drawn. In the spring, even the aquarium blossomed with life:

> De los nudos de sus estolones salen los brotes de *Vallisneria*, de color rojizo ahora; pero que al desarrollarse llenarán la pecera de hermosas cintas verdes y de tallos espirales con su flor al ras del agua. El *Potamogeton* brota también y sus hojas parecen plumas de un verde tierno. Entre estas armonías de color, nadan y se agitan, con sus nuevos trajes de un azul plateado, nuestros pequeños peces que se han conservado perfectamente durante el invierno ocultos entre las rocas del fondo.[80]

> [From the stolon's knots emerge the buds of *Vallisneria*, still reddish in colour; but as they grow they will fill the fishbowl with lovely green tendrils and spiralling stems, then blossom on the surface of the water. The *Potamogeton* is sprouting as well, its leaves looking like tender green feathers. Between these harmonies of colour our little fish emerge swimming and darting in new suits of silvery blue; they have survived the winter intact, hidden among the rocks below.]

Sensat published numerous arguments for nature study, science education, and open-air education in major journals which confirm her dedication to awakening in children an intellectual and spiritual fascination with the world around them. In one particularly suggestive example, she drew readers into a series of moments in the life of the school, describing the children's reactions and creating a wider frame of humanist reference, what she called the *other* side of instruction: one which privileged the 'íntima belleza de las cosas creadas para un goce superior de la vida y una mayor elevación espiritual' [intimate beauty of things created for the superior enjoyment and spiritual elevation of life].[81] In every instance, whether pupils were studying and naming the parts of a plant, foraging and drawing from nature, peering into ponds or walking in the mountains, her descriptions are carefully narrated with the Latin names of each specimen and attentive questions posed to the girls on what they saw and observed. In the process, both boys and girls were urged to take their own exploration and engagement seriously, drawing up maps of their

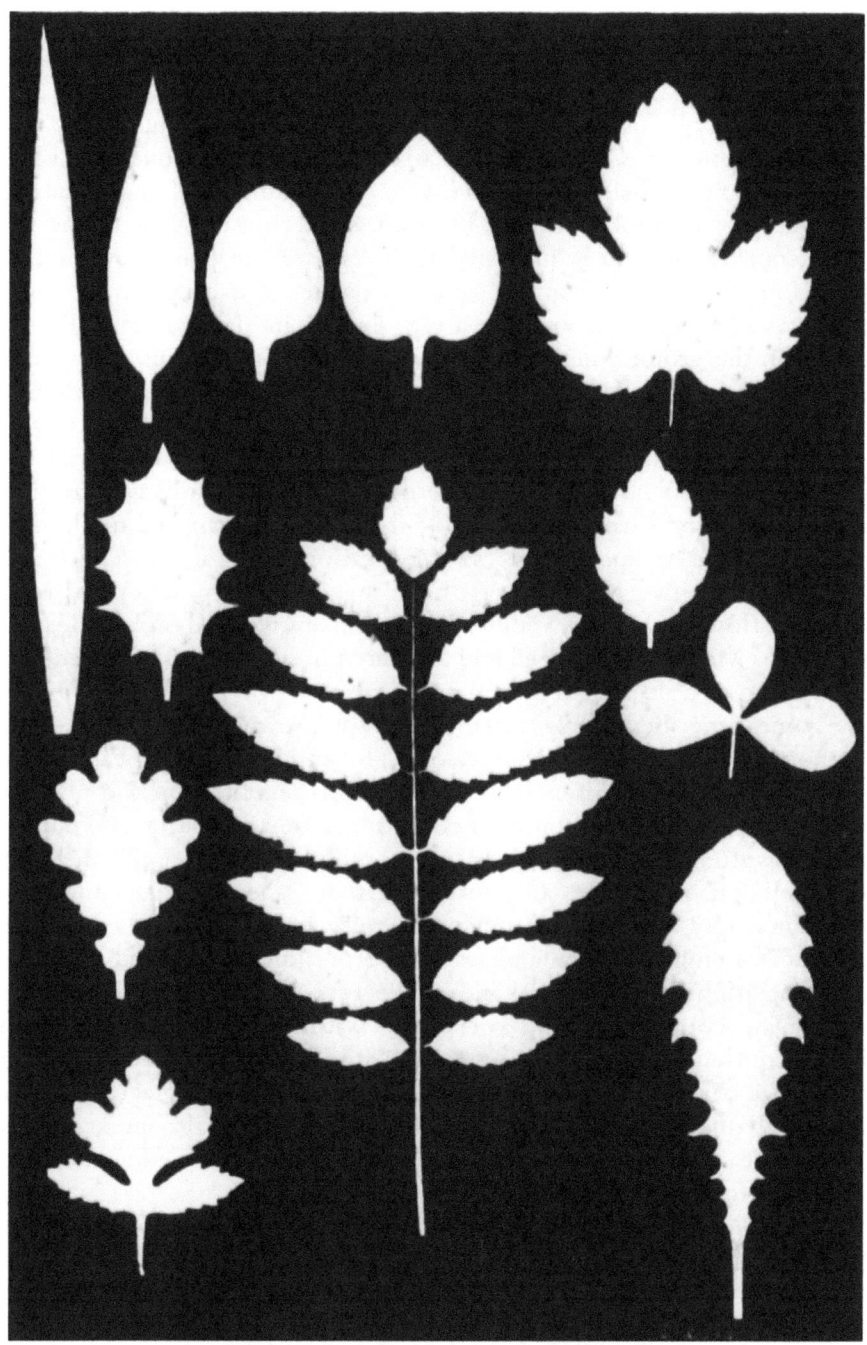

Fig. 4.3. Pressed leaves served as a botany lesson in a 1930s active-school classroom.
Source: José Mallart y Cutó, *La educación activa*, 4th edn
(Barcelona: Editorial Labor, 1935), p. 151.

neighbourhoods or the city of Barcelona, Egypt and the Nile, or the circulation of blood through the chambers of the heart, as described and illustrated in a work by a student named María Gallén.[82]

Sensat's pedagogy focused on drawing out the voices of her pupils through conversation: in one instance, she describes asking a class where one could find the 'children' of a plant she held in her hand. One girl volunteered, and matching 'her actions to her words', took hold of a blossom, scattering its seeds to the ground. '¡Ah, estos son los hijos de la planta!' [Ah, these are the plant's own children!], Sensat exclaimed, 'De estas semillas caídas en la tierra, nacerán en su tiempo las nuevas plantas semejantes en un todo a esta que les ha dado origen' [From these seeds fallen on the ground, new plants will be born, just like this one which gave them life].[83] From the seeds taking root in children's minds to the development of children themselves within a larger society, this was a pedagogy attentive both to questions of origin and futurity, both in lessons imparted and the social goals of the school. Sensat was not alone in these efforts. Nature study was considered a fundamental aspect of learning, inseparable from the open-air and modern school. In Sensat's classes as in subsequent New-Educational and active-school methods across Spain, lessons involved discovery, handling, and incorporation of the natural world. Leaves, flowers, pebbles, and hand-drawn maps were all tools for learning, as teachers such as Mallart synthesized and furthered in similar nature-based exercises over the coming two decades (Fig. 4.3).

At the same time, Sensat's sensorial pedagogy also pursued a social goal, one which echoed those pursued by Montessori. The children coming each day to the mountains were urban children who should most benefit from the physical and health-giving aspects of active, outdoor education. Their education and nurturance, with conscious attention to underlying social problems, was not only an act of *amor* towards childhood, it was also an effort to further society's highest moral values. The open-air school as practiced on Montjuïc was an effort to 'salvage imperilled human values' of environmental and aesthetic profundity. It pursued these through corresponding attention to physical and intellectual activity, liberty and discipline, work and play, cooperation and sociability within a small and experimental educational community.[84] Sensat's work is a significant example of how broader theories of open-air exploration and nature study were put into practice, developing these and localizing them within a rooted social and regional context. In districts across Spain, teachers trained in hygienic practices of new education initiated experimental efforts of their own.

One such teacher was Margarita Aranda, a pedagogue who had previously worked in sanatoria and *colonias escolares* on the northern coast, Oza and Pedrosa, for fourteen years.[85] Marrying the urban open-air school with the hygienicist measures of the *colonias escolares*, Aranda began running a summer open-air school in Madrid's Ciudad Lineal district from 1929. By this point, it was well accepted that open-air schools, playgrounds, and gardens were essential to the child's total 'organic and intellectual development', as one school hygiene officer, Octavio Vilariño, termed their significance the following year.[86] Such institutions were the product of late nineteenth-century hygienicist efforts, hosting urban children deemed most sickly and undernourished for summers of revitalization. Children's nutrition, exercise, physical growth, and strength were carefully documented on detailed *fichas* and charts over the course of the summer. Various projects had been run on a small scale by the ILE and local governments since 1892. But with reformers arguing that children's welfare plummeted as soon as they returned to the city, they further campaigned to extend the benefits of the *colonias* to residents of the city itself.[87]

Reformers shared a common rhetoric of returning the city to organic structures in which children, like the cities in which they lived, could develop holistically. Since the late nineteenth century, planners and pedagogues found common ground in the appalling conditions of urban life, with its poor air, malnutrition, and disease. Activists had long called for government intervention, suggesting the model of open-air schools — often as simple as open pavilions or a garden — as a cost-effective solution for a cash-strapped city.[88] Yet problems persisted, despite public campaigns. The reformer Miguel Gómez Cano wrote in 1924 of Madrid's shamefully high infant mortality rates, calling on doctors, pedagogues, philanthropists, and government agencies to push for improvements in children's wellbeing.[89] The action he proposed was the expansion of *colonias escolares* to existing city schools, while building new ones in the outskirts of Madrid (Fig. 4.4). This hygienicist, pedagogical effort aligned with efforts already underway.

When Madrid engineer and inventor Arturo Soria y Mata had proposed and initiated a radical expansion of the city's core in 1882, he described his urban design as a forward-looking solution to green the city and improve residents' welfare. Envisioned as a fifty-three-kilometre linear band hugging eastern Madrid, the Linear City was intended to facilitate light, air, and transport for its residents. Citing Max Nordau's notion of degeneration, his Compañía Madrileña de Urbanización suggested that the district would counter degradation and improve urban health and welfare.[90] Its design was consciously organic: a long central avenue Soria referred to as the 'spinal cord' of the city branched off into transversal 'arteries' and 'capillaries'. Each house had a mandated minimum amount of open green space for health and play, considered as fundamentally entwined. This central vertebra, in turn, connected residents directly to central Madrid. The lungs of the city were made up of thousands of trees the Company planted at annual *fiestas del árbol*, or 'arbour days', celebrated with children's recitations of songs and poems, a tradition first established in the regenerationist atmosphere of the late nineteenth century then partially revived in a Madrid-centred, patriotic inculcation of nationalism under Primo de Rivera, as Alejandro Quiroga has documented.[91]

Where Soria y Mata undertook a spatial reform, pedagogues such as Aranda and her contemporaries were engaged in one of outreach and practice. One resident of the Ciudad Lineal was Domingo Barnés, among the first to advocate for open-air schools in Madrid. Funded by the JAE, Barnés travelled to Britain in 1908 with a group of pedagogues to visit the Franco-British Exhibition in Shepherd's Bush, where he was struck by an exhibition about open-air schools. He described several in detail, from Berlin's 1905 Waldschule to British and American examples, urging

FIG. 4.4. Children boarding a bus to an open-air school on the outskirts of Madrid.
Source: Pedro Roy Herreros, *Planes escolares de la Villa y Corte: Parques infantiles,*
excursiones escolares, escuelas al aire libre, colonias escolares y plan económico
(Madrid: Imprenta Municipal, 1929), p. 67.

their importation to Spain.[92] As seen with Sensat and the Escola del Bosc, open-air schools included formal instruction in traditional subjects, but in a health-giving environment of gardens and three-walled classrooms. Four years after Barcelona's establishment of the Escola del Bosc and the beginning of Sensat's work there, local efforts in Madrid led to the establishment of its own Escuela del Bosque in 1918. By 1928, with Barnés serving as vice-president of the advisory board of the Ciudad Lineal's Compañía Madrileña de Urbanización, personal links were key to smaller local efforts in the district. The district and the city at large supported the work of Aranda, then-director of Madrid's Colegio La Milagrosa, with small grants, as well as making numerous efforts to design services and initiatives around children's health and education. The 1931 *Guía de la Ciudad Lineal* notes that in addition to private academies and Catholic schools, several 'open-air schools' were in operation in the district. Underscoring the home-grown nature of this effort, neighbours were called upon publicly to volunteer their garden space to the cause.[93]

Aranda had sole responsibility for one such open-air project from 1929. Her work in the Ciudad Lineal followed the models of open-air education laid out according to international standards: a day balanced between academic instruction, gymnastics, free play, and excursions into the countryside and forests, described as the product of their teacher's 'espíritu progresivo' [progressive spirit]. In contrast to the efforts of Montessori and Sensat, Aranda's smaller project is lesser known or documented. Even at the time it seems to have gone largely unrecognized, though a spattering of newspaper articles depicted this example of a local philanthropic effort. The most evocative of these portrayals comes from that of a visit from reporter Manuel Reverte to Aranda's *colonia* in the Quinta de Chamartín in 1931 (Fig. 4.5). When Reverte and a photographer approached, they encountered children running around gaily under the trees; the children stopped at their arrival and approached shyly to examine their camera. Aranda explained that they were not used to receiving visitors. Surprised, Reverte concurred: 'Llegamos a creer que son muy pocas las personas que están enteradas de su existencia' [We believe very few people know of its existence].[94]

As depicted by her visitors, Aranda's school was spread out in the extensive, hillside grounds of a hotel, converted for the children. Set with pines and eucalyptus trees, the building had the all-important 'aire sano del Guadarrama' [healthy air of the Guadarrama] running freely through the rooms, rustling their curtains like 'banderas de paz' [flags of peace]. Reverte emphasized the initiative's healthful benefits. Aranda herself, the director, organizer, and 'alma' of the initiative, was described as 'joven y fuerte, con el rostro tostado por el sol y el aire' [young and strong, with a face toasted by the sun and air]. Her pupils, meanwhile, ran around the grounds 'medio desnuda, con los cuerpecitos tostados por el sol' [half naked, their small bodies toasted by the sun]. As pictured elsewhere in the publication, they gathered to do calisthenics in long, haphazard lines, and Reverte described them bathing in a 'chorro cristalino y fresco' [crystalline, fresh spring] and sunbathing, a treatment known as heliotherapy and celebrated by international open-air school advocates.[95] Aranda saw physical interventions as a direct effort to counterbalance the poor educational environments to which the children were subjected during the winter, in closed, stuffy, and crowded classrooms. She also saw sensorial interventions as central to her mission, specifically including teaching for deaf and blind children, if not billing the camp as a school for *sordomudos* as such. In addition to a teaching staff of four female assistants and two male professors, the students were visited by a doctor each day to measure and record their health and growth.[96]

Reverte's coverage was richly illustrated with photographs of the children engaged in various aspects of the daily curriculum. One encounters a class of deaf and blind children doing written work at long tables in an open courtyard, a class he describes as guided by a teacher but focused on children's interactions with one another through sign and written language. In another image, children gather around their teacher at a piano to undertake singing and rhythmic games; on a facing page, a larger group undertakes outdoor exercises, while others sit cross-legged, reading on a terrace during a break. Each image manifests the pointedly hybrid nature of the school: in one, wide windows and plants growing along the wall demonstrate that the students were not shut up indoors but seated in an outdoor courtyard; elsewhere, behind the piano and nestled in a trellis hangs a sign for 'colonias escolares', askew and overgrown by verdant vines. Such natural incursions point to the intentional interplay of interior and exterior, classroom and the outdoors, which were to be one and the same.

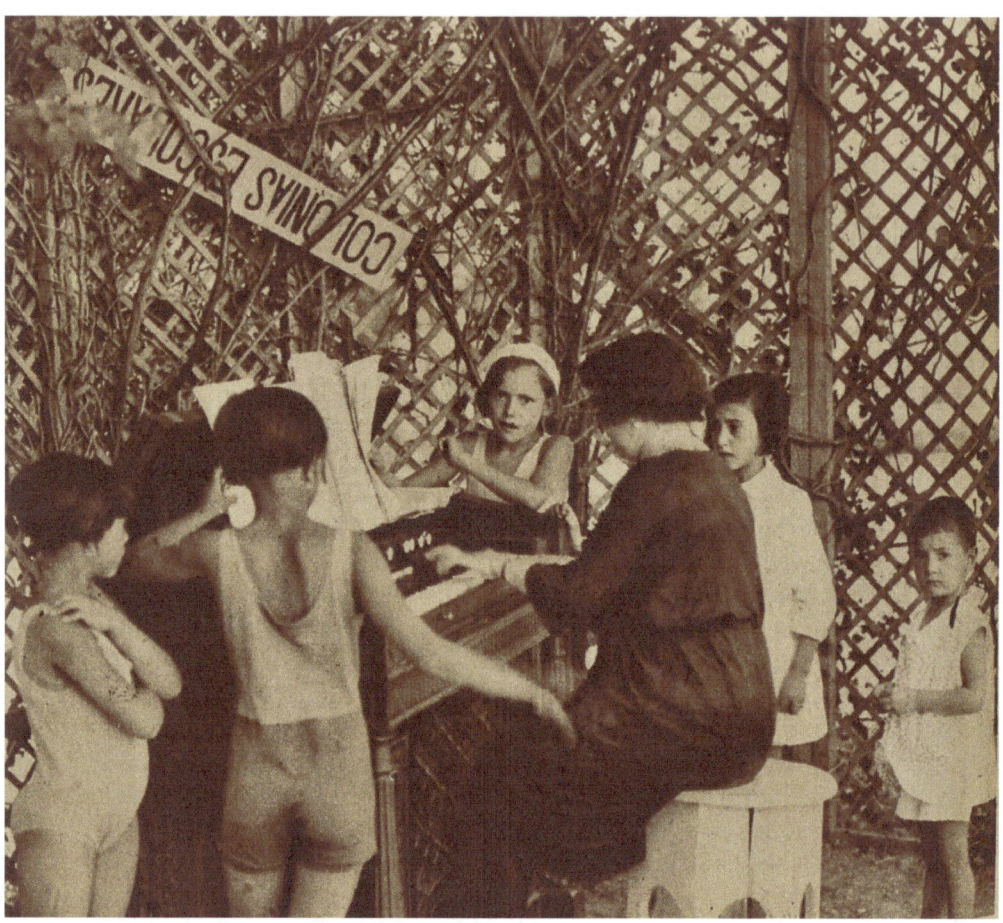

FIG. 4.5. Children of all ages gathering around the piano as a teacher, possibly Aranda, plays. Source: Manuel Reverte, 'La colonia escolar de la Ciudad Lineal', *ABC*, 19 August 1931, pp. 6–7 (p. 6).

Alongside the legacies of Montessori and Sensat, Aranda's summer school was one small example of an aligned local initiative responding to social need. Unlike larger and better established schools such as Granada's Escuelas del Ave María, Madrid's Escuela del Bosque, or Barcelona's Escola del Mar, Aranda's was a temporally-bound, philanthropic social project for children of poor or modest means, undertaken on a personal initiative, with modest support from private foundations, government, and individual donations. Yet its reach was significant: some 120 children, male and female, were in Aranda's care at the time of Reverte's writing. That number was limited only by resources, which included a subvention from the Rotary Club, funds from schools for deaf and blind children from which a number of her summertime attendees came, contributions from individual families with means, and occasional contributions from the Ministry of Education. The rest Aranda topped up herself. Throughout the summers, she would meet her students in central Madrid each day to ensure their safe arrival in the Ciudad Lineal and arranged a reduced-price train ticket for their daily commute — a small (two pesetas per month) transportation cost that, it was argued, the government should provide for all urban children.[97] Taking advantage of the Ciudad Lineal's location, connectivity, and philanthropic leanings of residents and administrators, Aranda's work brought open-air principles to bear on urban education. Through such efforts, ideas of sensorial and physical education were not limited to schools subscribing to the Montessori method nor to Spain's open-air flagship schools at the sea or in the mountains. They also informed individual and localized efforts.

Across the wider patchwork of Spanish schools, as indicated by Luis Bello's 1926 journalistic advocacy for the rural, underfunded 'escuelas de España', there remained a larger effort to be undertaken.[98] Yet as these examples suggest, principles of physical health and sensorial integrity began to filter into practice through concerted importation, translation, and internationalization by teachers trained in Spain's *escuelas normales* and abroad. Building on theories of play and sensation, individual practitioners enacted small-scale projects of social and cultural renewal, while regional and district-level governments supported efforts to experiment with international principles of open-air education and sensorial learning. The dialogue between theory and practice was reciprocal, and from the very first, the nature of play was on the line. It was on the one hand a utilitarian biological process of training for life, while on the other figures such as the teacher Teodoro Causí and philosopher Manuel García Morente argued for play as a spontaneous flourishing of children's very being. Building on play theory, international models of active learning were celebrated as a way to enact holistic education through physical activity. These debates were entertained by those working in a psychological realm; those seeking political and municipal reforms; and even by writers such as Jarnés, who imagined from an interior frame a child's passage into adult rationality through sensorial integration. Whether viewed within the framework of well-known experimental models such as the Montessori method or enacted in local efforts of open-air education, sensorial principles informed a holistic view of the child. Holding perceptual experience, physical activity, and environmental orientation as central, new models sought to prioritize children's developmental vitality. Moving from distance to proximity, observation to contact, theory to practice, they positioned children's social, cultural, and ethical 'humanization' as a function of play between developing self and world.

Notes to Chapter 4

1. Julián Izquierdo Ortega, *Filosofía española (Tres ensayos: Ortega y Gasset, o la vida; Turró, o la ciencia; Unamuno, o la religión)* (Madrid: Ediciones Argos, 1935), p. 26.
2. Benjamín Jarnés, 'Un niño descalzo', *Meseta*, 1 (1928), 4.
3. While I have not been able to locate Aranda's vital dates, a chronology of her career can be ascertained. She completed her teacher-training *oposición* in 1915. After her work on the northern coast, Aranda directed the Colegio La Milagrosa in Madrid, the *colonias escolares* in Ciudad Lineal and Miraflores de la Sierra, taught in Soria's Velilla de los Ajos and was appointed in 1936 to Madrid's Escuela Nacional Mixta de Cubas, where she also served after the Civil War. See, for instance, Anon., 'Ministerio de Obras Públicas', *Gaceta de Madrid*, 4 March 1936, pp. 1837–38, and José Ibáñez Martín, 'Orden de 7 de Mayo de 1947', *Boletín Oficial del Estado*, 18 June 1947, p. 3434.
4. *Diccionario de pedagogía*, ed. by Sánchez Sarto, II, 2910.
5. Guillén, 'Cinco florinatas', p. 8.
6. For an overview of play in the Spanish reform tradition, see María de Borja i Solé, *El juego como actividad educativa: instruir deleitando* (Barcelona: Universitat de Barcelona, 1984) and Andrés Payà Rico, 'La actividad lúdica en la historia de la educación española contemporánea' (unpublished doctoral thesis, Universitat de Valencia, 2007), pp. 30–142. Play continues to be a key educational policy issue. As has been demonstrated by research groups in developmental psychology and education, children's playtime correlates with linguistic, social, and cognitive skills; see David Whitebread and others, *The Importance of Play: A Report on the Value of Children's Play with a Series of Policy Recommendations* (Brussels: Toy Industries of Europe, 2012), <http://www.importanceofplay.eu> [accessed 1 April 2018].
7. Teodoro Causí, *Bosquejo de una teoría biológica del juego infantil* (Madrid: Calpe, 1924), p. 18.
8. García Morente, 'El mundo del niño'. In considering Causí's view of human progress I refer both to the ontogenetic perspective of Ernst Haeckel (1834–1919) as well as a humanistic conception of historical evolution put forward in the introduction to Causí's work. There, he considers pedagogy as 'la afirmación del hombre' across his (mankind's) entire scientific, philosophical and cultural evolution; see Causí, *Bosquejo de una teoría biológica del juego infantil*, pp. 11–12.
9. Valentina Fernández Vargas, Luis Lorenzo Navarro, and Juan Bosch-Marín, *El niño y el joven en España (siglos XVIII–XX): aproximación teórica y cuantitativa* (Barcelona: Anthropos, 1989), p. 10.
10. Arturo Soria y Mata, *El talentómetro: reglas para construir un aparato medidor del talento* (Madrid: Imprenta de la Compañía Madrileña de Urbanización, 1902), p. 31.
11. Juarros, *La crianza del hijo*, p. 113, and José Eleizegui López, *Los juegos en la infancia: guía médicopedagógica para padres y maestros* (Barcelona: Sociedad General de Publicaciones, 1900); Ricardo Rubio, 'Hay que enseñar a jugar', *La Escuela Moderna*, 20 (1901), 85–87 (pp. 85–86).
12. Lorenzo Luzuriaga, 'La biología de los niños en relación con la educación', *El Sol*, 5 November 1918, p. 8.
13. Barnés Salinas, 'La función biológica de la infancia', pp. 41–42.
14. Ibid., pp. 49–50.
15. José Mallart y Cutó, 'El trabajo agradable y el problema de la educación activa', *Boletín de la Institución Libre de Enseñanza*, 45 (1921), 176–84, 211–20 (pp. 177, 178).
16. Mallart y Cutó, *La escuela del trabajo*, p. 39. On Mallart's presence in Geneva, see Joan Soler i Mata, 'The Rousseau Institute of Geneva's Influence on and Presence in Catalan Pedagogy in the First Third of the 20th Century', *Catalan Social Sciences Review*, 1 (2012), 58–87 (p. 72).
17. The most significant early texts on play and its biological roots were by Karl Groos, in separate studies of humans and animals: *The Play of Animals*, trans. by Elizabeth L. Baldwin (London:

Chapman & Hall, 1898), and *The Play of Man*, trans. by Elizabeth L. Baldwin (London: William Heinemann, 1901). Buytendijk's work continued this line; see his *Wesen und Sinn des Spiels: Das Spielen des Menschen und der Tiere als Erscheinungsform der Lebenstriebe* (Berlin: Kurt Wolff, 1933), translated as *El juego y su significado: el juego en los hombres y en los animales como manifestación de impulsos vitales*, trans. by Eugenio Imaz (Madrid: Revista de Occidente, 1935).

18. Causí, *Bosquejo de una teoría biológica del juego infantil*, p. 18.

19. Ibid., p. 45.

20. Ibid., p. 38.

21. Ibid., p. 25.

22. Ibid., p 103.

23. Ibid., p. 25.

24. John Dewey, *The Child and the Curriculum*. 27th edn (Chicago: University of Chicago Press, 1963), p. 23. See also John Dewey, *La escuela y el niño*, trans. by Domingo Barnés (Madrid: Ciudad Lineal, 1926), pp. 41–42. On the reception of Dewey's pragmatism in Spain, see Gonzalo Jover, 'Readings of the Pedagogy of John Dewey in Spain in the Early Twentieth Century: Reconciling Pragmatism and Transcendence', in *Democracy and the Intersection of Religion and Traditions: The Readings of John Dewey's Understanding of Democracy and Education*, ed. by Rosa Bruno-Jofré and others (Montreal: McGill-Queen's University Press, 2010), pp. 79–130.

25. Dewey, *The Child and the Curriculum*, pp. 5–6.

26. García Morente, 'El mundo del niño', pp. 116–17.

27. Ibid., pp. 117–18.

28. Ibid., p. 118.

29. Ibid., p. 119.

30. Ibid., p. 120. In the words of Wolfgang Köhler, speaking in Barcelona in 1927, 'el juego no es cosa de broma [...]. Se trata, pues, de un juego serio' [Play is not a laughing matter [...] it is a *serious* game]: 'El problema de la psicología de la forma', p. 66.

31. García Morente, 'El mundo del niño', p. 120.

32. Ibid., p. 121.

33. Ibid., p. 122.

34. Ibid. Pedagogue Anselmo González wrote that a child's adoption of the pronoun *yo* constituted a critical stage in their intellectual development, between the self and the surrounding world: A. Anselmo González, *Nacimiento y evolución de la inteligencia (Formad el espíritu de vuestros hijos)* (Madrid: M. Aguilar, 1930), p. 132.

35. Joaquim Xirau considered Charlotte Bühler and her husband Karl Bühler's work as part of a longer tradition of humanistic psychology, from the Renaissance to the Gestalt psychologists. Charlotte Bühler's research on human development constituted 'un estudi de la vida — de la vida en la seva totalitat — cal partir de la unitat vital psicofisiològica [i] les lleis fonamentals de la seva evolució' [a study of life — life in its totality — which draws from vital psycho-physiological unity [and] the fundamental laws of its evolution]; see Joaquim Xirau i Palau, 'Bibliografies. Charlotte Bühler: Der menschliche Lebenslauf als psychologisches Problem', *Revista de Psicologia i Pedagogia*, 1.1 (1933), 87–89 (p. 88).

36. Benjamín Jarnés, 'Un niño descalzo', *Meseta*, 1 (1928), 4.

37. Michel de Certeau, *The Practice of Everyday Life*. trans. by Steven Rendall (Berkeley: University of California Press, 1984), p. 110.

38. Jarnés, 'Un niño descalzo'.

39. Ibid.

40. Ibid.

41. Herbert Spencer, *Education: Intellectual, Moral and Physical* (New York: D. Appleton, 1896), p. 153.

42. Francisco Santamaría Esquerdó, *Los sentidos: lecciones de psicometría, dadas en la Escuela de Criminología de Madrid*, 2nd edn (Madrid: Suárez, 1918), p. 257.

43. Juarros, *Educación física y moral del niño*, p. 41. As president of the Federación Española de Gimnasia (1933–36) alongside advocacy of Freudian psychoanalysis, eugenics, and sexual reform, Juarros, like others, would apply work on childhood to human development as a whole.

44. Zaragüeta, *El estudio del niño*, p. 10.

45. Jaén and Peinado, *Manual de paidología*, p. 135.

46. Zaragüeta, *El estudio del niño*, p. 10.

47. See Purificación Lahoz Abad, 'El modelo froebeliano de espacio-escuela: su introducción en España', *Historia de la Educación*, 10 (1991), 107–34.

48. Jean Piaget and Bärbel Inhelder, *The Child's Conception of Space*, trans. by F. J. Langdon and J. L. Lunzer (London: Routledge & Kegan Paul, 1956), pp. 19–20. On Piaget's 'biological' approach see Hans G. Furth, *Piaget and Knowledge: Theoretical Foundations* (Englewood Cliffs: Prentice-Hall, 1969), pp. 12–13.

49. Zaragüeta, *El estudio del niño*, p. 16. According to the Real Academia Española's *Diccionario de la lengua española* (2001), cenestesia is defined as a general awareness of inhabiting one's body; cinestesia refers to the sensation of movement through space.

50. Juan Zaragüeta, *Conciencia y organismo* [offprint from the journal *Ensayos de Cultura Médica*] ([Madrid]: s.n., 1932), pp. 46, 48.

51. Joan Roura i Parella and Felipe Panizo Gambón, *Contestaciones al cuestionario de pedagogía de las oposiciones a Escuelas Nacionales* (Madrid: Imprenta Editorial Colón, 1923), p. 57.

52. Ibid., p. 89.

53. David Katz, *Der Aufbau der Tastwelt* (Leipzig: J. A. Barth, 1925), published in Spanish as *El mundo de las sensaciones táctiles*, trans. by Manuel García Morente (Madrid: Revista de Occidente, 1930). Katz's work, as with Freud's, is an example of a corpus in which Spain, which often considered itself as intellectually behind the times, anticipated the English-speaking world. A first English translation of Katz was published only in 1989; see Susan J. Lederman, 'D. Katz "The World of Touch"', *Perception*, 19.4 (1990), 556–57 (p. 556).

54. Katz, *Der Aufbau der Tastwelt*, p. 40.

55. Katz, *El mundo de las sensaciones táctiles*, pp. 252–54.

56. Mira y López, *Psicología evolutiva del niño y el adolescente*, p. 77.

57. A rich visual sample of these toys remains on display at the Museo Torres García in Montevideo; see Joaquín Torres García, *Aladdin: juguetes transformables* (Montevideo: Museo Torres García, [2005]), and *Torres-García, construcciones en madera*. ed. by Marc Domènec Tomàs (Madrid: Guillermo de Osma Galería, 2000); 'Al Magisterio Nacional Primario: Propósito', *Biblion*, 2 (1933), 4.

58. Maria Montessori, 'El método Montessori y la educación moderna', *Revista de Pedagogía*, 1 (1922), 201–04 (p. 202).

59. Juan Palau Vera, 'Prefacio', in *El método de la pedagogía científica aplicado a la educación de la infancia en la 'Case dei Bambini'*, ed. by Maria Montessori (Barcelona: Araluce, 1913), pp. xi–xiv. See also Francesca Comas Rubí and Bernat Sureda García, 'The Photography and Propaganda of the Maria Montessori Method in Spain (1911–1931)', *Paedagogica Historica*, 48.4 (2011), 571–87 (p. 573).

60. On her early incorporation and subsequent influence in Catalonia, see Sáiz and Sáiz, 'La estancia de María Montessori en Barcelona, pp. 201–02, and on the wider scope of Montessori's career, see above all Rita Kramer, *Maria Montessori: A Biography* (Oxford: Blackwell, 1978).

61. Maria Montessori, *La auto-educación en la escuela elemental*, trans. by Juan Palau Vera (Barcelona: Araluce, 1920), p. 89.

62. Ibid., p. 33.

63. Maria Montessori, *The Montessori Method: Scientific Pedagogy as Applied to Child Education in 'The Children's Houses' with Additions and Revisions by the Author* (London: Heinemann, 1912), p. 107.

64. Anon., 'Las escuelas Montessori: donde se educa a los niños jugando', *Alrededor del Mundo*, 671 (1912), 296–97 (p. 297).

65. Montessori, *The Montessori Method*, pp. 137–47. This movement reflected a wider interest in gymnastics in Italian educational thought; see, for instance, Edmondo de Amicis's 1891 *Amore e ginnastica* (Atripalda: Mephite, 2004) and Suzanne Stewart-Steinberg, *The Pinocchio Effect: On Making Italians, 1860–1920* (Chicago: University of Chicago Press, 2007), pp. 157–65.

66. Montessori, *The Montessori Method*, p. 167. Angeline Stoll Lillard, in *Montessori: The Science Behind the Genius* (Oxford: Oxford University Press, 2005), analyses the bases, from movement to cognition, rewards to motivation, of Montessori's 'anthropological pedagogy'.

67. Montessori, *The Montessori Method,* pp. 185–209.

68. Anon., 'Las escuelas Montessori', p. 297.

69. Leonor Serrano, *La pedagogía Montessori: estudio informativo y crítico* (Madrid: Sucesores de Hernando, 1915), and Ezequiel Solana, *María Montessori: exposición crítica de sus métodos de educación y enseñanza* (Madrid: n.p., 1915). Serrano would carry on her advocacy of the Montessori system through the 1920s, alongside works on the education of the 'woman of tomorrow'; see Leonor Serrano, *El método Montessori* (Madrid: Revista de Pedagogía, 1928), and *La educación de la mujer de mañana,* ed. by María del Carmen Agulló Díaz (Madrid: Biblioteca Nueva, 2007).

70. Maria Montessori, *L'autoeducazione nelle scuole elementari* (Rome: P. Maglione & C. Strini, 1916).

71. Domingo Barnés Salinas, 'Revista de Revistas: Francesas: *La Revue', La Lectura,* 14.161 (1914), 214–20 (p. 216).

72. Antonio Zozaya, 'La cuenta del golfo', *Vida Socialista,* 25 June 1911, pp. 4–5.

73. *Diccionario de pedagogía,* ed. by Sánchez Sarto, II, 2159.

74. See Sáiz and Sáiz, 'La estancia de Maria Montessori en Barcelona', p. 205. Dramatic changes, ostensibly made on grounds of financial stability and structural efficiency, were announced on 12 April 1924 in a pronouncement by the Barón de Viver (Darius Rumeu i Freixa, 1886–1970); see 'L'Institut d'Estudis Catalans', *La Publicitat,* 12 April 1924, p. 4.

75. *Diccionario de pedagogía,* ed. by Sánchez Sarto, II, 2159.

76. See validations of the Montessori method and its relationship to outdoor and special education respectively in texts such as Vaquero Cantillo, *Las escuelas al aire libre,* and Tomàs Busquet i Teixidor, 'La educación de los niños psico-anormales en la provincia de Barcelona', *Infantia Nostra,* 8.72 (1929), 80–90.

77. See María del Mar del Pozo Andrés, 'La utilización de parques y jardines como espacios educativos alternativos en Madrid, 1900–1931', *Historia de la Educación,* 12–13 (1993/94), 149–84, and Francisco Javier Rodríguez Méndez, 'Renouvellement architectural et pédagogie de plein air en Espagne (1910–1936)', in *L'École de plein air: une expérience pédagogique et architecturale dans l'Europe du XXe siècle,* ed. by Anne-Marie Châtelet (Paris: Éditions Recherche, 2003), pp. 148–60.

78. José Mariano Bernal Martínez, 'De las escuelas al aire libre a las aulas de la naturaleza', *Areas,* 20 (2000), 171–82 (p. 178).

79. Barcelona, Biblioteca Rosa Sensat, 'Diaris de Rosa Sensat i Vilà (1914–1928)', first notebook (1914–15), Memòria Digital de Catalunya, <http://mdc.cbuc.cat/cdm/compoundobject/collection/arxiurs/id/260> [accessed 1 February 2018].

80. Rosa Sensat i Vilà, 'Momentos escolares', *Revista de Pedagogía,* 9.101 (1930), 196–204 (p. 202).

81. Ibid., p. 197.

82. Barcelona, Biblioteca Rosa Sensat, 'Escola del Bosc de Montjuïc: Treball de varis alumnes' (1923), AD020.

83. Sensat i Vilà, 'Momentos escolares', p. 199.

84. Rosa Sensat i Vilà, 'La escuela al aire libre', *Revista de Pedagogía,* 8.85 (1929), 15–22 (p. 16).

85. Manuel Reverte, 'La colonia escolar de la Ciudad Lineal', *ABC,* 19 August 1931, pp. 6–7 (p. 6).

86. Octavio R. Vilariño, *La infancia y la naturaleza: estudio sintético de la influencia que ejercen, en el desarrollo orgánico e intelectual del niño, las colonias escolares, los jardines de la infancia y los campos de juego* (Madrid: Librería Médica, 1930).

87. García Trejo, *Escuelas al aire libre,* p. 18.

88. For plans and proposals, often featuring diagrams of school layouts built around gardens and open space, see Juan Pomareda Soler, *La escuela al aire libre y los paseos escolares: programas y guía práctica de la educación de los niños en el campo* (Madrid: Pedro Núñez, 1902); Germán Penedo, 'La escuela en el campo', *La Correspondencia de España,* 8 May 1909, p. 1; and Nieves García y Gómez, *Las colonias escolares y las escuelas al aire libre en su aplicación al mejoramiento de la salud y de la enseñanza primaria* (Madrid: A. Ungría, 1914).

89. Miguel Gómez Cano, *Las colonias escolares del Ayuntamiento de Madrid* (Madrid: Imprenta del Asilo de Huérfanos, 1924), p. 5.

90. Compañía Madrileña de Urbanización, *La reintegración al campo y la Ciudad Lineal* (Madrid: Imp. de la Ciudad Lineal, 1928), p. 4.

91. On the organization of green space, see Anon., 'La Ciudad Lineal, lejos', *La Ciudad Lineal*, 14.385 (1909), 1493–94; Quiroga, *Making Spaniards,* pp. 120–21.

92. Barnés Salinas, 'Escuelas al aire libre', pp. 62–83.

93. Anon., 'Escuelas al aire libre en la Ciudad Lineal', *La Ciudad Lineal*, 34.823 (1930), 129.

94. César García Iniesta, 'Una estadística escolar equivocada urge la rectificación del Alcalde', *Heraldo de Madrid*, 23 January 1930, pp. 8–9 (p. 9); Reverte, 'La colonia escolar de la Ciudad Lineal', p. 6.

95. Reverte, 'La colonia escolar de la Ciudad Lineal', p. 6.

96. Ibid., p. 7.

97. Ibid., p. 6; García Iniesta, 'Una estadística escolar equivocada urge la rectificación del Alcalde', p. 9.

98. Bello, *Viaje por las escuelas de España.*

PART III

Spirit

CHAPTER 5

Art and the Mind:
Childhood and the New *Ingenium*

El Arte es un recreo del espíritu.
[Art is a recreation of the spirit.]
Ángel Ferrant, 'Diseño de una configuración escolar' (1932)

In 1928, Salvador Dalí, Lluís Montanyá, and Sebastià Gasch included a denunciation of derivative art for children in their famous Manifest Groc [Yellow Manifesto]. Signed in Barcelona and considered one of the most significant statements of the Catalan and indeed European avant-garde, the manifesto denounced the putrid, the stale, and the passé while celebrating the fast, the spontaneous, and the new: films, boxing matches, beach games, jazz, science, and the poets, playwrights, and artists of a new age.[1] Signalling how critical a culture of childhood was to avant-garde projects, the last three entries stand out:

> DENUNCIEM les metzines artístiques per a ús infantil, tipus: *Jordi* (Per a l'alegria i comprensió dels nois, res de més adequat que Rousseau, Picasso, Chagall...)
> DENUNCIEM la psicologia de les noies que canten 'Rosó, Rosó...'
> DENUNCIEM la psicologia dels nois que canten: 'Rosó, Rosó...'.[2]

> [WE DENOUNCE artistic poisons fed to children, in the line of *Jordi* (for children's gaiety and understanding, nothing better than Rousseau, Picasso, Chagall...)
> WE DENOUNCE the psychology of girls who sing 'Rosó, Rosó...'
> WE DENOUNCE the psychology of boys who sing 'Rosó, Rosó...'.]

What in this invocation of art for children, including popular songs and literature, was so objectionable? In pursuit of an ideal of imaginative and aesthetic liberty, the manifesto's authors singled out a children's magazine, *Jordi*. This publication featured richly-illustrated pages with colourful illustrations, prose stories, dialogues, cartoons, and 'how-to' instructions for children on everything from making shadow puppets to constructing toys and tools. From a modern educational perspective, the magazine fulfilled all the goals to which a cosmopolitan education could aspire: the feisty independence of the child (usually an urban, well-to-do boy), an inquisitive and can-do attitude, and the tools to construct one's own learning and daily experience through action and exploration. The manifesto's criticism, rather, seemed to posit that bourgeois cultural products intended to mimic the worlds of children were reductive and didactic. To awaken the mind of the child, all that was needed was good art and literature. Such works opened themselves to viewers of all ages, sharpened aesthetic sensibilities, and stirred the imagination. Artists and reform pedagogues alike called for the use of creative design, simple forms, and abstraction to open new vistas onto the unknown, whether through art, products, or toys.

In the fight for new, vanguard forms of culture, children's art and production came to stand both for technoscientific modernity (children's drawings as inseparable from psychological probes and analyses) and spiritual liberation (through celebrations of the liberty of children's art). Artists admired and upheld children's own artistic production — as poets did their stories and poems — for their imaginative transcendence. Meanwhile in Spain, as internationally, artistic interest coincided with serious study of children's drawings as windows on to the mind. Psychologists studied children's drawings as tools for reading and analysing their developing worldviews.[3] Claims for children's mental, emotional, and 'spiritual' development therefore came hand in hand with discussions of how they interacted with art. Through engagement with a diverse range of psychologists, pedagogues, and ultimately artists and writers, this chapter juxtaposes two seemingly divergent forms of response to children's art, namely the psychotechnic and the creative, in order to understand how they came together.

Why and how did these two spheres coincide? As teachers, pedagogues, and psychologists looked towards the images created by and for children, their artistic and poetic colleagues declared their belief in a mutual affinity: an aesthetic of childhood in modern art and of artistic intervention in modern childhood. Using drawing and writing as exemplars of a wider progression of knowledge production, art historian Barbara Wittmann has argued that the physical, graphical nature of children's drawings transformed these sketches and scribbles into instruments of technoscientific modernity. Yet these were 'weakly structured' tools, better suited to stimulating and transforming the larger 'synchronic structures' of the child's consciousness than to strictly reproducing and recording the mind.[4] Imagination and interpretation were needed. A host of psychometric tests of spatial awareness, object recognition, and visuo-physical processing arose that are typically read as normative measures. With avant-garde artists drawing on the same wells of theory, including notions of the primitive, the evolutionary, and the *naïf*, the celebration of children's art must be read within an accompanying fascination with the imaginative, spiritual liberties of the mind.

Aforementioned figures such as the sculptor Ángel Ferrant (1890–1961) and critic Sebastià Gasch (1897–1980), among others, drew on a rich vein of popular and academic interest in children's drawing as expression. They pioneered studios, workshops, and models of reform that incorporated psychological principles of the early global reach of the mind. More broadly, as suggested in analyses undertaken by the children's book author, critic, and intellectual Manuel Abril (1884–1943), the development of art intersected with larger questions about the wider spiritual aspects of human society. Enacting ideas of 'humanization' through Ortega's 'dehumanization' and the history of art, Abril sought not simply to understand changing worldviews but to understand what defined the evolving human spirit.

The notion of studying children's own production to better understand their mental development became critical during the early twentieth century in both a psychotechnic and vanguard artistic frame. Mental tests and probes of professional orientation had a long history, including in Spain. Works such as Juan Huarte de San Juan's *Examen de ingenios para las ciencias* [The Examination of Men's Wits] (1575), republished in 1930, for instance, provided an 'authentic' Spanish model for accessing and classifying talent and mental ability, *ingenium*, to set one on a suitable course of life and study.[5] By the early twentieth century, within a larger psychological and psychoanalytic frame, a new notion of aptitude had taken hold: the child as artist par excellence. Children's visual and creative production was used by the scientific community as a measure of mental function — much as graphology had been used from the mid-nineteenth century to bolster expertise in criminal cases or to identify particular psychiatric conditions.[6] The chief innovation in this domain was the psychometric test, which offered comparative insights into performance and aptitude. Following Alfred Binet and Theodore Simon's development of the first intelligence test in France in 1906, early tests were designed to help teachers reach children according to their strengths and developmental progress, not to sort and divide them by social and racial categories as they arguably came to do.

Surveying the impact of early intelligence tests, historian of science John Carson has argued that early twentieth-century psychologists found in tests a form of language and a viable technology that validated their professional authority.[7] As tests grew in ubiquity, they became central to teachers' and psychologists' collaborative work in classrooms and laboratories. As early as 1926, an editorial in the *Revista de Pedagogía* suggested, all too soon, that the apogee of the 'test' was past. It acknowledged, however, that these measures would leave an indelible imprint on society:

> Como todas las modas, esta de los 'tests' no duró mucho tiempo. Pero, a diferencia de lo que ocurre con la vida social, las modas en la ciencia no desaparecen totalmente, sino que los estudios que las representan dejan de ocupar el primer plano de interés, para incorporarse al cuerpo de doctrina a que pertenecen.[8]

> [Like all fashions, this one of 'tests' did not last long. But, unlike in social life, fads in science never completely disappear. These studies may no longer occupy the first rank of interest, rather becoming incorporated into a larger body of doctrine.]

The boom in intelligence tests would give way to a new craze, the editorial suggested, proposing holistic movements such as Gestalt psychology as the likely next wave in pedagogy. Such a process of import, adaptation, and institutionalization was both conscious and self-understood.

Through a converging perspective, a close linkage between children's art and primitivist, Expressionist, and abstract art has been well-documented by psychologists and historians of art alike.[9] Influential studies of children's art served to establish an integral connection between visuality and the mind, both for teachers and psychologists seeking objective measures and for vanguard artists seeking to buck naturalism, derivative work, and traditional artistic instruction. Such scholarship included Karl Lamprecht's 1906 article 'Les Dessins d'enfant comme source historique' on the genealogy of children's art, George-Henri Luquet's 1913 *Les Dessins d'un enfant*, and Georges Rouma's *Le Langage graphique de l'enfant* of the same year. Children's drawings across developmental ages could be isolated and examined in major works from Georg Kerschensteiner (1905) to Marcel Braunschvig (1914).[10] The psychiatrist Robert Gaupp's popular manual of child psychology, translated into Spanish in 1927, featured an entire chapter on assessing the child's aptitude and knowledge through drawings. All of these and others contributed the base sources and even illustrations from which both teachers trained in psychometrics and vanguard artists such as Ferrant drew in their studies and pedagogical engagements. Meanwhile, children's art was not merely a passive and natural entity to be foraged and collected. It could also be nurtured and developed, as in the work of influential pedagogues abroad such as Viennese child-art pioneer Franz Čižek (1865–1946) who made famous a thoughtful, creative pedagogy of art and expression that took hold within the New Education fellowship and beyond.

Through international visits to model schools and study at institutes abroad, teachers and psychologists lauded new pedagogies of art and integrated a flood of international portrayals of the child as artist. Within children's art, it was understood, were concrete reflections of the world in which they lived. Galician doctor and paidologist José Eleizegui López in 1929 described children's drawings as windows onto their 'fisonomía mental':

> Y de estos dibujos son de los que podemos obtener datos para formar o completar la fisonomía mental del niño. Esos trazados que a una mirada inexperta nada dicen, muestran detalles de intuición, de cómo refleja el modelo interno, cuáles son sus preferencias de colorido, la manera de percibir y comprender su capacidad retentiva, y, sobre todo, y en cantidad no despreciable, nos muestran el círculo de sus intereses y la intensidad del recuerdo de éstas o de las otras imágenes.[11]

> [From these drawings we can obtain the information needed to shape or complete the child's mental physiognomy. These traces, meaningless to an inexpert eye, reveal details of intuition and reflect their interior framework: their favorite colours, their ways of perceiving and retaining information, and above all, in no small part, the range of their interests and intensity of the memory made by these or other images.]

Thus, in addition to drawing what children knew of the objects they saw, they represented the total environment in which they lived. This vision, in turn, helped paidologists, teachers, and parents understand the 'mental physiognomy' of their charges. Eleizegui even published research showing the effects of children's environments on imaginative production, indicating that children in sunny Madrid drew the sun at rates up to ten times higher than their light-starved northern equivalents in Bilbao. The influence of their surrounding environments had its clearest influence during children's earliest years, when they were considered in direct communication with the world.[12] With children's own production an expression of their entire worldview, the 'mundo del niño' was critically tied to its representations on the page.

In this way, children's drawings were never far from the individual and collective psyche. Just as these spontaneous products gave insight into the environment the children perceived, the images children created could also be used to reveal broader qualities of nation and world. There was, thus, a critical political dimension to the use of children's art as well as its psychometric significance. Building upon public interest internationally, an exhibition and contest of children's drawings was organized in Geneva in 1929. According to Spanish psychologist César Juarros, Spain had sent no works of importance, despite publicity by the Spanish Red Cross and the *Revista de Pedagogía*. With national pride on the line, he suggested that children's drawings revealed something profound about the nation from which they came. They acted as a sort of Freudian subconscious, for as long as the psychological characteristics of each nation appeared in its children's hands, the threat of international conflict and difference remained: 'El pasado, lo instintivo, lo inconsciente, de los froidianos, sigue y seguirá, probablemente, por tiempo indefinido, pudiendo más que el presente, lo adquirido, lo consciente. Así dícenoslo la diversidad psíquica de los dibujos infantiles' [The past, the instinctive, the Freudian subconscious, persists and will probably do so indefinitely, more powerful even than the present, the acquired, the conscious. Such is what we learn from the psychical diversity of these children's drawings].[13] Juarros's prophecy would, arguably, later be fulfilled in the thousands of children's drawings of war and violence collected in schools and *colonias* during the Civil War, published widely abroad as both propaganda and elegy. Many of the analyses of these works were conducted and published by those pedagogues most invested in the psychotechnic use and analysis of children's writing and drawing during the 1920s and early 1930s, including the pedagogues Mercedes Rodrigo and Regina Lago, whose related tests and tools are discussed below.[14]

Interest in children's own creative production coincided with the flourishing of the psychometric test, embraced by educators across political, religious, and educational spectrums. Visual tests and an array of mental measures — typically reliant on a predominant visual component, either eliciting children's responses to images or analysing how they illustrated prompts — were closely linked not only to empirical diagnostics, but also to the psychological and spiritual declarations that artists drew from children's art itself. As the declarations of the Manifest Groc made clear, not all children's art, nor all art aimed at children, was alike: only the liberating freedom of new, creative, vanguard production was seen to truly expand children's personhood. Introducing the teaching of art in schools and among artists, this chapter analyses how considerations of child art influenced the intellectual development of Spain's avant-garde within and alongside an omnipresent psychometric context. Bringing educators' various efforts towards a wider view of human creative development, it highlights various tools and approaches for capturing the ineffable, that is, the shifting nature and individuality of each child.

Testing the Imagination: Visuality and a Measure of the Mind

In 1933, the journalist Carlos Delgado Olivares authored a brief article in the *Heraldo de Madrid* to mark the publication of a new Spanish translation of Marcel Proust's *À la recherche du temps perdu*.[15] Delgado's discussion focused on Proust's evocation of memory through mental imagery. For Proust, a sip of tea elicited a childhood world in its full visual splendour. But, Delgado wrote, the child's perceptual world differed radically from that of an adult. Relying on the work of Gestalt psychologist Kurt Koffka, he compared Proust's use of imaginative images to the memory-images that represented the 'essence' of childhood perception. For the adult, objects were obscured by a haze of abstractions, whether physical (whiteness, roundness) or moral (goodness, virtue). In contrast, children's contact with the world was direct and unfiltered. Signalling the visuality of children's minds, Delgado repeated an anecdote gleaned from Koffka's writings: the four-year-old daughter of a colleague allegedly asked, '¿Por qué no podemos ver lo que acabo de decir?' [Why can't I see what I have just said?].[16] If an utterance had presence and force, why was it not as manifestly visible as any other physical thing? The notion that not all concepts could be seen and placed on paper was foreign to children. In this imaginative world of the visual, the child's perceptions and memories could be elicited, encouraged, recorded — and analysed, at least in part, by an adult viewer.

Principally, this work of analysis was done through psychometric tests and probes. Early tests were designed to require minimal equipment and training. Seeking to encourage the spread of tests in Spanish schools in 1922, pedagogue Mariano Sáez Morilla summarized three valid methods of studying the child:

> 1.° Experiencias de laboratorio, hechas por medio de aparatos.
> 2.° Experiencias hechas por medio de *tests* que no exigen aparatos, que duran poco tiempo y que los mismos niños por reacción, nos proporcionan una prueba del estado de sus facultades psíquicas; memoria, atención, etc.
> 3.° Los cuestionarios y las encuestas, sea para completar los datos recogidos por los otros métodos o como medio supletorio cuando no puedan aplicarse los *tests* ni las experiencias de laboratorio.[17]

> [1. Laboratory experiments, conducted with the aid of various apparatuses.
> 2. Experiments carried out through tests, brief in duration and requiring no equipment, in which children's own responses reveal their state of mental functioning: memory, attention, etc.
> 3. Questionnaires and surveys, to obtain information either excluded by the above means or as a supplement when neither tests nor laboratory experiments may be conducted.]

These were to be the tools of the modern pedagogue, capable of providing necessary insight into an individual child's aptitudes and capabilities. As Spanish teachers began adopting and adapting mental tests in earnest, efforts were made to distinguish between the forms of knowledge that might be solicited. 'No es solo la *capacidad* cuantitativa la que puede ponerse de manifiesto en las pruebas mentales, sino también la *aptitud* cualitativa del niño de hoy' [it is not only the quantitative *ability* that can be demonstrated through mental tests, but also the qualitative *aptitude* of the child of today], psychologist Juan Zaragüeta argued in 1919.[18] Quantitative

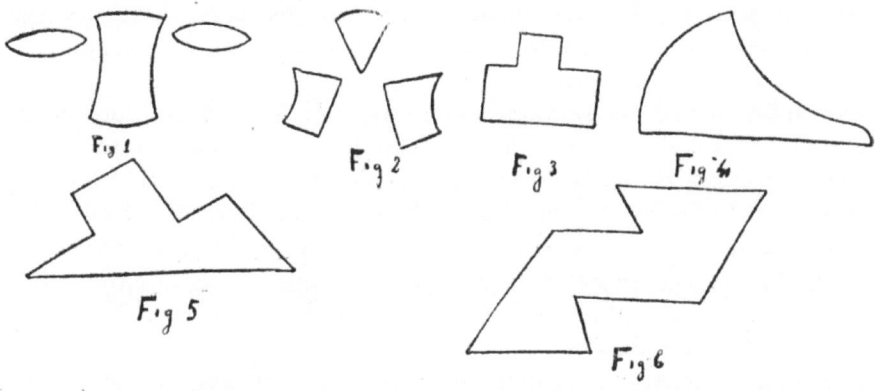

FIG. 5.1. A test by Emilio Mira y López probing children's spatial abilities.
Source: Emilio Mira y López, 'Pruebas para la determinación de los tipos de
inteligencia en los niños', *Archivos de Neurobiología, Psicología, Fisiología, Histología,
Neurología y Psiquiatría*, 7 (1927), 3–37 (p. 19).

and qualitative understandings of data implied difference in the interpretation
and use of that data. In order to understand the child as a physical and mental
whole, pedagogues sought evidence from which they aimed to educate in a more
appropriate, individualized form. Using codified results, pedagogues looked to
enact what Eleizegui, a decade later, termed 'oportunismo fisiológico', that is, the
tailoring of education to different developmental stages. Posing overly challenging
cognitive tasks to a young child was like demanding fruit from a sapling, he wrote:
premature, unnecessary, and ill-advised. Others concurred, elaborating the need
for data, tests, and observations, both to identify and treat 'abnormality' as well as
to identify 'gifted' children, a process urgently suggested for the children of both
rich and poor.[19]

The mastery and adaptation of international models and analytical tools formed
part of a larger path to disciplinary professionalization and scientific modernity
within the teaching profession.[20] One of the earliest exponents of psychometric
measures, for instance, was Madrid pedagogue and professor Anselmo González,
who during the early 1920s promoted simple classroom tests. The exercises could be
applied by any teacher across the country, 'sin aparatos' [without equipment], and
were therefore among the earliest, most extensively applied probes.[21] Yet many of
those most invested in a technoscientific approach to measuring and categorizing
the mind, such as Emilio Mira y López, offered notes of caution. In introducing a
range of measures, he argued presciently that children possessed a 'multiplicidad'
of intelligences. Because there was no one standard form of intelligence, tests must
evaluate not the *quantity* of data tests provided, but also their form and *quality*.[22] In
a number of different exercises, Mira sought to do just that, using a series of fixed
shapes to probe children's ability to invert and reconstitute configurations of shapes
over time (Fig. 5.1). The goal was to measure *Augenmaß,* translated as 'medida del ojo,

golpe de vista' [measurement by the eye, *at a glance*], that is, the ability to synthesize 'las formas, tamaños y distancias' [forms, sizes, and distances].[23] Mira suggested that children's creativity led them to a wide variety of linkages and responses. This effect stemmed from an intensely felt, cohesive, and intellectual experience of form and idea, or in his words, 'las *constelaciones* de imágenes, ideas y recuerdos, presentes en el subconsciente en el momento de la prueba' [the *constellations* of images, ideas, and memories present in their subconscious at the time of the test].[24] Relying on children's mental flexibility as seen through visual intelligence, Mira suggested the mind's impulse to complete, enclose, or link diverse elements into a unified constellation of parts. Psychometric tests were promising not because they offered a decisive number, as one might imagine today, but because they also allowed room for a multiplicity of intelligences.

By measuring their visual, spatial, and synthetic abilities in the classroom, teachers could evaluate students' progress and encourage their capacities. A clear process of translation, adaptation, and implementation can be observed, as Miguel Ángel Cerezo Manrique and others have shown in expositions of the growth of psychometric tests in Spain alongside models and precedents gleaned from international psychologists.[25] Such tests walked a fine line between stimulating the child's creativity and seeking to evaluate the mind through quantitative analysis. Many relied, in addition to verbal or mathematical abilities, on qualities of spatial and visual ability. A common procedure was to present children with an image of a sketched scene or a complex painting by, say, Francisco Goya (1746–1828) and have children narrate descriptively their representations of perspective, line, form, and space, as was done in tests conducted in schools by teacher Bonifacio Arrabal. In a 1922 report he argued that children's future work and production would rely on their creative imagination. Suggesting more about his own intellectual affinities than those of his students, Arrabal cited the Dada and Futurist movements as evidence for the rise of creativity in modern culture. All acts of the imagination, he suggested, elevated a constructed mental image over the existing world. Like memories, these acts were a necessary 'composición irreal, obra de artífice'.[26] While the connection of avant-garde art to children's psychology was widespread, creativity itself was celebrated in notably developmental terms.

The psychometric emphasis on imagination and visuo-spatial ability drew from a broader paidological well. The young pedagogues Joan Roura i Parella and Felipe Panizo Gambón, for instance, in 1923 described various tools that could be used to 'measure' the development of imagination. Children's auditory or visual memory could be tested with an image shown for ten seconds, removed, and replaced. The child was then asked to recall its details, while their 'clarity' of visual imagination could be tested by asking the subject to invert words or syllables, measuring errors, omissions, or additions of letters. Drawing upon González's school tests 'sin aparatos', Roura and Panizo described further probes using Rorschach-style inkblots to elicit images, drawings to elicit stories, and free writing exercises on a given theme — the latter judged both quantitatively (through, for example, the length of the essay) and qualitatively (at the teacher's discretion).[27] The incorporation of verbal and visual techniques by pedagogues demonstrates an acute interest in the visuo-imaginative function of the child's mind, alongside the tests' surrounding insights into children's greater proficiency with verbal, spatial, and numerical cues.

Notable Spanish tests of intelligence adapted foreign models and, through comparative means, sought to understand something about the Spanish child — not just his or her mental frame, but their environmental conditions as a whole. These included most notably Mercedes Rodrigo's and Pedro Rosselló's 'Escala Popular de Madrid', revised from the work of Swiss pedagogue Édouard Claparède, Rodrigo's teacher and later Rosselló's colleague at Geneva's Institut Jean-Jacques Rousseau. Rodrigo's and Rosselló's test evaluated boys and girls on memory, vocabulary, arithmetic, writing and drawing, and general reasoning based on small pictures of scenes and objects. The results could be compared and sorted by gender, age, and social class, as well as between Spanish and Swiss public schools (to Spain's detriment). According to Rodrigo and Rosselló, the tests showed more than individual development; their results went so far as to lay bare questions of 'injustice', the 'material and spiritual penury' occasioned by societal striations. Winning the 1923 prize from the *Revista de Pedagogía*, the scale was adapted and put into practice in other regions of Spain, for instance in Córdoba the following year.[28] The spread of psychometric tests was furthered with Rodrigo's and José Germain's subsequent adaptation of Lewis Terman's 1916 Stanford-Binet Intelligence Scales, a work reviewed in 1930 by leading Madrid psychiatrist José Sacristán.[29]

That same year, in 1930, Regina Lago de Comas (1897–1966) described a series of drawing-based tests that she and colleagues had conducted to test children's development of spatial perspective within their environments. Lago was a prominent pedagogue from Palencia, trained at the Escuela de Estudios Superiores de Magisterio and, after two years of experimental psychology studies in Geneva (1928–30), then teaching at the Escuela Normal de Lugo.[30] Having studied at the Institut Jean-Jacques Rousseau with professors and colleagues such as Claparède and Piaget, her work suggested that infantile perception, gleaned through drawing, offered the most promising points of difference and investigation in child psychology. Counterintuitively, but following established conventions in the psychology of children's art, Lago explained through her own tests' results the common understanding that children's realities were predominantly intellectually rather than perspectively accurate. Children drew an intuitive mental view of the world, freed of the conventions of representational perspective. She used the ideas of juxtaposition and syncretism, proposed as keys to infantile thought, as way to understand the phenomenon of children's own views of the world: their *'realismo intelectual'*. Children saw objects not as adults would imagine them, but rather as schematic types that represented all the child's knowledge of them.[31]

How might drawings reflect the demands and limitations, and promise, of understanding children's phenomenological experiences of the world? Lago began by soliciting children's drawings to gain access to their mode of thought. The process was not meant to be universal for all children, but diachronic across a child's development. If one were to collect all the drawings done across his or her development, this evidence would give the surest insight into the 'proceso formativo de su pensar, a la génesis de la noción de *objeto* que se da en un *espacio* y que está en *relaciones variables* con otros objetos' [the formative process of thought, the genesis of the notion of the *object,* which is located in *space* and is in *variable relations* with other objects]. With this development in mind, she designed a series of tests to determine how spatial perspective influenced children's representations. With a hundred subjects from ages five to fourteen, Lago sought to collect results that emphasized description rather than statistics. She asked children to imagine and draw a specific object familiar to them. Next, she revealed the object and asked the children to judge how well they had represented it, comparing the drawings to their memories of the objects or scenes. The qualitative results were, she suggested, a rich source for psychologists, giving them access to the 'influencias mutuas entre el pensar infantil y las exigencias de una adaptación a la realidad exterior percibida en un momento y una posición dadas' [mutual influences between children's thought and their adaptation to an exterior reality perceived at a given moment and from a certain perspective].[32] With this statement, Lago integrated psychological notions of progressive development with a perspectivist depiction of the child.

By breaking results down by points in time and space, psychologists such as Lago sought to use art to define perceptions and representations of space. According to Lago, an egocentric, subjective 'realismo intelectual' predominated until about the age of seven. Children would draw objects not in accordance with conventional perspective, but as types — towers from the side, stairs with parallel edges — thus producing anti-perspectival representations. They would follow their idea of an object rather than the illogical distortions of visual perspective, because they lacked 'una noción definida, intelectualizada, del espacio' [a defined, intellectualized notion of space]. Then came a period of struggle between 'realismo intelectual' and an increasingly strong 'realismo visual', leading to a *bricolage* of these two tendencies: the latter nascent, the former increasingly subjugated. From about eleven years onward, children began to show capability in perspective, demonstrating that they had moved beyond an egocentric and 'primitive' motor space. They began to develop adult visual realism — what she called an 'intellectualized, objective, geometric space'.[33] Lago likened the adolescent's realization of space to man's Renaissance 'discovery' of artistic perspective, as young people absorbed logic and science, akin in their minds to society's integration of relativity and new scientific principles. Connecting broader societal paradigm shifts to the child's mental development, she suggested that visual and spatial tests were central to a larger project of intellectual renovation.

Fascination with children's visual abilities and tendencies was impossible to divorce wholly from larger contexts of psychometric testing and analysis, nor was doing so the ultimate aim for most pedagogical reformers. Progressive Spanish pedagogues demonstrated the tension manifest in all diagnostic efforts, namely how to incorporate both an internally holistic understanding of the child's worldview and an externally imposed, clinical understanding of development. Numerous actors attempted to access children's abilities and experience from different angles of methodological approximation. All appealed to the objectivity of science — principally a psychological understanding of the child's mental structure and development — to make their claims. Efforts such as those by Lago, Arrabal, Mira, and others constituted a middle ground: a collective effort to understand the relationship between the mind and its environmental space, to delineate differences between the adult's and the child's view of the world, and to garner significant, legitimate results through experiential and descriptive terms. Drawing on a deeper background of the psychology of child art, a reading of their works suggests that it was not simply avant-garde fascination with primitivism or the Freudian subconscious which motivated pedagogical reformers to embrace drawing as a tool in both education and evaluation. Rather, there were concrete methodological goals underlying efforts to elaborate the visual 'world of the child'. New psychological methods both affirmed and bolstered the work of avant-garde artists looking to transcend the limitations of pure pedagogy.

Drawing the World of the Child: Infantile Sketches and the Psyche

Children's drawings, as Ángel Ferrant declared in 1933, were something 'eterno, permanente, BIOLÓGICO'.[34] Ferrant saw children's art arising irrepressibly, essential to growth across history and borders. Yet such art is also rooted in particular cultures, times, and spaces of production. Spanish teachers' uses of drawing drew from a wide body of scholarship in European psychological, psychoanalytic, and psychiatric works, but interest in children's art extended beyond any one school of thought. Artists such as Ferrant solicited, collected, and promoted children's drawings as a validation of larger aesthetic projects. Whereas psychometric tests focused on quantifying results, art and expression were posed as providing more authentic insight into how the child viewed the world. With the child understood to be in direct contact with the 'essence' of objects, meaningless scrawls transformed into insights into evolving perceptions. As teachers, psychologists and artists grew enamoured of 'el dibujo infantil', they looked to children's art as a key to the mind.

In 1922, Spain's first journal of neuropsychiatry, the *Archivos de Neurobiología, Psicología, Fisiología, Histología, Neurología y Psiquiatría* which Ortega y Gasset had founded with Gonzalo Lafora and José Sacristán three years before, published an extended study of the psychological convergences between modern art, children's art, and works produced by schizophrenic patients. The author of this particular article, the prominent psychiatrist Lafora, described the child as akin to a Cubist, free to bypass visual laws in order to expose a more individual, liberated, and authentic view of the world.[35] Lafora melded diverse sources from German psychiatrist Ernst Kretschmer to Unamuno, Friedrich Nietzsche, and Freud to argue that artistic representations of space were a manifestation of the modern subconscious. In this regard, children, along with primitive man and schizophrenic patients, created 'arte cerebral por excelencia' as a direct result of their symbolic, subjective, and stylised representations of the world.[36] Such a description was by no means unusual, but amply confirms how closely images of the child-artist were aligned methodologically with scholarly studies of both the modern mind and of modern art. Describing the child's altogether foreign spatial sense, Lafora stated:

> El niño, desconocedor de la representación de la perspectiva y del espacio, nos muestra las casetas y los caballos en planos distintos de aquellos que están el resto de las cosas y la superficie del mar. La realidad visual aparece aquí trastornada ante el esfuerzo de evocación del niño, que como un cubista prescinde de las leyes visuales y de las tradiciones estéticas.[37]

> [The child, to whom representations of perspective and space are foreign, shows us the little houses and horses on levels distinct from the surface of the sea as well as from everything else. Visual reality appears disturbed by the child's effort to evoke it, as they disobey visual laws and aesthetic traditions like a Cubist.]

In interpreting a selection of children's drawings, he suggested, viewers must learn how to draw out the essence, the 'conjunto' and 'Weltanschauung' of the child's mind. The question for Lafora was one of coherency. Should such visual representations be perceived and understood as a whole or as a series of parts: 'un todo o solo como una aglomeración, en la que reúnen las unidades que él tenía en su imaginación' [a whole or only an agglomeration, in which the units that he had in his imagination come together]? This was a query which was at once psychological, perceptual, and concerned with the relationship of form, compositions, and Gestalt to inner thought and perception.[38] In the images he reproduced, juxtaposed with comparable sources from contemporaneous avant-garde art, Lafora aimed to show how children began with what they knew of the world, as in their depiction of a bullring, using a direct rather than perspectival approach (Fig. 5.2). Supported by a relatively univocal, and growing, line of scholarship, Lafora suggested that the child intuitively drew what he *knew* of the object, rather than how representative convention would depict it.

Psychological studies of the developing mind gave the celebration of children's art an intellectual force. Using drawing as a lens to view the workings of the child's mind, psychologists and artists alike emphasized points of difference from that of the adult. Analyses of children's art across Europe became standard psychological references, alongside visuo-imaginative tests such as Rorschach ink blots, advocated to Spanish teachers as a psychological tool by at least 1928.[39] Critical were those drawings known as 'memory-images', summoned from memory, versus either a modelled drawing from life or one of pure fantasy. The capacity to remember and re-imagine was seen as crucial to childhood. Children had, for instance, a greater capacity for 'eidetic imagery', or sensorial after-images, said to be a key indicator of cognitive difference between children and adults. As Sacristán recounted in 1927, the German psychologist Erich Rudolf Jaensch (1883–1940) described the phenomenon by which children recalled a memory in concrete visual terms — to 'volver a ver', or re-see, a mental image with sensorial immediacy.[40] Sacristán argued that interest in this topic signalled a willingness to recognize not just the

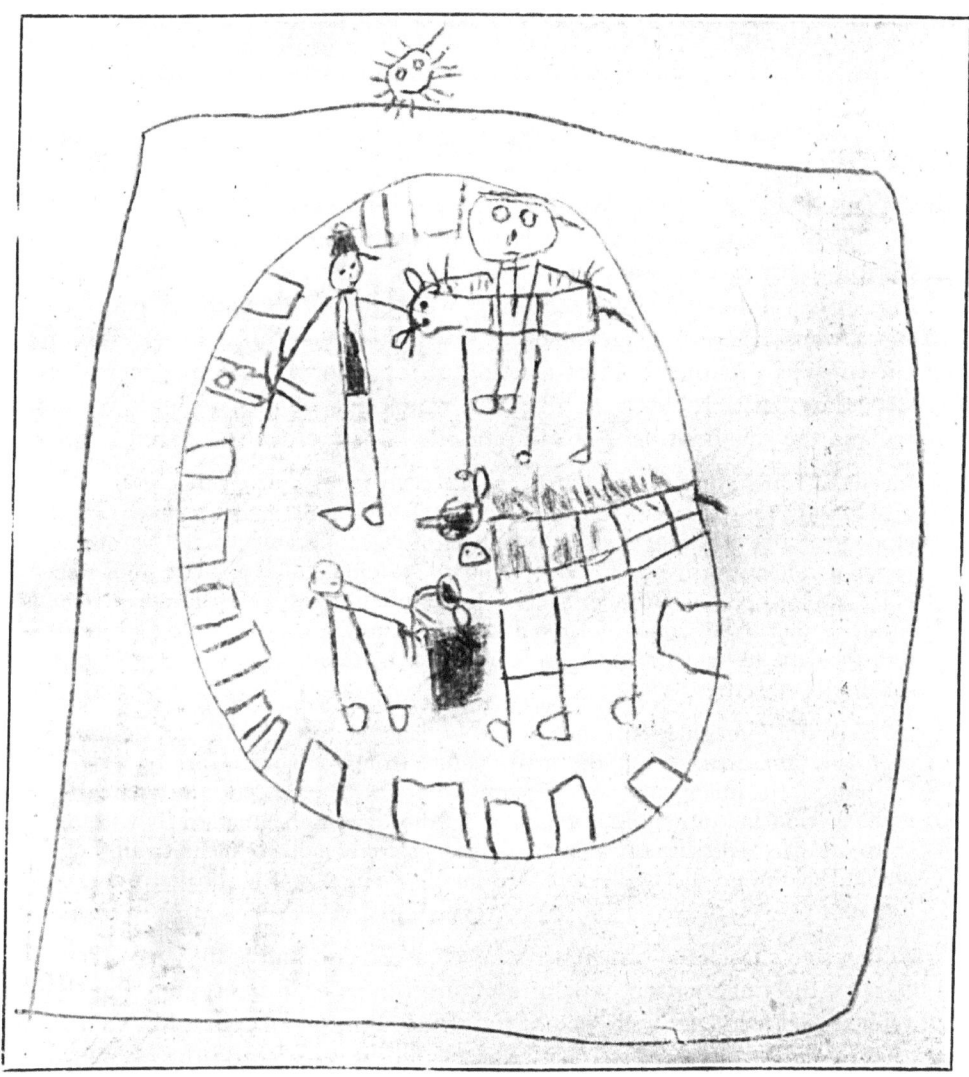

FIG. 5.2. A bullring as seen by a seven-year-old child.
Source: Gonzalo R. Lafora, 'Estudio psicológico del cubismo y expresionismo',
Archivos de Neurobiología, Psicología, Fisiología, Histología, Neurología y Psiquiatría, 3
(1922), 119–55, pl. 4 (Fig. 22).

quantitative differences between children and adults, but also qualitative ones: the range of the child's psyche, 'el núcleo esencial y definidor del alma del niño' [the essential, defining nucleus of the child's mind].[41] In calling up after-images, children accessed a vital, direct recollection of their worlds.

Qualities of vivid, imaginative recall made infantile art of utmost interest to Spain's avant-garde. Sebastià Gasch, one of Spain's most dedicated proponents of children's art and a co-signatory of the Manifest Groc, argued in 1930 that children were capable of creating great art precisely because they drew from memory and the imagination — from what they knew intuitively to be true, rather from imitation or a rote observation of reality. Children were not realist painters painstakingly seeking to transcribe an image's perfect correspondence onto canvas, but rather individual minds catching hold of fleeting glimpses of a subjective reality. Gasch urged Catalan artists to leave behind the imitations of realism and to embrace memory and the imagination — to imbibe the liberty of a child-gaze:

> En efecto: la imaginación, prisionera cuando el artista se somete voluntariamente al naturalismo, vuela libremente cuando el artista pinta de memoria. Sin el control del naturalismo, la imaginación hace libremente de las suyas, engendrando así un arte que tiene mucho de creación y muy poco de imitación [...]. Que los que tengan imaginación, le permitan, pues, volar libremente sin trabas. Y que cedan el naturalismo a los impotentes, a los pobres de espíritu, a todos los que no sabiendo crear, se han de ver tristemente reducidos a la tarea subalterna de imitar.[42]

> [Indeed: the imagination, imprisoned when the artist willingly submits to naturalism, soars when the artist paints from memory. Unrestricted by naturalism, the imagination freely roams where it will, engendering an art that is all creation and little imitation [...]. So let those with imagination fly without trusses. Let us cede naturalism to the impotent, to the poor of spirit, to all those who, knowing not how to create, are sorrily reduced to the subaltern task of imitation.]

Gasch suggested that pre-eminent artists such as Picasso and Joan Miró (1893–1983) had liberated the imagination, separating conventions of visual representation from what they recognized as the essence of the thing. Proponents of child-art arrived at their aesthetic positions against a vast background of research on the exceptionality of childhood vision and liberty, one which could not be read apart from ideas of primitivism and the natural world in which children lived. As Gasch wrote, both 'los salvajes y los niños, que pintan de memoria, son a menudo más reales que los pedestres naturalistas, y que nos dan una imagen de la realidad mucho más potente y exacta' [savages and children, who paint from memory, are often more authentic than run-of-the-mill naturalists, for they impart to us a more potent and exact vision of reality].[43] By glorifying memory and the imagination as higher forms of access in art, Gasch celebrated the child's ability to represent the world more honestly than in the codified, representational renderings of the adult hand.

But in order to vivify art, unfettered imagination was needed. Following the example of schools in France, Belgium, Switzerland, Britain, and elsewhere, Spanish schools began to integrate the pedagogy of art in ways that anticipated and built upon notions of children's perception and active learning. From the early twentieth century, pedagogues began consciously to revive and reform instructional art teaching. Shifting from artistic education as the inculcation of culture and training of technical ability, they joined international pedagogues and artists focusing upon the child's imagination and vivacity. An early pioneer in the creative teaching of art in Catalonia was Francesc Galí (1880–1965), who founded his own *noucentista*-influenced academy in 1906 as well as the Consell d'Investigació Pedagògica, later the Consell de Pedagogia, in 1913. As Inés Ortega Cubero has detailed, Galí's school became a centre for artistic and intellectual activity and attracted figures such as Miró, Josep Llorens i Artigas, Enric Ricart, Francesc Domingo, Rafael Sala, and later Josep Ràfols, Marian Espinal, and Joaquín Torres Garcia. The school was founded on the premise that art could not be taught, but would flourish under appropriate guidance. An 'educación integral' through the cultivation of the senses was encouraged, from music to literature — Bach, Shakespeare, Goethe, Dostoevsky — and through natural excursions. Galí's practical instruction went beyond the purely visual, incorporating exercises in perception and tactile senses. Blindfolding the pupil and having them draw objects based on touch or presenting them with an object from an unfamiliar angle, he sought to develop a new representation of reality.[44] Through Galí's school came a rising generation of artists interested in pioneering various experimental models of learning, engaging, and entertaining the child.

These included the aforementioned Catalan-Uruguayan artist Torres García (1874–1949) who began teaching in Colegio Mont d'Or in 1907, founded by pedagogue Joan Palau i Vera on progressive Fröbelian, Montessori, and New Educational principles. At Mont d'Or, Torres García's experience as a teacher underlay his conviction that the act of drawing and creating was essential to children's mental and spiritual development. During a decade in which his first three children (Olimpia, Augusto, and Ifigenia) were born, Torres García began sketching and creating hundreds of toys and wood-block objects designed to align with children's developing psychology and tendencies: their tendency towards fundamental forms, their sensorial primacy towards grasping and moving, and the physical construction and deconstruction of those objects around them (Fig. 5.3).[45] From early training with Antoni Gaudí, designing stained-glass cathedral windows (1903–04), to his later focus upon fundamental elements of circles, squares, and blocks in toys that could be composed and articulated at will, Torres García's universal constructivism began as a joint artistic-pedagogical exploration in the origins of form and shape. As his career boomed, he professionalized his operation, moving to Italy for cheaper production and establishing a company called Aladdin Toys from 1924. From such an abiding substratum of playful children's art, Torres García brought a childhood essentiality to views of form, manifest in his foundation of the Cercle et Carré group in Paris in 1929, work with the Grupo de Arte Constructivo in Madrid with Benjamin Palencia, Maruja Mallo, José Moreno Villa, and his theories of constructivism and structuralism in Montevideo after 1934.[46]

Fig. 5.3. Torres García's woodblock parrot and related toy models integrated children's psychology with constructivist design. Source: Joaquín Torres García, *Loro*, c. 1922–23, oil on wood; model for Aladdin Toys, reverse of box top, c. 1930. Courtesy of the Museo Torres García.

JOUETS ALADIN   Modèle déposé par J. Torrès-Garcia

The act of drawing was similarly a focus of model institutions such as the JAE's Instituto-Escuela. The archives of the Retiro school, today the IES Isabel la Católica in Madrid, contain dozens of *cuadernos escolares* created by secondary pupils to document and synthesize their everyday experiences. Instruction in drawing, painting, sculpture, and relief-making were central to the curriculum, with one teacher, Jacinto Alcántara Gómez, advocating a 'visión sensorial de la naturaleza', arguing that colourful work tapped into a uniquely Hispanic, Velázquian approach to art that countered the 'intellectualism' of technical, form-driven drawings. These works are more advanced than the pre-pubescent 'child art' of modernist fantasy. They display a solid foundation in outline, perspective, and detail, whether in sketches of biological specimens or cultural and excursionist field trips around Madrid and its environs.[47] The practice of the illustrated *cuaderno escolar* would remain central to Republican education, while collections of stories and drawings were published by school presses such as that sponsored by Barcelona's Escola del Mar, with its journal *Garbí*. The latter began with primarily adult-contributed photographic and graphical content, but eventually populated its pages almost entirely with children's sketches from the early 1920s to mid-1930s. Teachers at rural as well as urban schools similarly initiated classroom presses, operated and printed by the children themselves.[48]

Elsewhere in Madrid, namely in Cuatro Caminos, pedagogue and school director Ángel Llorca and his colleagues at the Grupo Escolar Cervantes translated artistic theory into a pedagogy of the imagination for primary school children. Here, the art curriculum taught children to employ free and spontaneous forms in drawing then, only in older years, to submit to instructive, methodical, technical instruction. Through travel and study visits, Llorca had come into contact with the work of Viennese pedagogue Franz Čižek, around whom the classroom teaching of art in Europe had undergone a revolution, towards a theorized valorization of the imaginative and individual practice of art. Spanish pedagogues came into contact with his work through presentations and conferences abroad, integrating these into their practice. Llorca collected brochures on child art during his stay at the New Education Fellowship conference in Locarno in 1927, to which he travelled with Spanish colleagues in a delegation funded by the Junta para Ampliación de Estudios. The conference featured lectures by Čižek on how to use art as a tool for 'creative formation' in childhood.[49] In addition to using great art as a spur for discussion, in which Llorca asked children to work in groups and describe what they saw in paintings by Goya or Diego Velázquez (1599–1660), he implemented methods of reading instruction by which the very kinaesthetic act of writing and drawing acted as a precursor to the more rational modes of spelling and composition.[50]

To the extent that children's developing motor abilities allowed, drawings were the closest approximations of the psyche that teachers could foster. Influential pedagogues of art under the ambit of the Institución Libre de Enseñanza included Elisa López Velasco (1884–1936[?]), a colleague of Llorca's who published widely on the teaching of art and the notion of drawing as a form of visual language. Her manual was cited by scholars and practitioners of child art through the mid-century, notably by the novelist Josefina Aldecoa (née Rodríguez Álvarez, 1926–2011), who in 1959 praised López Velasco's focus on vivacity, movement, and spontaneity and claimed that she had been the first pedagogue to imbibe and communicate this spirit of creativity through children's drawing.[51] As collected in the records of Justa Freire (1896–1965), a colleague at the Grupo Escolar Cervantes, López Velasco's manuscript on the practice of drawing in primary school argued for its primacy over other forms of learning. According to her, education had passed from the filling (*llenar*) of the mind with knowledge towards the projection of interior forms: namely, the shapes of the child's own mind. The act of drawing constituted a unique language of its own: 'El dibujo por tanto es un lenguaje y más universal que la lengua materna' [Drawing is, therefore, a language and one more universal than any mother tongue].[52]

Imaginative activity manifested on paper from the expression of subconscious, pre-rational sensations, in an almost psychoanalytic sense: 'las múltiples sensaciones visuales, táctiles y musculares dan vida a su conciencia' [the multiple visual, tactile, and muscular sensations that give life to their consciousness].[53] Whether depicting a human body, a house, or a horse, children gave visual form to the world around them. As was done with theories of globalist learning, López Velasco drew on a vocabulary of perceptual understanding across the five senses to argue for the importance of considering children's early drawings within a new understanding of education. These constituted a 'dibujo lenguaje' that moved outward towards representative content, 'dibujo técnico'.[54] Summarizing the historical progress of art education, López Velasco described an evolution from classical education towards the sensorial, humanistic teachings of the Renaissance, to rigid nineteenth-century pedagogies focused on analytical, geometrical designs and knowledge. Finally, she shifted to the present: drawing as intuitive visual language. Summarizing Kerschensteiner's claim that language, drawing, and manual work formed the 'linguistic triad' of childhood, she subsumed the mental, spiritual, and physical aspects of development into art. Visual intelligence brought out the whole child.[55]

A unified emphasis on primary, visual, physical creation came through not just in primary-school classrooms such as those of Llorca or López Velasco. The pedagogue Victor Masriera made it his mission, for instance, to introduce a systematic form of art-based pedagogy, *dibujo escolar*, into Spain's schools across primary and secondary schools, using simple schematic shapes for the objects of everyday life that led increasingly towards technical instruction. While less aesthetically innovative than the aforementioned methods, Masriera developed exercises to sharpen artistic ability through visual-manual exercises. Two-dimensional and three-dimensional models, switches in perspective, comparisons of forms and sizes, combinations of shapes and revolving bodies all formed part of his programme.[56] Ultimately, however, these methods were just that: methods. As Freire wrote in a series of handwritten classroom notes for fellow teachers, all of the ideas she and colleagues such as López Velasco engineered were secondary to the care embedded in them:

Las indicaciones metodológicas que caben en un capítulo, como las que llevan muchas páginas, de uno o varios libros, no sirven para nada en la escuela, si antes, el maestro no las ha hecho carne suya y pone [...] en ellas la vida que vivifica, el cuidado que hace cuidadosos, el entusiasmo que entusiasma y [...] que abre en el niño horizontes amplios y caminos nuevos.

[The methodological instructions that fit in a chapter, or across many pages or books, are useless if, the teacher has not first made them his own flesh and blood and brought [...] to these the life that vivifies, the care that makes others take care, the enthusiasm that enthuses and [...] that opens in the child wide horizons and new paths.]

The values of liberty, individual spiritual development, and hands-on physical experience that Freire advocated culminated in a focus upon art education.

Alongside teachers' celebrations of children's art and production, a series of exhibitions fuelled the popularization of children's art: first a 1925 exposition of children's art in the Parque del Retiro, followed by a well-received 1926 exhibition showcasing images created by children at Mexican open-air schools.[61] In 1927, Madrid's Lyceum Club Femenino sponsored an exhibition of Spanish children's toys, and the next year drawings from children enrolled in the society's in-house nursery.[62] Featuring the show in a headline article in *La Voz*, art critic Juan de la Encina (Ricardo Gutiérrez Abascal, 1883–1963) applauded the women who had organized the show, noting that their work was based on a solid foundation of international scholarship.[63] His analysis did the same. He drew attention to children's early representations of the human figure, depicted at its most basic, a stick figure or 'monigote': a circle for the head or belly, with protruding lines for limbs, a familiar sequence from studies such as those of Georges Rouma, whose images of children's drawings were frequently reproduced in comparable Spanish manuals. Delighting in the art of six-year-old Sonia Araquistáin, the critic praised her charming, freely-drawn *monigote* depictions of Goya's *Marquesa de Pontejos* or *Maja vestida*, drawn from memory.[64] According to him, adults must cultivate children's 'espontaneidad estética' [aesthetic spontaneity] and not cloud works with academic practice. They should approach tactfully and respectfully the 'impulsión sagrada' of the child's nascent personality, allowing their pupils to synthesize the world individually.[65]

Visual art was, finally, a crucial component of the Second Republic's rural outreach and *misiones pedagógicas,* which among other initiatives brought reproductions of great Spanish masterpieces including Goya and Velázquez, El Greco (1541–1614) and Bartolomé Esteban Murillo (1617–1682) to the countryside via a travelling Museo del Pueblo.[57] Through such efforts, but also through their own teaching engagements, artists of the Spanish avant-garde advanced children's art as part of a cultural and political framework. Artists such as Maruja Mallo (1902–95) joined with writers and dramatists in travelling, teaching, and becoming personally invested, in her case placed as a teacher in Ávila in 1933. As Roberta Quance has shown through her analysis of an anonymous article in the avant-garde journal *Diablo Mundo*, 'El niño, genio natural' (1934), Mallo's efforts were received in accord with celebratory representations of children's perspective and unity of vision. For the author, children's drawings from Mallo's classroom illustrated the notion of the child as artistic 'genius'.[58] By drawing from life, and particularly from memory itself, the author noted that children were forced to discern and to distinguish: 'se veía forzado a dar por sí mismo una interpretación de las cosas' [they were forced to give an independent interpretation of things]. In doing so, children formed an entirely new language and mode of expression. A turn towards freer, open creation simultaneously constituted a denial of prior modes of art, as renounced by the Manifest Groc. Here, disparaged were the 'viejos profesores' [old teachers] fixated on hands transcribing models 'maquinalmente' [mechanistically]. Such rigidity had had an adverse effect on children, on their 'espíritu' and its development, it was contended.[59] In addition to her teaching, Mallo would illustrate an Italian folktale for children, published in 1935 by José Bergamín's *Cruz y Raya* and printed by poet Manuel Altolaguirre.[60]

By popularizing children's art as both a form of quantitative insight and qualitative inspiration, teachers and public figures made way for the celebration of free drawing and creative art in schools. Together, various models looked to employ, further, and integrate art education into the classroom. Seeking to synthesize such diverse efforts and reforms as part of a coherent movement, teacher Rafael Verdier in 1935 advocated an 'estética en la escuela' in his address at the Semana Pedagógica de la Nacional in Málaga.[66] Through the domain of art, he suggested that faculties of philosophical 'intuition' and 'aesthetic emotion' must be cultivated, in opposition to pure reason and rationality.[67] These qualities must be fostered for the sake of individuals' personal and spiritual development. By engaging with the most fundamental creations of the self, those of early childhood, artists and teachers theorized pedagogy through the visual. While psychologists found ways to quantify, diagnose, and examine children's prodigious imagination through various test-based measures, a corresponding cultural and political celebration looked to the spontaneously generated products of children's minds for inspiration. Artists sought to access and nurture children's individuality and perspective through pencil and paint — a humanization of art even amidst its self-conscious 'dehumanization', in Ortega's famous term.

Embodying Spirit: Ferrant, Abril, and the Rehumanization of Art

> Se deja al chico que vea, que invente, que interprete, que se recree re-creando el mundo entero. Cada individuo tiene que nacer, y el mundo tiene en cada uno que nacer, o no sentiremos jamás la unión de nuestro espíritu y el mundo.

> [Let the child look, invent, interpret, and seek recreation in re-creating the entire world. Each individual must be born, and the world must be born within each of us, if we are ever to sense the union of our spirit and the world.]

> Manuel Abril, 'Comentarios a nuestros grabados' (1933)

Celebrations of children's art proved an iterative cycle. As pedagogues and teachers theorized children's scribbles and adapted classroom methods, artists drew inspiration from children's production and contributed writings, odes, and new experiments. A notable shared educational and aesthetic fascination with children's visual and imaginative creativity characterizes the aforementioned writings of sculptor Ángel Ferrant and the critic and writer (including of children's stories and theatre) Manuel Abril, which both provide new windows into this cycle of reciprocal exchange. In different ways, their works sought to reconcile what they saw as the primitive, essential aspects of childhood with its alleged enduring, spiritual qualities, which could be recaptured and renewed through art. Like many of his contemporaries, Ferrant was fascinated with children's drawings, collecting examples from around the world and a wide library on the psychology of children's art. He even collaborated with Lorca, designing marionettes for the poet's play *Retablillo de San Cristóbal* in 1935. But it was through Ferrant's direct work with children at Barcelona's Escola del Mar and Madrid's Asociación Auxiliar del Niño, specifically its *club infantil*, that he furthered a view of children as chiefly creative experimenters.[68] Abril, meanwhile, sought through various critical, journalistic explications of art and childhood to isolate what defined human culture, including through analyses of contemporary art (such as Ferrant's work) and children's visual presences.[69] Together, their contributions provided a synthesis of the developing human as spiritual, imaginative, and inventive, humanized through the act of artistic creation.

Children's first markings supposedly gave insight into the workings and development of their minds. But why were pedagogies of art treated with such interest by an avant-garde audience of artists and social reformers? Ferrant, in addition to his early sculptural production and work with ADLAN (Amics de l'Art Nou [Friends of New Art]) after 1932, embraced childhood as both a social cause and artistic inspiration. With their playful participation in artistic initiatives and workshops in schools and after-school clubs, artist-teachers like him melded scholarship and practice. Through his own art, pedagogical work, and publications, he moved at the forefront of the artistic avant-garde and creative education during the 1930s. Born in Madrid, Ferrant trained as a sculptor. His first major work was a bas-relief sculpture of a schoolgirl writing at a desk, *La escolar*, which won a national prize in 1925. The pupil is all calm yet coiled energy. She leans into the paper, grips her pen and holds herself in steady concentration, long legs braced against a baseboard (Fig. 5.4). This work marked the beginning of Ferrant's interest in the nexus of childhood and art. In contrast, however, to sensitive children's busts made by contemporaries such as Joan Rebull (1899–1981), Ferrant's subsequent work rarely depicted children in anything nearing representative fashion. Rather, a tendency towards abstract and organic form aligned with his interest in disparate natural objects — stones, seashells — in playful *objetos hallados* of 1932 and found-object sculptures of the 1940s and 1950s, the pedagogical echoes of which scholar Clara Eslava has convincingly drawn out within a broader aesthetics of nature and life.[70] It also led, as with Torres García, to the creation of interactive toys, namely a series of paper 'arsintes' begun in 1933, as well as writings on the cultivation of sensorial, plastic, and technical abilities. These works all drew from a view of creativity and whimsy, of play and creation, inspired by work with children.

FIG. 5.4. Ferrant's depiction of a girl studying, dedicated to Rafael Barradas, won the 1926 national sculpture prize. A copy hangs at the Madrid's Instituto Ramiro de Maeztu, the Instituto-Escuela's post-war successor. Source: Ángel Ferrant, *La escolar*, 1925, painted plaster, 67 × 41 × 5 cm. Courtesy of the Asociación Colección Arte Contemporáneo, Museo Patio Herreriano, Valladolid.

As a young professor in Barcelona, Ferrant first came into contact with the aesthetics of child art through a circle of enthusiasts of children's design and illustration. Ferrant was a regular attendee of Uruguayan artist and children's book illustrator Rafael Barradas's 'Ateneíllo del Hospitalet' *tertulia* from 1927, along with Gasch, Torres García, and others.[71] With Gasch, Ferrant visited Barcelona's experimental Escola del Mar on the Barceloneta in 1931. Struck by the imagination and vitality of its pupils, Ferrant would carry on a correspondence with school director Pere Vergés and his pupils into the 1950s. Collected in the Museo Patio Herreriano's Archivo Ferrant in Valladolid, hundreds of images (including drawings by Gasch's son, Emili, or 'Mili') serve as a record of Ferrant's close engagement with these children. In tune with the attitudes of reciprocity and care between child and teacher put forward by New Education reformers, they also demonstrate a clear familiarity with Ferrant as an important presence in the classroom. One drawing is labelled 'Ángel', for Ferrant, written in a child's hand. The fact that child and teacher would be on a first-name basis is notable, but the appreciation seems to have been mutual. Through regular correspondence with the Escola del Mar, Ferrant amassed an extensive number of drawings and letters from the children in Barcelona as well as a wealth of richly coloured, expressionistic acrylic images demonstrating a global interest from Argentina to Japan. Many of the drawings from the Escola del Mar can be found reproduced and examined in contemporaneous articles on children's art, as well as appearing in subsequent texts published in the 1950s by a new generation of scholars and reformers such as Josefina Aldecoa, whose first monograph studied children's art and included numerous drawings and paintings drawn from Ferrant's collection.[72]

The drawings from the Escola del Mar demonstrate a marked familiarity and warmth between child and teacher. An article, 'Resplandor y proyección de los dibujos infantiles' [Splendour and Scope of Children's Drawings], published in the architectural journal *AC* in 1933, echoes the sense of mutual respect Ferrant sought to cultivate. His praise of children's art and its development formed part of the issue's focus upon the architecture of the primary school in the future modern, 'functional' city. Published alongside extensive examples of cutting-edge school design by leading architects such as Josep Lluís Sert (1902–83), Ferrant's contribution looked to the imaginative qualities that an open, ventilated, health-giving school could foster. Taking the Escola del Mar as his starting point, Ferrant lauded children's art for its natural qualities. In recounting the work of the school's pupils, Ferrant opened with an epigraph lauding his pupils' receptivity:

> En las manitas de los 'nanos' de la Escuela de Mar de la Barceloneta, vi la plumilla de un tierno aparato registrador preciso, fiel, y refinadamente sensible a todo fenómeno imaginativo de repercusión lineal.[73]

> [In the little hands of our children at the Escuela de Mar on the Barceloneta, I watched the nib of a tender recording instrument, precise, faithful, refined and sensitive to all imaginative phenomena of line and form.]

Children, in the act of drawing, acted as a precise connection between environment and imagination. As the pen moved in their hands, it recorded and fixed their worlds. In writing of children's drawings, Ferrant followed his predecessors in the psychology of art in speaking of these as a manifestation of instinct, a natural, indeed 'biological' force inseparable from the essential being and nature of childhood. Drawing was as pleasure-driven and reflexive as throwing a stone at glass and seeing it shatter. The act produced pleasure, but only once such pleasure could be prolonged beyond the mere act of putting pen to paper could the child be said to be truly drawing. To draw, as he defined it, was to organize marks and forms in relation to one another, creating a larger thought.[74] In essence, art was communication: a form of language that moved beyond scribbles towards structure and meaning. Drawing was a way of making ours the thought of another. Posing drawing as both a biological and expressive act, Ferrant sought to incorporate principles of spontaneity, directness, and energy into its cultivation.

Acknowledging a shift in society as a whole, Ferrant proposed in 1932 the establishment of a network of institutes for the 'plastic arts' — sculpture and visual arts — based on a foundation of manual, hands-on experimentation. Ferrant's plan, 'Diseño de una configuración escolar' (Fig. 5.5), aimed at reforming drastically the organizational structure of art education through the establishment of a national network, the so-called Escuelas Federadas de Artes Plásticas del Estado (EFAPE). First published in *Arte* in 1932, the 'Plan Ferrant', as it came to be known, sought to bring youthful energies to bear on a larger curricular system, one that could also provide 'plenitud' and the 'satisfacción auténtica de nuestras necesidades espirituales' [authentic satisfaction of our spiritual needs'].[75] The envisioned plan moved in intersecting angles and axes, from 'intuición' [intuition] to 'conciencia' [awareness], incorporating 'espíritu' [spirit] and 'técnica' [technique]. Courses in the first stage were limited to exercises of initiation, definition and experimentation; only in the second and third stages did the student move toward formal technical education, vocational workshops and specialization. A circle labelled 'education' is the central point around which, and toward which, all leads.

In conceptualizing an organizational scheme, Ferrant drew on a fundamental philosophy of new education and its perceived advantages:

En vez de	Años....................	Momento
» » »	Polvo..................	Limpieza
» » »	Solemnidad..........	Familiaridad
» » »	Academismo........	Inspiración.[76]

[Instead of	Years....................	Moment
» » »	Dust......................	Cleanliness
» » »	Solemnity..............	Familiarity
» » »	Academicism.......	Inspiration.]

It was with this turn towards the collective, towards a re-design of national institutes and workshops along clear lines, that Ferrant sought to shift the pedagogical field. This was, in a sense, an expected fulfilment of his thought: the Spanish children's art pioneer and teacher Gabriel García Maroto (1885–1969) had envisioned, in his 1927 imaginative projection of a post-dictatorship Spain, that Ferrant would someday take the reins of an invigorated Escuelas de Bellas Artes in Madrid.[77] Like

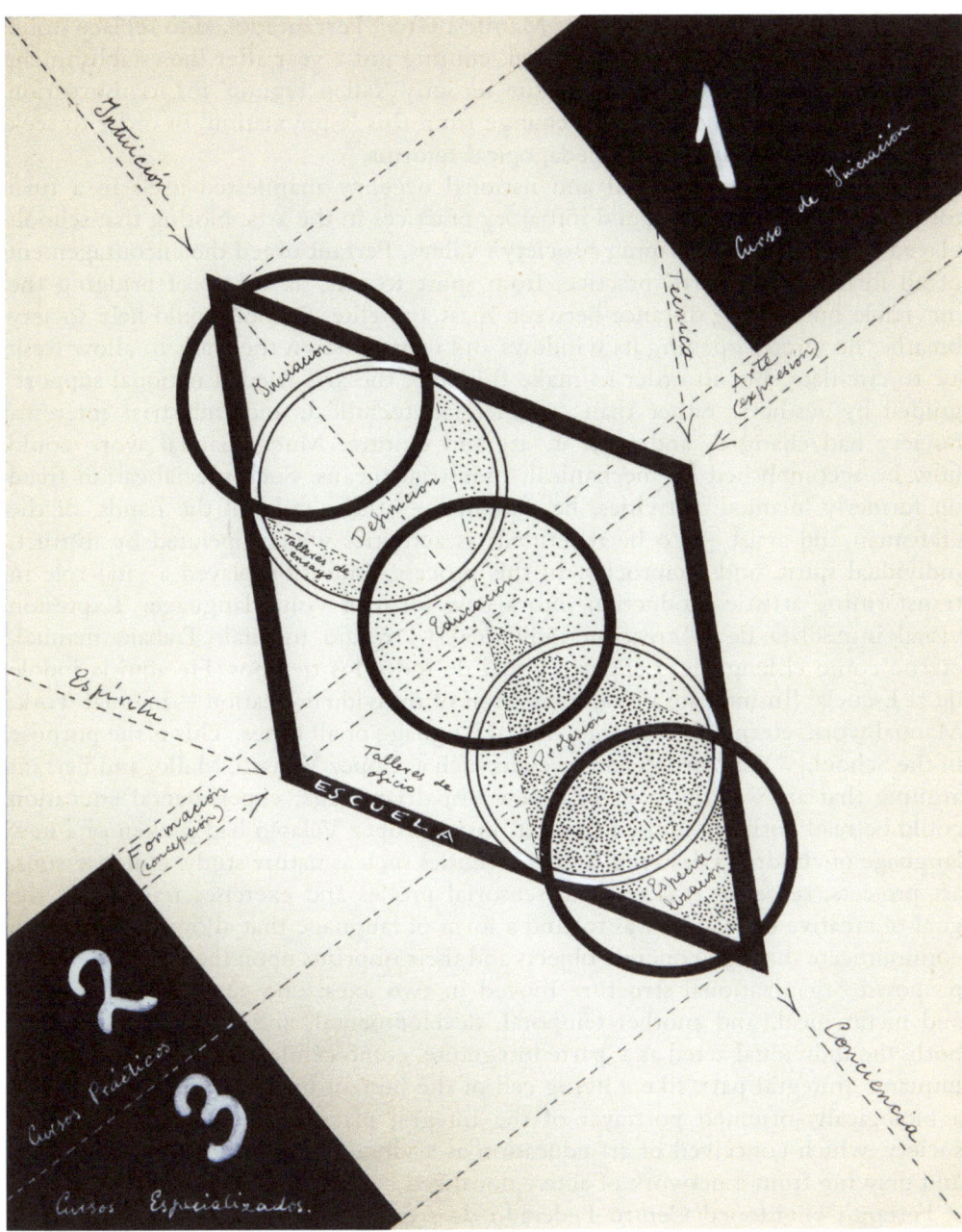

FIG. 5.5. For Ferrant, 'education' began with one's own intuition, incorporating spirit, formation, technique and artistic expression. Source: 'Gráfico de "Diseño de una configuración escolar"', 1932. Courtesy of the Archivo Ángel Ferrant, Asociación Colección Arte Contemporáneo, Museo Patio Herreriano, Valladolid.

Dalí, Montanyá, and Gasch in their Manifest Groc, Ferrant looked to replace stolid political and social mores. His proposal, coming just a year after the establishment of the Spanish Republic, critiqued the recently 'fallen regime' for its usurpation of rights and urged the nation to emerge from this 'asphyxiation' in order to seek 'transcendence' through major pedagogical reforms.[78]

This expression of political and national urgency manifested itself in a turn towards sensorial, intuitive, and initiatory practices in the arts. Noting that schools played a central role in shaping a society's values, Ferrant urged the encouragement of all forms of 'spiritual' practice, from sport to arts, as a way of bridging the inevitable but stifling distance between mass and elite. Schools could help society breathe, he wrote, opening its windows and tearing down the walls to allow fresh air to circulate. But in order to make this step, the arts needed national support, guided by aesthetic rather than commercial, technical, and industrial interests. Society had changed, and with it, art and culture. Much manual work could now be accomplished by mechanical, industrial means. Such specialization freed up formerly 'manual' activities, he reasoned — those tasks of the hands, of the craftsman and artist — to be redefined: as activities which operated by instinct, individual spirit, and reciprocity. In this process, education played a vital role in transforming artistic production into a new form of visual language: 'Expresión visual inmediata de la creación individual = trabajo manual. Trabajo manual, eterno como el lenguaje. Lenguaje visual de todos los tiempos. He aquí la índole de la Escuela' [Immediate visual expression of individual creation = manual work. Manual work, eternal as language. Visual language of all times. This is the purpose of the School.][79] With artists and teachers such as López Velasco, Mallo, and Ferrant arguing that art was the basis of a new visual language, experimental education could be read within a revised context. Just as López Velasco had spoken of a new language of children's drawing, and as activities such as nature study, object lessons, art projects, cuadernos escolares, and sensorial probes and exercises reinforced, the goal of creative education was to find a form of language that allowed children to communicate through concrete objects and their imprints upon the world. Ferrant's proposed organizational structure moved in two axes: one geographical, spatial, and hierarchical, and another temporal, developmental, and skills-based. Within both, the individual acted as a 'parte integrante, como célula viva que es del cuerpo humano' [integral part, like a living cell of the human body that it is].[80] This was a biologically-oriented portrayal of the integral place of the individual within society, which conceived of art education as a vibrant central body radiating into and drawing from a network of active, localized centres of practice.

Ferrant's envisioned Centro Federado de Artes Plásticas de Estado (CEFAPE) represented that larger body. With a conference hall, museum, cinema, garden, library, studios, and offices, it would showcase the vibrancy of a national network of production. Each individual school, section, or department would be designed according to modern principles of light, air, and space, teaching painting, sculpture, or mixed media. Like the Bauhaus or Vienna's Kunstgewerbeschule, which Ferrant had visited on a trip funded by the JAE in 1927, teaching would be designed by a

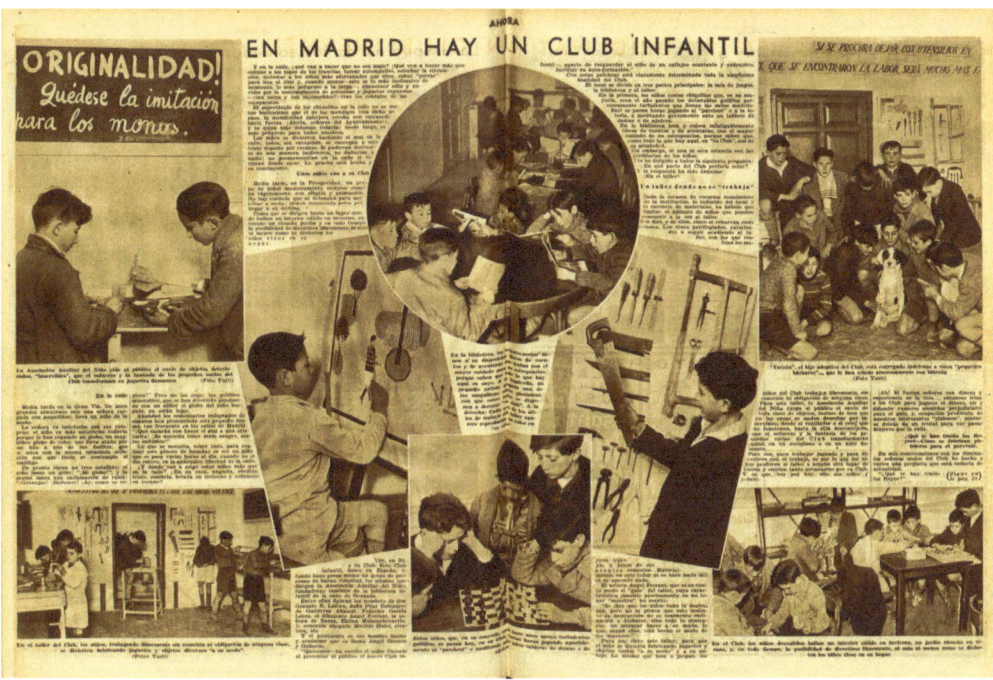

FIG. 5.6. Boys in the workshop of the *club infantil*, under the aspirational reminders of Ferrant's banners. Source: 'En Madrid hay un club infantil', *Ahora*, 16 January 1936, p. 18.

conjunction of experts in these respective areas, from architects to sculptors.[81] In this way, he aimed not for the reinforcement of embedded conventions but for the establishment of creative interdisciplinary hubs. In the design of the early courses of the EFAPE one finds the base of a pedagogy he would soon implement with children in Madrid. In a curriculum divided into three phases, as seen in Fig. 5.5, first would come introductory courses focused on free expression, followed by practical courses that built technical skills, before theoretical and practical specialization and advanced experimentation in a given area. During early play, the burgeoning artist would begin to create. Through a range of materials (paper and pencil, clay and plaster, cardboard, metal, wood), and a variety of perspectives (music and cinema, architecture, sculpture, carpentry, metalwork, construction), artistic formation was to begin on a broad base before developing its focus. Ferrant noted in closing that this proposal need not be implemented on a total national, material, physical scale to prove successful. Rather, its principles could be enacted on any number of smaller and individual, practical levels in schools and workshops.

Indeed, such was precisely what Ferrant would enact with ADLAN from 1935 in Madrid. In cooperation with the Asociación Auxiliar del Niño, he took a leading role in the establishment of a club for urban children in what was intended to be a social project of urban uplift. The latter Association opened a library for children, girls and boys, on the Calle de Granada in Pacífico that year; four months later, they inaugurated a recreational youth club. Led by Ángel de Ossorio, the effort involved prominent members of Madrid society. Lorca, Lafora, and lawyer Matilde Huici, among others, were named as collaborators. Notable supporters, including Carmen Conde and husband Antonio Oliver, donated to the cause.[82] Due to space constraints the club was initially limited to boys — particularly those considered to be at most social risk, referred to in publicity about the club as 'golfillos' — with the aim of a subsequent, co-educational expansion. In addition to a garden for outdoor play, the club was organized into three areas: a recreational room; a library; and finally, a workshop, the *taller de niños*. This was Ferrant's domain, or, more properly, that of the child-artists themselves.[83] Contemporaneous photographs show a space filled with boys engaged in all kinds of active pursuits: playing draughts, reading, painting, building puppets, and using tools (Fig. 5.6).

Ferrant is noted as the 'guide' in the school's efforts in art and construction, and his stamp is notable in its design, execution, and public outreach. From the banners hung around the walls with thought-provoking quotations and aphorisms on art and life (his hundreds of what he called 'pancartas' [placards]) to the club's model of the interactive, art-based workshop, Ferrant saw this project as melding child-centred pedagogy, social aid, and artistic experimentation. In order to supply the workshop with objects children could adapt, Ferrant issued a public call for old, discarded belongings of no use to their owners, noting that in the hands of children these would take on new life and transform into things of wonder and delight (Fig. 5.7). His workshop was designed with contemporaneous representations of children's (boys') active natures in mind. Ferrant noted:

> Se dice que los niños todo lo destrozan, pero no se piensa que este instinto de destrucción no es realmente inclinación a deshacer, sino todo lo contrario: un intentar hacer a su modo, lo que, según ellos, está hecho al modo de los mayores.[84]

> [They say that children destroy everything, but it never occurs to us that this destructive instinct is not in fact an inclination to unmake, but rather the opposite: an effort to create in their own image something which, from their perspective, was made for grown-ups.]

Children's tendencies to throw objects beyond their reach, and as they grew older to take things apart, rip them open, or otherwise engage with them physically became in Ferrant's view positive evidence for creativity. In the *taller*, Ferrant sought to give them the space to build a suitable world on their own terms.

An urge towards play and experimentation for which Ferrant argued in his 'Diseño para una configuración escolar' was equally on display in his own creation of a range of children's toys and tools. Alongside theoretical and practical interventions in artistic experimentation, his art played with toy-like constructions, namely sets of shapes, outlined and cut from paper, which children could arrange into an infinity of forms and human elements (Fig. 5.8). This project was what he called his 'arsintes': sets of many small pieces in various series of simple, essential shapes which came together to form a multitude of adaptable forms. With these products, he sought from 1933 to create a 'synthetic art' that would allow the individual child to create and manipulate their own imaginative forms.[85] Based on

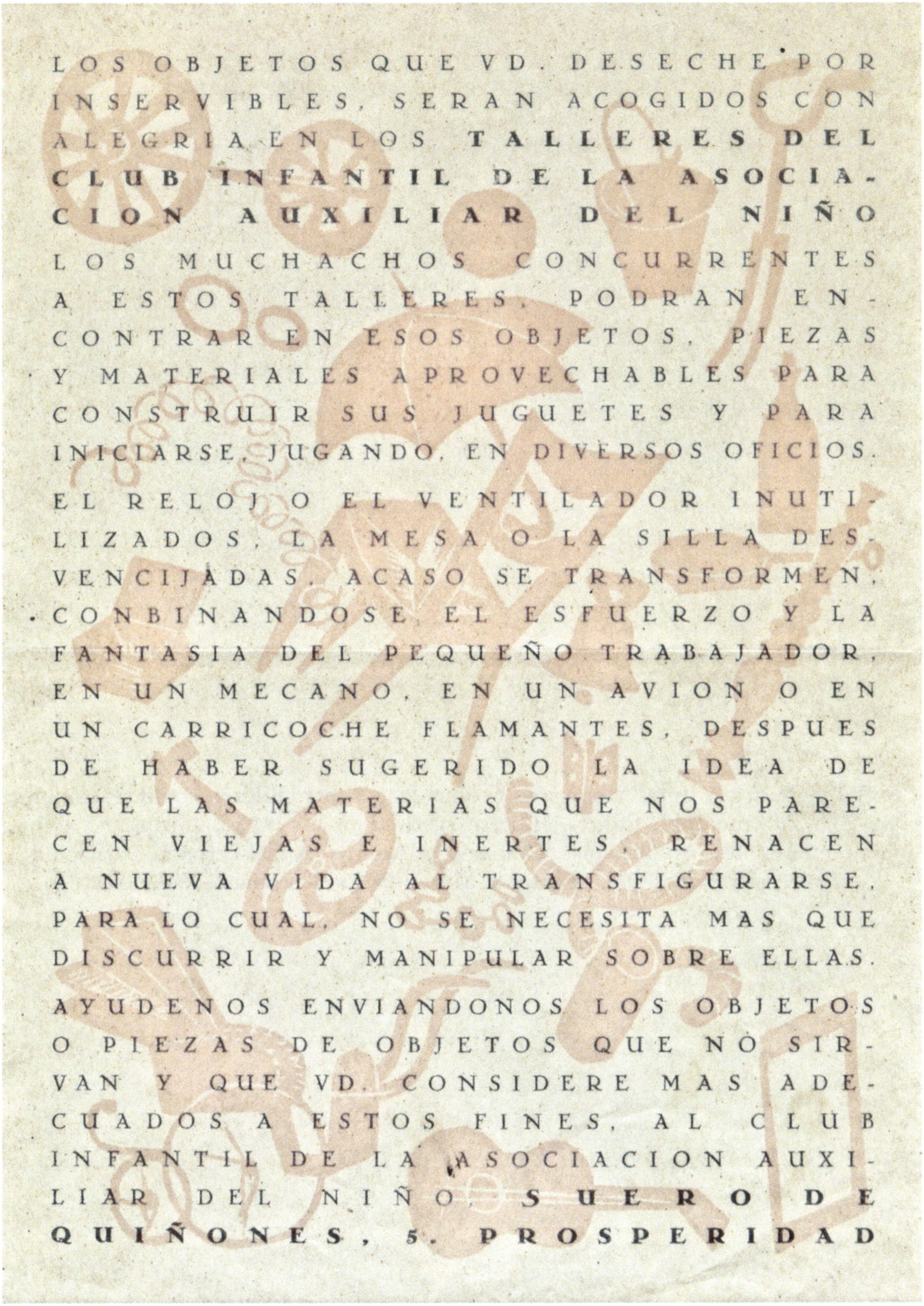

LOS OBJETOS QUE VD. DESECHE POR INSERVIBLES, SERAN ACOGIDOS CON ALEGRIA EN LOS **TALLERES DEL CLUB INFANTIL DE LA ASOCIA-CION AUXILIAR DEL NIÑO** LOS MUCHACHOS CONCURRENTES A ESTOS TALLERES, PODRAN ENCONTRAR EN ESOS OBJETOS, PIEZAS Y MATERIALES APROVECHABLES PARA CONSTRUIR SUS JUGUETES Y PARA INICIARSE, JUGANDO, EN DIVERSOS OFICIOS. EL RELOJ O EL VENTILADOR INUTILIZADOS, LA MESA O LA SILLA DESVENCIJADAS, ACASO SE TRANSFORMEN, CONBINANDOSE EL ESFUERZO Y LA FANTASIA DEL PEQUEÑO TRABAJADOR, EN UN MECANO, EN UN AVION O EN UN CARRICOCHE FLAMANTES, DESPUES DE HABER SUGERIDO LA IDEA DE QUE LAS MATERIAS QUE NOS PARECEN VIEJAS E INERTES, RENACEN A NUEVA VIDA AL TRANSFIGURARSE, PARA LO CUAL, NO SE NECESITA MAS QUE DISCURRIR Y MANIPULAR SOBRE ELLAS.

AYUDENOS ENVIANDONOS LOS OBJETOS O PIEZAS DE OBJETOS QUE NO SIRVAN Y QUE VD. CONSIDERE MAS ADECUADOS A ESTOS FINES, AL CLUB INFANTIL DE LA ASOCIACION AUXILIAR DEL NIÑO **SUERO DE QUIÑONES, 5. PROSPERIDAD**

FIG. 5.7. Ferrant's poster called for donations of old household objects, which, through the child's imagination, would be reborn 'to new life through transfiguration'.
Source: 'Cartel de la Asociación Auxiliar del Niño'. Courtesy of the Archivo Ángel Ferrant, Asociación Colección Arte Contemporáneo, Museo Patio Herreriano, Valladolid.

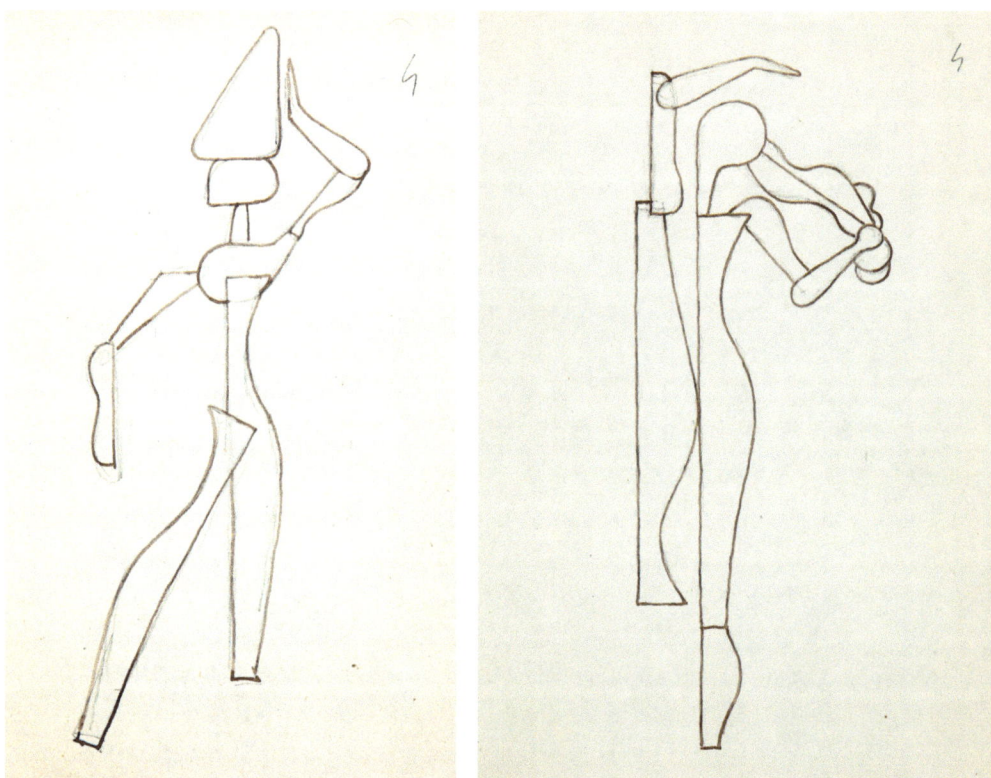

FIG. 5.8. Ferrant's 'arsintes' comprised various shapes that children could re-combine into moveable figures. Here, a set based on ancient vase forms.
Source: 'Arsintes: Ánfora', 1935. Courtesy of Archivo Ángel Ferrant, Asociación Colección Arte Contemporáneo, Museo Patio Herreriano, Valladolid.

children's urge towards experimentation and construction, the objects also fit into a wider frame of contemporaneous vanguard art. The project's very name, 'arsintes', gestures at the holistic, integral impulse of Ferrant's efforts: he sought to combine a Latin *ars*, art, with a drive towards *sintaxis* or *síntesis*, unifying of separate forms into larger elements of meaning. This was an activity pointedly synthetic in nature, drawing on art, nature, and form to create new worlds in the mind and imagination of the child in a constructive, re-creative way. As Ortega Cubera has documented, Ferrant's various 'arsintes' drew inspiration from ancient to new forms, from vases to mannequins, and ranging in style from 'grotesque' to 'organic'.[86]

In line with the protestations of the Manifest Groc about the unnecessary and undesirable intellectual reduction of children's magazines and culture, artists and illustrators created works that served as innovative design in their own right. One striking example of this tendency was the product of illustrator and graphic designer Emeterio R. Melendreras (1905–86), in a work introduced by editor J. Demuro, pseudonym of Juan Ortiz, a publisher in the Ciudad Lineal interested in children's 'auto-educación' through interactive play and projects.[87] Works such as *La pintura por el recorte geométrico a base de rectas y curvas* (1934) provided a notable visual conflation of pedagogical impulse and avant-garde influence. Melendreras's illustrations, unlike Cubist art which multiplied depth and enlarged perspective by the layering of angles and views, are a simple form of abstraction that flattened the world to the level of the page, as in Constructivist and Bauhaus design. The author invited children to create their own versions of this world from one dimension, to spring it into life from a spare and representative outline. Each of these images, like those of Ferrant and others, were designed to inspire children's developing manual abilities, instructing them in the use of scissors, paper, and glue to model their world as they saw fit: 'no es necesario que copies exactamente' [it isn't necessary to copy them exactly], Demuro assured children in a brief foreword, for 'Dentro de poco, los modelos no te harán falta' [soon you won't even need the models]. The drawings were accompanied by simple dialogue and ideas to stimulate the child's imagination and curiosity about the figures outlined here, or the world they evoked, with untranslatable puns:

> ¿En qué se parece un payaso y un pelotón?
> En que el pelotón está lleno de aire,
> y el payaso de don-aire.

[What do a clown and a ball have in common? | The ball is filled with air, | and the clown with hot air.]

The text accompanies a winking clown composed of circles and triangles, red and black and yellow forms, beside a ball composed of four green, red, yellow, and blue quarter-circles, one of several such arrangements easily replicated and arranged in new forms (Fig. 5.9).[88] Such a denaturalized and universal range of form in each of these artists' works aligned with a cognitive and Gestaltist psychological frame, in which children were understood to view the world in contrasts, in blocks of form and colour, reciprocally and actively.

FIG. 5.9. Children were encouraged to take scissors to paper and create new stories to accompany their resulting designs. Source: Emeterio Ruíz Melendreras, *La pintura por el recorte geométrico a base de rectas y curvas*, ed. by J. Demuro, 1st edn (Madrid: Juan Ortiz, 1934), n.p.

Through texts, toys, and constructions, principles of abstraction, line, and form worked in the service of the constructivist pedagogy put forward by Piaget and others from the 1920s onwards, in which children learned by building actively upon the knowledge they possessed.[89] They echoed intelligence and other visual tests that relied on shape, form, and contrast to evaluate individual development. In the distillation of form towards abstraction and in the encouragement of active engagement, children's art met graphic design and pedagogical reform. Just as Ferrant envisioned a form of educational humanism through the EFAPE, children's art formed the basis of a national project building upon children's art. These principles simply required that reformers align their teachings with fundamental notions of liberty and play, moving from experimentation towards technical prowess, so that the body of the larger educational structure would also represent Ferrant's 'peso del espíritu' [weight of the spirit].[90]

Manuel Abril and the Spiritual Mission of Art

Amidst the intervention of intellectuals and artists in efforts such as Madrid's *club infantil*, the Second Republic decreed the start of a highly visible form of cultural outreach: the *misiones pedagógicas*, which from May 1931 enlisted leading intellectuals and artists to bring art and culture to small towns and neglected rural areas.[91] Essayist and children's author Manuel Abril early documented this culturally iconic educational effort within a larger effort to isolate the human element in art and childhood alike. From the canvas to the living child of the *misiones*, until the start of the Civil War, Abril sought to understand what it was about art that could capture fleeting human qualities — muted, stilled, held in time — making these at once eternal and enduring. These writings revolved around questions of what the human was, how art could capture that sense of life and how art itself could be, in the process, lifted and vivified. Two works are crucial to Abril's elucidation of the human: first his defence and explication of Ortega's *La deshumanización del arte* (1925), in which Abril developed a framework for spiritual development beyond human representation, and secondly, his writings on the 'humanized' images of children within art and photography. Together, these moved from a cultural critique of the *misiones* towards a view of the human in art, with childhood in the balance.

Abril's writings embodied concrete debates on how to vivify education through culture. While the *misiones* represented the spirit of outreach and democratization of the Second Republic, neither were they comprehensive nor was their 'mission' uncritically applauded.[92] Amidst celebration of the missions' accomplishments by the Patronato de Misiones Pedagógicos, an early response came from Abril himself when he published several photographs of children and 'missionaries' in the journal *Arte* in 1933. In a commentary, he suggested that it was not trinkets of culture that were needed, but access to human experience, understood as childlike, primary, and conserved in the rural.[93] Abril suggested that efforts to transport high art and culture to rural villages were of limited value, an elite task of 'colonización espiritual' which could only ever have a superficial effect on its intended recipients:

> La carga de cultura, ¿en qué consiste? En unos gramófonos, en un cine, a veces en la compañía de La Barraca, en unas cuantas copias de Velázquez, El Greco, Ribera. A los chicos que nunca oyeron ni vieron otra cosa que lo más elemental de su rincón aldeaniego, se les da quintaesencia de cultura.
> Esto nos parece a nosotros un grave error desde varios puntos de vista.[94]
>
> [The weight of culture: of what does it consist? A few gramophones, a cinema, sometimes the La Barraca theatre company, a few copies of Velázquez, El Greco, Ribera. For kids who have never heard or seen anything beyond the rudimentary in their rural village, it gives them a quintessence of culture.
> This seems to us a grave error in many respects.]

In essence, the missions should not teach what *culture* was, but must rather engage with the experiences of these children themselves, who understood most fundamentally what *life* was. This statement built upon a guiding pedagogy of 'being', of existence: 'La pedagogía que enseña a ser tendrá siempre ventajas radicales sobre la que enseña a aprender' [A pedagogy that teaches how to be will always have radical advantages over one that teaches how to learn].[95] Abril's critique brings to mind that of Carmen Conde, a fellow writer who participated amply in the outreach of the *misiones* (Fig. 5.10). As seen in Chapter 2, Conde depicted literature as a vivifying force that could capture the living, dawning childlike aspects of art. This process was not so simple.

FIG. 5.10. Missionaries visiting the village of La Murta in 1935, including Carmen Conde (indicated with an arrow on the left), listen to a recording. Source: Courtesy of the Legado Carmen Conde, Patronato Carmen Conde-Antonio Oliver, Cartagena.

The essence of the pedagogical missions was the fruits of Spanish culture, passed down through education: the word, above all, lived and written, but also art, music, film, and theatre. Against a governing mainstream of pedagogical authority, 'el método, el sistema, el orden, la moderación, la experiencia, en suma, la inhibición' [method, system, order, moderation, experience, in sum, inhibition], young missionaries sought to instil and foster a new spirit even within the missions' own outreach, seeking not to reproduce culture per se but to stimulate the 'choque de la realidad misma, al contacto con aquel aspecto de la acción misionera en que la producción espontánea, la libre creación y la originalidad dominan' [clash with reality itself, towards contact with that aspect of missionary action in which spontaneous production, free creation, and originality dominate].[96] Abril was sympathetic to this ambition. A living, breathing vision of pedagogical outreach was more relevant in visual art than in any other field, Abril suggested, for art relied on human emotions that could not be taught, delivered, or packaged. New educationalists promoted pedagogies that focused upon active learning and physical, visual, and imaginative contacts with the world. With art, children could draw from a fount of creativity and first-hand contact.

What was that essentiality so natural to children? Without doubt the answer lay in enquiries into how humans developed from 'primitive' to cultivated, animal to spiritual life — throughout which an innate humanity burgeoned in the growing child. In 1933, in an article entitled 'Humanización y desnaturalización, o lo humano y lo demasiado humano' [Humanization and Denaturalization, or the

Human and All-Too-Human], Abril argued that the Spanish public had taken up Ortega's notion of the 'dehumanization' of modern art in overly broad strokes. In art's turn to 'dehumanization' was the 'infrahumana', a biological, animal state, counterposed with a spiritual, abstracted humanity of a higher order: the 'sobrehumano'.[97] In Abril's argument, these two tendencies came into balance.

Art formed part of a process of 'humanization': the denaturalization of the animal and the development of a transcendent, shared culture. Abstraction and rationality defined the limits and extensions of human capability. It was, thus, in art's turn to abstraction that it became most human. As in discussions of children's 'global' perception and poetic access, which came from the conviction that children synthesized the world in a direct, concrete, and unfiltered manner, theories of artistic development marked children's ability to think progressively more rationally over time. A dichotomy between the part and the whole held as individuals developed analytical and abstract thinking:

> Para analizarlo lo abstrajo, o sea lo aisló, separándolo del resto del proceso en donde estaba integrado, resulta que el hombre pierde, al abstraer, la integridad de la función y pierde la conciencia del conjunto vital conforme gana en conocimiento intelectual de una de las partes.[98]

> [In order to analyse the abstract, that is to isolate it, separate it from the entire process in which it was integrated, man loses, in that act of abstraction, the integrity of function; he loses his awareness of the vital confluence as he gains intellectual knowledge of one of its parts.]

Abstraction, in this sense, was the singular process of human intellectual development. By willing grandeur in art, thought, or technology, humanity defined itself beyond the animal sphere: 'lo espiritual del hombre, pueda, por engreimiento, quererse emancipar de lo terreno en demasía, y, por querer lo más, pierda lo menos' [man's spiritual nature may seek, in its conceit, to emancipate itself from the earthly and, in its desire to gain everything, risk losing it all.][99]

If Abril's humanity struck an ambivalent balance between the physical and the spiritual, the mundane and the heavenly, the animal and the angelic, what might this mean for the 'human' development of art itself? Modern, non-representative art was that which was most human, he (with Ortega) suggested. Representative art relied on the human body. If humans were bound to their bodies, so too should art reflect exclusively that form. But, he asked, who could claim that the biological world was limited to that of corporality? The artist did not work with the tools of body or soul exclusively, but used paints, material, things of the world, as a medium of expression. The artist set out to put on canvas that which was most human: thought, emotion, and invention. The development of technology represented this uniquely human balance. Like human flight, whose invention drew imaginatively from the forms of birds, angels, and motors to create something uniquely human, art was defined by human balance. It made use of all that humans did not inherently, *naturally*, possess, but that which they invented. Through abstract form, the peak of human invention was reached. Between the natural and the 'angelic', Abril suggested the human position lay somewhere in between:

> Entre uno y otro pecado está la posición humana — mixta, de equilibrio —,
> que consiste en inventar, inventar algo que participa de la materia, de lo físico
> y de lo espiritual, de lo metafísico, pero sin supeditarse exclusivamente ni a lo
> uno ni a lo otro.[100]

> [Between one sin and the other is the human position — mixed, in equilibrium
> — borne of invention, inventing that which draws from the material world,
> physical and spiritual, and from the metaphysical, without any one taking
> precedence over the other.]

Arguing that wherever human values could be found, one encountered a continual process of 'humanization and denaturalization', Abril's argument fitted into
a wider field of enquiry into the development of the child, both what children
represented in their natural, 'pure' selves and in their development of human values
of awareness, communication, personality, and morality.

Closing his essay on the 'human' in art with this description of a higher,
spiritual, and denaturalized realm, Abril unknowingly prefigured a claim made by
the Uruguayan pedagogue Jesualdo Sosa in his 1950 *La expresión creadora del niño*,
namely that development was not a fixed state or line, but a process of continual
alternation. Sosa, a prominent teacher and theorist, described children as liminal,
flickering, and changeable in their perceptions of the human aspects of things: 'ante
su imaginación las figuras y cosas sufrirán un continuo proceso de humanización
y deshumanización' [before their imagination figures and objects will suffer a
continual process of humanization and dehumanization].[101] Creating a frame for
shifts of 'humanization and dehumanization' in the child, Abril pointed towards
a hybrid conception of art and spirit. Two years later, in another exposition of *La
deshumanización del arte,* he closed with a seven-point list of Ortega's points and his
interpretations. The last and final word he gave was this:

> En fin, 7.°, 'el arte, según los artistas jóvenes, es un arte sin trascendencia'. (Y
> nosotros: ... sin trascendencia absoluta o total: incapaz de suplantar a lo absoluto;
> incapaz de ser Dios; pero, en cambio, capaz de ser sagrado. El arte concebido
> de este modo es el único camino que, aparte la santidad y su vía, lleva a un
> concepto sacro de la creación y del espíritu.)[102]

> [Lastly, 7., 'art, according to the young artists, is an art without transcendence.'
> (And we say: ... without total or absolute transcendence: incapable of supplanting
> the absolute; incapable of being God; but, instead, capable of being sacred. Art
> understood in this manner is the only way, other that saintliness and its path,
> that leads to a sacred conception of creation and the spirit.)]

Marrying abstract representation to a marked sense of spirit, he argued for a higher
purpose in art, embodying the essence of the flickering and emerging human
condition.[103]

Abril's examination of humanization in the framework of art and education came
to a head in 1936, when he published *Los niños en la fotografía y en la arte*. A work
consisting solely of classical paintings, contemporary photographs, or cartoons of
children (see Fig. 2.1 above) with brief facing texts, he pinpointed the aspects that
brought out their shifting personhood — an attentive gaze, a hungry mouth, chubby

hands, a laugh — in essence, their human punctum. 'El niño es flor, es cachorrillo, es juguete y es... persona humana' [The child is a flower, a puppy, a toy and... a human being], he wrote. With these words, Abril began to introduce some of the myriad roles the child had taken on in Western visual representation.[104] One could find the figure of the child in a museum, mute and immortalized in oil, or behold the living child, a vibrant, breathing, 'inagotable' [inexhaustible] biological force. In Goya's *Manuel Osorio Manrique de Zúñiga*, a noble, beribboned child serenely holds a leashed bird as three cats gaze outward. The child was, in Abril's eyes, here 'un juguete más, sin deje de ser humano' [one more toy, without any human trace], alongside the 'realismo vulgar' of his small, animal 'amigos'. Yet a clear, awakened humanity he found in the open gaze of a child painted by Rembrandt, 'humanísima' in its expression for one simple reason: the painting captured the soul, 'el alma', not in living vitality but in 'la vida "parada", eternizada' [life 'stopped', made eternal], transcending the mundane to reach a higher, 'infrahuman' plane.[105]

From classic works of art to contemporaneous photography, the child formed part of a wider history of humanistic development. Writing of Picasso's *Paulo en arlequín* [Paulo as a Harlequin], Abril described the artist's son as drawn with 'una ternura y un encanto inmaterial que compagina lo humano con esa seriedad sobrehumana' [a tenderness and immaterial enchantment that combines the human with a kind of suprahuman sobriety], an element of balance he posed as common to all masterpieces.[106] In the bright eyes of an infant captured by photographer Hedda Walther, staring out of the frame while teething on a big rubber ring, the child's gaze was the 'gran misterio humano' from birth. Unlike all other beings, only the human child, 'el niño, el ser humano', offered a gaze of such enraptured 'asombro y de atención' [surprise and attention], taking in the world both physically and visually. In the child's look, the viewer saw not physical beauty but a moral and spiritual awakening: 'una personita humana en sus albores: la atención, la sorpresa, el candor' [the dawning of a tiny human being: in attention, surprise, and candour].[107]

In closing these reflections, Abril included several images of children at the *misiones* he had earlier critiqued. Whether in the figure of a girl in a field standing shyly, fingers nervously in her mouth, listening as a 'missionary' read a story, or the delighted, illuminated faces of three boys watching a show, he suggested, living reality exceeded the efforts of realist painters. These children exhibited that true life, 'la vida, la espontaneidad, la riqueza' [life, spontaneity, and richness] that only human life could. His was not a shift in position from his earlier writings on the *misiones*, and if anything these odes romanticized the figure of the child all the more. But what he sought within these images of adorned children, playing children, crying children, reading children, was their human thread, that spark of awakening, of *soul* that was at the base of all art and culture.

In their discussions of the sensorial, the creative, the human, and the spiritual, the essential goal for both Ferrant and Abril, as for so many artists engaged in pedagogical reform, was to enact a progressive development of self and spirit, from birth to adulthood. They were not alone in this effort. Drawing upon a foundation of experimentation and scholarship, conceptions of children's art shared by vanguard artists pointed towards the inextricable bond formed between the inner experience of childhood and its physical traces. Creative work overlapped with a larger psychological interest in unpacking the mental and spiritual life of the child. On the one hand, as this chapter has shown, psychologists and teachers explored the life of the mind through psychometric and visual tests, one frame and mode among many measures used to solicit knowledge and insight. On the other, through children's drawings and all manner of art education, a wide array of educators looked to isolate a nexus of interior reality and external representation. From the visual probes and sketches embraced by psychologists and teachers towards modernist and avant-garde art, psychologists and pedagogues used art in new frames to read children's individual development.

Ultimately, how were theories of psychological development through art employed in broader discussions of creativity, spirituality, and the 'humanization' of the Spanish child? Children's drawings were not only an arbiter of intelligence but a measure of children's personhood and development. Amidst larger movements narrowing pedagogy towards technical skill and specialization, vanguard reformers granted children the dynamic satisfaction of recreating their own world on the page. Among this movement were individuals influenced by pedagogical, psychological, and social depictions of childhood and the mind — Llorca, Mallo, López Velasco, Barradas, Ferrant, Abril, and many others — who looked to bring new psychotechnic and creative ideas to bear on both their own educational outreach in schools and on a nationwide level of institutional reform. In their celebrations of children's art, they aimed to foster not primarily technical or creative ability but, more fundamentally, a form of aesthetic plenitude through vitality and human expression. Through the practice of art, reformers looked to amplify physical, intellectual, and spiritual development in the growing individual and society as a whole.

Notes to Chapter 5

1. Aránzazu Ascunce Arenas, in *Barcelona and Madrid: Social Networks of the Avant-Garde* (Lewisburg: Bucknell University Press, 2012), pp. 28–30, uses the genesis of the Manifest Groc as a prime example of collaboration networks. She notes that Dalí credited Gasch with the idea and himself with its writing; Lorca would publish the work in Spanish translation in the second and final issue of his new, Granada-based magazine *Gallo* that year.

2. Jaime Brihuega, *Las vanguardias artísticas en España, 1910–1931* (Madrid: Ediciones Cátedra, 1979), p. 161.

3. On *fin de siècle* psychology of children's art, see *La psicología del arte en España (1898–1923): antología de textos fundacionales*, ed. by Jorge Castro Tejerina (Oviedo: KRK Ediciones, 2018). With Spain's leading historians of psychology unpacking the work of central figures such as Ramón y Cajal, Lafora, and Juan Vicente Viqueira (1886–1924), Castro Tejerina and others have argued that interest in children's art drew from regenerationist efforts and furthered critical interests in the individual and society.

4. Barbara Wittmann, 'Symptomatologie des Zeichnens und Schreibens: Verfahren der Selbstaufzeichnung', in *Spuren erzeugen: Zeichnen und Schreiben als Verfahren der Selbstaufzeichnung*, ed. by Barbara Wittmann (Zurich: Diaphanes, 2009), pp. 7–20. In English, on drawings as tools in the psychoanalytic work of Melanie Klein, see also Barbara Wittmann, 'Drawing Cure: Children's Drawings as a Psychoanalytic Instrument', *Configurations*, 18.3 (2010), 251–72.

5. Juan Huarte de San Juan, *Examen de ingenios para las ciencias* (Madrid: La Rafa, 1930). See Joyce E. Chaplin and Darrin M. McMahon's narrative of a Renaissance elision of pre-existing concepts of the classical Latin *ingenium* with new, superhuman notions of genius in their 'Introduction' to *Genealogies of Genius*, ed. by Joyce E. Chaplin and Darrin M. McMahon (Basingstoke: Palgrave Macmillan, 2016), pp. 2–3.

6. One such work was written by Werner Wolff (1904–57), a psychologist who, after training with Gestalt psychologist Max Wertheimer in Berlin, spent formative years in exile from Nazi Germany affiliated with the laboratory of Mira y López in Barcelona (1933–36). On Wolff's lecture series in Madrid in 1934, see Anon., 'Curso del profesor Wolf [*sic*] en el Instituto Psicotécnico', *Revista de Escuelas Normales*, 12 (1934), 27–28. Wolff was concerned with children's drawing and the inner life of the child, and broadly with human psychology; see his *The Personality of the Preschool Child: The Child's Search for His Self* (London: William Heinemann, 1947), and *Diagrams of the Unconscious: Handwriting and Personality in Measurement, Experiment and Analysis* (New York: Grune & Stratton, 1948).

7. John Carson, *The Measure of Merit: Talents, Intelligence, and Inequality in the French and American Republics, 1750–1940* (Princeton: Princeton University Press, 2007), p. 161.

8. Anon., 'El estudio del niño', p. 558.

9. On this relationship see above all Jonathan David Fineberg, *The Innocent Eye: Children's Art and the Modern Artist* (Princeton: Princeton University Press, 1997), and, from a psychological perspective, Howard Gardner, *Artful Scribbles: The Significance of Children's Drawings* (New York: Basic Books, 1980), and Claire Golomb, *Child Art in Context: A Cultural and Comparative Perspective* (Washington, DC: American Psychological Association, 2002). From a Spanish and Latin American historical perspective, Emmanuel Guigon's edited catalogue is essential; see *La infancia del arte: arte de los niños y arte moderno en España* (Teruel: Museo de Teruel; Logroño: Cultural Rioja, 1996).

10. Karl Lamprecht, 'Les Dessins d'enfant comme source historique', *Bulletin de l'Académie royale de Belgique*, 9–10 (1906), 457–69; Georges-Henri Luquet, *Les Dessins d'un enfant* (Paris: 1913); G. Rouma, *Le Langage graphique de l'enfant* (Paris: F. Alcan, 1913); Georg Kerschensteiner, *Die Entwicklung der zeichnerischen Begabung* (Munich: Carl Gerber, 1905); Marcel Braunschvig, *El arte y el niño: ensayo sobre la educación estética* (Madrid: D. Jorro, 1914); Robert Gaupp, *Psicología del niño*, trans. by Antonio Vallejo Nágera, 4th edn (Barcelona: Editorial Labor, 1936).

11. Eleizegui López, *Biología de la edad escolar*, p. 320.

12. Ibid., p. 300.

13. César Juarros, 'Desde la cuneta: dibujos de niños', *Mundo gráfico*, 19.899 (1929), 49–50 (p. 50).

14. See, for example, Regina Lago de Comas, 'La guerra a través de los dibujos infantiles', *Educación y Cultura*, 1 (1940), 422–36. Several were famously published in Aldous Huxley, *They Still Draw Pictures! A Collection of Sixty Drawings Made by Spanish Children During the War* (Oxford: Oxford University Press, 1939), and in José Antonio Gallardo Cruz, *El dibujo infantil de la evacuación durante la Guerra Civil española (1936–1939)* (Málaga: Universidad de Málaga, 2012). Many hundreds of these drawings are collected in the Biblioteca Nacional de España as 'Dibujos de los niños de la guerra', catalogued by child-artist's name, <http://www.bne.es/es/Catalogos/BibliotecaDigitalHispanica/Colecciones/> [accessed 1 November 2018].

15. Carlos Delgado Olivares, 'Proust y la imagen', *Heraldo de Madrid*, 27 July 1933, p. 23. Taking over from Pedro Salinas, who translated the first two volumes, Unamuno's son-in-law José María Quiroga Plá had recently published a new translation of Marcel Proust's *El mundo de Guermantes* (Madrid: Espasa-Calpe, 1932).

16. Delgado Olivares, 'Proust y la imagen', p. 23.

17. Sáez Morilla, *Introducción al estudio de la paidología y pedagogía moderna*, p. 30.

18. Zaragüeta, *El estudio del niño*, p. 24.

19. Eleizegui López, *Biología de la edad escolar*, p. 9. Anon., 'El problema de los niños pobres superdotados', *Unión Patriótica*, 15 July 1927, p. 1; Madariaga, 'La selección corporativa de los "superdotados"'.

20. Such a path to technoscientific modernity has been argued, for instance, in the case of teacher Llorenç Cabós y Badia, who translated and adapted the Binet-Simon, Yerkes, Bridges and Hardwick, and Terman intelligence tests for Barcelona public schools from 1920. He

subsequently graduated to tests of his own creation, building a stereograph to measure pupils' spatial orientation and abilities; see Mülberger, Balltondre, and Graus, 'Aims of Teachers' Psychometry', pp. 7, 17.

21. A. Anselmo González, *Técnica de psicología experimental sin aparatos: manual de investigación psicológica* (Madrid: Sucesores de Hernando, 1921), and *Nacimiento y evolución de la inteligencia*. See Annette Mülberger, 'Appropriation of Psychological Testing in the Spanish Pedagogical Context', in *The Circulation of Science and Technology: Proceedings of the 4th International Conference of the ESHS, Barcelona, 18–20 November 2010*, ed. by Antoni Roca Rosell (Barcelona: SCHCT-IEC, 2012), pp. 626–35 (p. 633).

22. Mira y López, 'Pruebas para la determinación de los tipos de inteligencia en los niños', p. 3; see also an interest in Rudolf Steiner's anthroposophic notion of a 'pluralidad de almas' [plurality of souls] in Castillejo, '¿Malgastamos la niñez de nuestros hijos?', p. 1. Mira's and others' claims for broadening the bounds of intelligence(s) through notions of diversity and multiplicity came half a century before the Harvard psychologist Howard Gardner made the idea of 'multiple intelligences' famous in *Frames of Mind: The Theory of Multiple Intelligences* (New York: Basic Books, 1983). Mira's article formed part of a larger unpublished work entitled *¿Qué van a ser nuestros hijos?*, its title representative of a wider social dialogue on the futurity of childhood.

23. Emilio Mira y López, 'Las pruebas de imaginación visual (espacial) en la escuela', *Revista de Pedagogía*, 3.32 (1924), 281–84 (p. 282).

24. Ibid., p. 284.

25. See Cerezo Manrique, *Los comienzos de la psicopedagogía en España, 1882–1936*.

26. Bonifacio Arrabal, 'Ensayo sobre la imaginación de los niños', *Revista de Pedagogía*, 1.5 (1922), 169–74 (p. 170).

27. Roura i Parella and Panizo Gambón, *Contestaciones al cuestionario de pedagogía de las oposiciones a Escuelas Nacionales*, p. 91.

28. Mercedes Rodrigo and Pedro Roselló, 'Revisión española de los "tests" Claparède (primera serie): escala popular de Madrid', *Revista de Pedagogía*, 2.15 (1923), 81–92 (pp. 89–91). See also further adaptations, including that of Juan Ocaña Torrejón and Alfredo Gil Muñiz, *Ensayo sobre revisión española de los 'tests' Claparède: (primera serie): escala de Villanueva de Córdoba* (Villanueva de Córdoba: Talleres Tipográficos Pedrajas, 1924).

29. José M. Sacristán, 'Libros: Germain (J.) y Rodrigo (M.): *Pruebas de inteligencia* – Madrid, La Lectura, 1930', *Revista de Pedagogía*, 9.108 (1930), 569.

30. On Lago's contributions see Carmen García Colmenares, 'Regina Lago, una psicóloga comprometida con la infancia durante la guerra civil española', *CEE Participación Educativa*, 14 (2010), 211–20.

31. Lago de Comas, 'El realismo intelectual', pp. 391–92. With her spouse, pedagogue and anthropologist Juan Comas, she would continue psychometric testing during the coming years; see for example Juan Comas and Regina Lago, *La práctica de las pruebas mentales y de instrucción* (Madrid: Publicaciones de la Revista de Pedagogía, 1933).

32. Ibid., pp. 393–94, 396.

33. Ibid., p. 397.

34. Ángel Ferrant, 'Resplandor y proyección de los dibujos infantiles', *AC*, 3.10 (1933), 34–35 (p. 35).

35. Gonzalo R. Lafora, 'Estudio psicológico del cubismo y expresionismo', *Archivos de Neurobiología, Psicología, Fisiología, Histología, Neurología y Psiquiatría*, 3.2 (1922), 119–55 (p. 130). See Enrique Lafuente Niño, 'La contribución de Gonzalo R. Lafora a la psicología del arte', *Revista de Historia de la Psicología*, 27.2–3 (2006), 71–79.

36. Lafora, 'Estudio psicológico del cubismo y expresionismo', p. 123. He followed scholars such as Lamprecht and Rouma in tracing visually the child's ontological recapitulation of human development.

37. Ibid., pp. 132–33.

38. Ibid., p. 141.

39. Psychologist Daniel Widlöcher has argued that the visual principles of Gestalt psychology, in particular, gave scientific weight to a growing interest in children's artistic production during the early twentieth century. As argued by the Gestalt psychologists, perception resulted from a

totality of sensorial impressions. These impressions were interpreted and synthesized according to individual mental structure, such that creative production — writing, drawing, sketches — might give insight into the workings of development; see *L'Interprétation des dessins d'enfants* (Sprimont: Mardaga, 1998), p. 8. On the adoption of Rorschach tests, see María Soriano and César Juarros, 'El método de Rorschach en los niños', *Revista de Pedagogía*, 7.74 (1928), 66–69.

40. José M. Sacristán, 'El fenómeno eidético', *Revista de Pedagogía*, 6.61 (1927), 1–6 (p. 1). Other Spaniards also made contact with Jaensch on this topic. For instance, a professor from Santander named Antonio Encinas visited Jaensch in the early 1920s, concluding that eidetic images were 'key to the phenomena in Spain'; see Erich Rudolf Jaensch, *Eidetic Imagery and Typological Methods of Investigation* (London: Kegan Paul, Trench, Trubner & Co., 1930). Encinas sought to shed light on puzzling cases relating to miraculous visions in Limpias, Spain, from 1918, as documented in William A. Christian, *Moving Crucifixes in Modern Spain* (Princeton: Princeton University Press, 1992). Encinas's examination of eidetic phenomena appeared in the Jesuit cultural journal *Razón y Fe* in 1924; see his 'Imágenes eidéticas: sus propiedades y naturaleza', *Razón y Fe*, 69.275 (1924), 273–88. Sarah Wright cites the case as a possible referent for the 1955 film *Marcelino, pan y vino*; see the corresponding chapter in her *The Child in Spanish Cinema*, pp. 23–58.

41. Sacristán, 'El fenómeno eidético', p. 1.

42. Sebastià Gasch, 'Creación e imitación', *La Gaceta Literaria*, 4.73 (1930), 13.

43. Ibid.

44. Inés Ortega Cubero, 'Ángel Ferrant, profesor de vanguardia: estudio de la didáctica personal del artista a través de su legado documental presente en el Museo Patio Herreriano' (unpublished doctoral thesis, Universidad de Valladolid, 2007), pp. 324–27.

45. Inés Ortega Cubero, *Ángel Ferrant, profesor de vanguardia* (Valladolid: Junta de Castilla y León, 2009), pp. 123, 129.

46. On this chronology, his educational and cultural associations, and a far larger assortment of the hundreds of toys and sketches he began creating in Catalonia, see Cecilia de Torres and Susanna V. Temkin, 'Chronology: Documentary Materials', Joaquín Torres-García Catalogue Raisonné, <http://torresgarcia.com/chronology/documentary_materials.php> [accessed 8 May 2018].

47. Personal communication with Encarnación Martínez Alfaro, IES Isabel La Católica, Madrid, 19 June 2013. The pedagogical rationale for such works was surveyed in Francisco Benítez Mellado, 'El dibujo técnico en el Instituto-Escuela', *Revista de Pedagogía*, 7.79 (1928), 312–19. On the establishment and practices of the Instituto-Escuela, see Encarnación Martínez Alfaro, *Un laboratorio pedagógico de la Junta para Ampliación de Estudios: el Instituto-Escuela Sección Retiro de Madrid* (Madrid: Biblioteca Nueva, 2009). One such method for instructing students in a daily practice of journal-writing, drawing, and map-making is detailed by Rafael Verdier and Rafael Gutiérrez, 'Del hacer en la escuela: una unidad de trabajo escolar', *Escuelas de España*, 3.25 (1936), 12–29.

48. Martínez Alfaro, *Un laboratorio pedagógico de la Junta para Ampliación de Estudios: el Instituto-Escuela Sección Retiro de Madrid*, p. 139. See, among many other examples of the dissemination of school presses nationwide during the Second Republic, the work of pedagogue Herminio Almendros, 'La imprenta en la escuela', *Revista de Pedagogía*, 11.130 (1932), 448–53.

49. Ángel Llorca, '2D/2.2. Impresos, direcciones y folletos de Congresos Internacionales', in *Archivo digital 'Los viejos papeles'* (Madrid: Fundación Ángel Llorca, [1925–27]).

50. Llorca, *El primer año de lenguaje*, p. 124.

51. See Elisa López Velasco, *La práctica del dibujo en la escuela primaria*, 4 vols (Madrid: Espasa-Calpe, 1933) and Josefina Rodríguez Álvarez [Josefina Aldecoa], *El arte del niño* (Madrid: CSIC, Instituto San José de Calasanz de Pedagogía, 1959). On the contributions of López Velasco to Spanish art education, see Antonio Cuenca Escribano, 'La obra de Elisa López Velasco', *Arte, Individuo y Sociedad*, 15 (2003), 73–81, and 'Evolución de la enseñanza del dibujo en la escuela', *Tendencias Pedagógicas*, 14 (2009), 335–51 (pp. 339–45).

52. On Kerschensteiner's influence upon notions of visual language, see Cecilia Valbuena, 'La obra de Elisa López Velasco: la enseñanza del dibujo orientada por la Escuela Activa', *Actas del XVIII Coloquio de Historia de la Educación*, 2.3 (2008), 261–73 (pp. 265–68). López Velasco's, Freire's and Llorca's extensive notes and files are preserved at the Fundación Ángel Llorca in Madrid, and

available in digitalized form through the foundation's online database; see Justa Freire, '4.D/4.2: Didáctica del dibujo según Justa Freire', in *Archivo digital 'Los viejos papeles'* (Madrid: Fundación Ángel Llorca, [early-mid-1920s]), <http://www.fundacionangelllorca.org> [accessed 9 February 2018].

53. Ibid.

54. Ibid., p. 7.

55. See Kerschensteiner, *Die Entwicklung der zeichnerischen Begabung.*

56. Víctor Masriera Vila, 'El dibujo en la escuela primaria', *Revista de Pedagogía,* 1.12 (1922), 441–47, 'Cómo se enseña el dibujo', *Revista de Pedagogía,* 2.21 (1923), 346–51, and 'El dibujo y las oposiciones restringidas', *Revista de Pedagogía,* 6.72 (1927), 566–70.

57. For a rich visual overview of the artistic, cultural, and theatrical work undertaken by the *misiones pedagógicas,* see the exhibition catalogue *Las misiones pedagógicas: 1931–1936,* ed. by Eugenio Manuel Otera Urtaza (Madrid: Sociedad Estatal de Conmemoraciones Culturales, Residencia de Estudiantes, 2006). Jordana Mendelson has demonstrated in her work on photography and propaganda how the *misiones* were exhibited and furthered in the eyes of the Spanish public and international audiences: 'Las misiones pedagógicas en la prensa de 1935 a 1938', *Boletín de la Institución Libre de Enseñanza,* 40–41 (2001), 61–79.

58. Roberta Quance, 'Maruja Mallo and the Interest in Children's Art during the Second Spanish Republic', *Bulletin of Hispanic Studies,* 90.7 (2013), 803–18 (pp. 808–09). Quance narrows in on María Zambrano as the likely author, based on her friendship with Maruja Mallo and related contributions to *Diablo Mundo.* On *Diablo Mundo* and Zambrano's involvement, see Nigel Dennis, *Diablo Mundo: los intelectuales y la Segunda República: antología* (Madrid: Editorial Fundamentos, 1983), p. 21.

59. Anon., 'El niño, genio natural', *Diablo Mundo,* 1.5 (1934), 5.

60. Signing by the name of 'Mary Mall', Mallo illustrated an Italian folktale (*Las siete cortezas de tocino*) in the series *Cuentos de Basile* published by Ediciones del Árbol in 1935. See Andrea Puente, 'Ilustración para niños en la España de los años 10, 20 y 30', *Peonza: Revista de Literatura Infantil y Juvenil,* 117 (2016), 13–22 (p. 21).

61. Ortega Cubero, 'Ángel Ferrant: profesor de vanguardia', p. 330. The Mexican *escuelas al aire libre,* directed by pedagogue Alfredo Ramos Martínez, were a unique example of the genre, though here seemingly devoid of their roots and similar examples among the international New School movement. *Escuelas al aire libre,* if not focused exclusively on painting, had been successfully operating in Barcelona since 1914 and Madrid since 1918, as detailed in Pozo Andrés, 'La utilización de parques y jardines como espacios educativos alternativos en Madrid, 1900–1931'.

62. Quance, 'Maruja Mallo and the Interest in Children's Art during the Second Spanish Republic', pp. 810–11.

63. Juan de la Encina, 'Los dibujos de niños en el Lyceum', *La Voz,* 2 July 1928, p. 1. Encina was the art critic for Bilbao's *Hermes* (1917–22), curated the 1919 *Exposición Internacional de Pintura y Escultura,* and served as a member of the organizing committee for the 1925 *Ibéricos* exhibition in the Retiro, with Manuel Abril, Juan Ramón Jiménez, and others; see Ascunce Arenas, *Barcelona and Madrid,* pp. 129–30, 195.

64. Daughter of Trudy Graa de Araquistáin, a prominent Lyceum member, and Luis Araquistáin, later ambassador to Germany (1932–36) and France (1936–39), Sonia's early art would flourish into professional talent. As a student at the progressive Suffolk school Summerhill, her playful pen and ink drawings illustrated the story *The Last Man Alive* (1936) by the school's founder Alexander Sutherland Neill. In 1941 she exhibited at the Leger Galleries in London and was working with other artists at a shared studio in London before her internationally-reported suicide in 1945 at the age of twenty-three. See London, Tate Archive, J. Leger & Son, 'Leger Galleries Private View Card for "Exhibition of Contemporary Continental Art"', TGA 20052/2/11/6; and EFE, 'Sonia Araquistáin se mata, arrojándose desde un séptimo piso', *ABC,* 6 September 1945, p. 25.

65. Encina, 'Los dibujos de niños en el Lyceum', p. 1. A popular interest in children's art and representations of the world extended into adult's representations of children themselves, as in Austrian émigré photographer Adrienne Junger Chapiro's 1934 exhibition of portraits of

children — often the sons or daughters of fellow artists. Exhibited at the Palacio de la Biblioteca Nacional by the Sociedad Española de Amigos del Arte, several of her photographs were later analysed by critic Manuel Abril in his 1936 work on visual representations of childhood; see *Los niños en el arte y en la fotografía* (Madrid: M. Aguilar, 1936). Junger is pictured in Anon., 'Una exposición artística', *Ahora*, 24 October 1934, p. 17.

66. José Julio Castro, 'Semana Pedagógica de la Nacional en Málaga', *Escuelas de España*, 2.22 (1935), 464–69.

67. Ibid., pp. 465–66.

68. As with Ortega's conflation of the child and scientist, these comparisons skewed masculine. While the New Education Fellowship and Republican government pointedly applied pedagogical principles towards co-education, practice and perceptions of gender differed on a larger societal level, including in Ferrant's artistic workshop for boys.

69. See Manuel Abril, 'L'escultor Ángel Ferrant o les tres gràcies de la forma', *Gaseta de les arts*, 2 (1929), 133–37. The Archivo Ferrant at the Museo Patio Herreriano in Valladolid holds Ferrant's library, consisting of dozens of works bridging philosophy of education (Giner, Cossío, Decroly), psychology, and psychoanalysis (Jung, Adler, Spranger), and the interpretation of children's art and aesthetics (Luquet, Braunschvig, Kerschensteiner, Gasch, Torres García), among others.

70. See Clara Eslava, *Mutación poética: naturaleza viva en el imaginario de Ángel Ferrant, 1945–1950* (Alzuza, Navarra: Fundación Museo Jorge Oteiza, 2017), pp. 7–54. This volume accompanied a comprehensive exhibition on Ferrant at the Museo Oteiza in 2017, curated by Eslava, which in a nod to Ferrant's own efforts included a creative workshop and events for schoolchildren in a dedicated space connected to the gallery itself.

71. As part and parcel of his promulgation of cultural movements such as *vibracionismo* and *clownismo*, Barradas was an active illustrator of children's books, magazines, and cartoons, from the poster for Madrid's 1919 Teatro de los Niños, Gómez de la Serna's children's books, and the costumes for Lorca's 1920 *El maleficio de la mariposa*. Given these interests, Barradas was also a likely force for Ferrant's 1935 collaboration on the design of theatrical marionettes with Lorca. On this *tertulia*, see Ortega Cubero, 'Ángel Ferrant: profesor de vanguardia', pp. 319–20; Federico García Lorca and Sebastián Gasch, *Cartas a sus amigos* (Barcelona: Ediciones Cobalto, 1950), pp. 87–88.

72. See Rodríguez Álvarez, *El arte del niño*.

73. Anon., 'La escuela en la "ciudad funcional" ', *AC*, 3.10 (1933), 15–30 (p. 15); Ferrant, 'Resplandor y proyección de los dibujos infantiles', p. 34.

74. Ibid.

75. Ángel Ferrant, 'Diseño de una configuración escolar', *Arte*, 1.1 (1932), 12–18 (p. 13). On the reception of the Plan Ferrant among fellow artists, including the minor polemic it created in the Catalan press, see Javier Pérez Segura, *Arte moderno, vanguardia y estado: la Sociedad de Artistas Ibéricos y la República (1931–1936)* (Madrid: Consejo Superior de Investigaciones Científicas, 2003), p. 181.

76. Ferrant, 'Resplandor y proyección de los dibujos infantiles', p. 19.

77. Gabriel García Maroto, *La nueva España 1930: resumen de la vida artística española desde el año 1927 hasta hoy* (Madrid: Biblios, 1927), pp. 18, 80–88.

78. Ibid., p. 13.

79. Ibid., pp. 14, 15.

80. Ibid.

81. Ignacio Asenjo Fernández, 'Ángel Ferrant: el anhelo de las influencias pedagógicas', *Arte, Individuo y Sociedad*, 25.1 (2013), 11–29 (p. 18); Inés Ortega Cubero, 'Ángel Ferrant y la Escuela de Artes y Oficios de Viena', *Pulso: Revista de Educación*, 32 (2009), 25–54.

82. Anon., 'En Madrid hay un club infantil', *Ahora*, 16 January 1936, p. 18; Cartagena, Legado Carmen Conde, Patronato Carmen Conde-Antonio Oliver, letter from Norah Borges to Carmen Conde, sig. 015 01402.

83. Anon., 'En Madrid hay un club infantil'.

84. Ibid.

85. See an introduction to the 'arsintes' as a vanguard pedagogical artistic project in Ángel Ferrant, Antonio de Lara Gavilàn, and Emeterio R. Melendreras, *Tres propuestas para niños, 1930–1935*, ed. by Carlos Pérez (Valencia: Institut Valencià d'Art Modern, 1999).

86. Ortega Cubero, *Ángel Ferrant, profesor de vanguardia*, pp. 222–51.

87. See Emeterio Ruíz Melendreras, *La pintura por el recorte geométrico a base de rectas y curvas*, ed. by J. Demuro (Madrid: Juan Ortiz, 1934). Juan Ortiz published numerous books that brought together graphic design and active learning, including a series of vibrant books showing children how to transform everyday food and objects into new scenes. See his *46 trabajos manuales hechos con corcho, sandía, limón, cerezas, cañas, etc.* (Madrid: Ortiz, n.d.) and teacher Luis Llácer Asencio's vividly illustrated, active-learning text *Actividades escolares con hojas, frutos y semillas* (Valencia: J. Vicente Pont Ferrer, 1934). Juan Ortiz published pedagogical texts grounding this active learning, for example Alexander J. Deschamps, *La auto-educación en el método Decroly*, trans. by Emilia Elías de Ballesteros (Madrid: Juan Ortiz, 1932). I am grateful to Andrea Puente of Mundo Pintado (<https://mundopintado.blogspot.com> [accessed 1 May 2018]) for graciously sharing her knowledge and a related article.

88. Melendreras, *La pintura por el recorte geométrico a base de rectas y curvas*, n.p. Ferrant's and Melendreras's work is joined in Pérez's IVAM collection by illustrator Tono's flattened, outlined paper animals (*El arco de Noé* [Noah's Ark]), published in *Crónica*, 1933–36. The latter's clever shapes formed a collection of 'recortables', starting with a stout bull and building up to dozens of other animals, all of which the child could cut out, fold, and play with at will; see Carlos Pérez, 'Tono: humorismo y vanguardia', *Boletín de la Institución Libre de Enseñanza*, 42–43 (2001), 175–80.

89. On constructivist art and its influences on Bauhaus, De Stijl, and other design movements, see Stephen Bann, *The Tradition of Constructivism* (New York: Da Capo Press, 1974). On a parallel track, on Piaget's path to psychological 'constructivism', see Barry J. Wadsworth, *Piaget's Theory of Cognitive and Affective Development: Foundations of Constructivism*, 5th edn (White Plains: Longman, 1996).

90. Ferrant, 'Diseño de una configuración escolar', p. 20.

91. On the *misiones* and their wider educational context, see *Las misiones pedagógicas: 1931–1936*, ed. by Otero Urtaza, as well as Holguín, *Creating Spaniards*, pp. 145–52.

92. Almost half of the villages visited were within close reach of Madrid, in Castilla la Vieja and León, giving the initiative the sense of a 'Madrid-based enterprise with a marked predominance of Castilian culture', and little outreach to Catalonia, Aragón, Valencia, or the south; see Ginsborg, *Family Politics*, p. 241. The Patronato released a first report in 1934, documenting some seventy missions across hundreds of towns and celebrating the more than three thousand libraries created (as well as documenting Unamuno's visit to one travelling theatre), see Anon., 'La juventud en los pueblos', *Diablo Mundo*, 1.4 (1934), 7.

93. Manuel Abril, 'Comentarios a nuestros grabados', *Arte*, 2.2 (1933), 27–28 (p. 27). In a more celebratory, reflective vein, Abril also published three images of the *misiones* in *Los niños en el arte*, pp. 88–93. In one, a girl listens intently to a story from an eager 'missionary'; children gather around to hear a story read aloud; boys' faces light up as they watch a play being performed. Comparing the latter scene to a work of nineteenth-century realism, Abril suggested that this was true life: '¿Hay una sola obra de la pretendidamente realistas que nos ofrezca la vida, la espontaneidad, la riqueza de estas expresiones de estos chicos de Castilla escuchando una "función" de los pedagogos trashumantes?' [Is there a single work from the supposed Realists that can offer us the life, the spontaneity, the richness of expression of these Castilian boys listening to a 'production' by these migrating pedagogues?]. See *Los niños en el arte*, pp. 90–92.

94. Abril, 'Comentarios a nuestros grabados', pp. 27–28.

95. Ibid., p. 28.

96. Anon., 'La juventud en los pueblos'.

97. Manuel Abril, 'Humanización y desnaturalización, o lo humano y lo demasiado humano', *Arte*, 2.2 (1933), 20–25 (p. 21); José Ortega y Gasset, *La deshumanización del arte e ideas sobre la novela*, in *Obras completas*, III, 353–419.

98. Abril, 'Humanización y desnaturalización, o lo humano y lo demasiado humano', p. 23.

99. Ibid., p. 24.

100. Ibid., pp. 24–25.

101. Jesualdo Sosa, *La expresión creadora del niño*, 2nd edn (Buenos Aires: Editorial Poseidón, 1950), p. 142.

102. Manuel Abril, 'Sobre la deshumanización del arte', *Cruz y Raya*, 1.2 (1935), 154–63 (p. 163).
103. See also Manuel Abril, *De la naturaleza al espíritu: ensayo crítico de pintura contemporánea desde Sorolla a Picasso* (Madrid: Espasa Calpe, 1935).
104. Roland Barthes, *Camera Lucida: Reflections on Photography*, trans. by Richard Howard (New York: Hill & Wang, 1981), p. 27. Abril, *Los niños en el arte*, p. 10.
105. Abril, *Los niños en el arte*, pp. 26, 16.
106. Ibid., p. 34.
107. Ibid., pp. 42, 61. The potentially problematic nature of his claims should also be noted as children matured. The latter quotation on the 'dawning' of the human accompanies a portrait by the photographer Rúa of a pre-pubescent youth, 'Encarnita', wrapped in a towel, cropped hair tousled after a bath. As frames of 'childhood' gave way to those of 'humanization' and maturation, so too were gender and sexualization inextricable from these readings.

CHAPTER 6

Early Plenitude:
A Phenomenology of the
Child's Spirit

Me parece, evocando mi niñez a través de los años, que sentíamos entonces
confusamente en el fondo del alma la trabazón de todo.

[It seems to me, recalling my childhood after so many years, that we began to
feel then, in our deepest selves, the coming-together of the whole.]

Miguel de Unamuno, *Recuerdos de niñez y de mocedad* (1908)

From December 1930, a series of vignettes in the *Heraldo de Madrid* asked various
well-known figures to recount their earliest memories. Collected under the title of
'La infancia de la gente conocida' [Childhoods of the Famous] and published over
the course of the next three weeks, the series echoed a larger question being asked by
teachers, scholars, writers, and bureaucrats alike: how does childhood frame the life
one lives and the person one becomes? Of note within this popular genre of writing
were a number of recollections which introduced in a deeper autobiographical and
intellectual sense the lives of 'gente conocida': Miguel de Unamuno's *Recuerdos
de niñez y de mocedad* [Memories of Childhood and Youth] (1908), Juan Ramón
Jiménez's *Platero y yo* (1914), and Santiago Ramón y Cajal's *La infancia de Ramón y
Cajal, contada por él mismo* [Ramón y Cajal's Childhood, Told by Himself] (1921)
were prominent examples of this trend. While such pieces arguably tapped into a
circulating Freudian fascination with early childhood as the key to one's subsequent
life, these reflections were in effect closer to what the philosopher Gaston Bachelard
has called a 'poetics of reverie' built around childhood and its enduring influence
on the self. Like Proust's recuperations of sensations long past, it was understood
that the adult might draw upon the heightened sensations of childhood to 'renew'
a 'primitive simplicity' through brief instances of wonder. Engaging with the
'lively, full', 'human' act of consciousness, Bachelard posed language, the poetic
imagination, as the only way to bridge pure psychological and phenomenological
methods. Through the 'added light' of an expanding consciousness, one's own
acting and evolving self might be renewed in the present.[1]

Through reverie also comes a sense of reverence. In the neo-humanist theory
and literature of education read in this chapter, this sense of reverence extended to
the people and things that shaped one's present and across which a stable self was

forged. Through novellas, essays, and poetry of childhood, prominent intellectuals evoked a deep-seated childhood abiding in the developing and future self. As this book shows, representations of childhood were approached from a multiplicity of angles and approaches, incorporating psychological, physical, medical, religious, and political concerns. But these partial views would not be complete without a total view of human experience which went beyond any one of these lenses, namely a spiritual and transcendent sense of the very human core. As this chapter argues, among Spain's leading reformist educational circles during the 1920s and 1930s a 'spiritual' view of education constituted not primarily a doctrinal or religious view, but rather an understanding of childhood as part of a larger process of personal, historical, and cultural evolution.

One's burgeoning sense of self depended on individual struggle and evolution through development, drawing from a stream of philosophical and humanistic thought to find its fulfilment, ultimately, in notions of love and reciprocity: between child and adult, past and present, interior and exterior worlds. This was the sense of widening engagement that the pedagogue Adolfo Maillo described as a 'sensación de plenitud humana, de superabundancia espiritual' [sensation of human plenitude, of spiritual superabundance] gained through poetry.[2] As in Maillo's description of education, notions of the child's *alma* co-existed alongside a metaphysical notion of *espíritu*. The term *espíritu* was often applied in strictly psychological contexts to refer to the mind and its operation, but by the late 1920s it had arguably overtaken and merged with *alma* within a neo-humanist conception of development, plenitude, and transcendence. This latter term was not strictly related to the mind, but rather embraced all aspects of the child's developing personhood.[3] Because any concepts of soul existed alongside and in close connection with Christian rhetoric, I employ the term 'spirit' to convey most literally the sense of *espíritu* and the *espiritual* examined here. Doing so acknowledges both the more religiously bound connotations of the 'soul' and a psychological rendering of *espíritu* as 'intellect'. To speak of a humanist 'spirit' of education, therefore, was not merely a question of translation. It was also one of liberation, including among the intellectuals who defined vanguard educational philosophy through the Second Republic.

How was such a neo-humanist philosophical and literary perspective theorized? Within a politically secular context came fierce articulations of a human spirit forged through education, taking a foundation of human development and transcendence as their *raison d'être*. Moral, ethical, and indeed spiritual aspects of childhood could only be encompassed by considering personhood as a whole, echoing an integral view of the self as fostered by the confluence of mystical, Krausist, and Catholic influences within early twentieth-century Spanish education reform. Throughout theological and pedagogical history, notions of the child's soul were inseparable from discussions of broader values and development. Yet as Thomas Popkewitz has argued about the pedagogical 'soul' in early twentieth-century scientific discourse, histories of education have too often reduced the soul to scientific categories of mind and reason. Such narratives ignore how the soul was 'transmogrified' in pedagogical theory, not into analytical or religious categories of upbringing but into a more all-encompassing ideal: that of a rich inner life and conscious expansion of personhood. Concepts of the soul in early twentieth-century pedagogy were therefore simultaneously connected to transnational cosmopolitan values of reason, science, and the developing 'biography' and unfolding narrative of the self.[4]

This chapter analyses such a spiritual view of education through texts that contrast scientific and transcendent interpretations of self and development. Notably, it focuses on works by three men who take up questions of fatherhood and the youthful, adolescent struggle at their cores. In each can be read a pronounced turn from overly scientific, empirical, and limiting pedagogies towards transcendent understandings of the ideal role of education in shaping the self. Through texts such as Miguel de Unamuno's short novel or 'nivola', *Amor y pedagogía* [Love and Pedagogy] (1902, expanded 1934); Joaquim Xirau's *L'amor i la percepció dels valors* [Love and the Perception of Values] (1936) with its section entitled 'Amor y pedagogía', his *Amor y mundo* [Love and World] (1940); and finally Joan Roura's *Educación y ciencia* [Education and Science] (1940), I trace the major lines of argument that characterized a transcendent educational humanism among Spanish intellectuals. Unamuno's critique of a destructive, stifling scientific pedagogy set the terms by which reformist pedagogues such as Xirau responded during the Second Republic, defending a pedagogy of individual spiritual development. At the same time, values of vitality and spiritual plenitude were embraced by a wide spectrum of writers and intellectuals during the intervening years, including by poets who sought to align language to the heart of phenomenological experience. For this reason, finally, I read a humanistic notion of spirit towards its wider use and incorporation in the cultural sphere: Jorge Guillén's poetry of childhood and its relation to memory, self, and world.

According to Xirau, the legacy of Spanish educational humanism had passed from Ramón Llull and Juan Luis Vives onward through Cervantes, Góngora, and others, and towards the modernity of figures such as Julián Sanz del Río, Francisco Giner de los Ríos, and Manuel B. Cossío. These *hommes de lettres* were principally concerned with education and its relation to life, Xirau argued, and saw Spain's chief problem as one of education. In his writings on Cossío and the Institución Libre de Enseñanza, Xirau noted that, as in the work of Vives, all 'esfuerzos del espíritu' [spiritual efforts] converged and were derived from the educational question.[5] Xirau and Roura, along with Emilio Mira y López, led the University of Barcelona's Seminari de Pedagogia, at the forefront of Spain's educational and psychometric research from the late 1920s. Educated in pedagogy in Madrid and considered members of the so-called philosophical Escuela de Barcelona under Jaume Serra Húnter, Xirau, and Roura offer an essential counterpoint to the monolithic presence of *institucionistas* such as Giner, Cossío, and Ortega.[6] Between the ILE in Madrid and the Seminari in Barcelona, pedagogical research in Madrid and Barcelona functioned less as opposed poles than as complementary nodes of reform.[7] Xirau, in particular, was profoundly influenced by Cossío, seeing in his pursuit of pedagogy and art history the gentle, insightful culmination of a tradition of Spanish humanism and in whose reverent hands education itself became a transcendent 'obra de arte' [work of art].[8]

Given their deep training and engagement both in *krauso-institucionalismo* and international philosophies of education, both Xirau and Roura are crucial bridges from the holistic enquiries of the 1920s to neo-humanist and exilic perspectives after the Civil War. Building on provocative portrayals of education by figures such as Unamuno, both pedagogues sought an ideal of total human formation in a celebration of the *Geisteswissenschaften,* a conception of the human sciences that went beyond strict empiricism to embrace experience, phenomenology, and culture. Pioneered by Wilhelm Dilthey in 1883 and furthered by Eduard Spranger in the field of pedagogy, elaborations of a *ciencia del espíritu* in Spain sought to distinguish — as Unamuno had done in *Amor y pedagogía* — positivistic science from humanistic education. With and alongside the advocacy and imaginative work of poets, writers, and artists, they sought to formalize in both theory and practice an ideal of 'espiritualismo en la educación' [spiritualism in education]. That spirit stood for an integral development of the child's very personhood.[9] In drawing distinctions between biological, psychological, and spiritual growth, essays such as Ortega's 1925 'Vitalidad, alma, espíritu' cut to the heart of this matter. Within a larger field of discussion on the role of biology and consciousness in human development, Ortega's essay drew distinctions between mechanical intelligence and spiritual intuition, asking how one might recognize the ineffable, the whole self, the *ser*, from the many elements that made it up. Just as water was more than the sum of hydrogen and oxygen, a person could not be reduced to a simple past, present, or future:

> Pues esa pre-cosa es el ser de la cosa, y es lo que hay que buscar [...]. En cambio, el ser y la definición, la pre-cosa, nos muestra la cosa en statu nascendi, y solo se conoce bien lo que, en uno u otro sentido, se ve nacer.[10]

> [For this pre-thing is the being of the thing, and it is what must be sought [...]. In contrast, the being and its development, this pre-thing, shows us the thing in *statu nascendi*; and one only truly knows that which one has, one way or another, seen being born.]

Within educational philosophy, the child was the ultimate 'pre-cosa'. It was the 'ser de la cosa' of humanity, the being-in-formation that could not be viewed analytically as a product of input and output, but only holistically over time, as an individual shaped by his or her environment, by social bonds, and by unquantifiable spiritual depths.[11] Writing of the potential of pedagogy to revive and vitalize society, Ortega called for the revival of 'esa trastierra espiritual' [this spiritual after-land], far richer and more abundant than the merely utilitarian.[12] Through terms such as *alma* and *espíritu*, *intuición* and *plenitud*, philosophical and poetic writings posed their opposition to narrow rationalism and positivism. More than that, they drew upon a sense of 'reverie' to move towards reverence for human life itself. Intellectuals sought a new and more expansive science to encompass ideals of vitality and a physically-attuned expansion of the spirit.

Love and Pedagogy: Unfolding Education from Unamuno to Xirau

Educar és en essència amar.

[To educate is, essentially, to love.]

Joaquim Xirau i Palau, *L'amor i la percepció dels valors* (1936)

Between Unamuno's 1902 publication of *Amor y pedagogía* (1864–1936) and the expanded re-publication of the *nivola* in 1934, practices and theories of pedagogy and education worldwide underwent fundamental shifts. Unamuno's story of a father intent on raising his son as a genius drew on concrete objections to prevailing tendencies in science and education. Given the focus on holistic education throughout this work, it may not be entirely surprising that Unamuno's original title for his educational satire of 1902 was not *Amor y pedagogía* but *Todo un hombre*.[13] In Unamuno's own writings, from the *nivola* to poetry to essays, one can trace this thread of totality and plenitude of the self. By 1936, the year of his death, Unamuno would describe the self as the 'hombre entero y verdadero, con su completo organismo espiritual encarnado en el corporal' [the whole, true man, with his complete spiritual organism incarnated in the corporal]. The individual, often called a 'microcosmos' or a 'pequeño mundo', was, he noted, better understood as an 'universo individual — y personal — dentro del vasto mundo' [individual — and personal — universe, within the vastness of the world].[14] At the *nivola*'s heart was the question of how to shape that 'hombre entero', and how a fullness of spirit could be gained.

Using *Amor y pedagogía*'s two editions as a framework, namely its sections entitled 'Apuntes para un tratado de cocotología' [Notes for a Treatise on Cocotology] (1902) on the art of paper-folding, and 'Apéndice' (1934), an appendix treating paper birds, I suggest that beyond Unamuno's satire of an overly limiting, calculated view of pedagogy lay a wider advocacy not just for a neo-humanist *Bildung* but for a philosophy of education based on unconditional love. Such, indeed, was the framework advocated and furthered by Xirau two years later, when his essay 'Amor i pedagogia' drew on Unamuno's titular terms to reconfigure the meaning of education itself.[15] Central to the book's construction is a series of origami birds, the *cocottes* that populate *Amor y pedagogía*'s meta-frame. Unamuno was known for his fondness for paper-folding and the hundreds of tiny birds and other animals he created. In coverage documenting his love for his *cocottes*, such as one article published in *Estampa* in 1932, Unamuno holds his first grandchild, Miguel Quiroga Unamuno (Fig. 6.1), while in another image, his grown son Pablo and daughter María fold birds while a delighted toddler-aged Miguelín plays with the paper creations. Unamuno took pride in being 'inventor' and 'creator' of these forms, yet saw children themselves as their ultimate creators and spirits. The form of each bird was so 'pure' and 'exalted' that he would 'atribuirle un espíritu, y aún supone que las manos del niño, al fabricar una cocotilla, están movidas por el Poder Supremo' [attribute to them a spirit, supposing that the hands of the child, in making a little cocotte, were moved by the Supreme Power]. Salamanca was the birds' home, its rivers, stones, and trees: the 'valle natal de las espirituales pajaritas' [valley in which

FIG. 6.1. Miguel de Unamuno holding his first grandchild, Miguel Quiroga Unamuno, c.1930. Source: Courtesy of the Casa-Museo Unamuno.

FIG. 6.2. A meeting of Unamuno's cocottes. Source: José Suárez,
50 fotos de Salamanca ([1932]). Courtesy of the Casa-Museo Unamuno.

these spiritual paper birds were born].[16] In coverage of his stay at the Residencia de Estudiantes in 1932, Unamuno is depicted sitting calmly, folding and shaping a figure, while additional photographs by José Suárez show a veritable arc of animals arranged around a table for tea or prancing across a table, their tiny feet folded upwards as they jump (Fig. 6.2).

Unamuno, a father of nine with his wife Concepción Lizárraga (1891–1934), frequently mused upon his children — as well as his paper birds — in his prolific poetic production. He patently had real, physical children and grandchildren against whose living realities the absurdities of pedagogical methodologies and rationalist approaches could be contrasted. As seen in his sketches of his own children, their shifting profiles and faces, from birth through childhood (Fig. 6.3), Unamuno understood what it was to watch a child grow and change over time. Contrasted with the satirical framework of scientific empiricism he draws between the empirically, experimentally-crazed Don Avito and his son Apolodoro, such images bring out the humanist and interpersonal concerns at the heart of the educational project. While critiques of *Amor y pedagogía* have analysed Unamuno's wider view of education and, in the case of Leslie Harkema, its take on youth and adolescence, the work's framing texts, the 'Apuntes' and 'Apéndice', responded critically to specific positivist tendencies in pedagogy.[17] They not only laid bare the

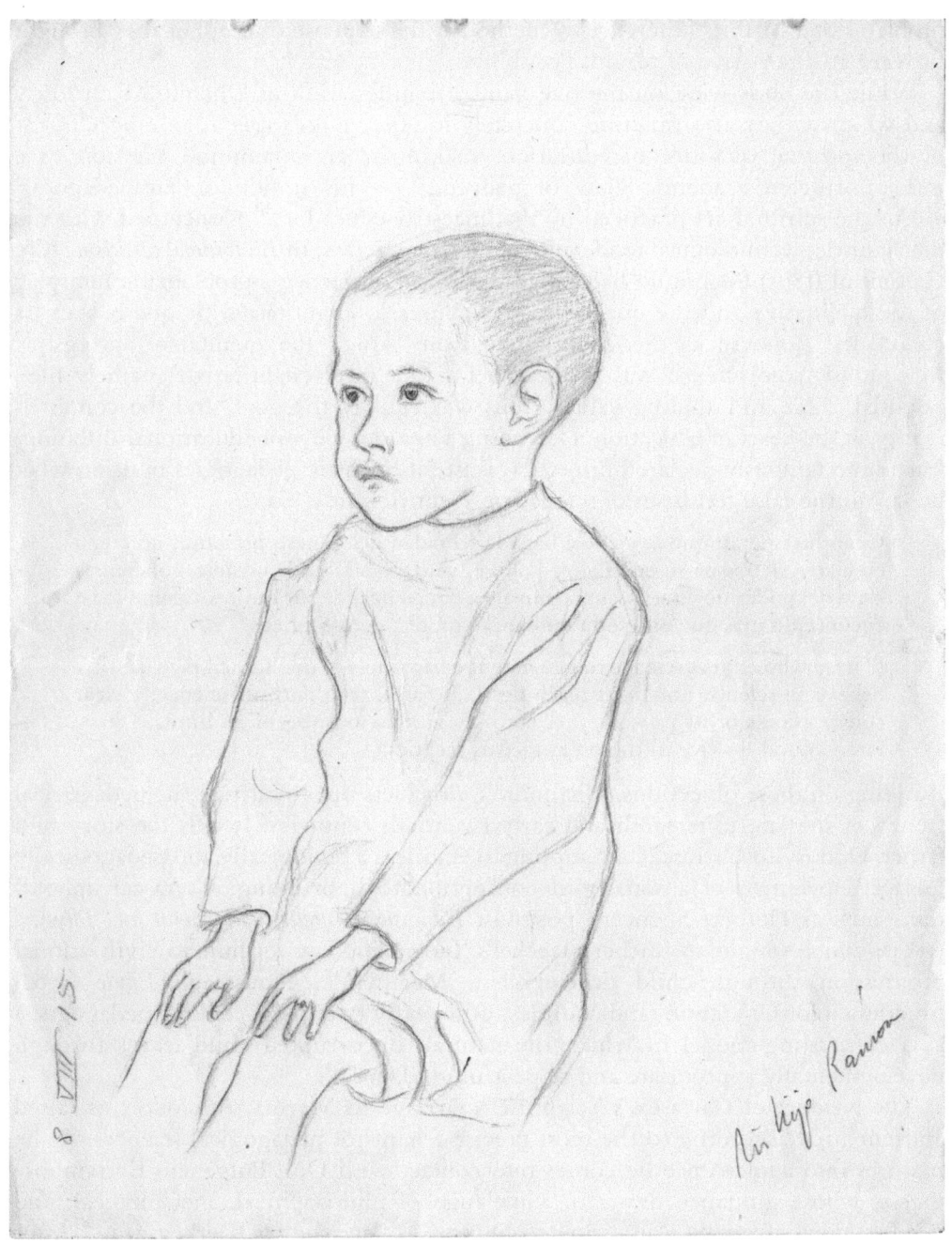

FIG. 6.3. In Unamuno's sketches of his own children, the geometry of his *cocottes* gives way to living curves and lines. Source: Miguel de Unamuno, 'Mi hijo Ramón' (1915). Courtesy of the Casa-Museo Unamuno.

problems of a stifling adherence to method at the expense of life, but they brought forward an alternative of playful possibility.

While the birds were on the one hand a manifestation of Unamuno's curiosity and whimsy, they also function concretely in *Amor y pedagogía* as an embodiment of the spiritual qualities of education, making clear Unamuno's aversion to a pure, unfiltered academic view of pedagogy — his notion of 'antipedagogía' versus the spiritual art practiced by the 'maestro-educador'.[18] Concerned with the mechanistic, technological tendencies of modern society, in *En torno al casticismo* [On Casticism] (1895) Unamuno had called the world of science a problematic interplay of the qualitative and the quantitative: 'se busca lo cuantitativo de que brotan las cualidades!' [one seeks the quantitative from which the qualitative springs!].[19] In contrast, true science was the search for the 'intra-cuantitativo', namely life's essential, vital, and abiding values. This was equally the goal, and the contested reality, at the heart of education. Defending a broader view of educational ambition, Unamuno famously declared himself against rationalistic pedagogies built on what he saw as the false fetishism of science or 'cientificismo':

> Cuantos esperan que la ciencia haga la felicidad del género humano, no creen en ella y menos en su enseñanza [...]. Fe, verdadera fe en la ciencia, conciencia clara del poder de ésta, lo cual equivale a conciencia de sus límites, apenas la he encontrado más que en esos a quienes se moteja de escépticos.[20]

> [Those who expect science to generate the happiness of the human race, neither believe in science nor in its teachings [...]. Faith, true faith in science, a clear consciousness of its powers, that is to say a consciousness of its limits, I have rarely found — save in those branded as sceptics.]

Building on these objections, Unamuno's *nivola* sets out to satirize the pedagogical frenzy of the late nineteenth and early twentieth centuries. It tells the story of a father, Don Avito Carrascal, attempting to engineer a biologically and pedagogically 'perfect' specimen of a son, from conception to upbringing. Carrascal upholds texts such as Herbert Spencer's positivist *Education: Intellectual, Moral and Physical* (1861), which sought to further Haeckel's 'biogenetic law' of human civilizational progression through child development. Meanwhile, Rousseau's *Émile* (1762) functioned for Unamuno (and countless other early twentieth-century pedagogues) as a contrasting model in which the natural, uncorrupted child learns through developmentally appropriate and respectful guidance.[21]

The product of Carrascal's 'scientific' marriage to Marina, Apolodoro is raised and nurtured according to the most precise tenants of pedagogical sciences. As he matures into adolescence he comes into contact with Don Fulgencio Entrambos-mares, whose guidance draws in a melange of philosophical, metaphysical, and nihilist views, from St Augustine to Spinoza, Nietzsche to Kierkegaard.[22] After Apolodoro suffers a crisis of faith, torn by conflicting models of philosophy, faith, and a youthful love, his eventual suicide acts as a renunciation of the scientific pedagogy that formed him. His father's, Don Avito's, effort to educate methodically is presented as a desperate act of paternal love, against which the young Apolodoro turns to a human love beyond the scientific, philosophical, or intellectual. In that struggle, Apolodoro conforms to that adolescent 'youthful faith [...] capable of resistance' that Harkema calls critical to Spanish writings: compared to that of childhood, the adolescent faith is less passive, less innocent, and more fiercely able to challenge the encompassing worldviews of childhood. As in Apolodoro's struggle, only adolescence, only youth itself, allowed for the possibility of a 'true faith', tested and forged by struggle and conviction.[23]

Around the *nivola* are a series of paratexts that reinforce and enrich this critique, including a treatise supposedly written by Don Fulgencio Entrambosmares. This contribution, 'Apuntes para un tratado de cocotología' stands in for Entrambosmares's *obra maestra* on paper-folding. Supposedly a fragment of his envisioned two-volume *Tratado crítico comparativo de cocotología racional* [Critical Comparative Treatise on Rational Cocotology], the 'Apuntes' function as a concise critique of positivism and its exacting, dissecting portrayals of physical and empirical reality, in this case, the child in formation. In defining 'la ciencia que trata de las pajaritas de papel' [the science of paper birds], Entrambosmares terms his discipline 'cocotología', from the French nursery word *cocotte* (versus hybrid Greek and Latin terms such as *papyrornithiología*).[24] From Entrambosmares's precise elaboration of the boundaries and divisions of the science to diagrams of the *cocottes*' embryology, anatomy, origin, and purpose, Unamuno parodied the diagnostic work undertaken by early twentieth-century paidologists and pedagogues who, in their zeal to professionalize and proclaim, lost sight of the proverbial forest for the trees and the ineffability of spirit for the physical, measured body and mind.[25] His birds function as a warning of blinkered analysis that threatened to exclude the living self in development.

Unamuno's devotion to his *cocottes* pose the key to the humanist puzzle at the work's heart. His playful interest in origami and paper-folding was well known. In a 1928 article entitled 'Unamuno als Bildhauer' [Unamuno as Sculptor], German journalist Edda Reinhardt related a meeting that she and a group of visitors held with Unamuno. Speaking of Spanish politics, philosophy, and literature, he brought forth the paper birds he loved to fold, the fantastical creatures immortalized in *Amor y pedagogía*'s paratext 'Apuntes para un tratado de cocotología' of 1902. Reinhardt's article was introduced and translated by Manuel García Blanco for *La Gaceta Literaria* in 1930.[26] In this account, Reinhardt described their conversation meandering from Spanish rural poverty, to philosophy, to the Basque language, before Unamuno began reading from the 1928 German translation of his 1925 *L'agonie del cristianisme*. But the magic of the visit began when he pulled out a piece of paper and set to work: 'Rápidamente y seguramente trabajaban sus manos, plegaban, doblaban y alisaban de nuevo' [Rapidly and confidently his hands moved, bending, folding, and smoothing again]. Unamuno, the eternal teacher, recounted to his audience how the creations arose, years before: 'comencé a hacer dobleces, así, y apareció el animal. ¡Como usted ve, severamente cubista!' [I began to fold, like this, and suddenly the animal appeared. As you can see, severely Cubist!].[27]

Reinhardt emphasized the creative aspect of Unamuno's unusual hobby, telling her German readers that while his philosophical works were well-known in Spain, few were acquainted with these delicate paper novelties and the spirit from which they sprung. Reinhardt's sketch suggested a man melding respect for form and precision with inventive creativity. These were objects of impeccable mathematical and inductive spirit, as a simple piece of paper became transformed into a lively three-dimensional creation. In turn, García reminded his Spanish readers that, for Unamuno, these paper figures were archetypes of a divine geometry, in which, allegedly, the *cocottes'* underlying purpose was to challenge children's developing senses of form and reality. To 'inquietar la psique en germen de la niñez' [to disquiet the child's nascent psyche], something which should matter to all those concerned with 'los primeros pasos de la humanidad' [the first steps of humanity].[28] Thus did García address the metaphorical purpose of these tiny creations springing from Unamuno's hands: their relation to pedagogical thought, and the unfolding and realisation of individual lives. As Unamuno advised his visitors, glue and scissors were superfluous, for the animals' forms were all there, immanent — they needed only to be folded, doubled, and projected to take shape. These 'living' *cocottes*, thus, can be read as the physical legacy of those birds elaborated in the 'Apuntes'.

During the third of a century that transpired between Unamuno's original critique of 1902 and its 1934 expansion and re-publication, the world had changed radically. From his elaboration of the paper birds' archetypal perfection in the earlier 'Apuntes', therefore, Unamuno's 'Apéndice' of 1934 moved rather towards a 'visión cocótica del universo' which attempted to demonstrate logically how these creatures grew to view and understand the world.[29] This new *Amor y pedagogía* appeared both amidst sweeping educational reforms and unprecedented political currents that would make its arguments all the more prescient. The Primo de Rivera government had come into power, occasioning Unamuno's attendant and very public exile in France and the Canary Islands (1924–30), then fallen again and the Second Republic established. Roughly two generations of young teachers had been funded for pedagogical studies in new methods abroad; numerous active and open-air schools had opened their doors, while institutions such as the Institución Libre de Enseñanza had grown and formalized their educational work. Yet even as the Second Republic put forward socialist educational reforms in Spain, the rise of National Socialism in Germany threatened a liberal order and made education a cornerstone of patriotic and nationalist consolidation.

The risks of ceding education to blinkered pedagogies were thus clear. Born from a triangular, trapezoidal differentiation of *cocotte*-Adam and *cocotte*-Eve, the *cocottes'* world was a geometrical universe. Within it, the pedagogue Entrambosmares notes that his analysis of love — erotic, filial, and conjugal — cannot help but veer dangerously away from objective science and into philosophical territory in approaching its structure and outlook. As Entrambosmares narrates this imaginary paper bird's worldview:

> Cabe conjeturar que sea la visión y por tanto la contemplación del mundo que tenga la cocota. Es decir, su *Weltanschauung,* para mayor claridad. Visión y contemplación estrictamente cúbicas [...] la cocota o pajarita de papel ve una puesta de sol en el mar como el acostarse de una svástica en una greca.[30]

> [We may conjecture that such is the vision and therefore perspective that the *cocotte* has on the world. That is to say, its *Weltanschauung,* for total clarity.

> Strictly cubical vision and contemplation [...] the *cocotte* or paper bird sees the
> sun setting in the sea like a swastika dipping into a Greek frieze.]

With a line-drawing depiction of a cubist swastika dipping below a line of block-shaped geometrical waves, Entrambosmares transforms the human setting sun into that which a paper *cocotte* would perceive. To see the world through the eyes of the paper bird would be to know it as a geometrical block, whereas to be human is to view the world in organic, living terms. Yet danger beckoned, as reflected most transparently in Unamuno's invocation of a swastika, 'la hoy tan famosa cruz gamada o ganchuda, la svástica de los racistas de allí y de aquí' [today's infamous hooked or twisted cross, that swastika of racists here and everywhere]. His critique of this geometrical world is political, but also pedagogical in evoking the limitation that ideologies provide to the infinity of potential, nascent views and visions. The absurdity of reducing the complex physical, mental, spiritual development of any creature — a bird, a child, a person — to a series of geometrical lines and forms is patent. Through this new text, questions of national regeneration and post-positivist critiques began to turn towards broader notions of universality, humanism, and transnational solidarity between and among human individuals.

These political currents and critiques were inextricable from the work's larger celebration of the plenitude and inviolability of individual development. Through obscure and obtuse discussions of form and function, the paratexts serve to vindicate the ineffable spiritual aspects of childhood — all that could not be explained or contained within their boundaries. In Unamuno's conclusion to the 'Apéndice', in effect a treatise on a treatise, he dismissed Entrambosmares's meandering into the science and anatomy of 'cocotología' with what seems at once the most honest and complicated statement in the text:

> Concluyo, pues, antes de que se me agríe el humor y dejando este tono me avíe a
> otro en que vierta todo el asco que me producen los pedantes investigacionistas,
> que no investigadores. Tengamos la fiesta en paz, y ahoguemos en amor, en
> caridad, la pedagogía.[31]

> [Thus shall I conclude, before my humour is exhausted and I leave this polite
> tone aside to venture into another with which I can pour out my disgust for
> researching pedants, who do not deserve to be called researchers. Let us keep
> the peace, and drown pedagogy in love and charity.]

Leaving science, and scientific pretenders, aside, Unamuno invoked timeless spiritual principles: love, charity, peace. Whether these brought faith, disillusionment, or a tragic drowning of certainty, he closed by suggesting that these three were the only trinity on which a solid educational philosophy could be built. Creating an etymological pun on his birds into the verb 'aviarse', Unamuno suggested the continual depths to which meaning, duality, and understanding could be taken — as well as the personification, in the children-bird metaphor, to which his *pajaritas* could be subjected.

Through the lens of *Amor y pedagogía*, Unamuno's protestations against pedantic, methodological, and rationalist pedagogy testified to another ideal: universalism and plenitude of individual development, against a tide of technological and specialist modes that reduced the child to a mere product of pedagogy or nationalist modes of viewing the world through one fixed and given lens. In his vivid physical and literary creation and re-creation of the *cocottes*, Unamuno suggested that the task of the teacher and the interlocutor was to temper rationality with other modes of understanding, balancing the rationality of *pedagogía* with the irrationality of love in all its educational repercussions. From knowledge to experience arose a new source of understanding. Tragedy and its transcendence were the shared inheritance of humanity, as Unamuno's closing line of *Amor y pedagogía* suggests: upon Apolodoro's suicide, torn between competing philosophies and earthly love, simply, 'El amor había vencido' [Love had won].[32] The teacher's role was to bring students to see this 'dual version' of the world, to provide a 'gesture of universal solidarity with the human endeavour', as has been argued about the responsibility of higher education.[33] Unamuno's *cocottes*, those mystical, divine, marvellous, surprising animals, were not only a representative presence in his pedagogical work, but a reminder of the universal ties between the child's developing spirit and wider world.

Love and World: Xirau's Articulation of the Pedagogical Spirit

Two years after the re-publication of Unamuno's *Amor y pedagogía*, Xirau took up the problem of pedagogical love in philosophical form. In his 1936 essay 'Amor i pedagogia' and subsequent monograph *Amor y mundo* (1940), Xirau expounded upon a specific conception of love and pedagogy that went hand in hand.[34] Instead of considering whether these terms — and by extension, their positivist and metaphysical values — could co-exist, he argued that the concepts and actions themselves must be re-defined. Whereas love saw perfection in the other, pedagogy sought to reform and idealize. Pedagogy, a loving pedagogy, must be oriented not towards reform but an expansion of spirit. While Unamuno's text stands alone, it also benefits from being read in the context of contemporaneous philosophy of education. Paired with Xirau's work on pedagogical love, it represents a base for and response to growing currents of advocacy in a humanist philosophy of spirit.

As pedagogy in Spain and abroad became ever more specialized and empirical in its methods, educators, intellectuals, and poets spoke out with vigour to defend the child's inner life and experience. In 1933 Xirau had published an article entitled 'La pedagogía y la vida', summarizing the problem facing parents and teachers: 'Qué vamos a hacer del niño?' [What shall we do with the child?].[35] Questions of curricula and methodology were secondary, he argued, to essential considerations of human value. How should a child's spirit be oriented? How could educators go beyond science to encompass human life in its infinite totality? Suggesting that pedagogy was a subset of biology (if defined as the study of life), Xirau argued that *human* life was far more complex and contingent than biology allowed. To foster in children a realization of their own humanity must be the goal of education.[36] Yet this was no simple task. In order to 'formar hombres' [educate men] one needed to understand 'qué son los hombres' [what men are] — in other words, to agree upon 'la esencia y el fin' [the essence and the purpose] of human life. Like others before him, Xirau posed education as a problem that transcended the disciplinary bounds of biology, psychology, or the physical sciences. It was also one that could be addressed concretely in practice: Xirau and his wife Pilar Subías joined fellow intellectuals in sending their own children to schools they saw as attuned to new educational values, in this case enrolling young Ramón Xirau in a Montessori school.[37]

Through Xirau's subsequent writings on the role of spiritual love, one also gains a clearer picture of why a philosophy of *pedagogical* love occupied such a central place in Spain's pre-Civil War educational literature. Xirau noted that terms of love had long been used for the emotional bond between student and teacher. This linkage went back to Platonic dialogues: 'Desde entonces amor y pedagogía han ido siempre juntas' [Since then, love and pedagogy have always gone hand in hand].[38] Xirau's argument depended on a distinction between 'amor cristiano' and '*eros* platónico'.[39] Calling Xirau the 'philosopher of love', Manuel Durán suggests his approach was inspired by St Paul and St Augustine, revering the Christian love of *agape*, God's love for man and the reciprocal love it awakes: a 'supreme love' from above that fosters love in the beloved.[40] From Unamuno's *erostratismo* — the pedagogue's fruitless search for immortality through the pupil, production, the other — one moves towards Xirau's understanding of education not as an idealized and hierarchical *amor,* but as reverence for the totality of the spirit. In the tradition of *Liebesphilosophie,* Xirau drew from Goethe and Scheler, whose writings defended an '*ordo amoris*' which placed love at the centre of a divine order.[41]

The centenary of Goethe's death in 1932, in particular, had brought out a celebration of humanistic precedents in Spain. Both Ortega and Xirau, among others, dedicated significant works to Goethe that year, amidst a wave of celebration of new educational precedents.[42] Placing Xirau's thought in this wider intellectual context, Conrad Vilanou Torrano has shown how Xirau integrated various humanisms into his philosophy of education, from the Greek *paideia* to the Latin *humanitas,* medieval *studium* to Renaissance *sapientia* and neo-humanist *Bildung.* According to Vilanou, for Xirau education was a vital and spiritual imperative: 'una acción vivificadora, o, lo que es lo mismo, de espiritualización porque la vida — biológica y espiritual — constituye un todo unitario' [a vivifying action, or what is equivalent, of spiritualization because life — biological and spiritual — constitutes a unitary whole].[43] Xirau's notion of love made sense of a complex world, forging a 'cosmovisión, una filosofía holista' that philosophically echoed views of the body and its 'functional unity' put forward by contemporaries such as August Pi i Sunyer.[44] Such a 'cosmovision' was built upon a solid scientific base. Yet it depended upon human experience.

Xirau would use this sense of an 'amorous' encounter throughout his pedagogical writings, defining education as the recognition of human life as a course of evolution in which 'ésser home significa obrir amorosament l'esperit a totes les forces de la vida' [to be human is to open one's spirit in love to all forces of life].[45] In particular, Xirau's 1936 *L'amor i la percepció dels valors* posited love as the key to a philosophical hierarchy of values. Ranging from desire to sensation, Xirau's closing section, 'Amor i pedagogia', turned to education. Pedagogy, he suggested, was the heart of the philosophical problem of love. Only by addressing how one educates another could one understand what it means to love, and to live, in a world of value. Xirau opened this work with what he called a tired cliché, that education is the exercise of love between student and teacher, setting out to recover the term's 'vitalitat i la seva veritat', its vitality and veracity. Love was not, nor could it be, 'pedagogical', because the act of educating constituted the bestowal of a new reality: transforming something from what it was, to what it should be; introducing new qualities and eliminating defects. Education was an act of reform 'que aspira a millorar la realitat present mitjançant la seva conversió' [that aspires to improve the present reality by means of its conversion]. This 'discipline of reform' recalls Unamuno's two pedagogues, Entrambosmares and Carrascal, both seeking to shape the young Apolodoro into their respective images. To approach pedagogy as a purely reformist activity, however, transgressed Xirau's sense of unconditionality. Love esteemed an object as it was. To correct was to suspend, momentarily, that love. While education created change, respect must come first: 'Educar, és, més aviat, portar cada cosa a la seva pròpia plenitud, amb tot respecte i reverència' [To educate is rather to bring each thing towards its own plenitude, in total respect and reverence].[46] Through respect, one could approach the mutually enriching relationships that influenced, beyond knowledge or content, one's lifelong thinking and way of being in the world.

In sum, Xirau posed three possible approaches to pedagogy. The first was reform: changing the child's very nature. Such reformist action implied that the child's reality was imperfect and it simultaneously demanded that a 'perfecció ideal' be applied to each and every child. This approach was not an attitude of love, an emotion which must involve total respect. Xirau's second framework took the opposite approach. It shied away from imposing change on the child in the name of respecting individual autonomy. The educator met the child passively. He, or she, allowed the child to flourish according to natural laws, aiming to 'obrir les fonts de la vida espontània' [open the founts of spontaneous life]. Yet neither could this naturalistic approach constitute education. Education demanded discrimination. It required that the educator evaluate, judge, and select: to 'valorar, estimar els valors i les jerarquies' [appreciate and respect these values and hierarchies] with wisdom and discretion.[47] Finally, as a third approach, Xirau proposed a compromise between these two poles. Love and education were not only compatible, but inseparably bound. Love and pedagogy, he wrote, 'es completen, s'estimulen i es redueixen, en últim terme a unitat' [they complete each other, stimulate each other and can be reduced, ultimately, to unity]. The two terms upheld the holistic unity of the child's development.

Within this total framework, the role of the adult was not to disrupt but to enhance the fullness of the child's inner life. In this respect, Xirau argued that a certain Rousseauian laissez-faire was essential to allow independence of mind and spontaneity of spirit. Yet an entirely detached approach to guarding the child's natural development — as emulated by certain New Educational methods of free play and exploration — was insufficient. A pedagogy of 'deixar viure' [let them live], he concluded, was no pedagogy at all. Xirau's distinction between intervention and observation provided a bridge from a biological to a spiritual framework. Defining human life as that which aspired to more than itself, he suggested that education gave the child access to an unknowable, transcendent reality beyond the physical world:

> La vida humana no és una activitat que termini en ella mateixa. No és vida una vida que no consisteixi en res més que en anar vivent [...]. La vida de l'home és sempre un viure per alguna cosa que la reclama. No és una realitat purament immanent sinó que es transcendeix a ella mateixa i es consagra a les formes més diverses de l'objectivitat.[48]

> [Human life is not an activity fulfilled by itself. A life that does not go beyond simply living is not a life [...]. Human life is always a living for something that demands its attention. It is not a purely immanent reality but one which transcends itself and consecrates itself to the most diverse forms of objectivity.]

Thus, rather than a pedagogy of simply 'letting' the child develop, Xirau proposed one of 'fer viure' [make them live] — to intervene only such that children develop a rich sense of the life around them. He drew on Cossío's notion of 'vivificar', of enriching vital and spiritual life and providing the means for the child to live an 'authentic' life. But this was an authenticity predicated on all that was unreal, unknown, and unquantifiable about our existence: 'Es tracta, per tant, en tot moment, de produir quelcom que no existeix, de portar a plena actualitat virtualitats, de conduir la vida — cada vida — a plenitud' [It is a matter of producing, therefore, at all times, something that does not exist, bringing the virtual into concrete existence and guiding life — each life — towards plenitude].

Xirau's notion of plenitude encapsulates the notion of spiritual holism raised in this chapter. Plenitude through spiritual fulfilment relied on a love which respected the intactness of the self while distinguishing an inherent hierarchy of values. The teacher who sought to foster such plenitude understood the human spirit as contingent and variable, multifaceted and complex. Thus the task of the educator was to embrace the totality of this spirit, to recognize and nurture its vitality and layers of reality:

> Hi ha en ella múltiples plans de realitat i de valor que s'estructuren en una dimensió de profunditat. Posar-los en evidència, donar-los-hi vigència i vigor, treure-los a primer pla, ordenar-los en recta jerarquia, és justament l'obra de l'educació. L'activitat educadora no es proposa suplantar una realitat per una altra, ni suprimir ni anorrear res, sinó portar una realitat virtual a tota la seva plenitud d'ésser i de valor.[49]

> [In every spirit are multiple layers of reality and value structured in a dimension of depth. To evidence these, to give them force and vigour, to bring them into the light and order them properly, is the true work of education. Education is not an attempt to supplant one reality for another, nor to suppress or obviate anything, but to bring an imagined reality towards its own plenitude of being and value.]

It was on this point, for Xirau, that love and education coincided. There could be no love without education, for the presence of love drew new values into the world, qualities previously unnoticed and unsuspected. Nor could education (that is, 'educació', not 'pedagogia') happen without a spirit of love, for love developed higher values in the child:

> Educar no és sinó descobrir amb mirada delicada totes les aptituds i capacitats de l'educand i fer-les efectives [...]. Tal és la formació de la personalitat, l'educació del caràcter, el descobriment de les aptituds i de la vocació.[50]

> [To educate is to discover, with the most delicate glance, all the aptitudes and capacities of the educand and to turn these to action [...]. Such is the formation of the personality, the education of character, the discovery of aptitudes and callings.]

Character, personality, aptitude: all of these qualities composed the evolving plenitude of spirit that Xirau sought to promote. These were not merely theoretical: values and aspects of character and orientation were, too, what closely aligned psychologists and pedagogues sought to discover through investigative means, as demonstrated by Xirau's close collaborations with Mira and others at Barcelona's Institut Psicotècnic and Seminari de Pedagogia and by the influence of psychologists such as Claparède.[51] Yet Xirau took a qualitative, philosophical view of the use of these processes. Any such probes or interventions were worthless without a broad view of education that had a rich spiritual plenitude at its core.

For Xirau, the child possessed unmatched and perfect values, including ingenuity, spontaneity, joy, agility, and vitality, which must be treated with respect and dignity. Xirau's vision of pedagogical love was powerful and reciprocal. According to a strict philosophical 'hierarchy of values', love was a seeking-out of the superior, a movement from inferiority to superiority. In that sense, the 'current' of love would move upwards from child to teacher. The teacher's goal was to make children fall in love: with them, with knowledge, with the world. It was to 'enamorar, suscitar en el deixeble l'amor i l'atracció que promouen sempre les realitats superiors' [to seduce, to elicit in the disciple the love and attraction that higher realities always foster] and to foster through this enthusiasm an elevation towards increasingly higher values.[52] For precisely this reason, Xirau argued, a 'totalitarian' approach to education was impossible. All things, all people were in their essence deserving of love:

> L'amor no distingeix humils i poderosos, grans o petits. Busca en cada cosa, tots els valors que posseeix i pot posseir, descobreix gràcies i virtuts recòndites [...]. La mirada amorosa salva tot el que toca.[53]

> [Love does not distinguish between the humble and the powerful, the great or the small. It seeks in each thing all the values that it does and can possess, it discovers graces and hidden virtues [...]. The loving glance saves all that it touches.]

Xirau's elaboration of a philosophical *amor cristiano* would be more explicit by 1940, with the publication of his *Amor y mundo*.[54] This love was neither authoritarian nor patriarchal, for only in reciprocity, he wrote, could love be perfect. There was a dialectical quality to this love based upon the inherent value in each and every human spirit. The student also taught the teacher. In short, the dialectic of education was a dialectic of love.[55]

Such a dialectic was intuitive and irrational. Love preceded, superposed, and outweighed rational knowledge. It left quantities, values, and intellect aside. It was not a weighing of positive and negative values, but an 'integral' determination by the heart. In this vein, Xirau described pedagogical love as an embrace of plenitude in another: the 'intuïció immediata del seu valor total i incondicionat, estimació indivisible de la seva personalitat, amb tots el seus valors i tots els seus defectes' [direct intuition of the total and unconditional value of another, an indivisible esteem for their personality, in all its values and imperfections].[56] Xirau accorded spiritual value to each individual — and, most notably, to each child, from birth through all stages of development. Giving and receiving love through the educational act, this imagined child moves towards that vital wholeness embedded in his own inherent humanity. This love spreads and grows as it is given: 'Enamora el que es lliura gratuïtament *per gratia* i amb gràcia, el que pels camins de la vida vessa damunt del pròxim la font abundosa de la seva vida espiritual' [We fall in love with he who devotes himself to others *per gratia* and with grace; he who, along the paths of life, lets overflow upon his neighbours the abundant spring of his spiritual life].[57] In education as in life, Xirau was concerned with the spiritual wholeness of the self in its relation to others.

Such transcendent considerations, which echo through his pedagogical work during and following the Civil War, epitomize the impulses towards a spiritual, intellectual, and ethical wholeness within the rapidly professionalizing domains of paidology, pedagogy, and educational theory. While the educationalist Theodore J. Haarhoff asserted that the descent from humanism to holism was 'lineal and direct', the reverse seems also to have been true.[58] Concepts of holism directly underpinned concerted gestures of humanistic engagement within the pedagogical field. Building upon a base of critique and perspective established by works such as Unamuno's *Amor y pedagogía*, neo-humanist philosophers and pedagogues such as Xirau embraced the holistic principles and psychotechnic tools of the early twentieth century in order to transcend them, seeking an education that was both scientifically and spiritually sound. As others would do, he looked to articulate a thread of the human spirit which could be fostered only by love.

Making Education Whole: Roura i Parella on the Sciences of the Spirit

In 1934, Joan Roura, a student of Xirau in the ambit of the Seminari de Pedagogia in Barcelona, published an essay entitled 'Les tres pedagogies' [The Three Pedagogies]. Both in his early thinking and in subsequent writings and lectures, Roura sought to define a new, phenomenological ideal of education in line with a renewed humanist understanding of culture. Published in the same year as Unamuno's expanded *Amor y pedagogía* and a thread he would later expand in his monograph *Educación y ciencia* (1940), this early article provides a foundation for understanding the various educational approaches that figures such as Unamuno and Xirau saw as jostling for dominance, from religious to empirical to hermeneutic schools of thought. Considered together with Unamuno, Xirau, and the active practices pioneered by teachers melding open scientific approaches to knowledge, his work gives a conceptual frame to a shared integral, humanistic view of spirit.

Roura was well integrated in the mainstream of Spanish educational reform, having qualified at Madrid's Escuela de Estudios Superiores del Magisterio (1919–23) under the country's leading lights in pedagogy and New Education, including Domingo Barnés and Luis de Zulueta.[59] It was here that he, like many young teachers, began to integrate new scientific thought into a nascent philosophy of education. These considerations would culminate in his doctoral thesis of 1937, published as *Educación y ciencia* in Mexico after the Civil War.[60] Roura had recently studied in Berlin (1930–32), where he absorbed work from Heideggerian philosophy to holistic psychologies and educational theory. There he also briefly studied under German economist Werner Sombart, upon whose 1930 text *Die drei Nationalökonomien* [The Three National Economies] he modelled his essay.[61] Sombart argued that three models had shaped and regulated economic attitudes across history; Roura suggested that these three paths could be understood within any sector of culture, including human societies' foundational activity of raising and educating its young. These approaches were, in brief, a metaphysical attitude, a natural-scientific one, and a human-scientific approach. These three outlooks had led to three forms of economic development: first, a normative, ethical mode of judging, assessing, and evaluating; second, an analytical approach of positivist or quantitative explanations; and third, an interpretive and iterative outlook. These categories mingled and evolved across time and cultures, with all three aiming at the essential questions of knowledge: '(1) what ought to be, (2) what is, (3) why'.[62] Building upon these categories, Roura suggested applying Sombart's ideas to educational thought in order to understand the past, present, and future of the field. There were three *ur*-pedagogies, he argued, which mapped onto the schema outlined above: a normative one of morals and ideals (one might think of religious education): a pedagogy of positivist science (such as the *über*-rationalist models Unamuno parodied in *Amor y pedagogía*); and finally, a phenomenological, hermeneutic perspective on education (along the lines of the experimental, dialogical models Roura sought to develop for Spain).

Roura's interest in Dilthey and Spranger encapsulated this synthetic impulse, but he also drew on diverse scientific scholarship including that of August Pi i Sunyer, Ramon Turró, William James, Wolfgang Köhler, Jakob von Uexküll, and others to move from atomistic towards holistic modes of understanding development within a wider social context.[63] His portrayal of pedagogy built chiefly on Dilthey's model of the *Geisteswissenschaften,* namely the cultural, historical, spiritual dimensions of human understanding. The distinction Dilthey drew between differing methods in natural and social sciences proved a rich fount not only for Roura, but also for figures including Giner, Cossío, and Ortega.[64] This interest, as noted, sprang from his years in Berlin, where he studied education with Eduard Spranger, psychology and child development with Gestalt psychologists Köhler and Kurt Lewin, aesthetics with Max Dessoir, and philosophy with Nicolai Hartmann, Max Scheler, and Werner Jaeger.[65] The approach of the *Geisteswissenschaften* that he discovered there was precisely what he believed was lacking in Spain. In a letter home in 1932,

Roura wrote that pedagogy in Spain was still widely considered a 'second class' science because it had yet to embrace this new, 'rebellious' methodological approach to knowledge:

> En nuestro país los hombres de ciencia siguen considerando la medida, el número, como un símbolo mágico [...]. En España la introducción del número, de la medida, de la ley en su sentido físico-matemático en el campo de la Pedagogía con el intento de darle la categoría de ciencia, de 'primera clase', ha contribuido [...] a obscurecer la esencia del problema pedagógico.[66]

> [In our country men of science still consider the measure, the number, to be a magical symbol [...]. In Spain the number, measure, and law in the physical-mathematical sense have been introduced within pedagogy in order to give it the status of a 'first class' science, which has contributed [...] to obscuring the essence of the pedagogical problem.]

Pedagogy, Roura argued, must stand at the forefront of developing its own standards of clarity and precision, embracing its identity as a 'science of the spirit'. Pedagogy must draw from life itself, using its endless complexity as the raw material on which to build a new science, 'un todo estructurado y ordenado' [a structured and ordered whole].[67] Through a modulation of science, Roura sought to carve out a newly defined space for neo-humanist, experience-based practice. He first published on pedagogy as a 'ciencia del espíritu' in Barcelona during the Second Republic and was instrumental in bringing Eduard Spranger to lecture in Barcelona in October 1933, translating these lectures for the *Revista de Psicologia i Pedagogia*. Coinciding with Ortega's exegesis of Dilthey's philosophy in 1933–34, Roura lectured on Spranger's pedagogical philosophy at the Instituto Psicotécnico in Madrid, discussing the role of history, culture, ethics, and love within education, and at the Universidad Internacional de Santander, where he urged teachers to understand life within the wider 'unidad viva' of human culture.[68]

Roura's doctoral thesis built on this consolidating view of the individual as a spiritual microcosm of the whole. *Educación y ciencia* took as its central concern man's biological and spiritual dimensions. Yet in its focus upon education as the central task of society, it kept the real and the remembered child at its heart. After decades of bickering between disciplines, professionals had lost sight of the child under their gaze:

> Médicos, psicólogos y maestros han disecado el alma infantil en todas sus posesiones. Pero diríase que entre ese enorme caudal de conocimientos se nos esfuma la imagen del niño, considerado como un todo. Su contorno se nos pierde en el análisis de su vida psíquica.[69]

> [Doctors, psychologists, and teachers have dissected the child's soul into its many elements. But amidst this wealth of knowledge, the image of the child, seen as a whole, vanishes before our eyes. Its outline is lost in the analysis of its psychic life.]

This depiction of the child 'considerado como un todo' acknowledged medical, psychological, and social views of character and behaviour, yet suggested that analytical approaches were insufficient. Missing, above all, was the totality of the *alma* in its progressive, dynamic development. He drew from the rhetorical concept of the 'mundo del niño' as discussed by García Morente and Dewey while drawing attention back to the child's very soul.

Here, as in his subsequent *Spranger y las ciencias del espíritu* (1944) and *Conceptos fundamentales del pensamiento de Dilthey* (1946), Roura advocated for an education based upon transcendent, holistic notions of human experience.[70] The soul, the all-encompassing and evolving spirit, was inextricable from the individual shaped by the world from birth to death. This mutual connection between self and world was, on the most basic biological level, built upon layers and levels: primarily of internal and external 'ósmosis y endósmosis', through the 'dialectic' of metabolism, the very basis of human life itself. That breathing, growing being of *Bios* also existed within social and cultural worlds, including those of perception and reaction, Uexküll's *Merkwelt* and *Wirkwelt* — as well as, critically, a spiritual domain that moved beyond pure life towards choice, significance, and liberty.[71] Subject to natural laws yet not limited by them, this 'hombre' abided in a contingent world of interrelationships and subjective histories, in which the 'estructura espiritual' was determined by the very structures of one's surrounding world.[72] Through relationships, the self expanded through spiritual communion:

> Una afinidad electiva orienta al hombre a través del mundo espiritual. Todo lo que encuentra un eco en su alma se incorpora a su imagen del mundo. Cada individuo tiene su mundo particular de vivencias [...] hemos de aprender a ver en esta infinita variedad de formas, infinitas irradiaciones de la vida divina. Así nace el respeto y la reverencia a toda vida humana y un sentido integrador en la vida social.[73]

> [An elective affinity orients man across the spiritual world. Everything that finds an echo in his soul is incorporated into his image of the world. Every individual has his own world of experiences [...] we must learn to see in this infinity of forms the infinite irradiations of divine life. This is how respect and reverence for all human life and a sense of integration in social life are born.]

Drawing upon Goethe's 'elective affinities', a basis for the role of the *Geisteswissenschaften* in education, Roura looked to bring spiritual purpose to pedagogical action. Through recognition of the amplitude of divinity and communion in everyday life, society might begin to construct an education in alignment with the workings of the individual and his known world.

As Josep Cullell i Ramis has characterized Roura's view of personhood, Roura desired neither to *naturalize* nor to *spiritualize* man, but to find a dissonant coexistence of these dimensions: 'una física i l'altra [...] no física, que s'integren en aquella unitat' [one physical and the other [...] non-physical, integrated into that unity].[74] He described the relationship between body and spirit according to neither a Descartian philosophical nor a Christian religious tradition, but rather as simple reality within which the distinction between 'organic' and 'spiritual' life clarified what it meant to develop as a spiritual whole. As Roura outlined in *Educación y ciencia*, spiritual life developed in a way entirely distinct from organic life. An organism grows in predictable ways under the influence of its environment, according to preceding structures. Personal development, on the other hand, is dynamic and open: 'el espíritu ha de hacer de sí mismo, el que él es' [the spirit must make of itself, what it is], in an process driven by 'esfuerzo, afán, entusiasmo' [effort, eagerness, enthusiasm]. The human spirit followed no set course, rather needing to 'aprender a hablar, a escribir, a orientarse en el mundo' [to speak, to write, to orient himself in the world] with a certain liberty of realization.[75] One's freedom to will drew from the same source identified by phenomenologically-minded New Educationalist reformers. But the idea that the child should take an active role in learning went beyond child-centrism to encompass a wider view of the unfolding self and the self in the world. In Roura's phrasing, life sought plenitude through differentiation, from birth to death, becoming itself a vital unity:

> Vivir significa diferenciarse e integrarse sin cesar. La unidad amorfa, indiferenciada, se convierte en una unidad diferenciada, en una estructura en la que las partes tienen solo sentido a partir del todo. Diferenciación e integración del cuerpo, del alma y del espíritu que a su vez se integra en un todo: el hombre. El todo es uno y las partes son a su vez un todo.[76]

> [To live is to become ceaselessly distinguished and integrated. An amorphous, undifferentiated unity becomes a differentiated one, part of a structure in which the parts only make sense within the whole. Differentiation and integration of the body, the soul, and the spirit, which in turn become a whole: man. The whole is one and the parts are, in their turn, whole.]

The language of holism in this declaration is unmistakeable. The growth of any part of the self could not be isolated from a larger sense of internal dynamism which, as a whole, developed over time. As Roura argued, no criteria existed by which to evaluate such transformation. While physical changes could be measured scientifically, this was impossible for the human spirit: 'El curso de la vida, la historia individual, el tiempo interior, son inaccesibles a medidas exactas' [The course of life, individual history, interior time, cannot be captured in exact measures].[77]

However sweeping in scope, Roura's philosophical texts on education kept the child at the heart of human biological and spiritual development. He traced the child's engagement with the world from what he called an 'undifferentiated unity' of *ego* and environment: 'En la infancia el niño vive en el mundo y con el mundo. El niño se encuentra confundido con el medio ambiente' [The child lives in the world and with the world. The child cannot be distinguished from the environment].[78] Yet maturation demanded distinguishing the self from the world. Roura's view of infancy drew on child psychologists including William Stern, Karl Bühler, David Katz, and Jean Piaget, all of whom reinforced the idea that the child experiences time, space, and selfhood in way qualitatively different from the adult, lacking perceptual connections of space and time to anchor reality.[79] He expanded this argument beyond biology to ask whether children also possessed a spiritual difference which facilitated their early 'magical' thinking — and whether this thread could be followed across history and culture.[80] With children understood as initially incapable of distinguishing the limits of their selves from the world around them, child and world were bound by an 'unión vital'. Rather than a *yo*, the child had only an all-encompassing *nosotros*, the union of 'el hombre y el mundo'. Roura drew on Piaget's and Lucien Lévy-Bruhl's notions of 'participation' in the world by both the 'primitive' and the child, in which the 'mundo del niño' appeared to adults as a magical sphere of fantasy and will. Some objects took on an exaggerated character; others vanished. A table could become a castle, a piece of wood a doll. The child made no distinction between thoughts, dreams, and realities, believing that everything originated with or through the self. With the Gestalt psychologist Kurt Lewin, Roura emphasized temporal disjunction: the infant was 'presente y nada más que presente' [present and nothing more than present].[81] The past and future existed, but only for brief and shifting periods, and not as a primary guiding scaffold across an axis of time.

As Roura recounted, Spranger described human spiritual development as progressing through a 'coordinate system' of three reference points: first, changes in the tenor of one's own perception; second, changes in one's worldview; and third, the reciprocal relationship between self and world. Using these three criteria, he proposed to understand individual life qualitatively along the temporal axis of development. This was but one way to understand notions such as Bergson's 'creative evolution', which posed the individual as a constant and dynamic *becoming* in the world. Within a mass of space and time, the child began to select from his environment, Uexküll-like, objects of significance.[82] The world transformed from merely exterior to 'circundante', exerting a mutual and active influence:

> Para el niño que acaba de nacer el mundo exterior no es todavía mundo circundante. Vive en un mundo ausente de objetos. Mejor todavía: su cuerpo con sus necesidades es el único objeto. Pero este estado dura poco. Pronto empieza a orientarse en el mundo. El pecho de la madre, la botella de leche, el delantal rojo de la nodriza... El mundo exterior deviene mundo circundante. El hombre lo construirá durante toda su vida.[83]

> [For the newborn child the exterior world is not yet the surrounding world. He lives in a world without objects. Better yet: his body, with its own necessities, is the only object. But this state does not last long. Soon he begins to orient himself in the world. A mother's breast, a bottle of milk, the nanny's red apron... The exterior world becomes the surrounding world. Man will construct it his whole life long.]

As adolescence approached, however, the infantile communion of *nosotros* was understood to rupture into a violent 'cesura' between self and world.[84] In Roura's telling, adolescence broke the 'unidad de la vida infantil' [unity of childhood], making way for chaos, disruption, and anarchy. New appetites and desires struggled with the residual structures of childhood, as the developing person turned from inner to outer life. Duelling forces of fantasy and love were seen as driving these changes in the developing self. Fantasy bound the child to all he had left behind, while *eros* began to drive him towards the self he would become.[85]

Adolescence functioned as a test of all that pedagogy sought to do: to accompany the developing child towards an unknown future self. Guided by a developing *Weltanschauung* and competing social, erotic, and emotional bonds, Roura contended that the adolescent's vision of the world was shaped by a mediation of self and surroundings. His *alma* was irrevocably shaped by its commerce with the world in ways distinct from mere biological and physical influence: 'Los contenidos espirituales le imprimen su propia ley' [Spiritual elements impose their own law].[86] Just as the adolescent assimilated the surrounding culture, he was assimilated by it, becoming an integral piece of a wider cultural whole. The adolescent began to articulate himself in social life, 'no sin dolor, no sin lucha' [not without pain, or struggle], as in Unamuno's account of Apolodoro's maturation. Society at once represented a limitation of one's own expanding, solidifying individuality, as an equilibrium was continually sought. The mature, 'spiritual' self arose from this gradual shift away from *ego* and towards the world. The purpose of education was to facilitate an integration of the various structures which made up the child's world, whether psychological, phenomenological, or spiritual.[87]

Roura's use of Gestalt psychology as a model was an explicit reminder of the humanist core at the heart of educational science. Just as various constituent quantities, orders, and significations formed a Gestalt, so too did man have constituent spiritual, psychical, and biological parts that made up his personal whole: 'En una estructura de gran complicación se vincula una vida y en esta vida se vincula, a su vez, un espíritu' [A life is bound within a complex structure, and in this life is bound, in turn, a spirit]. Building on various dialectics — man and world, inheritance and environment, spontaneity and receptivity — Roura positioned the developing self as an integration of opposing forces, building towards spiritual plenitude as in the harmony of 'música polifónica'.[88] His vision of education exalted the individual's progressive development:

> La escuela de la vida, la escuela activa, la genuina escuela nueva no rompe esa estructura horizontal de la vida, sino que [...] interpola contenidos de orden superior, contenidos espirituales y morales que son los que dan al hombre toda su dignidad y toda su grandeza.[89]

> [The school of life, the active school, the genuine new school does not break this horizontal structure of life, but rather [...] interpolates ever greater elements, spiritual and moral contents that grant man all his dignity and grandeur.]

The goal of this 'científico-espiritual' view of education was to develop the self in all possible fullness. Only through such efforts, he wrote, could a true education be achieved: 'Finalmente se puede considerar al hombre como *unitas multiplex*, como un todo y ver las relaciones de unas partes con otras y con el todo' [At last man might be considered as *unitas multiplex*, as a whole, seeing the relationships between each of the parts and with the whole].[90]

Thus, from the part to the whole, and from the self to the world, Roura used holistic principles to defend a notion of ineffable human spirit within biological and pedagogical modernity. Because he sought a view of education that drew from both the individual and collective human spirit, he saw an ideal pedagogy that lay beyond political divisions; an education that would seek relationality, globality, and universality, even if these values themselves had a clear political, ideological charge. Written during the Civil War and published in its immediate aftermath, Roura's advocacy of educational and scientific modernity was not limited to insular debates about scientific and pedagogical method. Rather, it gestured towards the ideals of an education that fostered a mutual relationship between developing self and world, a humanism defined by relationality. These terms integrated the child's inner experience into a wider dialogue on what it meant to be human — to be spiritually whole, reflective, and intact — even amidst the cataclysm of world war and exile. Together with Unamuno's caution against dogmatic applications of pedagogical method and Xirau's celebration of the power of an elevating love through education, Roura's work sought to lift the spirit towards a deeper sense of the expanding self in contact with the world.

Gathering Light: Childhood Reverie in Jorge Guillén's *Cántico*

> Hondo, el caudal. Dentro del hombre latía su infancia.
> [Deep, the source. Within the man beat his childhood.]
> Jorge Guillén, 'Prólogo' (1975)

All declarations on the nature and development of the human 'spirit' through education depended upon one common foundation: childhood. Present and past, continuity and rupture, life's beginning and its end: in describing the 'caudal' of childhood within the poetry of his friend Federico García Lorca, as in the epigraph above, or of one's own 'fondo del niño' [innermost child], the poet Jorge Guillén proposed an enduring spirit that inflected upon each life across its unfolding.[91] From Unamuno's 'love' to drown out pedagogy to Xirau's philosophical elaboration of a truly loving and reciprocal education, through Roura's gaze upon the person growing in all complexity, struggle, integration, and ultimate plenitude, new humanist educational thought was guided by a notion of abiding spirit that was shaped by encounters with the world. That radical contact was at the heart of Guillén's poetry. Through his extensive writings on childhood — both as memory and Bachelard's 'added light' of consciousness — I read a literary and spiritual 'humanization' of the child through a critical communion between self and world.[92]

   Widening reformist education from theory to (literary) practice, Guillén's *Cántico* [Canticle] celebrated childhood in the light of a humanist vindication of the total, gathering plenitude of experience. First published as a volume of seventy-five poems in 1928, *Cántico* matured organically through its three editions (1936, 1945, and 1950) to include more than three hundred poems by the time of its completion. Within this cycle were the very beginnings of life as well as each moment in its lived fullness. Philosopher Eugenio Frutos has called Guillén's poetic attitude one of 'jubilant existentialism', a term which applies seamlessly to his portrayal of the developing child.[93] A major voice of twentieth-century Hispanic literature, Guillén was an exponent of *poesía pura* and the oldest of a constellation of poet-friends of the Generation of 1927. Like those of peers, his depictions of childhood resonated with circulating poetic and paidological representations of childhood being and perception. Despite his reputation for challenging verse, with works spare and purified in their grace and exaltation of the everyday, Guillén's poems were contemporaneously anthologized by educators and used both to teach and to depict an essence of childhood.[94] Through such poems, a representation of childhood interiority developed alongside Guillén's personal engagement with poets, teachers, and pedagogues seeking to understand the 'world of the child'.[95]

Across *Cántico*'s evolution, Guillén put childhood at the centre of a tightly unified poetics of life. A sheer listing of titles suggests this quiet presence. Poems such as 'Niño', 'Nene', 'Hija pequeña', 'Un niño y la noche en el campo', 'El niño dice', 'Niño con atención', 'Niñez', 'Feliz insensato', 'Niñez antigua', or 'El infante' turn the adult gaze upon the child. Else Dehennin's 1977 analysis of *Cántico*'s semantic fields noted that *niño* is the most frequently used 'living, human' term in the first, 1928 work, but more commonly cited has been her finding that 'light', *luz*, prevails over 'air' as *Cántico*'s most frequent term overall.[96] Yet Guillén's portrayal of childhood, privileging perception, plenitude, time and instantaneity, light, breath, and contact, is inseparable from that view of human experience. Critics including Joaquín Casalduero, Ricardo Gullón, and Antonio Herrería are among those to have taken up Guillén's poems of childhood within their analyses of *Cántico*, though largely divorced from a wider temporal context of evolving representations of childhood as theme, aesthetic, and preoccupation.[97]

Guillén's *oeuvre* embodies a reverential attitude towards childhood inseparable from his larger poetic representation of life as a state of pure being. In his prologue to Lorca's 1975 complete works, Guillén drew attention to his late friend's affinity with children, noting that childhood was the 'primordial' aspect of Lorca's work — not as a theme, but as an attitude. What Guillén identified in Lorca's poetry as an 'hondura de infancia' [profundity of childhood], a 'fondo del niño' [innermost child], could equally be said to abide in Guillén's own poetry, from birth to presence to death.[98] Guillén's most famous lines on childhood are found in *Cántico*'s 'Los jardines' (1928):

> Tiempo en profundidad está en jardines.
> Mira cómo se posa. Ya se ahonda.
> Ya es tuyo su interior. ¡Qué transparencia
> De muchas tardes, para siempre juntas!
> Sí, tu niñez, ya fábula de fuentes.[99]

[Time in profundity is found in gardens. | See how it alights. Now it goes deeper. | Now its interior is yours. What transparency | Of many afternoons, forever together! | Yes, your childhood, now a fable of fountains.]

Many afternoons blur into one: childhood, a fable of fountains, a green blur of scent, sound, and image. Famously picked up by Lorca as the epigraph for his poem 'Tu infancia en Menton', this image of the 'fábula de fuentes' suggests the compressed temporality and sensorial perception Guillén finds in both the real, living child and the enduring 'niño en nosotros' (child in us), as Ortega called the inner vestige of childhood: maturation was not a suppression of childhood, but its integration.[100] As Guillén would write of Lorca's poetry, childhood beat within, persisting 'como pasado vivo' [as a living past] into the future.[101] It is precisely such an interiority across time, in the beholding of each moment, that characterizes Guillén's poetic vision of childhood's enduring presence. He first published 'Los jardines' in a suite including 'Cuna, rosas, balcón' in *Meseta* in 1928; Lorca would publish his verse as 'Ribera de 1910' in Concha Méndez's and Manuel Altolaguirre's *Héroe* in 1932.[102] Lorca's uptake of Guillén's lines reinforced the enduring quality of this perceived interior child through upheaval and chaos. Manuel Durán has noted that time here becomes as 'trabajado y humanizado' [cultivated and humanized] as a garden, accessible only through a Proustian recovery of the past — but does not delve into the phenomenological experience instilled by this deep childhood.[103]

Guillén dated *Cántico*'s origins to 1919 in Trégastel, Brittany. It was there that the poet met Germaine Cahen (1897–1947), whom he married in 1921 while working as a *lector* in Spanish at the Sorbonne (1917–23).[104] Their first child, Teresa, was born that year; son Claudio would follow in 1924. It was also during his time in Paris that Guillén began writing a series of playful fragments on childhood themes which he called 'airecillos' 'florinatas', 'ventoleras', and 'frivolidades' for Spanish readers while he corresponded from Paris for papers such as *España* and *La Pluma*.[105] Guillén and Cahen's growing family thus coincided with the birth of this work, as well as his first published writings on childhood. Guillén's sketch 'Dios se lamenta de que no puede viajar', for instance, takes a view of infancy as infinite possibility: he imagines God's melancholy as the 'eterno espectador de todos los horizontes', never able to discover new places, sights, and landscapes. The poet has God envying what he calls the naive 'feliz turista', that is, the infant first opening his eyes upon a new and foreign world: '¡Ser de veras nuevo, novel, novato en jornada de viaje! [...] ¡Imposible para Mí volver a nacer como el feliz turista! ¡Ah! ¡Quién dejara algunos ratos de ser Dios para no ser más que criatura imperfecta, vinculada a su paisaje' [To be truly new, novel, novitiate in this journey of life! [...] Impossible for me to be born again as the happy tourist! Ah! Who would not cease to be God for a few minutes to be nothing more than an imperfect creature, at one with its landscape].[106] Echoing the *n* of 'nuevo', 'novel', 'novato', 'noble', and 'nacido', Guillén's phrasing implicitly reminded the reader of critical missing *n*'s: *niño, niñez, natal*. In such a framing, to be a 'criatura imperfecta' becomes the most mundanely exalted state one can attain. Who would not envy the 'feliz turista', at the start of his or her own 'caminos reveladores' [revelatory paths] through the world?

The development of a soul before language, the pre-eminence of the moment, and the physical presence of the body in space were crucial aspects of the total aesthetic established here. These are visible throughout his work, from *Cántico*'s first edition of 1928, as meditations on its phenomenological qualities. Observing a boy, perhaps his son Claudio, splashing in the sea in 'Niño', Guillén describes the scene in revelatory terms:

> Claridad de corriente,
> Círculos de la rosa,
> Enigmas de la nieve:
> Aurora y playa en conchas.

Máquina turbulenta,
Alegrías de luna
Con vigor de paciencia:
Sal de la onda bruta.

Instante sin historia,
Tercamente colmado
De mitos entre cosas:
Mar solo con sus pájaros.

Si rica tanta gracia,
Tan solo gracia, siempre
Total en la mirada:
Mar, unidad presente.

Poeta de los juegos
Puros sin intervalos,
Divino, sin ingenio:
¡El mar, el mar intacto![107]

[Clarity of current, | The circles of the rose, | Enigmas of snow: | Dawn and
beach in a shell. | Turbulent machine, | The moon's joys | With patient vigour |
Salt of the brute wave. | Instant without history, | Tenacious culmination | Of
myths between things: | The sea alone with its birds. | Abundant in grace, |
Simple grace, always | Total in the glancing. | Sea, present unity. | Poet of
pure games | Without interval, | Divine, guileless: | The sea, the total sea!]

The child is evoked by only two words: the 'niño' of the title, and the 'poeta' of
its conclusion. Yet an entire state of childhood being is suspended between these
words. A poem celebrating the grace of a child on the beach is held together by
terms of roundness, instantaneity, and flow. From 'círculos de la rosa' to 'conchas',
the balance of natural shapes seems to echo the swirls of the ear, just as children
hold shells up and listen for the waves within. From the rhythmic 'alegrías de la
luna' to the corresponding regular 'onda' of the water below, a regular rhythm
resounds. The crepuscular and penumbral states of the 'aurora' and 'playa' are
brought together by the cyclical movement they contain.

    This state of youthful grace is 'total', 'sin intervalos', 'intacto' — in sum, one of
pure 'unidad'. Like Manuel García Morente's 'mundo del niño' of the same year,
the child-world was characterized by fluid passages of time in which, for the child,
'ser es ser presente' [being is being present].[108] Morente's *ser* for the child is thus
estar, akin to Guillén's declaration in 'Más allá' of being physically and mentally
present in the world: 'soy, más, estoy. Respiro. Lo profundo es el aire' [I am,
and more, I am here. I breathe. Deep is the air].[109] Both immediate and abstract,
the child is presented beyond time and space. He has a fluid existence: he plays,
alone with the sea and the birds above, games that are 'pure' and continual with a
grace that is 'total'. Each of these images accords with contemporaneous views of
childhood as a state wholly other than that of the adult. In perfect balance, as García
portrayed this infantile mentality, the 'sucesivos mundos' of experience are lived
in a steady stream of immediacy.[110]

Such an exceptional phenomenological representation of early childhood can be read most extensively in one major poem, 'El infante', which addresses the pre-verbal experience of infancy across some seven pages of verse. Describing a newborn, Guillén evokes first the child's pre-verbal existence: 'sin noción, sin vocablo va el sentido | Sintiéndose en un ser que existe y dura' [notionless, wordless sensation | Feeling himself as a being that exists and endures'. The child simply *is*, is being itself: 'Es el infante. No, no necesita | Vocablos, los vocablos de después' [He is the infant. No, he does not need | Words, the words that come later]. The infant exists in a pre-verbal world, resting in glowing repose, wordless on a bed of cambric and silk, in a beatified state of 'ignorante bienestar' [ignorant wellbeing].[111] This early, fleeting stage embodies a womb-like equilibrium in which words are superfluous:

> Se confía el infante. Ya está dentro,
> Profundamente dentro de un amparo
> Que se le impone y le trasforma en centro
> De inmensidad cerrada por un aro.
>
> Centro de cumbre: cuna. Mimbre, seda
> Guardan con precisión al desvalido
> — Que no lo fue jamás. El mundo rueda
> Suavizándole aún color y ruido.[112]

[The child trusts. He is deeply, | Profoundly under a protection | Which imposes and centres him | Encircled within immensity. | Centre of apex: cradle. Wicker, silk | Carefully guard the invalid | — Who never was such again. The world turns | Softening for him all colour and sound.]

The child is subject from birth to a transcendent power beyond the individual grasp. The world is 'imposed' on every individual life, which looks outward in turn. 'Centro de cumbre: cuna', Guillén writes. Each individual stands at the central axis of a total perspective on that world. Like the 'zenith' formed by sun, rose, and horizon in his poem 'Perfección', the child is the point that centres this tableau. The infant lies as naturally as the rose of that verse:

> Reposa,
> Central sin querer, la rosa,
> A un sol en cénit sujeta.[113]

[It rests, | Unwittingly centred, the rose, | Subject to a sun in zenith.]

The child is swaddled and rocked in its cradle as the world turns in its orbit, both at the world's centre and in perfect equilibrium with its movements.

The resting child embodies the integral perspective around which Guillén's larger view of the burgeoning human spirit resounds. Without language, the infant dreams within an 'ínsula sonora' [resonant island]; Guillén defamiliarizes the infant as a 'novedad de criatura' [novelty of a creature], an internally complete node within the 'realidad [...] extraña' [strange reality] of the material world. Yet as an early critic noted, in Guillén's 'islote', of childhood, his 'Kinderland', the supreme message was an 'exaltation of being'.[114] His emphasis on the reality of objects and their physical presence integrated childhood sensation into an overall poetics on engagement:

'El infante no dice más que vida, | [...] Que nada es tan real como la rosa' [The infant says nothing but life | [...] For nothing is as real as the rose].[115] Before words, the child first begins to engage with the surrounding world of material objects and atmosphere. An 'equilibrio' gives way to 'inquietud, manoteo' [restlessness, waving] of arms, legs in movement:

> Mundo, más mundo quiere con lo esbelto
> De sus pestañas, sombra a veces seria,
> Con lo rollizo de su puño vuelto
> Ya a una presión que pide una materia.
>
> ¡Materia capital! No la discierne
> La mano. ¿Superficie? No es sencilla.
> Universo confuso apunta en cierne
> Tal atracción que todo se le humilla.
>
> Sin poder, sin saber, pero no a ciegas,
> La criatura se dirige a eso:
> El enigma inmediato.[116]

[World, more world, these delicate eyelashes, | This sometimes serious shadow, demand; | And a chubby fist transformed into | Pressure seeking its material. | Supreme material! The hand does not | Discern it. Surface? Not so simple. | A diffuse universe presents, incipient, | The attraction before which all is subject. | Powerlessly, unknowingly, but not blindly, | The creature directs itself towards this: | The immediate enigma.]

In these lines, the material surfaces of the world are primary. The sensation of grasping and being grasped, the texture of foreign objects that greet these eager hands; such phenomena dominate and possess physical weight. Whether a taut fist or an entire world, the child seeks to draw all inward. The mouth is as avid as the hands: in animal 'grace', the body imposes its will for pleasure and satisfaction, as the mouth seeks the breast, milk, fingers, toys:

> La boca aguda
> Quiere satisfacer sus avideces.
> Todo contacto en goce se trasmuda.[117]

[The avid mouth | Will satisfy its hunger. | All contact is transformed into pleasure.]

In 'El infante', Guillén brings out that inner soul possessed by the nascent child through a communion of parent and child. He immerses the reader in the experience of beholding the infant in beauty and grace, while moving towards a recognition of opposing forces, namely the inevitable end of each individual life: birth and death, body and spirit. Even as the child's cry moves in tandem with the world, its 'harmony' co-exists with a larger chaos: 'Persiste en armonía con el coro | Solar ese desorden — sin pecado' [This disorder persists in harmony | With the solar chorus — sinless].[118] The child, from the earliest days, is in a state of continual instantaneity while irrevocably impelled towards an end. Guillén writes simply, beholding the infant:

Equilibrio tan justo excluye el Mal.
Es mucha la alegría entre las manos.

¿Frágil será el primor? Este volumen
Grosezuelo de brazos y rodillas,
Este decoro de la sien presumen
La gran corriente desde sus orillas,

Una oleada que meciendo impera,
General y fatal, arrulladora,
Con una pulsación que es una espera
Sin cesar anhelante de otra aurora.[119]

[Such perfect equilibrium excludes evil. | The happiness between our hands is great. | Fragile, this delicate thing? This imposing | Volume of arms and knees, | This holy ornament holds back | A great current from its banks, | A rocking wave that prevails | Generally, fatally, lullingly, | With a ceaseless pulsation that is the | Yearning expectation of another dawn.]

The final wave that rushes over each and every human will impose itself upon this infant life, an end to which all Guillén's protagonists are subject: 'el muro cano | va a imponerme su ley' [the white wall | will impose upon me its law], as he wrote in 'Muerte a lo lejos' [Death at a Distance].[120] Universal, fatal, this hint of darkness — or light — proves a counterweight to the revelatory promise of 'El infante'. The surety of an end ushers the child into the 'aurora' of a new age.[121]

Moving from the cradle to the child, Guillén's 'Hija pequeña' demonstrates how physical growth echoes the world's burgeoning in fullness and plenitude. The cry is creation, a form of auditory poetry that accompanies physical development in that world: 'La Creación a dar su poesía empieza. | ¡Tú creces!' [Creation begins to yield its poetry. | You grow!].[122] This 'tú', the child, is identified with natural shifts. The dawn, the dew, each apparition is as steady and imperceptible as the incremental growth of the infant. The transition between states is immaterial. It is the present moment, of contact and engagement, that matters. Guillén's emphasis upon contact and reciprocity develops in 'Feliz insensato' [Happy Fool], which opens with dialogue reminiscent of hide-and-seek or peek-a-boo, before moving into a larger vision of rejoicing. This cosmic world — objects, earth, and history as a whole — draws from a childhood root:

— ¿Dónde está, dónde estará?
— ¡Aquí está!
No deja de jugar el feliz insensato.
Como suma armonía
La Creación acoge este arrebato
Pueril. ¡Nadar, volar por la vacía
Primavera de un aire sin morada!
Y ascendiendo a su cumbre de alegría
Se arroja al sol más cándido la niñez confiada.[123]

[— Where is he, where could he be? | — Here he is! | The happy fool keeps playing. | As supreme harmony | Creation receives this childish joy. | To swim, to fly through the empty | Spring of a dwellingless air! | And ascending to the peak of joy | A trusting childhood is flung towards the most candid sun.]

A state of play holds infancy in suspended motion. Like the cinematographs of the early twentieth century, blurring frame by frame, the child achieves perfect wholeness, 'suma armonía', via flux and change.[124] In each jump, leap, or dive, the child's body melds with the environment. The force of childhood gathers and, 'ascending to its peak of joy', is impelled towards the sun. Like a young Icarus felled by his boundless spirit, each life for Guillén becomes a creation myth of its own. The progressively moving body becomes the unfolding history of the world:

> Ya todo es elemento
> De alguna encrucijada
> Donde el mundo no cesa
> De referir su historia como un cuento.[125]

[Now everything is a part | Of some crossroads | Where the world never stops | Telling its history as a tale.]

As the poet moves from the child's story to a larger 'cosmovision' and back, he focuses on the objects that fill that universe and give concreteness to one's surroundings. A simple table is given history and life through a child's imagination:

> Una mesa — no más, aquella mesa —
> Hoy descubre su fondo:
> Un secreto de gruta,
> Un islote redondo.
> ¡Niñez! Y todo, libre, se trasmuta.
> Basta la diminuta
> Persona.[126]

[A table — nothing more, that very table — | Discovers its root today: | A grotto's secret, | A round island. | Childhood! And everything, free, is changed. | This small person is | Enough.]

Objects come from the same elemental forces that give rise to all of life itself, including the body of the child: atoms, air, and elements forming trees, table, and body at once and continually, from the past into the future. On an imaginative level, they are transformed by the imagination of the growing child. That same table that adults view as a 'no más, aquella mesa' becomes a magical cave, an island on which to hide. Children wish to learn and grasp, know and explore the objects around them, 'conocer, escalar aquel sillón, | Tenderse en la tierna ladera' [to know, to climb that armchair | To lie down upon the soft hillside].[127] Through play they access a 'reality' not yet intellectualized:

> ¡Jugar, jugar en medio
> De esa masa de asedio
> Que en implacables círculos rodea
> De espesura al nacido:
> Nacido a realidad que aún no es idea,
> Y ya con él palpita![128]

> [To play, play amidst | This encroaching mass | That surrounds the newborn | In implacable, widening circles: | Born to a reality not yet idea | That palpitates with him!]

The world resounds, spins, and circles around the self. Indeed, the playful structure of this poem itself distinguishes 'Feliz insensato' from Guillen's other childhood poems. A poem imagining the unique delight of youth is structured in a deliberately recursive form, cycling back through the same lines as it began:

> La creación acoge este arrebato
> De fe como armonía
> Suma. ¡Juegue el feliz más insensato!
>
> — ¿Dónde está, dónde estará?
> — ¡Aquí está!¹²⁹

> [Creation receives this rapture | Of faith as supreme | Harmony. May he play, happy, reckless one! | — Where is he, where could he be? | — Here he is!]

The poem's circular structure moves one from infancy towards old age, with a return to childhood in this latter stage. The two voices that echo in the first and last lines seem those of a child and parent or grandparent seeking and finding each other time and again. Generations become a continually repeated quotation, two heartbeats in a cycle:

> Siempre doble el latido,
> Continúa la cita
> Prodigiosa: la luz y esa niñez.¹³⁰

> [A beat always doubled, | It carries on the prodigious | Quotation: light and that childhood.]

In this latter line resides that which makes childhood so central to the themes embraced in Guillén's work. First, there is the presence of *niñez* itself, in its prodigious growth towards fullness and maturity. Second, there is the sense of profusion that overflows these tightly controlled lines: more, more, more life, more air, more light: 'más, más, más, arrebata' [more, more, more, enrapture] as he proclaims to the coming dawn in 'Hija pequeña'.¹³¹

Childhood and light: in the spiritual communion between two individuals and two generations, these two nouns are drawn together as equally powerful. The entwinement of concepts of birth and light is well-established, both as a linguistically embedded relationship ('dar a luz', to give birth) and a view of constant birth and renewal through light that is developed across Guillén's poetry: 'the object responds, is there, becomes visible' through the presence of light.¹³² Yet here it is childhood that stands in the light. One is reminded of the afternoon sun of Guillén's eponymous poem, 'Luz natal' [Native Light], the final poem he wrote for *Cántico* in 1949, in his first, brief return to a Spain under Franco.¹³³ Looking upon his birth city of Valladolid from a height, the poet considers the traces — gouges — of history visible in the landscape, while recalling the same light on these hills of his childhood. It is not the shadows but the remembered light, that 'native light' which fills the narrator with wonder for the horizons his life has encompassed and may yet traverse, and which thus binds childhood to a vision of enduring luminosity. In Guillén's *oeuvre*, opening one's eyes, remembering, and seeing are all acts of active recovery and encounter. They are conscious returns to that deep interior garden, where the radiant 'transparencia | De muchas tardes' [transparency | Of many afternoons] is drawn together into a memory present, sudden and whole.

Why did Guillén return to the images of childhood he first began working through in his earliest writings as *Cántico* drew to a close? Each successive revision of the cycle, from 1928 until 1950, brought forward a more intimate, deeply developed view of infancy and childhood as both attitude *and* theme.[134] Juxtaposed with verses dedicated to his children and grandchildren, one could read these poems simply as the poet's coming to terms with mortality. Yet they signal a closer connection to ideas of development itself, indeed an embrace of all forms of awakening, perceiving, and acting to which spiritual growth is bound. Elaine Scarry has argued that all beauty involves a 'forward momentum', an attempt to replicate it, whether in song, in painting, in verse, or in the body of the infant.[135] There is an unmistakable element of praise in Guillén's invocation of the blue eyes, gentle curls, and graceful movements of his subjects. But in the intimate creation of a universalized state of childhood, there is another way in which beauty strikes. According to Scarry, it appears as both sacred and unprecedented. In such a reverent encounter with an other, beauty evokes both the 'newness' and 'newbornness' of the entire world. To stand in the presence of such beauty is an act of 'radical de-centring', in which one remains a fully embodied subject but experiences pleasure through proximity. Such beauty does not transform or change one. Rather, one stands in awe before it, willingly 'in the service of bringing new beauty into the world'.[136]

This is the sense in which Guillén acts as spectator of 'newbornness': the adult is an observer, decentred, renewing the present through new perceptions. Guillén noted, in a series of interviews published in 1979, that *Cántico* contained a number of poems related to children, including 'El infante'. He likened these poems to another kind of 'daily birth', that is, awakening each morning to see the world anew, suggesting this was the reason for *Cántico*'s abundance of dawns.[137] Such is the awakening of his poem 'Los nombres' [The Names], in which the 'Albor' [Daybreak] of the first line, opening its eyelashes to see the day, and the 'horizonte final' of the last stanza as the eyelashes close, hold an entire life's vision between them.[138] It is the dawn of the opening rose and the newborn baby in his 'Cuna, rosas, balcón' [Cradle, Roses, Balcony]: '¿Rosas? Pero el alba. | ...y el recién nacido!' [Roses? But the dawn. | ...and the newborn!], with all three 'dawns' given unmistakable physical form: 'Creaciones, masa | desnudez' [Creations, mass | nudity].[139] Such a 'primordial connection' between light, dawn, and birth was critically linked to the sense of 'contact' from which all 'vital actions' arise. Ultimately it was not merely visual, sonorous, or tactile contact that mattered, Guillén suggested, but the interior stirring of action and thought of one's primary engagement with the world.[140]

Guillén's representation of childhood in body and memory is distinguished by a sense of unity, plenitude, and clarity. The delicate care with which he traced the eyelashes, fingers, ears of the child — as finely drawn in spirals, curves, and circles as the roses or shells of his earliest verse — drew upon a parallel, contemporaneous humanistic view of childhood itself. Thus, when he wrote with wonder of the sleeping infant or the playing child he did so with a sense of transcendent beholding, conveying the ways in which a remembered childhood informed the subsequent days, thoughts, and actions of one's life. But it was not solely the impulse to recall one's own past that carried these poems forward, even as the enduring light of childhood cast its shadow towards an end. Rather, it was their instantaneous sense of awakening, beholding, and being that tied these poems to a larger vision of unfolding human spirit. In Guillén's work, this current dated from his first writings in Paris and ran through educators' adoption of his poems in 1930s Spain, toward his own poetic reckoning with childhood and life's end. In the reception, recording, and praise of childhood, Guillén transformed the earliest physical and mental awakenings into an enduring human experience of contact with the world.

Whether in the luminescent childhood reveries of Guillén, the adolescent struggles towards wholeness in Roura's view of human growth through education, or in the reciprocal love of education theorized by Xirau and enacted in literary and paper form by Unamuno, a neo-humanist vein of thought defended the awakening of a transcendent and abiding human spirit through childhood. Through memory, through philosophy, and through the poetic image, each of these observations of childhood anticipated Bachelard's 'added light' of consciousness in the very act of recalling, shaping, and educating another in mutual integrity. Within a rapidly modernizing and professionalizing educational field, such celebratory depictions acted as reminders of the human values for which pedagogical and psychotechnic methods must stand. Science provided critical guiding methods, that, as Roura suggested, must be harnessed and attuned to human endeavour. But ultimately it was the individual's continual engagement with the world that shaped their evolving growth and spiritual plenitude. Through contact and communion, through values of love and reverence, and through the vibrant poetic images of early perception, the human spirit was to be shaped and illuminated by the childhood at its core.

Notes to Chapter 6

1. Gaston Bachelard, *The Poetics of Reverie: Childhood, Language, and the Cosmos*, trans. by Daniel Russell (Boston: Beacon Press, 1971), pp. 4–6. A comparative study of these works' portrayals of childhood remains to be done; on the rich theoretical underpinnings of autobiography as poetic and symbolic project, see Richard N. Coe, *When the Grass was Taller: Autobiography and the Experience of Childhood* (New Haven: Yale University Press, 1984).

2. Adolfo Maillo wrote of culture, in this specifically the development of language and literacy, as expanding not solely the child's mind, but also a larger spiritual essence in 'El valor pedagógico de la poesía lírica', *Revista de Pedagogía*, 12.139 (1933), 294–300 (p. 295).

3. This usage mirrored the German, in which *Geist* was alternately posed as mind — a mental or intellectual capacity — and a wider conception of ineffable spirit. On the former, see, for example, Julián Sanz del Río, 'Psicología del niño: el espíritu en el niño', *Boletín de la Institución Libre de Enseñanza*, 16.363 (1892), 81–83. On the latter, see among many other paidological and psychological texts, for example, Domingo Barnés Salinas, *La salud del espíritu del niño* (Madrid: Ediciones Nuestra Raza, [1934]). Barnés surveyed the entire world of child development, in an attempt to understand sensation, language, emotion, art, free will and morality, and physical education as one larger, inseparable process.

4. Popkewitz, *Cosmopolitanism and the Age of School Reform*, p. 75.

5. Xirau i Palau, *Manuel B. Cossío y la educación en España*, pp. 17, 102.

6. Both took advantage of JAE funding for short stays at Geneva's Institut Jean-Jacques Rousseau; see Soler i Mata, 'The Rousseau Institute of Geneva's Influence on and Presence in Catalan Pedagogy in the First Third of the 20th Century', pp. 72–73. They worked also in the line of Catalan biologist and philosopher Ramon Turró i Darder (1854–1926), head of the Barcelona Laboratory of Medical Sciences, whose research on physiology and, in particular, the workings of hunger in 1912, posed a challenge to the physical/mental distinction. He suggested that perception of the external world is modulated primarily by physiological needs, an idea that would also have given credence to Decroly's idea of centres of interest, the physical needs that structure a child's learning. See Ramon Turró, *La base trófica de la inteligencia: conferencias dadas en la Residencia de Estudiantes los días 12 y 14 de noviembre de 1917* (Madrid, 1918).

7. Such reciprocity was well recognized. A 1934 editor's note in the *Revista de Pedagogía* suggested that to study philosophy, one went to Madrid, to study pedagogy, one must go to Barcelona; see Anon., 'Notas del mes: El estudio universitario de la Pedagogía', *Revista de Pedagogía*, 13.147 (1934), 135–36 (p. 136). There, the curriculum largely followed the example of Madrid's Escuela de Estudios Superiores de Magisterio with innovations instituted by Mira and Xirau; see Conrad Vilanou Torrano, 'Juan Roura-Parella (1897–1983) y los orígenes de la pedagogía universitaria en Cataluña', in *Pedagogía y educación ante el siglo XXI*, ed. by Julio Ruiz Berrio (Madrid: Departamento de Teoría e Historia de la Educación, 2005), pp. 171–202 (p. 181). Its journal, the Catalan-language *Revista de Psicologia i Pedagogia* (1933–36), covered topics ranging from psychology as a 'ciència de l'esperit' (1934) to studies of moral conduct, family environment, character, and intelligence, all of which pointed at a holistic view of influence and development. See, for example, Roura's translation of Eduard Spranger, 'Idees fonamentals de la psicologia com a ciència de l'esperit', *Revista de Psicologia y Pedagogia*, 2 (1934), 125–38, 239–56.

8. Xirau i Palau, *Manuel B. Cossío y la educación en España*, p. 14–18.

9. Teodoro Causí, 'El espiritualismo en la educación', *Revista de Pedagogía*, 8.87 (1929), 100–09.

10. José Ortega y Gasset, 'Vitalidad, alma, espíritu', in *Obras completas*, VI, 586.

11. Such ideas drew not only from Ortega's concepts of *circunstancia* but also a romantic *paisaje* of education: 'el paisaje educa mejor que el más hábil pedagogo' [the landscape educates better than the most able pedagogue]. Ortega wrote in 1906, as cited in María Teresa Caro Valverde and María González García, 'Valor educativo de la pedagogía romántica de la naturaleza en los escritos estéticos de Ortega y Gasset', *Cartaphilus*, 6 (2009), 33–34 (p. 33).

12. Jose Ortega y Gasset, 'Pedagogía de secreciones internas. I: Para Gregorio Marañón', *El Sol*, 26 March 1920, p. 5.

13. See Robert C. Spires, *Transparent Simulacra: Spanish Fiction, 1902–1926* (Columbia: University of Missouri Press, 1988), p. 158. For an early, focused reading of the work, see Manuel García Blanco, '*Amor y pedagogía*, nivola unamuniana', *La Torre*, 11 (1961), 443–78.

14. Miguel de Unamuno, 'Al hombre entero y verdadero', *Ahora*, 1 January 1936, p. 5.

15. Benito Galdós's work *Amor y ciencia: comedia en cuatro actos* (Perlado, Páez y Compañía, 1905) provides a fitting contrast. In *Signs of Science*, Pratt considers this play beside Unamuno's *Amor y pedagogía* (pp. 139–42).

16. Anon., 'Pajaritas de Unamuno', *Residencia*, 3.6 (1932), 176; Anon., 'Unamuno, residente', *Residencia*, 3.6 (1932), 177–78; Manuel Martín Agacir, 'Las pajaritas de papel de Unamuno', *Estampa*, 3 December 1932, pp. 15–16.

17. On Unamuno's 'poetics of youth' see Harkema, *Spanish Modernism and the Poetics of Youth*, pp. 38–90. More broadly, the text has been examined by, for example: Manuel Cifo González, 'Amor y pedagogía o el problema de la educación visto por Miguel de Unamuno', in *Miguel de Unamuno: estudios sobre su obra*, ed. by Ana Chaguaceda Toledano, 4 vols (Salamanca: Universidad de Salamanca, 2005), II, 329–47; and Gordon Minter, '*Amor y pedagogía*: An Object Lesson in Biography', in *Spain's 1898 Crisis: Regenerationism, Modernism, Postcolonialism*, ed. by Joseph Harrison and Alan Hoyle (Manchester: Manchester University Press, 2000), pp. 81–90.

18. Rafael Rubio Latorre, *Educación y educador en el pensamiento de Unamuno* (Salamanca: Ediciones Instituto Pontificio San Pío X, 1974), pp. 30–31; on Unamuno's educational thought see also Yvonne Turin's foundational work, *Miguel de Unamuno, universitaire* (Paris: S.E.V.P.E.N., 1962).

19. Unamuno, *En torno al casticismo*, p. 51.

20. Miguel de Unamuno, 'De la enseñanza superior en España', *Revista Nueva*, 1.18 (1899), 830–37 (pp. 832–33).

21. Thomas R. Franz, 'The Philosophical Bases of Fulgencio Entrambosmares in Unamuno's *Amor y pedagogía*', *Hispania*, 60.3 (1977), 443–51 (p. 448). Unamuno was by no means the only Spanish intellectual to rail against blinkered specialization, with Ortega notably warning against the dangers of semi-educated, technical ignorance in *La rebelión de las masas*.

22. Franz, 'The Philosophical Bases of Fulgencio Entrambosmares in Unamuno's *Amor y pedagogía*', p. 449.

23. Harkema, *Spanish Modernism and the Poetics of Youth*, pp. 57–58.

24. Miguel de Unamuno, *Amor y pedagogía* (Madrid: Espasa-Calpe, 1992), p. 183.

25. With its arcane and circuitous classifications of children's talent through discussions of Pythagoras, Archimedes, anarchism, numbers, form, and divinity, the 'Apuntes' seems directly to respond to the work of polymath Arturo Soria y Mata, founder of the Ciudad Lineal and author of the intriguing post-Darwinian analysis of the origin, unity, hierarchies, and even 'sexualities' of shapes; see his *Origen poliédrico de las especies: unidad, origen, reproducción y síntesis de las formas* (Madrid: Sucesores de Rivadeneyra, S.A., 1894), as well as his early venture into psychometrics *El talentómetro*. Unamuno's satirical take is also underpinned by the work of Gustav Theodor Fechner (1801–87), author of the pseudonymous *Vergleichende Anatomie der Engel* (1825) which set out to determine the precise anatomy of angels. Fechner concluded that every creature imagines the world after its own shape, just as Unamuno argued about the world of the *cocotte*.

26. Edda Reinhardt, 'Unamuno als Bildhauer (Unamuno, escultor)', *La Gaceta Literaria*, 4.78 (1930), 12. The topic clearly made an impression: García Blanco would revisit it in an extensive article three decades later in 'Amor y pedagogía, nivola unamuniana'.

27. Ibid.

28. Ibid.

29. Unamuno, *Amor y pedagogía*, p. 200.

30. Ibid., pp. 202–03. See also Adrian G. Montoro, 'La cruz y la greca en Unamuno', *MLN*, 95 (1980), 453–59.

31. Unamuno, *Amor y pedagogía*, p. 203.

32. Ibid., p. 158.

33. John Wyatt, *Commitment to Higher Education* (Bristol: Open University Press, 1990), p. 109.

34. On this relationship, see José Ignacio Sánchez Carazo's exposition of Xirau's 'conciencia amorosa' in the context of Xirau's entire philosophical *oeuvre*: 'Joaquim Xirau: una filosofía de ultimidades' (unpublished doctoral thesis, Universidad Complutense de Madrid, 1996), pp. 343–437.

35. Xirau i Palau, 'La pedagogía y la vida', p. 5.

36. Xirau might more precisely have spoken in such a scientific context of 'paidology', the study of the child, though use of disciplinary terms and their implications was fluid.

37. González-Agápito and others, *Tradició i renovació pedagògica*, p. 472. On Ramón's education (he became an eminent writer after the family's exile to Mexico), see, for example, Anon., 'Entrevista con Ramón Xirau, escritor y académico', *La Jornada*, 12 April 2004, <http://www.jornada.unam.mx/2004/04/12/02an1cul.php?printver=1&fly=> [accessed 1 December 2018].

38. Joaquim Xirau i Palau, *Amor y mundo* (Mexico: El Colegio de México, 1940), p. 221.

39. Conrad Vilanou Torrano, 'La formación, entre el amor y la plenitud: de J. W. Goethe a Joaquín Xirau', in *Ideales de formación en la historia de la educación*, ed. by Javier Vergara Ciordia, Fermín Sánchez Barea, and Beatriz Comella Gutiérrez (Madrid: Editorial Dykinson, 2011), pp. 399–436 (p. 399).

40. Manuel Durán and William Kluback, *Reason in Exile: Essays on Catalan Philosophers* (New York: Peter Lang, 1994), p. 22.

41. Vilanou Torrano, 'La formación, entre el amor y la plenitud', p. 429.

42. See, for example, Joaquim Xirau i Palau, 'La concepción del mundo de Goethe', *Revista de Pedagogía*, 11.124 (1932), 157–63, and José Ortega y Gasset, *Goethe desde dentro* (Madrid: Revista de Occidente, 1932). Goethe had long been celebrated as a model in Krausist-oriented Spanish

pedagogy, described in the *Boletín de la Institución Libre de Enseñanza* in 1922 as fostering a vision of the world as a 'totalidad orgánica', sensed in the creative life of nature, life, and birth and confirmed by the ordered structure of the world, as Goethe's educational ideal was described in Wilhelm Keiper, 'El ideal educativo de Goethe', *Boletín de la Institución Libre de Enseñanza*, 46 (1922), 97–104 (p. 99). Goethe's memoirs were edited and translated for children in Spain in 1924 (*La infancia de Goethe, contada por él mismo*, trans. by R. M. Tenreiro (Madrid: Editorial Reus, 1924)), following Ramón y Cajal's, in Editorial Reus's series of childhood memoirs.

43. Vilanou Torrano, 'La formación, entre el amor y la plenitud', p. 429. On Xirau's phenomenological views of education, see his 'Direcciones filosóficos: El idealismo', *Revista de Pedagogía*, 6.65 (1927), 209–15, 'Direcciones filosóficos: El realismo', *Revista de Pedagogía*, 6.71 (1927), 523–28, 'Filosofía y educación', *Revista de Pedagogía*, 9.106 (1930), 433–37, and 'La pedagogía y la vida'.

44. Vilanou Torrano, 'La formación, entre el amor y la plenitud', p. 402.

45. Joaquim Xirau i Palau, 'Idees fonamentals d'una Pedagogia', in *Obras completas*, 4 vols (Madrid: Anthropos, 1999), II, 443–55 (p. 454).

46. Joaquim Xirau i Palau, *L'amor i la percepció dels valors* (Tarragona: Tipografia Sugrañes, 1936), pp. 66, 67.

47. Ibid., pp. 67–68.

48. Ibid., p. 68.

49. Ibid., p. 69

50. Ibid.

51. By Claparède, I refer also to the broader New Education movement fostered under the auspices of the Institut Jean-Jacques Rousseau, so influential to the dozens of Spanish pedagogues who studied within its ambit in Geneva. See an early translation of Claparède's work that followed a summer course in Barcelona in 1920: Édouard Claparède, 'Rousseau y la significación de la infancia', *Revista de Pedagogía*, 1.1 (1922), 121–31. Claparède also cooperated with local psychologists to host the 1921 International Congress of Psychotechnics in Barcelona; see Institut d'Estudis Catalans, *Pedagogia, política i transformació social (1900–1917)* (Barcelona: Societat d'Història de l'Educació dels Països de Llengua Catalana, 2008), pp. 239–40.

52. Xirau i Palau, *L'amor i la percepció dels valors*, p. 69.

53. Ibid., p. 70.

54. This *amor cristiano* was to be the very presence of God. Comparing the Greek *eros* (bringing to mind Unamuno's cubist *cocotte* world) and *amor cristiano*, Vilanou Torrano sees two opposed worldviews, the Greek with its rationalism and 'geometric' logic, and a Christian 'cosmovisión' with orders of love and spiritual abundance; Joaquim Xirau i Palau, 'Volumen del tiempo (Las dimensiones del tiempo)', in *Obras completas*, I, 365.

55. Xirau i Palau, *L'amor i la percepció dels valors*, p. 71.

56. Ibid.

57. Ibid., p. 72.

58. Haarhoff, 'The Holistic Attitude', p. 103.

59. Molero Pintado and Pozo Andrés, *Escuela de Estudios Superiores del Magisterio (1909–1932)*, p. 133.

60. Roura i Parella, *Educación y ciencia*.

61. Werner Sombart, *Die drei Nationalökonomien: Geschichte und System der Lehre von der Wirtschaft* (Munich: Duncker & Humblot, 1930). Joan Roura i Parella, 'Les tres pedagogies', *Revista de Psicologia i Pedagogia*, 2.6 (1934), 164–89. Roura studied economics under Sombart during his two formative years in Berlin (1930–32), along with leading thinkers in aesthetics, Gestalt psychology and child development. On Roura's accompanying of Antonio Machado into exile, subsequent time in Mexico, and ultimate American academic career at Wesleyan University, see Conrad Vilanou Torrano, 'Joan Roura-Parella and his Presence in the United States', *Journal of Catalan Intellectual History*, 1.2 (2011), 131–47. Vilanou describes the neo-humanist view on education he developed, shaped by German *Bildung*, aesthetic philosophy of form, and even American Quaker thought, as one of process, giving form to the self across the span of life (p. 131).

62. Robert E. Park, 'Review: *Die drei Nationalökonomien*. By Werner Sombart', *American Journal of Sociology*, 36.6 (1931), 1071–77 (p. 1071).

63. Roura worked extensively on explicating and translating Spranger's books, including Eduard

Spranger, *Las ciencias del espíritu y la escuela*. trans. and ed. by Joan Roura i Parella (Buenos Aires: Losada, 1942). His 1935 course at the Universidad International de Santander focused on the philosophy of Dilthey and Spranger; see Joan Roura i Parella, 'La educación viva', *Revista de Pedagogía*, 14.157 (1935), 9.

64. Xirau noted both that Giner dedicated meticulous notes to Dilthey in his writings and that Cossío gave a course on Dilthey in 1914, but it was Ortega who turned this longstanding interest into a public sensation; see Xirau i Palau, *Manuel B. Cossío y la educación en España*, p. 102.

65. See Conrad Vilanou Torrano, 'La Pedagogía, ciencia de segunda clase. (En torno a un informe remitido por Juan Roura-Parella desde Berlín en Febrero de 1932)', *Historia de la Educación*, 24 (2005), 463–84 (p. 466). On Jaeger's work linking new educational and humanistic thought, see Christoph Horn, 'Werner Jaeger's *Paideia* and his "Third Humanism"', *Educational Philosophy and Theory*, 50.6–7 (2018), 682–91.

66. Vilanou Torrano, 'La Pedagogía, ciencia de segunda clase', p. 481.

67. Ibid., p. 482.

68. Anon., 'Don Juan Roura en el Instituto Psicotécnico', *El Sol*, 15 March 1933, p. 3; Roura i Parella, 'La educación viva'.

69. Roura i Parella, *Educación y ciencia*, pp. 54–55.

70. Joan Roura i Parella, *Spranger y las ciencias del espíritu* (Mexico: Minerva, 1944); *Conceptos fundamentales del pensamiento de Dilthey* (Havana: Universidad de La Habana, 1946).

71. Roura i Parella, *Educación y ciencia*, p. 9.

72. Joan Roura i Parella, *La pedagogía de Eduardo Spranger* (Buenos Aires: Editorial Losada, 1942), p. 11.

73. Roura i Parella, *Educación y ciencia*, p. 18.

74. Josep Cullell i Ramis, 'Joan Roura Parella: des de la totalitat', *Enrahonar: Quaderns de Filosofia*, 10 (1984), 78–84 (p. 80).

75. Roura i Parella, *Educación y ciencia*, p. 53.

76. Ibid., pp. 53–54.

77. Ibid., p. 54.

78. Ibid., p. 57.

79. Such an investigation is undertaken in Stern's *Psychologie der frühen Kindheit* (1923), on infantile perception of space and time.

80. Roura built on the work of German psychologist Charlotte Bühler, who considered the role of fantasy in the child's developing psyche. See Charlotte Bühler, *Das Märchen und die Phantasie des Kindes* (Leipzig: Barth, 1929), and, engaging in Spanish discussion of play and the school, 'Del juego al trabajo', *Revista de Pedagogía*, 11.125 (1932), 193–200. Bühler spoke at the Residencia de Estudiantes in 1932, allegedly contributing a 'palpitante nota científica en el ambiente médicopsiquiátrico' [resounding scientific note in the medical-psychiatric environment], on the difficulty of performing intelligence tests on young children. In order to obtain results that were not only qualitative but also quantitative, she designed new sets of tests tailored to the child's development; see Anon., 'La Profesora Bühler en Madrid', *El Sol*, 27 April 1932, p. 8.

81. Roura i Parella, *Educación y ciencia*, p. 55. See also Lewin's inclusion in Mira's 1935 manual of child psychology, in which he laid out his notion of field theory, applied to the child: the psychological forces in one's environment that shape development. See Kurt Lewin, 'Fuerzas del ambiente', in *Manual de psicología del niño*, ed. by Carl Murchison and Emilio Mira y López (Barcelona: Francisco Seix, 1935), pp. 735–77.

82. Roura i Parella, *Educación y ciencia*, pp. 54–55.

83. Ibid, pp. 60–61.

84. Gregorio Marañón, in particular, was concerned with the 'life-curve' of the individual; see Richards, 'Spanish Psychiatry c. 1900–1945', p. 833. Marañón's writings drew from Spranger's work on adolescence, arguing for clearer and more realistic teachings on youthful sexuality; see, for instance, *Amor, conveniencia y eugenesia* (Madrid: Historia Nueva, 1929), p. 104.

85. Roura i Parella, *Educación y ciencia*, pp. 58–60.

86. Ibid., p. 60.

87. Ibid., p. 137.

88. Ibid.

89. Ibid., p. 130.

90. Ibid., p. 119.

91. Jorge Guillén, 'Prólogo: Federico en persona', in Federico García Lorca, *Obras completas* (Madrid: Aguilar, 1969), pp. xvii–lxxix (p. xx). I draw out Guillén's early pedagogical writings and connections to Spain's educational avant-garde in greater depth and detail in Anna Kathryn Kendrick, 'Native Light: Jorge Guillén's Phenomenology of Childhood, 1923–1950', *Modern Language Review*, 113.3 (2018), 518–45.

92. Bachelard, *The Poetics of Reverie*, p. 5.

93. Eugenio Frutos, 'El existencialismo jubiloso de Jorge Guillén', *Cuadernos Hispanoamericanos*, 18 (1950), 411–26.

94. Guillén's poetry was also contemporaneously incorporated into classrooms through imaginative and rhetorical exercises. School director and teacher Ángel Llorca of Madrid's Grupo Escolar Cervantes used poems to help young pupils visualize and draw even before they could read. He also had older students copy out and illustrate writings by figures such as Alberti, Gabriel Miró, Gabriela Mistral, Santiago Ramón y Cajal and others, as a child named Juan Mira's illustration of Guillén's poem 'El ruiseñor' demonstrates. See Madrid, Fundación Ángel Llorca, Fondo Documental, 'Trabajos de los niños: copias de poemas', Bloque 5.B, Apartado 5.7, [early 1930s].

95. See García Morente, 'El mundo del niño'.

96. Alongside such metaphysical examinations of light, air, and space, the figure of the child in Guillén's work has gone almost entirely unexamined. See Elsa Dehennin, 'Continuidad y evolución en la obra poética de Jorge Guillén: los campos semánticos en "Cántico" y "Clamor" [1977]', in *Actas del Quinto Congreso de la Asociación Internacional de Hispanistas: celebrado en Bordeaux del 2 al 8 de septiembre de 1974*, ed. by François López Maxime Chevalier, Joseph Pérez, and Noël Salomon (Bordeaux: Instituto de Estudios Ibéricos e Iberoamericanos, Université de Bordeaux III, 2016), pp. 319–34 (pp. 322, 331). Her 'luz' finding is cited in Jorge Guillén, *Guillén on Guillén: The Poetry and the Poet*, trans. by Reginald Gibbons and Anthony L. Geist (Princeton: Princeton University Press, 1979), p. 18. See also Elisabeth Matthews, *The Structured World of Jorge Guillén: A Study of 'Cántico' and 'Clamor'* (Liverpool: Cairns, 1985), which analyses the order and harmony of twelve of Guillén's major poems, though 'El infante' is not included.

97. Casalduero suggests that precise biographical information (such as which child, in which crib, on which day) is irrelevant to Guillén's larger poetic project; this book reads these poems as literature, while also seeing them as inseparable from the social context of their genesis. See Joaquín Casalduero, *'Cántico' de Jorge Guillén y 'Aire nuestro'* (Madrid: Gredos, 1974), p. 185; Ricardo Gullón, 'El cuarto *Cántico* de Jorge Guillén', *Ínsula: Revista Bibliográfica de Ciencias y Letras*, 6.66 (1951), 3, 6; and Antonio Herrería, *'Cántico' en 'Orígenes': niñez en el Creacionismo* (n.d.), <http://www.auroraboreal.net/literatura/ensayo/1693-cantico-en-origenes-ninez-en-el-creacionismo#_ftn16> [accessed 1 November 2018].

98. Guillén, 'Prólogo', pp. xx.

99. Guillén, *Cántico* (1950), p. 315.

100. Ortega y Gasset, 'Un poeta indo (II)'. Drawing on Ortega's early phenomenological writings, I explore representations of infants' visual perception in Anna Kathryn Kendrick, 'Structuring the Mind: Domingo Barnés, Gestalt Perception and the Science of the Child, 1917–1933', *Bulletin of Spanish Studies*, 94.5 (2017), 795–820.

101. Guillén, 'Prólogo', p. xxi.

102. Jorge Guillén, 'Varios poemas', *Meseta*, 1.5 (1928), 1; [Federico García Lorca], 'Ribera de 1910', *Héroe*, 1.4 (1932), n.p. This enduring, internal childhood echoes sentiments voiced by Concha Méndez herself, whose poem 'No sé dónde' describes the search for self through a lost childhood ('Hoy aquí. ¿Y mañana? | No sé dónde mañana' [Here today. And tomorrow? I don't know where]), a search for her *alma* from streets to stars, returning ever to the green centre of childhood, 'al olvido primero | del jardín de mi infancia' [to the first forgetting | of my childhood garden]: 'No sé dónde', *Héroe*, 1.3 (1932), n.p.

103. Manuel Durán, 'Espacio y tiempo en dos poemas de *Cántico*', *Nueva Revista de Filología Hispánica*, 36.1 (1988), 455–65 (p. 462).

104. Biruté Ciplijauskaité, *De signos y significaciones. 1: Juegos con la vanguardia: poetas del 27* (Barcelona: Anthropos, 1999), p. 131.

105. For related imagery of childhood, of balloons flying from children's hands and of cities as sites of 'pureza infantil', imagined as a 'Ciudad de niños, ciudad límpida de niños nuevecitos', see Guillén, 'Cinco florinatas' and 'Sólo para pájaros', *España*, 9.365 (1923), 10.

106. Guillén, 'Cinco florinatas', p. 9.

107. Ibid., p. 27.

108. García Morente, 'El mundo del niño', p. 123.

109. Guillén, *Cántico* (1950), p. 18.

110. García Morente, 'El mundo del niño', p. 231.

111. Guillén, *Cántico* (1950), pp. 374, 381.

112. Ibid., p. 375.

113. Ibid., p. 240.

114. Georg Rudolf Lind, *Jorge Gulléns* Cántico*: Eine Motivstudie* (Frankfurt am Main: Vittorio Klostermann, 1955), p. 54.

115. Guillén, *Cántico* (1950), p. 381.

116. Ibid., pp. 377–78.

117. Ibid., p. 378.

118. Ibid.

119. Ibid., p. 379.

120. Ibid., p. 281.

121. Ibid., p. 379.

122. Ibid., p. 248.

123. Ibid., p. 114.

124. On the evolution of film as a pedagogical innovation, see Alicia Alted Vigil, 'El cine educativo en España (hasta 1936)', *Historia Social*, 76 (2013), 91–106, as well as, for example, Ángel Llorca, *Cinematógrafo educativo* (Madrid: [Sucesores de Hernando], 1917); Alexis Sluys, 'La cinematografía escolar', *Revista de Pedagogía*, 1.11 (1922), 401–10; and Miguel Gómez Cano, *El cinematógrafo y las escuelas ambulantes de puericultura* (Madrid: Escuela Nacional de Puericultura, 1927).

125. Guillén, *Cántico* (1950), p. 114.

126. Ibid.

127. Ibid., p. 115.

128. Ibid., p. 116.

129. Ibid.

130. Ibid.

131. Ibid., p. 248.

132. Joaquín González Muela, 'The Poetry of Jorge Guillén', *Bulletin of the John Rylands Library*, 69.2 (1987), 528–48 (p. 531).

133. Robert Havard, *Jorge Guillén: Cántico* (London: Grant & Cutler, 1986), p. 105; Guillén, *Cántico* (1950), pp. 338–50.

134. Guillén, 'Prólogo', p. xxii.

135. Elaine Scarry, *On Beauty and Being Just* (Princeton: Princeton University Press, 1999), p. 46.

136. Ibid., pp. 22, 117.

137. Guillén, *Guillén on Guillén*, p. 23.

138. Guillén, *Cántico* (1950), p. 26.

139. Ibid., p. 68.

140. Guillén, *Guillén on Guillén*, p. 23.

EPILOGUE

Childhood and the
Humanistic Promise of Holism

Lo permanente es el ser humano en todo el esplendor de su realidad como criatura abierta a la trascendencia. Lo cambiante son sus circunstancias; y todos los Humanismos que se han dado a lo largo de la Historia las han tenido en cuenta.

[What endures is the human being, in all the splendour of its reality as a creature open to transcendence. Only the circumstances change, something recognized by all the many Humanisms that have arisen over the course of History.]

Carmen Cárceles Laborde, *Humanismo en España: 1450–1650* (1993)

During the first decades of the twentieth century, a vanguard of Spanish educationalists worked towards the articulation of a humanistic ideal of education centred around the enigmatic figure of the child. As Carmen Cárceles Laborde has suggested of early modern Spain, every age defines the world through its own humanisms.[1] This book has argued that, through literature, art, philosophy, and science, a secular ideal of early twentieth-century Spanish humanism expressed itself through a fascination with the child in development. Translated into Spanish and published in the *Revista de Pedagogía* in 1934, an essay by the German reform pedagogue Peter Petersen (1884–1952) suggested that education was meant to bring out those most 'human' qualities in the child. Coinciding temporally with the publication of several works examined in this book, including Conde's *Júbilos*, Unamuno's re-issued *Amor y pedagogía*, and children's anthologies such as *Poesía infantil recitable*, the essay frames the varieties and qualities of human development sought through modern education. Whether goodness, loyalty, love, humility, compassion, sorrow, devotion, or respect, Petersen suggested, education fostered new qualities in the individual and thereby facilitated the 'revelation' of the self. For this reason, education was 'al mismo tiempo humanización, esto es, la compenetración y perfección espirituales de la forma humana' [simultaneously humanization, that is, the spiritual harmonization and perfection of the human form] — as defined by new and evolving humanisms over time.[2] Like Conde's and Borges's children vividly drawn in verse and image, 'preñadas de humanidad' [imbued with humanity] in the words of Mistral, the ideal of education was to foster in children the range and richness of human existence and experience.

The Phenomenological Project of Childhood

Beyond reformist efforts to understand and imagine the integral, 'whole' child of the future lay critical and unanswerable questions about the present. Teachers, artists, and intellectuals made the case for a new science of childhood built around dynamism and vitality, in accord with contemporaneous impulses in science, literature, art, and culture. Through their contributions, they successively defined and redefined the purposes and uses of education within nation and world. In seeking an objective understanding of children's experience, children's actions were presented as expressions of a totalizing — if still largely incommensurable — world of phenomenological experience. That these debates occupied a central place within broader sociological, political, and scientific discussions in Spain in the early twentieth century was crucial. This movement encompassed and embraced many separate phenomena which all, notably, sought terms of unity for the child's development. Throughout the 1920s and 1930s, a range of tendencies came together through pedagogical reform: educationalists' studied interest in Gestalt and holistic psychologies; the adoption of globalist reading methods through diverse methods in the classroom; valorizations of early language, imagination, and creativity; biological theories of functional unity and perception; notions of the world as a cognitively distinct whole for each being; explorations of child's play, sensorial engagement, and active learning; the rise of intelligence tests and an interest in children's art as a parallel form of probe or access to the mind; and fundamental reconsiderations of a larger notion of education as a vehicle for spiritual development. Shared throughout these engagements was a fascination with the enigma of the child and a larger investment in the questions of what it meant to be, and become most fully and consciously, human over the course of one's lifespan.

Educators articulated a spiritual, creative vitality that would grow from what Ortega termed the 'estratos profundos de vida psíquica' [deep layers of psychical life], in his pervasive writings on pedagogy so influential to a wide constellation of pedagogues in the 1920s.[3] Questions of the mind gestured at the temporal co-existence of past, present, and future in every individual. This psychical inheritance was what Unamuno portrayed as an individual's simultaneous 'preexistencia', 'per-existencia o sobre-existencia', respective temporal and spatial levels of abiding being. Present experience, Unamuno suggested, was co-existent with deep, pre-conscious memories of the 'ultra-cuna' [beyond the crib], the maternal, pre-natal 'cradle-world' that accompanied the child and adult throughout his life.[4] Whether understood as consciousness or soul, the human spirit was portrayed as born of the *ultra-cuna,* evolving through education and interpersonal interactions over time. Such a temporal dimension echoed through both psychological and philosophical depictions of childhood. As influenced by Dewey, the child's life — the 'mundo del niño' — was 'an integral, a total one', in which distinct experiences were knitted together with neither transition nor interval. The child's world was 'fluid and fluent', constantly expanding and contracting, its parts having 'no conscious isolation' or distinction.[5] From such psycho-pedagogical depictions of mental unity to subsequent poetic and artistic representations of childhood as pure being, human experience was posed as radically whole. Within this nexus, existence itself was total and contingent. It depended on a world shaped by the life of each individual, but it went beyond self-enclosure and ego-centrism.

Above all, a reciprocal notion of *vivencia*, or lived experience, was central both to the philosophical foundations and pedagogical manifestations of New Education. Knowledge was only as valid as the lived experiences that confirmed and constructed it. As individuals developed, their *vivencias* accumulated and acted upon their entire being. Over time, experience made for more than the quantitative sum of education and environment. These recollections became an emergent force inseparable from the whole person, as when Ortega suggested that maturity was not the 'suppression', but rather the 'integration' of childhood. These traces of early life remained and inflected upon one's existence and perception of the world: 'Y no sólo perduran aquellos breves trozos de nuestro personal pretérito que recordamos, sino todo él, íntegramente, colabora en nuestro ser actual, como en el fin de una melodía actúa su comienzo' [And it is not only these many glimpses of our own past that we remember, but our entire past, integrally; this past collaborates in the formation of our self, just as the final notes of a melody echo its beginning].[6] Ortega's 'personal preterite' constituted not just an individual's biography, but an entire lived experience. Echoing a Gestalt language of part and whole, melody and form, such descriptions characterized a distinct mode of phenomenological thought that melded science and a human reality.

Holism as New Humanism: A View from Spanish History

As historian Elías Díaz noted in his panorama from 'Institución' (the Institución Libre de Enseñanza) towards a post-dictatorship, democratic 'Constitución', the spiritual philosophy of Krausism functioned in Spain as a repository for humanistic values threatened under Francoism and emerging as an intellectual substratum in subsequent decades of democratization.[7] From points of post-war Republican exile, the defence of educational humanism was expressed with fervour. Speaking to a university audience in Puerto Rico during the early 1940s, Pedro Salinas contended that universities must seek to enrich students' moral and spiritual foundations, not just to train them in technical disciplines. He set out to envision the ideal student for a modern world, then sunk in the global crisis of the Second World War. Salinas depicted a student hungry for knowledge and truth, a lover of intellect and ideas, one who sought the inner 'sentido' [meaning] of the world and put faith in 'la cultura espiritual, del ejercicio del espíritu' [spiritual culture, the exercise of the mind]. This ideal, Salinas argued, must supplant a purely utilitarian, economically-oriented, mercenary mould of student. Furthermore, universities must take on the task of cultivating and fostering such an attitude. Otherwise, having lost their spark of 'espíritu', universities would cede their *raison d'être* and precipitate their own decline.[8] Within Spain itself, the simultaneous depuration of higher education institutions and the appointment of religious ideologues to positions of leadership in Spain should not be understated.[9] Yet certain decisive threads retained a flexible relevance in the rhetoric of a developing psycho-pedagogical field.

Given the spiritual aspects of Krausism, Spain's Catholic humanist traditions and a transnational rise of a 'Christian humanism' through the twentieth century, the question remains open to what extent an integral perspective on human development can viably be suggested through the Francoist period.[10] An explicitly national-Catholic framing, here within the Instituto Luis Vives of Madrid's Consejo Superior de Investigaciones Científicas (CSIC), meant that all knowledge was officially filtered through a trinitarian, religious dogma. From works during the 1920s and 1930s exploring Vives's legacy of a psychologically attentive pedagogy towards post-war incorporations of Vives by national pedagogical institutions, the trinity of mind, body, and spirit was posed in theological terms as one of an integral relationship within the developing self, towards others, and to God. 'Humanam mentem spiritum esse per quem corpus, cui est connexus, vivit, aptus cognitioni Dei propter amorem' [the human soul, vitally connected to body, lives in the knowledge and love of God]: scholar Fermín de Urmeneta y Cervera cited Vives's *De anima et vita* and its view of mind, body, and soul in a 1949 celebration of his pedagogy and its psychological bases.[11] Urmeneta y Cervera, as countless prior pedagogues, followed Vives in seeing the biological growth of the child's body towards adult decline and senility as an organic, physical surety, as natural as 'la subida y bajada del mar océano' [the rising and falling of the sea]. Humans were created from nature just as the cosmos was 'verificado' by God from void.[12] But where new educationalist reformers might have emphasized the biological roots of growth, leaving open the ineffable, transcendent aspects of spirit, an incommensurable difference was drawn in subsequent years between growth, explicable by biology; and creation, which evaded science's grasp and rendered it, thus, secondary to points of theology and national hierarchy.

Yet voices also emerged that connected intellectual production to wider currents. Carrying forward a contingent view of development in Spain, for example, were leading figures in literature, philosophy, and psychology, whose work drew on a phenomenological base. Intellectuals such as Luis Martín-Santos (1924–1964) spoke to questions of personal development in post-war writings, following Ortega in describing the circumscribed world of childhood ('el pequeño universo familiar') as exerting a continual moulding effect upon the evolution of the self across a lifespan: 'Dentro de la fluente sucesión de vivencias, solo el proyecto fundamental subsiste durante largo tiempo con una cierta constancia' [Within a steady succession of experiences, only the fundamental project subsists relatively constantly over time].[13] Like various contemporaries in medicine and psychology, including José Germain and Juan Rof Carballo (1905–1994), Martín-Santos's work was shaped by a base of phenomenological and experimentally-driven psychological research before the Civil War, including Gestaltist and cognitive theories, building upon a psychoanalytic framework. The fundamental project to be undertaken, for Martín-Santos, was the steady consolidation of an authentic self — 'al hombre, ser "en sí"' [towards man, being 'as such'] — through a totality of environmental influences, constraints, and liberties.[14]

Such an interiority contrasted with the new humanisms articulated in Enrique Tierno Galván's 1963 *Humanismo y sociedad*, which explored, among other defining

aspects of the modern humanism he sought to transcend, the subjective development of a unified self at the expense of a larger global solidarity. Together,
these currents — including Tierno Galván's, in urging the shift from a subjective,
aristocratic humanism towards an explicitly socialist, universalist understanding of
human interests and commonalities — represent recuperations and articulations of
new and abiding humanisms that shaped educational thought.[15] Over the course
of the twentieth century, such successive notions of self and society converged in
efforts to vitalize the body and the mind, engage the child's human spirit, and bring
the evolving self into contact with the world.

Rethinking Mind, Body, and Spirit: From Integrality to Totality

The efforts analysed in this book were products of a common rhetoric that would
shape Spanish education and intellectual life over the course of the early twentieth
century. Whether writing of the child's perceptual world, creating interactive,
vanguard toys, plays, or poems inspired by and apt for children's verbal access to the
world, or furthering open-air and sensorial methods of classroom activity through
nature study and creative projects, educators consciously linked the transnational
projects of child study and pedagogical reform to circulating theoretical currents
and debates. Intellectuals such as Ortega, García Morente, Xirau, and Abril; poets
including Conde, Lorca, and Guillén; artists in the circles of Mallo, Ferrant, and
others; and teachers from Verdier to Sensat to Freire furthered the New Educational
idea that experience must abide at the heart of inquiry.

Aligned in large part, but by no means exclusively, under the aegis of the ILE,
the richness, energy and continuity of educational reform suffered a decisive
rupture after 1936. With Franco's rise to power, many teachers sympathetic to the
Republic faced execution, imprisonment, and repression during and after the Civil
War. A 'systematic purge' displaced some fifty thousand public school teachers by
November 1937 and transformed the school into an explicit vehicle of patriotic
and religious indoctrination.[16] Among the thousands forced into exile were those
critically invested in pedagogical and educational experiments: Alberti, Camprubí,
Guillén, Jiménez, Roura, Salinas, Xirau, and many others. Scores of exiled teachers
and pedagogues contributed to a flourishing of humanistically-oriented pedagogical
work in Latin America. Among these stories are the leading psychotechnical career
forged by Emilio Mira y López in Argentina; the founding of the University of
Chile's Escuela Educadora de Párvulos by Matilde Huici, previously of Madrid's
Asociación Auxiliar del Niño; Mercedes Rodrigo's contributions to the field of
experimental psychology in Colombia; and pedagogues Regina Lago's and husband
Juan Comas's prolific scholarship in Mexico.[17]

Others carried on teaching within Spain, at private institutions and public
schools, rebuilding scholarship in education and psychology over the course of
the mid-century. The development of Spanish pedagogy has been described
as passing through various stages. While the early twentieth century was an
'embryonic', 'pre-formative' stage, the post-war period of 1939–70 constituted
decades of systematic 'reinvention and restoration', 'pre-constitutive' of a post-

1970 normalization and maturation of institutions.[18] Educators who participated in a post-war effort of 'reinvention and restoration' sought both a continuation of international engagement and an attempt to restore their dignity and creative practices in education. These included teachers such as Freire of Madrid's Grupo Escolar Cervantes, incarcerated for two years in the Ventas women's prison and only slowly regaining opportunities to teach through the 1940s and early 1950s — 'trapped' within Spanish history, as biographer Maria del Mar del Pozo Andrés has characterized her career.[19] Some teachers, like Verdier, carried on quietly working and publishing in limited thematic areas: orthography, left-handedness, children's stories.[20] Conde, the educationalist and writer whose poetic evocation of a classroom opened this book, embodied a more visible turn towards restoration; she continued writing and publishing prolifically from the early 1940s through to her death in 1996. The bulk of her immediate post-war publications took the form of fantastical and mythical children's stories and plays, signed by pseudonyms 'Florentina del Mar' or 'Magdalena Noguera'.[21] Conde joined voices such as Carmen Laforet, Ana María Matute, Susana March, and other post-war writers, poets, and novelists in reconstructing memories of childhoods past and stories re-imagined. Many of these works looked to memory, motherhood, and sensation, narrating human experiences of time, aging, and relationality through historical circumstance.[22]

Other teachers sought, slowly and within constraints, to recuperate and advance training and international pedagogical engagement under the early grip of national Catholicism. Immediately after the Civil War, in 1940, pedagogue Jimena Menéndez Pidal joined with pedagogues Carmen García del Diestro and Ángeles Gasset to reinvent the shuttered Instituto-Escuela as a new institution, the private Colegio Estudio. Negotiating religious beliefs and political connections, the founders operated with implicitly *institucionalista* methods. These included a firm adherence to co-education; a philosophy of active learning, favouring direct experience over textbooks; excursions organized to regions such as Spain's rural, impoverished Las Hurdes; music and theatre performances; and systems of democratically-organized student government.[23] Several open-air schools continued operating after the Civil War, notably the Escola del Mar of Barcelona, which moved to Montjuïc then Guinardó during the 1940s after the aerial bombardment of its grand Barceloneta seafront building in 1938. As earlier noted, director Pere Vergés would maintain his correspondence and cooperation with Ángel Ferrant on children's drawings through the 1950s. Equally, Ferrant's teaching manifested, as detailed by Clara Eslava, a fascination with the new and ever-newly created, the unceasing returns of the sea and the earth. His 'objects' of the early 1930s, many of which he purposefully destroyed in acts of creation and return, developed into his 'objetos hallados' [found objects] of 1945, small sculptures made from the shells, driftwood, and rocks of Galician shores and brought to rest in the heart of Madrid.[24]

Such individual efforts began in small ways to adapt and advance experimental principles and ideals within new contexts. Drawing on Ferrant's work on children's drawings in her own studies and publications, novelist Josefina Aldecoa, herself a child of Republican teachers, undertook concrete pedagogical initiatives to open an outlet for creative education under Francoism.[25] While writing a doctoral thesis on children's art at the University of Madrid in 1959, and as her daughter approached school age, she founded a co-educational private school to model what she and fellow intellectuals wanted to see in an evolving Spain.[26] She called the school the Colegio Estilo, founded on principles of art, music, and creativity and explicitly seeking to recover and carry on the work of the Institución Libre de Enseñanza. Under the direction of that same daughter, Susana Aldecoa, the school operated for almost sixty years before announcing its closure in 2019.[27] As a generation educated under the Second Republic and raised during the Spanish Civil War sought to begin this work of recuperation and reinvention in education, so too did writings and memory begin to reflect, and reflect upon, this process. In Aldecoa's 1983 *Los niños de la guerra*, such questions come full circle: what defines a generation? How had the Spanish Civil War — and diverse experiments previously — imprinted upon the very children whose lives and education it disrupted? And to revive Unamuno's 1932 question in the Introduction to the present book, how would Spanish children, as adults, view the society in which they were raised, and how had it in turn shaped and influenced those educated within it?[28]

Questions such as these are a necessary, if open, postlude to the possibilities set out by a range of protagonists across this book, whether they approached the 'problem' of childhood via scientific, sociological, literary, or artistic means. Through converging conversations on present society, its function, nature, and possibilities, children were drawn into a larger educational project that both built on a Spanish humanistic and Krausist tradition and consciously sought to engage with a wider world of scholarship. Studying and adapting models of pedagogy and psychometrics, early twentieth-century intellectuals and pedagogical allies across a range of institutions and alliances looked to integrate new modes of scientific modernity in the classroom. Seeking to counter what they saw as limiting, soul-stifling formulations of pedagogy, a wide range of educators drew upon currents of vitalism, holism, and New Educational rhetoric to promote the development of an active and imaginative world of play, language, and physicality. What must be done, they argued, was to understand how the child functioned, mentally, physically, and spiritually, and what fundamental values and skills should be inculcated to prepare them for a changing world. Their efforts extended from spiritual to material aspects of education, from stories to images to classroom models and toys. Educators critically engaged with the living, growing boys or girls in their care, whether in schools, summer camps and 'colonies', the *misiones pedagógicas*, or within their own homes, families, and communities. In line with circulating philosophical notions of vitality and becoming, they sought to equip the child to act upon the world with his or her being in totality, in fullest and gathering plenitude.

While pedagogy itself had an inherent aim, towards the 'humanization' of the child and a deepening of self and spirit, ultimately the world of the child remained, as teacher Francisco Carmona Nenclares described it in 1932, 'un mundo sin fines, ateleológico' [a world without ends, ateleological].[29] This was a purposely open-ended notion of existence, bridging the biological, the physical, and the spiritual;

an existence beyond the reach of adult understanding, yet ever abiding within the individual. Spanish educators of the early twentieth century oversaw a cultural reconfiguration of pedagogy which, in the midst of a societal frenzy for experimental psychotechnic tools and child-centred models and methods, simultaneously sought to transcend any one of these individual efforts.

True education — reformers argued — was not a collection of isolated practices, a summative process of input and output, but an entire approach to children's phenomenological experience and their evolving relationship to self and society. As philosophical, literary, and artistic thought converged, intellectuals looked to communicate the ultimate limits of pedagogical method and shift the focus towards individual children in changing circumstances and contexts. They reinforced the foundations of a humanistic approach to education: mutual respect and dialogue, free exercise of the imagination, and an active integration with the world through vital and lived experiences. Seeking the entwinement of body, mind, and spirit through the transnational lens of New Education, teachers and intellectuals pursued the enigma of childhood and its influence through aesthetics and literature. Through diverse notions of holism, humanism, and development, early twentieth-century Spanish educators joined with artists and writers to examine the growing child within a larger interpretive context. Engaging in an intellectual, literary, and artistic endeavour across disciplines, their celebration of the child sought to rethink the ends of education and reconfigure what it meant to be human.

Notes to the Epilogue

1. Cárceles Laborde, *Humanismo y educación en España*, p. 11.
2. Peter Petersen, 'Misión de la educación', *Revista de Pedagogía*, 13.148 (1934), 145–49 (p. 147). Known for his innovative 'Jena Plan', presented at the New Education Fellowship's conference in Locarno in 1927, Petersen's continued prominence through National Socialism exemplifies the ultimate bifurcations of pedagogical innovations. Later espousing ideas linked to race theory, Petersen's work can be both collected in studies of progressive, 'alternative schools' while also considered 'inseparable from anti-democratic and, ultimately, totalitarian tendencies'; see Ralf Koerrenz, Annika Blichmann, and Sebastian Engelmann, 'Peter Petersen and the Jena Plan School', in *Alternative Schooling and New Education: European Concepts and Theories* (Cham: Palgrave Pivot, 2018), pp. 87–104.
3. José Ortega y Gasset, 'Pedagogía de secreciones internas: la vida como suma y como unidad', in *El espectador* (Madrid: Calpe, 1921), III, 138–46 (p. 146).
4. Miguel de Unamuno, *Cómo se hace una novela* (Buenos Aires: Editorial Alba, 1927), p. 136, as cited in Alison Sinclair, *Uncovering the Mind: Unamuno, the Unknown and the Vicissitudes of Self* (Manchester: Manchester University Press, 2001), p. 221.
5. García Morente, 'El mundo del niño'; Dewey, *The Child and the Curriculum*, pp. 6, 5.
6. Ortega y Gasset, 'La psicología del cascabel', pp. 177–78.
7. Elías Díaz, *De la institución a la constitución* (Madrid: Editorial Trotta, 2009).
8. Pedro Salinas, *Defensa del estudiante y de la universidad* (Seville: Editorial Renacimiento, 2011), pp. 46–56.
9. For an encyclopaedic view of this process across fields, see *La universidad nacionalcatólica: la reacción antimoderna*, ed. by Luis Enrique Otero Carvajal (Madrid: Carlos III Universidad de Madrid, 2014), or, for example, in the field of physics, see *La física en la dictadura: físicos, cultura y poder en España 1939–1975*, ed. by Néstor Herran and Xavier Roqué (Bellaterra: Universitat Autònoma de Barcelona, 2012).
10. On evolving humanisms in Christian theology through the twentieth century, see *Re-envisioning*

Christian Humanism: Education and the Restoration of Humanity, ed. by Jens Zimmermann (Oxford: Oxford University Press, 2016).

11. Fermín de Urmeneta y Cervera, *La doctrina psicológica y pedagógica de Luis Vives* (Madrid: CSIC, Instituto San José de Calasanz de Pedagogía, Sección de Barcelona, 1949). See also Gregorio Marañón, *Luis Vives (un español fuera de España)* (Madrid: Espasa-Calpe, 1942); Juan Zaragüeta, *Las directrices de la pedagogía de Juan Luis Vives* (Madrid: Imprenta de Editorial Magisterio Español, 1945); and José Ortega y Gasset's 1940 *Vives, Goethe: conferencias* (Madrid: Revista de Occidente, 1961), one of several texts written upon his founding of the Instituto de Humanidades in Madrid in 1948. A fitting complement is Xirau's contemporaneous post-war, humanistic recuperation of Vives from Mexico; see his *El pensamiento vivo de Juan Luis Vives* (Buenos Aires: Editorial Losada, 1944).

12. Urmeneta y Cervera, *La doctrina psicológica y pedagógica de Luis Vives*, pp. 67–89.

13. Luis Martín-Santos, *Libertad, temporalidad y transferencia en el psicoanálisis existencial: para una fenomenología de la cura psicoanalítica* (Barcelona: Seix Barral, 1975), p. 43. Like Ortega, Roura, and others, Martín-Santos responded to Dilthey's *Geisteswissenschaften* and its delineation of a method for the human sciences. His doctoral dissertation applied Dilthey's ideas to psychopathology and psychiatry; see the editorial prologue to Martín-Santos, *Libertad, temporalidad y transferencia en el psicoanálisis existencial*, p. 20.

14. Martín-Santos, *Libertad, temporalidad y transferencia*, p. 13. See for instance the work of Juan Rof Carballo, particularly his idea of the post-birth 'urdimbre' [warp] that connected the human child to both mother and social-environmental surroundings: Consuelo Martínez Priego, 'Urdimbre afectiva y educación: aproximación a las ideas pedagógicas de Juan Rof Carballo', *Estudios sobre Educación*, 28 (2015), 139–54.

15. Enrique Tierno Galván, *Humanismo y sociedad* (Barcelona: Seix Barral, 1964), pp. 43–44. His line of argument recalls Republican predecessors for whom the 'humanization' of education was inseparable from its socialist aims and affiliations; see Llopis, *Hacia una escuela más humana*. In studies of Tierno Galván and others, Thomas Mermall has gone furthest in unpacking the development of post-Civil War humanisms; see *The Rhetoric of Humanism: Spanish Culture after Ortega y Gasset* (New York: Bilingual Press, 1976).

16. William J. Callahan, *The Catholic Church in Spain, 1875–1998* (Washington, DC: Catholic University of America Press, 2012), p. 370. On post-war repression of an unprecedented generation of female educators see, for example, the Goya award-winning documentary *Las maestras de la República,* dir. by Pilar Pérez Solano (Madrid: Transit Producciones, 2013) and the accompanying volume on female pedagogues' struggles for parity, often via socialist bodies such as the Federación de Trabajadores de la Enseñanza (FETE-UGT): *Las maestras de la República*, ed. by Elena Sánchez de Madariaga, 7th edn (Madrid: Catarata, 2014).

17. On these trajectories see, for example, Annette Mülberger, 'Un psicólogo abandona su mundo: el exilio de Emilio Mira y López', in *El exilio científico republicano*, ed. by José Luís Barona (Valencia: Publicaciones de la Universidad de Valencia, 2010), pp. 157–72, as well as other post-war re-orientations detailed in this volume.

18. Mainer Baqué, *La forja de un campo profesional*, p. 33. Mainer's work chronicles the importation of major pedagogical methods and the post-war continuities and transitions of teachers and social scientists who forged the discipline of pedagogy during the early twentieth century.

19. Pozo Andrés, *Justa Freire o la pasión de educar*.

20. Rafael Verdier: *Nene* (Málaga: Paidós, 1960), and *La enseñanza de la ortografía*; *Zurdera y destreza*; and *Cinco bolas y un misterio* (Málaga: n.p., 1973).

21. See Luís Ahumada Zuaza, 'El teatro para niños en la obra de Carmen Conde', in *Pasión por crear*, ed. by Francisco Henares y Caridad Fernández (Cartagena: Aglaya, 2008), pp. 117–33.

22. Conde's creative return to her own childhood is further explored in literary form in *Empezando la vida: memorias de una infancia en Marruecos (1914–1920)* (Tetuán: Ediciones Al-Motamid, 1955), published almost three decades after her poetic evocations in *Júbilos*.

23. See historian of psychology Helio Carpintero's 1981 address on her career, from his perspective of having taught philosophy at the Colegio Estudio during 1963–70: 'Jimena Menéndez-Pidal, educadora', *Estudio: Boletín de Actividades* (June 2013), 36–43; see also Elvira Ontañón, 'Jimena

Menéndez Pidal: la aventura de rescatar la ILE en tiempos de oscuridad', in *Treinta retratos de maestras*, ed. by Consuelo Flecha (Madrid: Cuadernos de Pedagogía, 2005), pp. 73–78.

24. Eslava, *Mutación poética*, pp. 7–54.

25. See Alison Ribeiro de Menezes, 'Family Memories, Postmemory, and the Rupture of Tradition in Josefina Aldecoa's Civil War Trilogy', *Hispanic Research Journal*, 13.3 (2012), 250–63. Raised in León as the child of *institucionista* parents, Aldecoa's upbringing is reflected in her trilogy moving from mother to daughter: the first volume imagines her mother's youth as a teacher in Guinea, where she uses image and movement, song and interactive methods to convey new words and ideas to her excited pupils: 'Yo dibujaba en la pizarra las cosas con sus nombres [...] "Palmera verde", decía yo' [I drew things with their names on the blackboard [...] 'Green palm tree,', I said]: Josefina Aldecoa, *Historia de una maestra* (Barcelona: Editorial Anagrama, 1990), p. 58.

26. Rodríguez Álvarez, *El arte del niño*. Her work shows the influence of Ferrant, Gasch, and López Velasco, as well as early twentieth-century scholars of children's art.

27. See an oral history of Colegio Estilo in Amelia Castilla, *Memoria de un colegio: 'Estilo', una experiencia de educación en libertad sobre la base de la comunidad* (Madrid: Biblioteca Nueva, 2002). The school's closure in June 2019 was explained on economic grounds; see ibid., 'El colegio Estilo cierra sus puertas', *El País*, 11 June 2019 <https://elpais.com/sociedad/2019/06/11/actualidad/1560271798_641394.html> [accessed 1 July 2019].

28. Unamuno, 'El niño es el padre del hombre', p. 1. On Aldecoa's effort of literary recovery, see her *Los niños de la guerra* (Madrid: Anaya, 2002). Documentation of the lives and legacies of the generation that experienced the Civil War as children extends beyond the early twentieth-century framework I have begun to outline, but on the experiences of a generation of 'children of war', including evacuees, see Verónica Sierra Blas, *Palabras huérfanas: los niños y la guerra civil* (Madrid: Taurus, 2009).

29. Francisco Carmona Nenclares, 'La psicología de la estructura y el mundo del niño', *Revista de Pedagogía*, 11.122 (1932), 55–66 (p. 66).

BIBLIOGRAPHY

I. Archives, Libraries, and Museums

Archivo de la Junta para Ampliación de Estudios (JAE), Residencia de Estudiantes, Madrid
Archivo Ferrant, Museo Patio Herreriano, Valladolid
Arxiu de Història de la Psicologia, Departament de Psicologia Bàsica, Evolutiva i de l'Educació, Universitat Autònoma de Barcelona
Biblioteca de la Associació de Mestres Rosa Sensat, Barcelona
Centro de Documentación de la Residencia de Estudiantes, Madrid
Bibliothek für Bildungsgeschichtliche Forschung, Berlin
Casa-Museo Unamuno, Salamanca
Centro Internacional de la Cultural Escolar (CEINCE), Berlanga de Duero
Fundación Ángel Llorca, Madrid
Ibero-Amerikanisches Institut, Berlin
Museo Torres García, Montevideo
Museo Sorolla, Madrid
Museu Abelló, Mollet del Vallès
Patronato Carmen Conde–Antonio Oliver, Cartagena

II. Newspapers and Journals

ABC
AC
Acción Gallega
Alrededor del Mundo
Anales de la Junta para Ampliación de Estudios e Investigaciones Científicas
Archivos de Neurobiología, Psicología, Fisiología, Histología, Neurología y Psiquiatría
Atenas
Arte
Boletín de la Academia de Ciencias, Bellas Letras y Nobles Artes de Córdoba
Boletín de la Institución Libre de Enseñanza
Biblion
Crónica
Cruz y Raya
Diablo Mundo
El Heraldo de Madrid
El Imparcial
El Sol
Escuelas de España
España
Estampa
Gallo
Garbí

Héroe
Ibérica
Mundo Gráfico
La Correspondencia de España
La Ciudad Lineal
La Escuela Moderna
La Esfera
La Gaceta Literaria
La Lectura
La Publicitat
La Vanguardia
La Voz
Madrid Científica
Meseta
Revista de Escuelas Normales
Revista Nueva
Revista de Occidente
Revista de Pedagogía
Revista de Psicologia i Pedagogia
Residencia
Sudeste
Unión Patriótica
Vida Socialista

III. Primary and Secondary Sources

Abril, Manuel, 'Comentarios a nuestros grabados', *Arte*, 2.2 (1933), 27–28
——*De la naturaleza al espíritu: ensayo crítico de pintura contemporánea desde Sorolla a Picasso* (Madrid: Espasa Calpe, 1935)
——'L'escultor Ángel Ferrant o les tres gràcies de la forma', *Gaseta de les arts*, 2.10 (June 1929), 133–37
——'Humanización y desnaturalización, o lo humano y lo demasiado humano', *Arte*, 2.2 (1933), 20–25
——*Los niños en el arte y en la fotografía* (Madrid: M. Aguilar, 1936)
——'Sobre la deshumanización del arte', *Cruz y Raya,* 1.2 (1935), 154–63
Ahumada Zuaza, Luís, 'El teatro para niños en la obra de Carmen Conde', in *Pasión por crear*, ed. by Francisco Henares and Caridad Fernández (Cartagena: Aglaya, 2008), pp. 117–33
Alberti, Rafael, *Lope de Vega y la poesía contemporánea seguido de* La pájara pinta, ed. by Robert Marrast (Paris: Centre de Recherches de l'Institut d'Études Hispaniques, 1964)
——*Marinero en tierra*, 1924 (Madrid: Biblioteca Nueva, 2017)
Alcántara García, Pedro, *Educación intuitiva y lecciones de cosas* (Madrid: Gras y Compañía, 1881)
Aldecoa, Josefina, *Historia de una maestra* (Barcelona: Editorial Anagrama, 1990)
——*Los niños de la guerra*, 1983 (Madrid: Anaya, 2002)
Almendros, Herminio, 'La imprenta en la escuela', *Revista de Pedagogía*, 11.130 (1932), 448–53
——'Libros: Antoniorrobles: veintiséis cuentos en orden alfabético', *Revista de Pedagogía*, 9.101 (1930), 236–37
Altamira, Rafael, Luis de Zulueta, and Alfredo Jara Urbano, *Pestalozzi in Albacete* (Albacete: Imprenta de Sebastián Ruíz, 1932)

ALTED VIGIL, ALICIA, 'El cine educativo en España (hasta 1936)', *Historia Social*, 76 (2013), 91–106

ÁLVAREZ DE CÁNOVAS, JOSEFINA, *Pedagogía del párvulo: estudio del niño español* (Madrid: Espasa-Calpe, 1943)

—— *Pequeñuelos: la enseñanza de la lectura por el método global (el libro en que aprendió a leer Mari-Sol)*, 6th edn (Madrid: n.p., [1943])

—— *Psicología pedagógica: estudio del niño español* (Madrid: Espasa-Calpe, 1941)

ÁLVAREZ JUNCO, JOSÉ, *La ideología política del anarquismo español: 1868–1910* (Madrid: Siglo XXI, 1976)

ÁLVAREZ PELÁEZ, RAQUEL, 'La búsqueda de un modelo institucional de protección a la infancia: institutos, guarderías y hogares infantiles: España 1900–1940', in *Salvad al niño: estudios sobre la protección a la infancia en la Europa Mediterránea a comienzos del siglo XX*, ed. by Enrique Perdiguero Gil (Valencia: Publicacions de la Universitat de València, 2004)

ANON., 'La Ciudad Lineal, lejos', *La Ciudad Lineal*, 14.385 (1909), 1493–94

—— 'Curso del profesor Wolf [*sic*] en el Instituto Psicotécnico', *Revista de Escuelas Normales*, 12 (1934), 27–28

—— 'Don Juan Roura en el Instituto Psicotécnico', *El Sol*, 15 March 1933, p. 3

—— 'En Madrid hay un club infantil', *Ahora*, 16 January 1936, p. 18

—— 'Entrevista con Ramón Xirau, escritor y académico', *La Jornada*, 12 April 2004, <http://www.jornada.unam.mx/2004/04/12/02an1cul.php?printver=1&fly=> [accessed 1 December 2018]

—— *La Escuela de Wickersdorf* (Madrid: La Lectura, 1926)

—— 'La escuela en la "ciudad funcional" ', *AC*, 3.10 (1933), 15–30

—— 'Escuelas al aire libre en la Ciudad Lineal', *La Ciudad Lineal*, 34.823 (1930), 129

—— 'Escuelas del Ave María en el Camino del Sacro Monte de Granada', *La Ilustración Artística*, 18.922 (1899), 555–58

—— 'Las escuelas Montessori: donde se educa a los niños jugando', *Alrededor del Mundo*, 671 (1912), 296–97

—— 'El estudio del niño', *Revista de Pedagogía*, 5.60 (1926), 557–58

—— 'La inteligencia de los monos: nuevos ensayos en el parque experimental de Suchum', *Mundo Gráfico* (1932), 8–9

—— 'La juventud en los pueblos', *Diablo Mundo*, 1.4 (1934), 7

—— '*Manual de Paidología*, por los señores D. Juan Jaén y D. José Peinado, inspectores de Primera Enseñanza', *España Médica*, 27 (1936)

—— 'Ministerio de Obras Públicas', *Gaceta de Madrid*, 4 March 1936, pp. 1837–38

—— 'El niño, genio natural', *Diablo Mundo*, 1.5 (1934), 5

—— 'Notas del mes: El estudio universitario de la Pedagogía', *Revista de Pedagogía*, 13.147 (1934), 135–36

—— 'El nuevo edificio del Instituto-Escuela, destinado a centralizar todas las secciones del Preparatorio, que suman más de un millar de alumnos', *Crónica*, 10 July 1932, p. 9

—— 'Pajaritas de Unamuno', *Residencia*, 3.6 (1932), 176

—— '*Poesía infantil recitable.* — José Luis Sánchez Trincado y R. Olivares Figueroa. — Aguilar. — Madrid', *Escuelas de España*, 2.13 (1935), 42–43

—— 'El problema de los niños pobres superdotados', *Unión Patriótica*, 15 July 1927, p. 1

—— 'El profesor Kohler [*sic*]', *La Época*, 6 April 1927, p. 4

—— 'La Profesora Bühler en Madrid', *El Sol*, 27 April 1932, p. 8

—— 'Reunión del Comité de Letras y Artes del Instituto de la Sociedad de Naciones', *Residencia*, 4 (1933), 106, 182

—— 'Una exposición artística', *Ahora*, 24 October 1934, p. 17

—— 'Unamuno, residente', *Residencia*, 3.6 (1932), 177–78

——'Vida docente: Visita de dos intelectuales chilenos', *La Vanguardia*, 18 April 1936, p. 9

——'Visita de dos ilustres personalidades americanas', *ABC*, 27 March 1935, p. 27

ARIÈS, PHILIPPE, *Centuries of Childhood: A Social History of Family Life*, trans. by Robert Baldick (New York: Vintage Books, 1962)

ARRABAL, BONIFACIO, 'Ensayo sobre la imaginación de los niños', *Revista de Pedagogía*, 1.5 (May 1922), 169–74

ASCUNCE ARENAS, ARÁNZAZU, *Barcelona and Madrid: Social Networks of the Avant-Garde* (Lewisburg: Bucknell University Press, 2012)

ASENJO FERNÁNDEZ, IGNACIO, 'Ángel Ferrant: el anhelo de las influencias pedagógicas', *Arte, Individuo y Sociedad*, 25.1 (2013), 11–29

ASH, MITCHELL, *Gestalt Psychology in German Culture, 1890–1967: Holism and the Quest for Objectivity* (Cambridge: Cambridge University Press, 1995)

BACHELARD, GASTON, *The Poetics of Reverie: Childhood, Language, and the Cosmos*, trans. by Daniel Russell (Boston: Beacon Press, 1971)

BALL, HUGO, 'Karawane', Academy of American Poets, <https://www.poets.org/poetsorg/poem/karawane> [accessed 1 December 2018]

BALLESTEROS Y USANO, ANTONIO, *El método Decroly* (Madrid: Publicaciones de la Revista de Pedagogía, 1928)

BALLTONDRE PLA, MÒNICA, and ANDREA GRAUS, 'The City of Spirits: Spiritism, Feminism and the Secularization of Urban Spaces', in *Barcelona: An Urban History of Science and Modernity, 1888–1929*, ed. by Oliver Hochadel and Agustí Nieto-Galan (London: Routledge, 2016), pp. 136–57

BANN, STEPHEN, *The Tradition of Constructivism* (New York: Da Capo Press, 1974)

BARBADO, MANUEL, 'Antecedentes escolásticos de la "Gestaltpsychologie"', *Revista de Filosofía*, 1.2–3 (1942), 371–76

BARNARD, G. WILLIAM, *Living Consciousness: The Metaphysical Vision of Henri Bergson* (Albany: State University of New York Press, 2011)

BARNÉS SALINAS, DOMINGO, *El desenvolvimiento del niño*, 2nd edn (Barcelona: Editorial Labor, 1933)

——*Ensayos de pedagogía y filosofía* (Madrid: La Lectura, 1921)

——*Escuelas al aire libre* (Madrid: Ministerio de Instrucción Pública y Bellas Artes, 1909)

——*Fuentes para el estudio de la paidología* (Madrid: Imprenta de la Revista de Archivos, Bibliotecas y Museos, 1917)

——'La función biológica de la infancia', *Boletín de la Institución Libre de Enseñanza*, 46.743 (1922), 41–51

——*Paidología*, ed. by José María Hernández Díaz (Madrid: Biblioteca Nueva, 2008)

——'Prólogo: Dewey y la filosofía pragmatista', in *La escuela y el niño* (Madrid: Ciudad Lineal, 1926), pp. 9–36

——'Revista de Revistas: Francesas: La Revue', *La Lectura*, 14.161 (1914), 214–20

——*La salud del espíritu del niño* (Madrid: Ediciones Nuestra Raza, [1934])

BAROJA, PÍO, *El árbol de la ciencia* (Madrid: Caro Raggio, 2012)

BARTHES, ROLAND, *Camera Lucida: Reflections on Photography*, trans. by Richard Howard (New York: Hill & Wang, 1981)

BAYÓN, DAVID, 'Libros: De Uexküll a Decroly', *Escuelas de España*, 3.4 (1931), 95–97

BELLO, LUIS, *Viaje por las escuelas de España* (Madrid: Magisterio español, 1926)

BENAIGES Y NOGUÉS, ANTONIO, 'Los niños ante *Platero y yo*', *Escuelas de España*, 3.29 (1936), 315–16

BENÍTEZ MELLADO, FRANCISCO, 'El dibujo técnico en el Instituto-Escuela', *Revista de Pedagogía*, 7.79 (1928), 312–19

BERGAMÍN GUTIÉRREZ, JOSÉ, 'La decadencia del analfabetismo', *Cruz y Raya*, 1.3 (1933), 61–94

BERGSON, HENRI, *L'Évolution créatrice* (Paris: Alcan, 1908)

——*Creative Evolution*, trans. by Arthur Mitchell (London: Macmillan, 1911)

BERNAL MARTÍNEZ, JOSÉ MARIANO, 'De las escuelas al aire libre a las aulas de la naturaleza', *Areas*, 20 (2000), 171–82

BLANCO Y SÁNCHEZ, RUFINO, *Paidología y paidotecnia: breve historia de la paidología* (Madrid: Tipografía de la Revista de Archivos, 1912)

BONILLA Y SAN MARTÍN, ADOLFO, *Luis Vives y la filosofía del renacimiento* (Madrid: L. Rubio, 1929)

BOON, GÉRARD, *Aplicación del método Decroly a la enseñanza primaria y la instrucción obligatoria*, trans. by Rodolfo Tomás y Samper (Madrid: Francisco Beltrán, 1926)

BORJA I SOLÉ, MARÍA DE, *El juego como actividad educativa: instruir deleitando* (Barcelona: Universitat de Barcelona, 1984)

BORRÁS LLOP, JOSÉ MARÍA, ed., *Historia de la infancia en la España contemporánea (1834–1936)* (Madrid: Ministerio de Trabajo y Asuntos Sociales, 1996)

BOYD, CAROLYN, 'The Anarchists and Education in Spain, 1868–1909', *The Journal of Modern History*, 48.4 (1976), 125–70

BRAUNSCHVIG, MARCEL, *El arte y el niño: ensayo sobre la educación estética* (Madrid: D. Jorro, 1914)

BRAVO-VILLASANTE, CARMEN, *Historia de la literatura infantil española* (Madrid: Doncel, 1972)

BRÉMOND, HENRI, *La poésie pure*, Academie Française (1925), <http://www.academie-francaise.fr/la-poesie-pure> [accessed 1 October 2018]

BRIHUEGA, JAIME, *Las vanguardias artísticas en España, 1910–1931* (Madrid: Ediciones Cátedra, 1979)

BRUNO-JOFRÉ, ROSA, and GONZALO JOVER, 'The Readings of John Dewey's Work and the Intersection of Catholicism: The Cases of the Institución Libre de Enseñanza and the Thesis of Father Alberto Hurtado, S.J. on Dewey', in *The Global Reception of John Dewey's Thought: Multiple Refractions through Time and Space*, ed. by Rosa del Carmen Bruno-Jofré and Jürgen Schriewer (London: Routledge, 2012), pp. 23–42

BÜHLER, CHARLOTTE, 'Del juego al trabajo', *Revista de Pedagogía*, 11.125 (1932), 193–200

——*Das Märchen und die Phantasie des Kindes* (Leipzig: Barth, 1929)

BÜHLER, CHARLOTTE, and HILDEGARD HETZER, *Tests para la primera infancia: pruebas del desarrollo para el primero al sexto años de vida*, trans. by Alejandro Chleusebairgue and Antonio Calero (Madrid: Editorial Labor, 1933)

BUSQUET I TEIXIDOR, TOMÀS, 'La educación de los niños psico-anormales en la provincia de Barcelona', *Infantia Nostra*, 8.72 (1929), 80–90

BUYTENDIJK, FREDERIK J., *El juego y su significado: el juego en los hombres y en los animales como manifestación de impulsos vitales*, trans. by Eugenio Imaz (Madrid: Revista de Occidente, 1935)

—— 'Sobre la diferencia esencial entre el animal y el hombre', *Revista de Occidente*, 14.153–54 (1936), 233–59, 24–53

——*Wesen und Sinn des Spiels: Das Spielen des Menschen und der Tiere als Erscheinungsform der Lebenstriebe* (Berlin: Kurt Wolff, 1933)

CALLAHAN, WILLIAM J., *The Catholic Church in Spain, 1875–1998* (Washington, DC: Catholic University of America Press, 2012)

CAMPOAMOR GONZÁLEZ, ANTONIO, *Juan Ramón Jiménez y Zenobia Camprubí: años españoles (1881–1936)* (Seville: Universidad Internacional de Andalucía, 2014)

CAPELLÁN DE MIGUEL, GONZALO, *La España armónica: el proyecto del krausismo español para una sociedad en conflicto* (Madrid: Biblioteca Nueva, 2006)

CAPITÁN DÍAZ, ALFONSO, *Breve historia de la educación en España* (Madrid: Alianza Editorial, 2002)

——'Humanismo pedagógico en la España contemporánea', *Revista Española de Pedagogía*, 60.223 (2002), 461–80

CÁRCELES LABORDE, CONCEPCIÓN, *Humanismo y educación en España: 1450–1650* (Pamplona: Ediciones Universidad de Navarra, 1993)

CARDA ROS, ROSA MARÍA, and HELIO CARPINTERO CAPELL, 'La Paidología de Domingo Barnés', *Boletín de la Institución Libre de Enseñanza*, 7 (1989), 3–28

——'Domingo Barnés: biografía de un educador avanzado', *Boletín de la Institución Libre de Enseñanza*, 12 (1991), 63–74

CARMONA NENCLARES, FRANCISCO, 'La psicología de la estructura y el mundo del niño', *Revista de Pedagogía*, 11.122 (1932), 55–66

CARO VALVERDE, MARÍA TERESA, and MARÍA GONZÁLEZ GARCÍA, 'Valor educativo de la pedagogía romántica de la naturaleza en los escritos estéticos de Ortega y Gasset', *Cartaphilus*, 6 (2009), 33–34

CARPINTERO CAPELL, HELIO, *Esbozo de una psicología según la razón vital* (Madrid: Real Academia de Ciencias Morales y Políticas, 2000)

——*Historia de la psicología en España* (Madrid: Eudema, 1994)

——'Jimena Menéndez-Pidal, educadora', *Estudio: Boletín de Actividades* (June 2013), 36–43

——'José Peinado y la influencia de Piaget en España', *Revista de Historia de la Psicología*, 18.1–2 (1997), 75–85

CARPINTERO CAPELL, HELIO, and ENRIQUE LAFUENTE, 'El método histórico de las generaciones: el caso de la psicología española', *Revista de Historia de la Psicología*, 28.1 (2007), 67–86

CARPINTERO CAPELL, HELIO, and VICENTA MESTRE, *Freud en España: un capítulo de la historia de la psicología en España* (Valencia: Promolibro, 1984)

CARPINTERO CAPELL, HELIO, and VICTORIA DEL BARRIO, 'La introducción de Piaget en España la figura y obra de Juan Jaén', *Revista de Historia de la Psicología*, 17.3–4 (1996), 186–93

CARSON, JOHN, *The Measure of Merit: Talents, Intelligence, and Inequality in the French and American Republics, 1750–1940* (Princeton: Princeton University Press, 2007)

CASADO, ÁNGEL, and JUANA SÁNCHEZ-GEY, eds., *Filósofos españoles en la Revista de Pedagogía (1922–1936)* (Santa Cruz de Tenerife: Ediciones Idea, 2007)

CASALDUERO, JOAQUÍN, *'Cántico' de Jorge Guillén y 'Aire nuestro'* (Madrid: Gredos, 1974)

CASTILLA, AMELIA, *Memoria de un colegio: 'Estilo', una experiencia de educación en libertad sobre la base de la comunidad* (Madrid: Biblioteca Nueva, 2002)

——'El colegio Estilo cierra sus puertas', El País, 11 June 2019 <https://elpais.com/sociedad/2019/06/11/actualidad/1560271798_641394.html> [accessed 1 July 2019].

CASTILLEJO, JOSÉ, 'La enseñanza plurilingüe', *La Escuela Moderna*, 53 (1931), 86–88

——'¿Malgastamos la niñez de nuestros hijos?', *El Sol*, 29 September 1932, 1

CASTRO, JOSÉ JULIO, 'Semana Pedagógica de la Nacional en Málaga', *Escuelas de España*, 2.22 (1935), 464–69

CASTRO TEJERINA, JORGE, ed., *La psicología del arte en España (1898–1923): antología de textos fundacionales* (Oviedo: KRK Ediciones, 2018)

CAUDET, FRANCISCO, *Las cenizas del fénix: la cultura española en los años 30* (Madrid: Ediciones de la Torre, 1993)

CAUSÍ, TEODORO, *Bosquejo de una teoría biológica del juego infantil* (Madrid: Calpe, 1924)

——'El espiritualismo en la educación', *Revista de Pedagogía*, 8.87 (1929), 100–09

——'La globalización de Decroly y la psicología de la estructura', *Revista de Pedagogía*, 9.103 (1930), 293–301

CEREZO MANRIQUE, MIGUEL ÁNGEL, *Los comienzos de la psicopedagogía en España, 1882–1936* (Madrid: Biblioteca Nueva, 2001)

CERNUDA, LUIS, 'Unas palabras sobre la poesía actual española', *Escuelas de España*, 3.29 (1936), 221–24

CERTEAU, MICHEL DE, *The Practice of Everyday Life*, trans. by Steven Rendall (Berkeley: University of California Press, 1984)

CERVERA, JUAN, *Historia crítica del teatro infantil español* (Madrid: Editora Nacional, 1982)

CHAPLIN, JOYCE E., and DARRIN M. MCMAHON, eds., *Genealogies of Genius* (New York: Palgrave Macmillan, 2016)

CHECA GODOY, ANTONIO, *Historia de la prensa pedagógica en España* (Seville: Universidad de Sevilla, 2002)

CHRISMAN, OSCAR, *Paidologie: Entwurf zu einer Wissenschaft des Kindes* (Jena: B. Vopelius, 1896)

CHRISTIAN, WILLIAM A., *Moving Crucifixes in Modern Spain* (Princeton: Princeton University Press, 1992)

CIFO GONZÁLEZ, MANUEL, 'Amor y pedagogía o el problema de la educación visto por Miguel de Unamuno', in *Miguel de Unamuno: estudios sobre su obra*, ed. by Ana Chaguaceda Toledano, 4 vols (Salamanca: Universidad de Salamanca, 2005), II, 329–47

CIPLIJAUSKAITÉ, BIRUTÉ, *De signos y significaciones. 1: Juegos con la vanguardia: poetas del 27* (Barcelona: Anthropos, 1999)

CIRAC, EUGENIO, 'El enigma', *Acción Gallega: órgano de la Federación de Sociedades Gallegas de Buenos Aires*, 12 April 1931, [n.p]

CLAPARÈDE, ÉDOUARD, 'Rousseau y la significación de la infancia', *Revista de Pedagogía*, 1.4 (1922), 121–31

CLEMINSON, RICHARD, 'Eugenics by Name or by Nature? The Spanish Anarchist Sex Reform of the 1930s', *History of European Ideas*, 18.5 (1994), 729–40

COBÓS, PABLO DE ANDRÉS, 'Bibliotecas infantiles: *En el Bazar más suntuoso del mundo* [por] Ramón Gómez de la Serna', *Escuelas de España*, 1.1 (1929), 126

COE, RICHARD N., *When the Grass was Taller: Autobiography and the Experience of Childhood* (New Haven: Yale University Press, 1984)

COLETES BLANCO, AGUSTÍN, 'Un apunte sobre la fortuna de Tagore en España', *Archivum*, 48–49 (1998), 171–73

COMAS, JUAN, 'Libros: Dottrens (R.) y M. (Emilia): l'apprentissage de la lecture par la Méthode Globale [...]', *Revista de Pedagogía*, 9.105 (1930), 425–27

COMAS, JUAN, and REGINA LAGO, *La práctica de las pruebas mentales y de instrucción* (Madrid: Publicaciones de la Revista de Pedagogía, 1933)

COMAS, MARGARITA, 'Algunos problemas biológicos', *Revista de Pedagogía*, 12.137 (1933), 211–17

——'L'herència i el medi en l'educació', *Revista de Psicologia i Pedagogia*, 1.4 (1933), 422–30

COMAS RUBÍ, FRANCESCA, and BERNAT SUREDA GARCÍA, 'The Photography and Propaganda of the Maria Montessori Method in Spain (1911–1931)', *Paedagogica Historica*, 48.4 (2011), 571–87

COMPAÑÍA MADRILEÑA DE URBANIZACIÓN, *La reintegración al campo y la Ciudad Lineal* (Madrid: Ciudad Lineal, 1928)

CONDE, CARMEN, *La composición literaria infantil (escuela primaria)* (Barcelona: Publicaciones Mujeres Libres, 1937)

——*Empezando la vida: memorias de una infancia en Marruecos (1914–1920)* (Tetuán: Ediciones Al-Motamid, 1955)

——'Júbilos (Poema del colegio)', *Meseta*, 1.5 (1928), 2

——*Júbilos: poemas de niños, rosas, animales, máquinas y vientos*, 2nd edn (Murcia: Sudeste, 1934)

——'Oda al gato Félix', *La Gaceta Literaria*, 3.56 (1929), 2

——*Por la escuela renovada* (Valencia: Cuadernos de Cultura, 1931)

Constitución de la República Española, 9 de diciembre 1931 ([Madrid]: n.p., 1931), <http://www. congreso.es/docu/constituciones/1931/1931_cd.pdf> [accessed 1 August 2018]

CUENCA ESCRIBANO, ANTONIO, 'Evolución de la enseñanza del dibujo en la escuela', *Tendencias Pedagógicas*, 14 (2009), 335–51

——'La obra de Elisa López Velasco', *Arte, Individuo y Sociedad*, 15 (2003), 73–81

CUESTA, JOSEFINA, MARÍA JOSÉ TURRIÓN, and ROSA MARÍA MERINO, 'Dos residencias universitarias femeninas en España, 1914–1915', in *La Residencia de Señoritas y otras redes culturales femeninas*, ed. by Josefina Cuesta, María José Turrión, and Rosa María Merino (Madrid: Universidad de Salamanca, 2015), pp. 11–30

CULLELL I RAMIS, JOSEP, 'Joan Roura Parella: des de la totalitat', *Enrahonar: Quaderns de Filosofia*, 10 (1984), 78–84

DALHEM, LOUIS, *El método Decroly aplicado a la escuela* ([Madrid]: La Lectura, 1924)

DE AMICIS, EDMONDO, *Amore e ginnastica* (Atripalda (Avellino): Mephite, 2004)

DECROLY, OVIDE, 'La función de globalización y su importancia pedagógica', *Revista de Pedagogía*, 2.23 (1923), 401–12

DEHENNIN, ELSA, 'Continuidad y evolución en la obra poética de Jorge Guillén: los campos semánticos en "Cántico" y "Clamor" [1977]', in *Actas del Quinto Congreso de la Asociación Internacional de Hispanistas: celebrado en Bordeaux del 2 al 8 de septiembre de 1974*, ed. by François López Maxime Chevalier, Joseph Pérez, and Noël Salomon (Bordeaux: Instituto de Estudios Ibéricos e Iberoamericanos, Université de Bordeaux III, 2016), pp. 319–34

DELGADO OLIVARES, CARLOS, 'Proust y la imagen', *Heraldo de Madrid*, 27 July 1933, p. 23

DENNIS, NIGEL, *Diablo Mundo: los intelectuales y la Segunda República: antología* (Madrid: Editorial Fundamentos, 1983)

DEPAEPE, MARC, RAF DE BONT, and KRISTOF DAMS, 'How Darwinism Has Affected Catholic as well as Non-Catholic Psycho-pedagogical Constructs in Belgium from the 1870s to the 1930s', *Paedagogica Historica*, 48.1 (2012), 51–66

DESCHAMPS, ALEXANDER J., *La auto-educación en el método Decroly*, trans. by Emilia Elías de Ballesteros (Madrid: Juan Ortiz, 1932)

DESCŒUDRES, ALICE, *El desarrollo del niño de dos a siete años: investigaciones de psicología experimental*, trans. by Jacobo Orellana Garrido (Madrid: Francisco Beltrán, 1929)

DEWEY, JOHN, *The Child and the Curriculum* [1902], 27th edn (Chicago: University of Chicago Press, 1963)

——*La escuela y el niño*, trans. by Domingo Barnés (Madrid: Ciudad Lineal, 1926)

DEXTER, THOMAS F. G., and ALFRED H. GARLICK, *Psychology in the Schoolroom* (London: Longmans, Green & Company, 1898)

DÍAZ, ELÍAS, *De la institución a la constitución* (Madrid: Editorial Trotta, 2009)

——*La filosofía social del krausismo español*, Colección ITS (Madrid: Editorial Cuadernos para el Diálogo, 1973)

DÍAZ DE REVENGA, FRANCISCO JAVIER, ed., *Carmen Conde: voluntad creadora (1907–1996)* (Murcia: Marcial Pons, 2007)

DÍAZ JIMÉNEZ, ENRIQUE, *Los fundamentos éticos, religiosos y psicológicos de la pedagogía de Luis Vives* (Madrid: n.p., 1929)

D'ORS, EUGENIO, *Grandeza y servidumbre de la inteligencia* (Madrid: Revista de Estudiantes, 1919)

DOTTRENS, ROBERTO, and EMILIA MARGAIRAZ, 'Método global de lectura: sus fundamentos psicológicos', *La Escuela Moderna*, 44.496 (1933), 40–48

DUBREUCQ, FRANCINE, 'Jean-Ovide Decroly (1871–1932)', *Prospects: The Quarterly Review of Comparative Education*, 23.1–2 (1993), 249–75

DURÁN, MANUEL, 'Espacio y tiempo en dos poemas de *Cántico*', *Nueva Revista de Filología Hispánica*, 36.1 (1988), 455–65

DURÁN, MANUEL, and WILLIAM KLUBACK, *Reason in Exile: Essays on Catalan Philosophers* (New York: Peter Lang, 1994)

EALHAM, CHRIS, *Anarchism and the City: Revolution and Counter-revolution in Barcelona, 1898–1937* (London: Routledge, 2005)

EFE, 'Sonia Araquistáin se mata, arrojándose desde un séptimo piso', *ABC*, 6 September 1945, p. 25

ELEIZEGUI LÓPEZ, JOSÉ, *Biología de la edad escolar* (Madrid: [Saez Hermanos], 1929)

—— *Los juegos en la infancia: guía médicopedagógica para padres y maestros* (Barcelona: Sociedad General de Publicaciones, 1900)

—— *La sexualidad infantil* (Madrid: n.p., 1936)

ENCINA, JUAN DE LA, 'Los dibujos de niños en el Lyceum', *La Voz*, 2 July 1928, p. 1

ENCINAS, ANTONIO, 'Imágenes eidéticas: sus propiedades y naturaleza', *Razón y Fe*, 69.275 (1924), 273–88

ESLAVA, CLARA, *Mutación poética: naturaleza viva en el imaginario de Ángel Ferrant, 1945–1950* (Alzuza, Navarra: Fundación Museo Jorge Oteiza, 2017)

FABIO, '¿Totalitarismo? (Holismo-Tradicionalismo)', *El Siglo Futuro*, 13 November 1934, p. 1

FERNÁNDEZ LÓPEZ, MARISA, 'Children's Literature Research in Spain', *Children's Literature Association Quarterly*, 27.4 (2002), 221–25

FERNÁNDEZ VARGAS, VALENTINA, LUIS LORENZO NAVARRO, and JUAN BOSCH-MARÍN, *El niño y el joven en España (siglos XVIII–XX): aproximación teórica y cuantitativa* (Barcelona: Anthropos, 1989)

FERRANT, ÁNGEL, 'Diseño de una configuración escolar', *Arte*, 1.1 (1932), 12–18

—— 'Resplandor y proyección de los dibujos infantiles', *AC*, 3.10 (1933), 34–35

FERRANT, ÁNGEL, ANTONIO DE LARA GAVILÀN, and EMETERIO R. MELENDRERAS, *Tres propuestas para niños, 1930–1935,* ed. by Carlos Pérez (Valencia: Institut Valencià d'Art Modern, 1999)

FERRIÈRE, ADOLPHE, *La ley biogenética y la escuela activa,* trans. by Lorenzo Luzuriaga (Madrid: Publicaciones de la Revista de Pedagogía, 1928)

FIGUERIDO, C. A., 'Psicología y pedagogía', *Revista de Pedagogía,* 13.150 (1934), 263–79

FINEBERG, JONATHAN DAVID, *The Innocent Eye: Children's Art and the Modern Artist* (Princeton: Princeton University Press, 1997)

FLECHA, CONSUELO, 'Alumnas y equipos directivos de la Residencia Teresiana de Madrid', in *La Residencia de Señoritas y otras redes culturales femeninas,* ed. by Josefina Cuesta, María José Turrión, and Rosa María Merino (Madrid: Ediciones Universidad de Salamanca, 2015), pp. 287–311

FLORES, MAXIMIANO, 'La enseñanza de la lectura', *Escuela Moderna*, 34.398 (1924), 802–24

FRANZ, THOMAS R., 'The Philosophical Bases of Fulgencio Entrambosmares in Unamuno's *Amor y pedagogía*', *Hispania*, 60.3 (1977), 443–51

FRASER, BENJAMIN, 'Unamuno and Bergson: Notes on a Shared Methodology', *Modern Language Review,* 102.3 (2007), 753–67

FREIRE, JUSTA, '4.D/4.2: Didáctica del dibujo según Justa Freire', in *Archivo digital 'Los viejos papeles'* (Madrid: Fundación Ángel Llorca, [early-mid 1920s]), <http://www.fundacionangelllorca.org> [accessed 9 February 2018]

FRUTOS, EUGENIO, 'El existencialismo jubiloso de Jorge Guillén', *Cuadernos Hispanoamericanos*, 18 (1950), 411–26

FURTH, HANS G., *Piaget and Knowledge: Theoretical Foundations* (Englewood Cliffs: Prentice-Hall, 1969)

GALDÓS, BENITO, *Amor y ciencia: comedia en cuatro actos* (Perlado: Páez y Compañía, 1905)

GALÍ, ALEXANDRE, ed., *Història de les institucions i del moviment cultural a Catalunya 1900–1936,* 24 vols (Barcelona: Fundació Alexandre Galí, 1979)

GALINO CARRILLO, ÁNGELES, ed., *Humanismo pedagógico en Pedro Poveda: algunas dimensiones* (Madrid: Narcea, 2000)

GALLAGHER, SHAUN, and DAN ZAHAVI, 'Phenomenological Approaches to Self-Consciousness', in *The Stanford Encyclopedia of Philosophy*, ed. by Edward N. Zalta (2016) <https://plato.stanford.edu/archives/win2016/entries/self-consciousness-phenomenological/> [accessed 1 May 2018]

GALLARDO CRUZ, JOSÉ ANTONIO, *El dibujo infantil de la evacuación durante la Guerra Civil española (1936–1939)* (Málaga: Universidad de Málaga, 2012)

GALLEGOS, PRESENTACIÓN, 'Humano, con el humanismo verdad', in *Humanismo pedagógico en Pedro Poveda: algunas dimensiones*, ed. by Ángeles Galino Carrillo (Madrid: Narcea, 2000), pp. 15–25

GARCÍA BLANCO, MANUEL, '*Amor y pedagogía*, nivola unamuniana', *La Torre*, 9 (1961), 443–78

GARCÍA COLMENARES, CARMEN, 'Regina Lago, una psicóloga comprometida con la infancia durante la guerra civil española', *CEE Participación Educativa*, 14 (July 2010), 211–20

GARCÍA INIESTA, CÉSAR, 'Una estadística escolar equivocada urge la rectificación del Alcalde', *Heraldo de Madrid*, 23 January 1930, pp. 8–9

GARCÍA LORCA, FEDERICO, *Obras completas*, 15th edn (Madrid: Aguilar, 1969)

—— 'Ribera de 1910', *Héroe*, 1.4 (1932), n.p.

GARCÍA LORCA, FEDERICO, and SEBASTIÁN GASCH, *Cartas a sus amigos* (Barcelona: Ediciones Cobalto, 1950)

GARCÍA MAROTO, GABRIEL, *La nueva España 1930: resumen de la vida artística española desde el año 1927 hasta hoy* (Madrid: Biblios, 1927)

GARCÍA MORENTE, MANUEL, 'El mundo del niño', *Revista de Pedagogía*, 7.74–75 (February-March 1928), 49–58, 116–25

—— *Obras completas, 1906–1936*, 4 vols (Barcelona: Anthropos, 1996)

GARCÍA TREJO, CATALINA, *Escuelas al aire libre: su organización en el extranjero; la que podría dársele en España; ventajas é inconvenientes del sistema* (Alicante: n.p., 1910)

GARCÍA Y GÓMEZ, NIEVES, *Las colonias escolares y las escuelas al aire libre en su aplicación al mejoramiento de la salud y de la enseñanza primaria* (Madrid: A. Ungría, 1914)

GARDNER, HOWARD, *Artful Scribbles: The Significance of Children's Drawings* (New York: Basic Books, 1980)

—— *Frames of Mind: The Theory of Multiple Intelligences* (New York: Basic Books, 1983)

GARFÍAS, FRANCISCO, 'Rabindranath Tagore en español', in Rabindranath Tagore, *Recuerdos* (Barcelona: Plaza & Janés, 1983), pp. 9–17

GASCH, SEBASTIÀ, 'Creación e imitación', *La Gaceta Literaria*, 4.73 (1930), 13

GAUPP, ROBERT, *Psicología del niño*, trans. by Antonio Vallejo Nágera, 4th edn (Barcelona: Editorial Labor, 1936)

GERMAIN, JOSÉ, *Kurt Koffka 1886–1941* (Madrid: n.p. 1945)

GINSBORG, PAUL, *Family Politics: Domestic Life, Devastation and Survival, 1900–1950* (New Haven: Yale University Press, 2014)

GLICK, THOMAS F., *Einstein in Spain: Relativity and the Recovery of Science* (Princeton: Princeton University Press, 1988)

GLICK, THOMAS F., ROSAURA RUIZ, and MIGUEL ÁNGEL PUIG-SAMPER, eds., *The Reception of Darwinism in the Iberian World: Spain, Spanish America and Brazil* (Dordrecht: Kluwer, 2001)

GOETHE, JOHANN WOLFGANG VON, *La infancia de Goethe, contada por él mismo*, trans. by R. M. Tenreiro (Madrid: Editorial Reus, 1924)

GOLOMB, CLAIRE, *Child Art in Context: A Cultural and Comparative Perspective* (Washington, DC: American Psychological Association, 2002)

GÓMEZ CANO, MIGUEL, *Las colonias escolares del Ayuntamiento de Madrid* (Madrid: Imprenta del Asilo de Huérfanos, 1924)

—— *El cinematógrafo y las escuelas ambulantes de puericultura* (Madrid: Escuela Nacional de Puericultura, 1927)

GÓMEZ DE LA SERNA, RAMÓN, *Cuentos para niños* (Madrid: Clan, 2004)

GÓMEZ TORRES, ANA, 'La carnavalización del teatro: los títeres y la ruptura del canon dramático', *Analecta malacitana: Revista de la Sección de Filología de la Facultad de Filosofía y Letras*, 17.2 (1994), 313–22

GONZÁLEZ, A. ANSELMO, *Nacimiento y evolución de la inteligencia (Formad el espíritu de vuestros hijos)* (Madrid: M. Aguilar, 1930)

—— *Técnica de psicología experimental sin aparatos: manual de investigación psicológica* (Madrid: Sucesores de Hernando, 1921)

GONZÁLEZ-AGÀPITO, JOSEP, and OTHERS, *Tradició i renovació pedagògica: 1898–1939. Història de l'educació: Catalunya, Illes Balears, País Valencià* (Barcelona: Abadia de Montserrat, 2002)

GONZÁLEZ MUELA, JOAQUÍN, 'The Poetry of Jorge Guillén', *Bulletin of the John Rylands Library*, 69.2 (1987), 528–78.

GRAHAM, JOHN T., *The Social Thought of Ortega y Gasset: A Systematic Synthesis in Postmodernism and Interdisciplinarity* (Columbia: University of Missouri Press, 2001)

GROOS, KARL, *The Play of Animals*, trans. by Elizabeth L. Baldwin (London: Chapman & Hall, 1898)

—— *The Play of Man*, trans. by Elizabeth L. Baldwin (London: William Heinemann, 1901)

GUIGON, EMMANUEL, ed., *La infancia del arte: arte de los niños y arte moderno en España* (Teruel: Museo de Teruel; Logroño: Cultural Rioja, 1996)

GUILLÉN DE REZZANO, CLOTILDE, *Los centros de interés en la escuela* (Madrid: Publicaciones de la Revista de Pedagogía, 1929)

GUILLÉN, JORGE, *Cántico* (Madrid: Revista de Occidente, 1928)

—— *Cántico*, 4th edn (Buenos Aires: Editorial Sudamericana, 1950)

—— 'Cinco florinatas', *España*, 9.354 (27 January 1923), 8–9

—— *Guillén on Guillén: The Poetry and the Poet*, trans. by Reginald Gibbons and Anthony L. Geist (Princeton: Princeton University Press, 1979)

—— 'Prólogo: Federico en persona', in Federico García Lorca, *Obras completas* (Madrid: Aguilar, 1975), pp. xvii–lxxix

—— 'Sólo para pájaros', *España*, 9.365 (1923), 10

—— 'Varios poemas', *Meseta*, 1.5 (1928), 1

GUILLÉN, MAURO F., *Models of Management: Work, Authority, and Organization in a Comparative Perspective* (Chicago: University of Chicago Press, 1994)

GULLÓN, RICARDO, 'El cuarto *Cántico* de Jorge Guillén', *Ínsula: Revista Bibliográfica de Ciencias y Letras*, 6.66 (June 1951), 3, 6

HAARHOFF, THEODORE J., 'The Holistic Attitude in Education', in *Our Changing World-view: Ten Lectures on Recent Movements of Thought in Science, Economics, Education, Literature and Philosophy*, ed. by Jan Christiaan Smuts and others (Johannesburg: University of the Witwatersrand Press, 1932), pp. 103–14

HAMELINE, DANIEL, 'Adolphe Ferrière (1879–1960)', *Prospects: The Quarterly Review of Comparative Education*, 23.1–2 (2000), 373–401

HARKEMA, LESLIE J., *Spanish Modernism and the Poetics of Youth: From Miguel de Unamuno to La Joven Literatura* (Toronto: University of Toronto Press, 2017)

HARRINGTON, ANNE, *Reenchanted Science: Holism in German Culture from Wilhelm II to Hitler* (Princeton: Princeton University Press, 1996)

HATFIELD, GARY, 'Koffka, Köhler, and the "Crisis" in Psychology', *Studies in History and Philosophy of Biological and Biomedical Sciences*, 43.2 (2012), 483–92

HAVARD, ROBERT, *Jorge Guillén: Cántico* (London: Grant & Cutler, 1986)

HERNÁNDEZ DÍAZ, JOSÉ MARÍA, 'Introducción', in Domingo Barnés, *Paidología*, ed. by José María Hernández Díaz (Madrid: Biblioteca Nueva, 2008), pp. 17–54

HERRAN, NÉSTOR, and XAVIER ROQUÉ, eds., *La física en la dictadura: físicos, cultura y poder en España 1939–1975* (Bellaterra: Universitat Autònoma de Barcelona, 2012)

HERRERÍA, ANTONIO, *'Cántico' en 'Orígenes': niñez en el Creacionismo* (n.d.), <http://www.auroraboreal.net/literatura/ensayo/1693-cantico-en-origenes-ninez-en-el-creacionismo #_ftn16> [accessed 1 January 2018]

HERRERO, FANIA, 'Mercedes Rodrigo (1891–1982), la primera psicóloga española', *Revista de Psicología General y Aplicada*, 56.2 (2003), 139–48

HOLGUÍN, SANDY, *Creating Spaniards: Culture and National Identity in Republican Spain* (Madison: University of Wisconsin Press, 2002)

HORN, CHRISTOPH, 'Werner Jaeger's *Paideia* and his "Third Humanism"', *Educational Philosophy and Theory*, 50.6–7 (2018), 682–91

HORTA, GERARD, *De la mística a les barricades: introducció a l'espiritisme català del XIX dins el context ocultista europeu* (Barcelona: Proa, 2001)

HUARTE DE SAN JUAN, JUAN, *Examen de ingenios para las ciencias* (Madrid: La Rafa, 1930)

HUERTA CALVO, JAVIER, 'Cervantes y Lorca: La Barraca', *Don Galán: Revista de Investigación Teatral*, 5 (2014), 1–20

HUXLEY, ALDOUS, *They Still Draw Pictures! A Collection of Sixty Drawings Made by Spanish Children During the War* (Oxford: Oxford University Press, 1939)

IBÁÑEZ MARTÍN, JOSÉ, 'Orden de 7 de Mayo de 1947', *Boletín Oficial del Estado*, 18 June 1947, p. 3434

INIESTA, ALF, 'La lírica y los niños', *Atenas*, 4.28 (1933), 226–27

INSTITUT D'ESTUDIS CATALANS, *Pedagogia, política i transformació social (1900–1917)* (Barcelona: Societat d'Història de l'Educació dels Països de Llengua Catalana, 2008)

IZQUIERDO ORTEGA, JULIÁN, *Filosofía española (Tres ensayos: Ortega y Gasset, o la vida; Turró, o la ciencia; Unamuno, o la religión)* (Madrid: Ediciones Argos, 1935)

JAEGER, HANS, 'Generations in History: Reflections on a Controversial Concept', *History and Theory*, 24.3 (1985), 273–92

JAÉN, JUAN, and JOSÉ PEINADO, *Manual de paidología*, 2nd edn (Madrid: Aguilar, 1935)

JAENSCH, ERICH RUDOLF, *Eidetic Imagery and Typological Methods of Investigation* (London: Kegan Paul, Trench, Trubner & Co., 1930)

JAMES, WILLIAM, *Principles of Psychology* (New York: Henry Holt, 1890)

JARNÉS, BENJAMÍN, *El convidado de papel: novela* (Madrid: Espasa-Calpe, 1935)

—— 'Un niño descalzo', *Meseta*, 1.2 (1928), 4

JIMÉNEZ GÓMEZ, HILARIO, *Alberti y García Lorca: la difícil compañía* (Madrid: Renacimiento, 2014)

JIMÉNEZ, JUAN RAMÓN, *Platero y yo: elegía andaluza* (Madrid: La Lectura, 1914)

—— *Poesía en prosa y verso (1902–1932), escogida para los niños*, ed. by Zenobia Camprubí [1932] (Madrid: Alianza, 1984)

JIMÉNEZ-ALONSO, BELÉN, and JOSÉ CARLOS LOREDO-NARCIANDI, '"To Educate Children from Birth": A Genealogical Analysis of Some Practices of Subjectivation in Spanish and French Scientific Childcare (1898–1939)', *History of Education*, 45.6 (2016), 719–38

JIMÉNEZ GARCÍA, ANTONIO, *El krausismo y la Institución Libre de Enseñanza* (Madrid: Cincel, 1985)

JIMÉNEZ-LANDI, ANTONIO, *La Institución Libre de Enseñanza y su ambiente*, 4 vols (Madrid: Editorial Complutense, 1996)

JOHNSON, R. NEILL, 'Juan Ramón Jiménez, Rabindranath Tagore, and "la poesía desnuda"', *Modern Language Review*, 60.4 (1965), 534–46

JONES, ANDREW F., *Developmental Fairy Tales: Evolutionary Thinking and Modern Chinese Culture* (Cambridge, MA: Harvard University Press, 2011)

JONGH-ROSSEL, ELENA DE, *El krausismo y la generación de 1898* (Valencia: Albatros Hispanófila, 1985)

JOVER, GONZALO, 'Readings of the Pedagogy of John Dewey in Spain in the Early Twentieth Century: Reconciling Pragmatism and Transcendence', in *Democracy and the Intersection of Religion and Traditions: The Readings of John Dewey's Understanding of Democracy and Education*, ed. by Rosa Bruno-Jofré and others (Montreal: McGill-Queen's University Press, 2010), pp. 79–130

JOYCE, JAMES, *A Portrait of the Artist as a Young Man* (New York: B. W. Huebsch, 1922)

JUARROS, CÉSAR, *La crianza del hijo* (Madrid: Mundo Latino, 1900)

——'Desde la cuneta: dibujos de niños', *Mundo Gráfico*, 19.899 (1929), 49–50

——*Educación física y moral del niño en la familia como preparación de su futuro desenvolvimiento integral* (Madrid: Imprenta Artística, Sáez Hermanos, 1918)

KATZ, DAVID, *Der Aufbau der Tastwelt* (Leipzig: J. A. Barth, 1925)

——*El mundo de las sensaciones táctiles*, trans. by Manuel García Morente (Madrid: Revista de Occidente, 1930)

KEIPER, WILHELM, 'El ideal educativo de Goethe', *Boletín de la Institución Libre de Enseñanza*, 46 (1922), 97–104

KENDRICK, ANNA KATHRYN, 'Native Light: Jorge Guillén's Phenomenology of Childhood, 1923–1950', *Modern Language Review*, 113.3 (2018), 518–45

——'Structuring the Mind: Domingo Barnés, Gestalt Perception and the Science of the Child, 1917–1933', *Bulletin of Spanish Studies*, 94.5 (2017), 795–820

KERSCHENSTEINER, GEORG, *Die Entwicklung der zeichnerischen Begabung* (Munich: Carl Gerber, 1905)

KEY, ELLEN, *The Century of the Child* (London: G. P. Putnam's Sons, 1909)

KINCHIN, JULIET, and AIDAN O'CONNOR, eds, *Century of the Child: Growing by Design, 1900–2000* (New York: Museum of Modern Art, 2012)

KOERRENZ, RALF, ANNIKA BLICHMANN, and SEBASTIAN ENGELMANN, 'Peter Petersen and the Jena Plan School', in *Alternative Schooling and New Education: European Concepts and Theories* (Cham: Palgrave Pivot, 2018)

KOFFKA, KURT, *Die Grundlagen der psychischen Entwicklung: Eine Einführung in die Kinderpsychologie* (Osterwieck am Harz: Zickfeldt, 1921)

——*Bases de la evolución psíquica: introducción a la psicología infantil*, trans. by José Gaos (Madrid: Revista de Occidente, 1926)

——*The Growth of the Mind: An Introduction to Child-Psychology*, trans. by Robert Morris Ogden (London: Kegan Paul, Trench, Trubner & Co., 1924)

——'Introducción a la Gestalt-Theorie: la percepción', in *La teoría de la estructura (la psicología novísima)*, ed. by Kurt Koffka, Robert Morris Ogden, and Eugenio Rignano (Madrid: La Lectura, 1928), pp. 9–97

KÖHLER, WOLFGANG, 'El problema de la psicología de la forma', *Anales de la Sección de Orientación Profesional de la Escuela de Trabajo [Barcelona]*, 3.3 (1930), 57–103

KOLBE, FREDERICK CHARLES, *A Catholic View of Holism* (London: Macmillan, 1928)

KOOPS, WILLEM and MICHAEL ZUCKERMAN, *Beyond the Century of the Child: Cultural History and Developmental Psychology* (Philadelphia: University of Pennsylvania Press, 2003)

KÖSSLER, TILL, 'Education and the Baroque in Early Francoism', *Bulletin of Spanish Studies*, 91.5 (2014), 673–96

——*Kinder der Demokratie: Religiöse Erziehung und urbane Moderne in Spanien, 1890–1936* (Munich: Oldenbourg, 2013)

——'Towards a New Understanding of the Child: Catholic Mobilization and Modern Pedagogy in Spain, 1900–1936', *Contemporary European History*, 18.1 (2009), 1–24

KOSTYLEFF, NICOLAS, *La crisis de la psicología experimental*, ed. by Domingo Barnés (Madrid: Daniel Jorro, 1922)

KRAMER, RITA, *Maria Montessori: A Biography* (Oxford: Blackwell, 1978)

KUHN, THOMAS S., *The Structure of Scientific Revolutions* (Chicago: University of Chicago Press, 1970)

LABANYI, JO, 'Memory and Modernity in Democratic Spain: The Difficulty of Coming to Terms with the Spanish Civil War', *Poetics Today*, 28.1 (2007), 89–116

LAFORA, GONZALO R., 'Estudio psicológico del cubismo y expresionismo', *Archivos de Neurobiología, Psicología, Fisiología, Histología, Neurología y Psiquiatría*, 3.2 (1922), 119–55

LAFUENTE NIÑO, ENRIQUE, 'La contribución de Gonzalo R. Lafora a la psicología del arte', *Revista de Historia de la Psicología*, 27.2–3 (2006), 71–79

LAFUENTE NIÑO, ENRIQUE, HELIO CARPINTERO CAPELL, and ALEJANDRA FERRÁNDIZ LLORET, 'The Introduction of Gestalt Psychology in Spain (1923–1936)', in *Psychologie im soziokulturellen Wandel: Kontinuitäten und Diskontinuitäten*, ed. by Siegfried Jaeger and others (Frankfurt am Main: Peter Lang, 1995), pp. 214–20

LAGO DE COMAS, REGINA, 'El realismo intelectual y la aparición de la perspectiva', *Revista de Pedagogía*, 9.105 (1930), 391–98

—— 'La guerra a través de los dibujos infantiles', *Educación y Cultura* (August 1940), 422–37

LAHOZ ABAD, PURIFICACIÓN, 'El modelo froebeliano de espacio-escuela: su introducción en España', *Historia de la Educación*, 10 (1991), 107–34

LAMPRECHT, KARL, 'Les Dessins d'enfant comme source historique', *Bulletin de l'Académie royale de Belgique*, 9–10 (1906), 457–69

LASAGA, JOSÉ, 'El mono fantástico (Notas sobre la "ciencia del hombre" de Ortega)', *Revista de Occidente*, 384 (2013), 5–22

LEDERMAN, SUSAN J., 'D. Katz, "The World of Touch"', *Perception*, 19.4 (1990), 556–57

LEDESMA RAMOS, RAMIRO, 'De la nueva psicología', *La Gaceta Literaria*, 3.54 (1929), 2

—— 'La Gestalttheorie', *La Gaceta Literaria*, 3.50 (15 January 1929), 2

LEÓN, MARÍA TERESA, *Rosa-Fría, patinadora de la luna* (Madrid: Ediciones de la Torre, 1990)

LEWIN, KURT, 'Fuerzas del ambiente', trans. by Luis Ortega Durán and Arthur Brooke, in *Manual de psicología del niño*, ed. by Carl Murchison and Emilio Mira y López (Barcelona: Francisco Seix, 1935), pp. 735–77

LEYSSEN, SIGRID, and ANNETTE MÜLBERGER, 'Psychology from a Neo-Thomist Perspective: The Louvain-Madrid Connection', in *So What's New about Scholasticism? How Neo-Thomism Helped Shape the Twentieth Century*, ed. by Rajesh Heynickx and Stéphane Symons (Berlin: Walter De Gruyter, 2018), 181–204

LILLARD, ANGELINE STOLL, *Montessori: The Science Behind the Genius* (Oxford: Oxford University Press, 2005)

LINARES, ANTONIO G., 'Del cuento al teatro, pasando por el guiñol', *La Esfera*, 8.379 (1921), 18

LINARES MAZA, ANTONIO, 'Diagnóstico de niños anormales y superdotados', *Revista de Pedagogía*, 10.117–18 (1931), 412–17, 56–64

LIND, GEORG RUDOLF, *Jorge Guilléns Cántico: Eine Motivstudie* (Frankfurt am Main: Vittorio Klostermann, 1955)

LITVAK, LILY, *A la playa: el mar como el tema de la modernidad en la pintura española de 1870–1936* (Madrid: Fundación Cultural Mapfre Vida, 2001)

LLÁCER ASENCIO, LUIS, *Actividades escolares con hojas, frutos y semillas* (Valencia: J. Vicente Pont Ferrer, 1934)

LLONGUERAS, JOAN, 'La gimnàstica rítmica i els estudis calistènichs d'E. Jaques Dalcroze a l'Escola Coral de Tarrasa [sic]', *La Ilustració Catalana (Feminal)*, 36 (1910), 6–8

LLOPIS, RODOLFO, *Hacia una escuela más humana* (Madrid: Editorial España, 1933)

—— *La pedagogía de Decroly* (Madrid: La Lectura, 1927)

LLORCA, ÁNGEL, '2D/2.2. Impresos, direcciones y folletos de Congresos Internacionales', in *Archivo digital 'Los viejos papeles'* (Madrid: Fundación Ángel Llorca, [1925–27])

—— *Cinematógrafo educativo* (Madrid: [Sucesores de Hernando], 1917)

—— *Más lecciones de cosas* (Girona: Dalmau Carles & Compañía, 1912)

—— 'Notas educativas escritas en 1942 para el proyecto de libro *La educación vivida*', Document 34, Archivo Digital 'Los viejos papeles' (Madrid: Fundación Ángel Llorca, 1890–1933), <http://www.fundacionangelllorca.org/materiales/archivo-digital-viejos-papeles> [accessed 1 September 2018]

—— *El primer año de lenguaje* (Madrid: n.p., 1923)

LLORCA Y RADAL, JESÚS, 'Los juegos rítmicos en la Escuela', *Anales de la Junta para Ampliación de Estudios e Investigaciones Científicas*, 18.18 (1926), 341–67

LÓPEZ, VICENTE, 'La escuela, embrión social', *Revista de Pedagogía*, 8.89 (1929), 208–14

LÓPEZ GARCÍA, JOSÉ RAMÓN, *Vanguardia, revolución y exilio: la poesía de Arturo Serrano Plaja* (Valencia: Pre-Textos, 2008)

LÓPEZ-MORILLAS, JUAN, *El krausismo español* (Mexico: Fondo de Cultura Económica, 1956)

LÓPEZ VELASCO, ELISA, *La práctica del dibujo en la escuela primaria*, 4 vols (Madrid: Espasa-Calpe, 1933)

LUQUET, GEORGES-HENRI, *Les Dessins d'un enfant* (Paris: Alcan, 1913)

LUZURIAGA, LORENZO, 'La biología de los niños en relación con la educación', *El Sol*, 5 November 1918, p. 8

—— *La educación de nuestro tiempo* (Buenos Aires: Editorial Losada, 1961)

—— 'La escuela de Rabindranath Tagore: "Morada de Paz": (Shantiniketan)', *El Sol*, 21 July 1919, p. 12

MACHADO, ANTONIO, *Soledades. Galerías. Otros poemas*, ed. by Geoffrey Ribbans (Madrid: Cátedra, 1983)

MADARIAGA, CÉSAR, 'La selección corporativa de los "superdotados"', *El Imparcial*, 22 February 1928, p. 1

Las maestras de la República, dir. by Pilar Pérez Solano (Madrid: Transit Producciones, 2013)

MAILLO, ADOLFO, 'El valor pedagógico de la poesía lírica', *Revista de Pedagogía*, 12.139 (1933), 294–300

MAINER BAQUÉ, JUAN, *La forja de un campo profesional: pedagogía y didáctica de las ciencias sociales en España, 1900–1970* (Madrid: CSIC, 2009)

MALLART Y CUTÓ, JOSÉ, *Colonias de educación* (Madrid: Revista de Pedagogía, 1931)

—— *La educación activa*, 4th edn (Barcelona: Editorial Labor, 1935)

—— *La escuela del trabajo* (Madrid: Revista de Pedagogía, 1928)

—— *Escuelas-asilos de artes y oficios para niños pobres, huérfanos y abandonados: su organización práctica y útil* (Madrid: Imprenta de la Ciudad Lineal, 1926)

—— 'El trabajo agradable y el problema de la educación activa', *Boletín de la Institución Libre de Enseñanza*, 45.735–36 (1921), 176–84, 211–20

MANJÓN, ANDRÉS, *Hojas educadoras del Ave-María. (Primer apéndice de las Hojas Coeducadoras). Educar es completar hombres* (Granada: Imprenta-Escuela del Ave María, 1907)

—— *Escritos socio-pedagógicos: educar enseñando* (Madrid: Biblioteca Nueva, 2009)

MARAÑÓN, GREGORIO, *Amor, conveniencia y eugenesia* (Madrid: Historia Nueva, 1929)

—— *Luis Vives (un español fuera de España)* (Madrid: Espasa-Calpe, 1942)

MARÍN ECED, TERESA, *Innovadores de la educación en España: becados de la Junta para Ampliación de Estudios* ([Ciudad Real]: Universidad de Castilla-La Mancha, 1991)

MARRAST, ROBERT, 'Prólogo', in Rafael Alberti, *Lope de Vega y la poesía contemporánea seguido de La pájara pinta* (Paris: Centre de Recherches de l'Institut d'Études Hispaniques, 1964)

MARTÍN AGACIR, MANUEL, 'Las pajaritas de papel de Unamuno', *Estampa*, 3 December 1932, pp. 15–16

MARTÍN-SANTOS, LUIS, *Libertad, temporalidad y transferencia en el psicoanálisis existencial: para una fenomenología de la cura psicoanalítica* (Barcelona: Seix Barral, 1975)

MARTÍNEZ ALFARO, ENCARNACIÓN, *Un laboratorio pedagógico de la Junta para Ampliación de Estudios: el Instituto-Escuela Sección Retiro de Madrid* (Madrid: Biblioteca Nueva, 2009)

MARTÍNEZ NAVARRO, ANASTASIO and OTHERS, *La Editorial Calleja: un agente de modernización educativa en la Restauración* (Madrid: UNED, 2002)

MARTÍNEZ PRIEGO, CONSUELO, 'Urdimbre afectiva y educación: aproximación a las ideas pedagógicas de Juan Rof Carballo', *Estudios sobre Educación*, 28 (2015), 139–54

MARTÍNEZ SARALEGUI, PEDRO, 'El significado del "test"', *Atenas*, 3.13 (15 October 1931), 15–17

MAS LÓPEZ, JORDI, *Josep Maria Junoy i Joan Salvat-Papasseit: dues aproximacions a l'haiku* (Barcelona: Publicacions de l'Abadia de Montserrat, 2004)

MASRIERA VILA, VÍCTOR, 'Cómo se enseña el dibujo', *Revista de Pedagogía*, 2.21 (1923), 346–51

——'El dibujo en la escuela primaria', *Revista de Pedagogía*, 1.12 (1922), 441–47

——'El dibujo y las oposiciones restringidas', *Revista de Pedagogía*, 6.72 (1927), 566–70

MATEOS, ELADIO, and ISMAEL RAMOS, 'Alberti en el teatro de las vanguardias: vida y fortuna de La pájara pinta', *Papeles del Festival de Música Española de Cádiz*, 1 (2005), 61–81

MATTHEWS, ELIZABETH, *The Structured World of Jorge Guillén: A Study of 'Cántico' and 'Clamor'* (Liverpool: Cairns, 1985)

MATUTE, ANA MARÍA, *Cuentos de infancia*, ed. by Ana María Moix (Barcelona: Ediciones Martínez Roca, 2002)

MAURER, CHRISTOPHER, 'Prologue', in *Collected Poems* (New York: Farrar, Straus & Giroux, 2002), pp. xi–lxiv

MAYAGOITIA ALARCÓN, ODALMIRA, *El análisis del mundo circundante por el niño, con referencia especial al niño anormal: la ortopedia mental en la educación del niño en su aspecto sensoperceptivo* (Mexico: Secretaría de Educación Pública, 1950)

MELENDRERAS, EMETERIO RUÍZ, *La pintura por el recorte geométrico a base de rectas y curvas*, ed. by J. Demuro (Madrid: Juan Ortiz, 1934)

MENDELSON, JORDANA, 'Las misiones pedagógicas en la prensa de 1935 a 1938', *Boletín de la Institución Libre de Enseñanza*, 40–41 (2001), 61–79

MÉNDEZ, CONCHA, 'No sé dónde', *Héroe*, 1.3 (1932), n.p.

MERCANTE, VÍCTOR, 'Correlación inversa de las crisis físicas e intelectuales', *Revista de Pedagogía*, 7.80 (1928), 362–68

MERLEAU–PONTY, MAURICE, and JACQUES PRUNAIR, *Psychologie et pédagogie de l'enfant: cours de Sorbonne, 1949–1952* (Lagrasse: Verdier, 2001)

MERMALL, THOMAS, *The Rhetoric of Humanism: Spanish Culture after Ortega y Gasset* (New York: Bilingual Press, 1976)

MINTER, GORDON, *'Amor y pedagogía*: An Object Lesson in Biography', in *Spain's 1898 Crisis: Regenerationism, Modernism, Postcolonialism*, ed. by Joseph Harrison and Alan Hoyle (Manchester: Manchester University Press, 2000), pp. 81–90

MIRA Y LÓPEZ, EMILIO, 'Las pruebas de imaginación visual (espacial) en la escuela', *Revista de Pedagogía*, 3.32 (1924), 281–84

——'Pruebas para la determinación de los tipos de inteligencia en los niños', *Archivos de Neurobiología, Psicología, Fisiología, Histología, Neurología y Psiquiatría*, 7.1 (1927), 3–37

——*Psicología evolutiva del niño y el adolescente*, 2nd edn (Buenos Aires: El Ateneo, 1944)

MISTRAL, GABRIELA, 'Carmen Conde, contadora de la infancia', in *Júbilos: poemas de niños, rosas, animales, máquinas y vientos*, 2nd edn (Murcia: Ediciones Sudeste, 1934), pp. 7–13

——*Pasión de enseñar (Pensamiento pedagógico)* (Valparaíso: Universidad de Valparaíso, 2017)

MOLERO PINTADO, ANTONIO, *La Institución Libre de Enseñanza: un proyecto de reforma pedagógica* (Madrid: Biblioteca Nueva, 2000)

MOLERO PINTADO, ANTONIO, and MARÍA DEL MAR DEL POZO ANDRÉS, *Escuela de Estudios Superiores del Magisterio (1909–1932): un precedente histórico en la formación universitaria del profesorado español* (Madrid: Universidad de Alcalá de Henares, 1989)

MONTERO VIVES, JOSÉ, 'Andrés Manjón: discurso leído en la solemne apertura del curso académico 1897–1898 en la Universidad Literaria de Granada', in *La construcción de la identidad pedagógica española: entre la Institución Libre de Enseñanza y las Escuelas del Ave María*, ed. by Remedios Sánchez García (Madrid: Editorial Síntesis, 2015), pp. 173–87

MONTESSORI, MARIA, *L'autoeducazione nelle scuole elementari* (Rome: P. Maglione and C. Strini, 1916)

——— *La auto-educación en la escuela elemental*, trans. by Juan Palau Vera (Barcelona: Araluce, 1920)

——— 'El método Montessori y la educación moderna', *Revista de Pedagogía*, 1.6 (1922), 201–04

——— *The Montessori Method: Scientific Pedagogy as Applied to Child Education in 'The Children's Houses'* (London: Heinemann, 1912)

MONTORO, ADRIAN G., 'La cruz y la greca en Unamuno', *MLN*, 95.2 (1980), 453–59

MORENO MARTÍNEZ, PEDRO L., 'Carmen Conde y una ilusión: la educación del pueblo', in *Carmen Conde: voluntad creadora (1907–1996)*, ed. by Francisco Javier Díez de Revenga (Murcia: Marcial Pons, 2007), pp. 97–110

MOREU CALVO, ÁNGEL C., 'Presència d'un psicòleg exiliat: Werner Wolff a Barcelona (1933–1936)', *Educació i Història: Revista d'Història de l'Educació*, 9–10 (2006/07), 270–83

MÜLBERGER, ANNETTE, 'Appropriation of Psychological Testing in the Spanish Pedagogical Context', in *The Circulation of Science and Technology: Proceedings of the 4th International Conference of the ESHS, Barcelona, 18–20 November 2010*, ed. by Antoni Roca Rosell (Barcelona: SCHCT-IEC, 2012), pp. 626–35

——— 'Un psicólogo abandona su mundo: el exilio de Emilio Mira y López', in *El exilio científico republicano*, ed. by José Luís Barona (Valencia: Publicaciones de la Universidad de Valencia, 2010), pp. 157–72

MÜLBERGER, ANNETTE, MÒNICA BALLTONDRE PLA, and ANDREA GRAUS, 'Aims of Teachers' Psychometry: Intelligence Testing in Barcelona (1920)', *History of Psychology*, 17.3 (2013), 206–22

MURRAY, PENELOPE, *Genius: The History of an Idea* (Oxford: Blackwell, 1989)

NAVARRO FLORES, MARTÍN, 'La paidología: su historia y su estado actual', *Boletín de la Institución Libre de Enseñanza*, 28.528–529 (1904), 72–77, 100–05

NIEVA-DE LA PAZ, PILAR, 'Concha Méndez y Manuel Altolaguirre: la memoria de una vocación teatral', *Anales de la Literatura Española Contemporánea*, 38.3 (2013), 257–83

NOBLE, FIONA, 'The Representation of the Child in Contemporary Spanish Cinema', in *La piel en la palestra: estudios corporales II*, ed. by Alba del Pozo García and Alba Serrano Giménez (Barcelona: Editorial UOC, 2011)

NÓVOA SANTOS, ROBERTO, *Cuerpo y espíritu: fragmentos para una doctrina genética y energética del espíritu* (Madrid: Compañía Ibero-Americana de Publicaciones, [1930])

——— *Physis y psyquis: fragmentos para una doctrina genética y energética del espíritu* (Santiago de Compostela: El Eco de Santiago, 1922)

——— *El problema del mundo interior* ([Santiago de Compostela]: s.n., 1920)

NUSSBAUM, MARTHA, *Not for Profit: Why Democracy Needs the Humanities* (Princeton: Princeton University Press, 2016)

OCAÑA TORREJÓN, JUAN, and ALFREDO GIL MUÑIZ, *Ensayo sobre revisión española de los 'tests' Claparède: (primera serie): escala de Villanueva de Córdoba* (Villanueva de Córdoba: Talleres tipográficos Pedrajas, 1924)

OLIVARES FIGUEROA, RAFAEL, *El estudio del niño y sus aplicaciones* (Madrid: Cuadernos de Cultura, 1933)

——'La invención poética en el niño', *Boletín de la Academia de Ciencias, Bellas Letras y Nobles Artes de Córdoba*, 14.45 (1935), 149–69

——'Unos cuantos niños precoces madrileños', *El Heraldo de Madrid*, 18 April 1931, p. 14

OÑATIVIA, OSCAR V., *Dimensiones de la percepción* (Tucumán: Universidad Nacional de Tucumán, 1963)

——*Método integral para la enseñanza de la lecto-escritura inicial* (Buenos Aires: Editorial Humanitas, 1967)

——*Percepción y acción* (Buenos Aires: Universidad de Buenos Aires, 1951)

ONTAÑÓN, ELVIRA, 'Jimena Menéndez Pidal: la aventura de rescatar la ILE en tiempos de oscuridad', in *Treinta retratos de maestras*, ed. by Consuelo Flecha (Madrid: Cuadernos de Pedagogía, 2005), pp. 73–78.

ORRINGER, NELSON R., 'Luminous Perception in *Meditaciones del Quijote*: Ortega y Gasset's Source', *Revista Canadiense de Estudios Hispánicos*, 2.1 (1977), 1–26

——*La filosofía de la corporalidad en Ortega y Gasset* (Pamplona: Servicio de Publicaciones de la Universidad de Navarra, 1999)

——*Lorca in Tune with Falla: Literary and Musical Interludes* (Toronto: University of Toronto Press, 2014)

ORTEGA BERENGUER, EMILIO, 'El problema educativo en la Segunda República', *Jábega*, 24 (1978), 29–32

ORTEGA CUBERO, INÉS, 'Ángel Ferrant, profesor de vanguardia: estudio de la didáctica personal del artista a través de su legado documental presente en el Museo Patio Herreriano' (unpublished doctoral thesis, Universidad de Valladolid, 2007)

——*Ángel Ferrant, profesor de vanguardia* (Valladolid: Junta de Castilla y León, 2009)

——'Ángel Ferrant y la Escuela de Artes y Oficios de Viena', *Pulso: Revista de Educación*, 32 (2009), 25–54

ORTEGA Y GASSET, JOSÉ, *Biología y pedagogía* (Costa Rica: J. García Monge, 1920)

——*La deshumanización del arte e ideas sobre la novela*, in *Obras completas*, 12 vols (Madrid: Revista de Occidente, 1983), III, 353–419

——*El espectador*, 8 vols (Madrid: Calpe, 1916–34)

——*Goethe desde dentro* (Madrid: Revista de Occidente, 1932)

——*Guillermo Dilthey y la idea de la vida* (Madrid: Revista de Occidente, 1964)

——'La inteligencia de los chimpancés', *El Sol*, 23 April 1927, p. 3

——*Meditaciones del Quijote* (Madrid: Publicaciones de la Residencia de Estudiantes, 1914)

——*Obras completas*, 12 vols (Madrid: Revista de Occidente, 1946–1983)

——'Pedagogía de secreciones internas, I: Para Gregorio Marañón', *El Sol*, 26 March 1920, p. 5

——*Personas, obras, cosas* (Madrid: Renacimiento, 1916)

——*¿Qué es filosofía?*, 2nd edn (Madrid: Colección Austral, 1965)

——*La rebelión de las masas* (Madrid: Revista de Occidente, 1930)

——*El tema de nuestro tiempo*, 12th edn, Colección Austral (Madrid: Espasa-Calpe, 1968)

——'Un poeta indo (I)', *El Sol*, 27 January 1918, p. 5

——'Un poeta indo (II)', *El Sol*, 3 February 1918, p. 5

——*Vives, Goethe: conferencias* (Madrid: Revista de Occidente, 1961)

ORTIZ, JUAN, ed., *46 trabajos manuales hechos con corcho, sandía, limón, cerezas, cañas, etc.* (Madrid: Juan Ortiz, n.d.)

OSSENBACH, GABRIELA, and ALEJANDRO TIANA FERRER, 'La contribución de la Junta para Ampliación de Estudios a la renovación pedagógica en España en el primer tercio del siglo XX', *Boletín de la Institución Libre de Enseñanza*, 63–64 (2006), 97–114

OTERO CARVAJAL, LUIS ENRIQUE, *La universidad nacionalcatólica: la reacción antimoderna* (Madrid: Carlos III Universidad de Madrid, 2014)

OTERO URTAZA, EUGENIO MANUEL, ed., *Las misiones pedagógicas: 1931–1936* (Madrid: Sociedad Estatal de Conmemoraciones Culturales, Residencia de Estudiantes, 2006)

OTIS, LAURA, *Organic Memory: History and the Body in the Late Nineteenth and Early Twentieth Centuries* (Lincoln: University of Nebraska Press, 1994)

PALACIOS, LUIS, *Instituto-Escuela: historia de una renovación educativa* (Madrid: Ministerio de Educación y Ciencia, 1988)

PALAU VERA, JUAN, 'Prefacio', in Maria Montessori, *El método de la Pedagogía científica aplicado a la educación de la infancia en la 'Case dei Bambini'*, trans. by Juan Palau Vera (Barcelona: Araluce, 1913), pp. xi–xiv

PALENCIA, BENJAMÍN, *Niños* (Madrid: Índice, 1923)

PALMÉS, FERRÁN MARÍA, 'Hacia la psicología experimental: impresiones de un viaje de estudios', *Ibérica*, 475 (1923), 267–71

——'La psicología gestaltista: introducción a su estudio crítico', *Pensamiento*, 1 (1945), 31–61

PARK, ROBERT E., 'Review: *Die drei Nationalökonomien*. By Werner Sombart', *American Journal of Sociology*, 36.6 (1931), 1071–77

PAYÀ RICO, ANDRÉS, 'La actividad lúdica en la historia de la educación española contemporánea' (unpublished doctoral thesis, Universitat de Valencia, 2007)

PELEGRÍN, ANA, MARÍA VICTORIA SOTOMAYOR, and ALBERTO URDIALES, *Pequeña memoria recobrada: libros infantiles del exilio del 39* (Madrid: Ministerio de Educación, Cultura y Deporte, 2008)

PELTA, RAQUEL, 'Salvador Bartolozzi: un ilustrador para una infancia moderna', *Boletín de la Institución Libre de Enseñanza*, 42–43 (2001), 189–97

PENEDO, GERMÁN, 'La escuela en el campo', *La Correspondencia de España*, 8 May 1909, 1

PERALTA SERRANO, ALICIA, 'El Padre Ferrán María Palmés y el laboratorio de psicología experimental del Colegio Máximo San Ignacio de Sarriá de Barcelona', *Revista de Historia de la Psicología*, 15.3–4 (1994), 461–75

PERDIGUERO GIL, ENRIQUE, ed., *Salvad al niño: estudios sobre la protección a la infancia en la Europa Mediterránea a comienzos del siglo XX* (Valencia: Publicacions de la Universitat de València, 2004)

PÉREZ, CARLOS, 'Tono: humorismo y vanguardia', *Boletín de la Institución Libre de Enseñanza*, 42–43 (2001), 175–90

PÉREZ DE AYALA, RAMÓN, *El país del futuro: mis viajes a los Estados Unidos (1913–1914 y 1919–1920)* (Madrid: Biblioteca Nueva, 1959)

PÉREZ GALÁN, MARIANO, *La enseñanza en la Segunda República* (Madrid: Edición Cuadernos para el Diálogo, 1975)

PÉREZ SEGURA, JAVIER, *Arte moderno, vanguardia y estado: la Sociedad de Artistas Ibéricos y la República (1931–1936)* (Madrid: Consejo Superior de Investigaciones Científicas, 2003)

PÉREZ-VILLANUEVA TOVAR, ISABEL, 'El liberalismo institucionista en la Residencia de Estudiantes', *Studia Historica: Historia Contemporánea*, 8 (1990), 77–88

PETERSEN, PETER, 'Misión de la educación', *Revista de Pedagogía*, 13.148 (1934), 145–49

PI I SUNYER, AUGUST, *Classics of Biology*, trans. by Charles M. Stern (London: Sir Isaac Pitman & Sons, 1955)

——*Dispersa y conjunta (ensayos)* (Caracas: C.A. Artes Gráficas, 1945)

——*La unidad funcional*, 2 vols (Mexico: Compañía General Editora, 1944)

PI I SUNYER, AUGUST, JESÚS M. BELLIDO, and PEDRO NUBIOLA, *La doctrina de las secreciones internas*, 2nd edn (Barcelona: Instituto Bioquímico 'Hermes', 1919)

PIAGET, JEAN, *The Child and Reality: Problems of Genetic Psychology*, trans. by Arnold Rosin (New York: Viking Press, 1974)

——*The Essential Piaget*, ed. by Howard Gruber and J. Jacques Vonèche (London: Routledge & Kegan Paul, 1977)

——*El estructuralismo* (Barcelona: Oikos-Tau, 1974)

——'El nacimiento de la inteligencia en el niño', *Revista de Pedagogía*, 5.60 (1926), 529–36

PIAGET, JEAN, and BÄRBEL INHELDER, *The Child's Conception of Space*, trans. by F. J. Langdon and J. L. Lunzer (London: Routledge & Kegan Paul, 1956)

PIAGET, JEAN, and PEDRO ROSSELLÓ, 'Note sur les types de description d'images chez l'enfant', *Archives de Psychologie*, 18.3–4 (1922), 209–10

POMAREDA SOLER, JUAN, *La escuela al aire libre y los paseos escolares: programas y guía práctica de la educación de los niños en el campo* (Madrid: Pedro Núñez, 1902)

POPKEWITZ, THOMAS S., *Cosmopolitanism and the Age of School Reform: Science, Education, and Making Society by Making the Child* (London: Routledge, 2008)

POVEDA, PEDRO, *Itinerario pedagógico*, ed. by Ángeles Galino (Madrid: CSIC, Instituto de Pedagogía, 1964)

POZO ANDRÉS, MARÍA DEL MAR DEL, 'Ángel Llorca: un maestro entre la Institución Libre de Enseñanza y la escuela nueva (1866–1942)', *Historia de la Educación*, 6 (1987), 229–48

——*Justa Freire o la pasión de educar: biografía de una maestra atrapada en la historia de España (1896–1965)* (Barcelona: Ediciones Octaedro, 2013)

——'La utilización de parques y jardines como espacios educativos alternativos en Madrid, 1900–1931', *Historia de la Educación*, 12–13 (1993–94), 149–84

POZO ANDRÉS, MARÍA DEL MAR DEL, and J. F. A. BRASTER, 'The Reinvention of the New Education Movement in the Franco Dictatorship (Spain, 1936–1976)', *Paedagogica Historica*, 42.1–2 (2006), 109–26

PRATT, DALE J., *Signs of Science: Literature, Science, and Spanish Modernity since 1868* (West Lafayette: Purdue University Press, 2001)

PROUST, MARCEL, *El mundo de Guermantes*, trans. by José María Quiroga Plá (Madrid: Espasa-Calpe, 1932)

PUENTE, ANDREA, 'Ilustración para niños en la España de los años 10, 20 y 30', *Peonza: Revista de Literatura Infantil y Juvenil*, 117 (2016), 13–22

QUANCE, ROBERTA, 'Norah Borges Illustrates Two Spanish Women Poets', in *Crossing Fields in Modern Spanish Culture*, ed. by Federico Bonaddio and Xon de Ros (Oxford: Legenda, 2003), pp. 54–66

——'Maruja Mallo and the Interest in Children's Art during the Second Spanish Republic', *Bulletin of Hispanic Studies*, 90.7 (2013), 803–18

QUIROGA, ALEJANDRO, *Making Spaniards: Primo de Rivera and the Nationalization of the Masses, 1923–30* (Basingstoke: Palgrave Macmillan, 2007)

RADCLIFF, PAMELA BETH, *From Mobilization to Civil War: The Politics of Polarization in the Spanish City of Gijón, 1900–1937* (Cambridge: Cambridge University Press, 1994)

RAMÓN Y CAJAL, SANTIAGO, *La infancia de Ramón y Cajal, contada por él mismo* (Madrid: Editorial Reus, 1921)

REINHARDT, EDDA, 'Unamuno als Bildhauer (Unamuno, escultor)', *La Gaceta Literaria*, 4.78 (1930), 12

REVERTE, MANUEL, 'La colonia escolar de la Ciudad Lineal', *ABC*, 19 August 1931, 6–7

RIBAGORDA ESTEBAN, ÁLVARO, 'Los orígenes del Instituto-Escuela: los grupos de niños de la Residencia de Estudiantes', in *Ciencia e innovacíon en las aulas: centenario del Instituto Escuela (1918–1939)*, ed. by Encarnación Martínez Alfaro, Leoncio López-Ocón Cabrera and Gabriela Ossenbach Sauter (Madrid: CSIC, 2018), pp. 47–70.

RIBEIRO DE MENEZES, ALISON, 'Family Memories, Postmemory, and the Rupture of Tradition in Josefina Aldecoa's Civil War Trilogy', *Hispanic Research Journal*, 13.3 (2012), 250–63

RICHARDS, MICHAEL, 'Spanish Psychiatry c. 1900–1945: Constitutional Theory, Eugenics, and the Nation', *Bulletin of Spanish Studies*, 81.6 (2004), 823–48

RICHET, CHARLES, 'Des limites de l'incrédulité', *Annales des Sciences Psychiques,* 18.7–8 (1908), 97–101

RÍOS, FERNANDO DE LOS, *El sentido humanista del socialismo* (Madrid: Biblioteca Nueva, 2006)

RODRIGO, MERCEDES, and PEDRO ROSELLÓ, 'Revisión española de los "tests" Claparède (primera serie): escala popular de Madrid', *Revista de Pedagogía,* 2.15 (1923), 81–92

RODRÍGUEZ ÁLVAREZ, JOSEFINA [JOSEFINA ALDECOA], *El arte del niño* (Madrid: CSIC, Instituto 'San José de Calasanz' de Pedagogía, 1959)

RODRÍGUEZ DE CORTÁZAR, JOAQUÍN, 'Escaparate de libros: Antoniorrobles: 26 cuentos infantiles. CIAP', *La Gaceta Literaria,* 4.74 (1930), 15

RODRÍGUEZ MATA, ÁNGEL, 'La escuela de Decroly y el método activo', *Revista de Pedagogía,* 1.3 (1922), 86–89

RODRÍGUEZ MÉNDEZ, FRANCISCO JAVIER, 'Renouvellement architectural et pédagogie de plein air en Espagne (1910–1936)', in *L'École de plein air: une expérience pédagogique et architecturale dans l'Europe du XXe siècle,* ed. by Anne-Marie Châtelet (Paris: Éditions Recherche, 2003), pp. 148–60

RODRÍGUEZ VICENTE, A., *Higiene de la edad escolar o paidocultura* (Madrid: CSIC, 1946)

RODRÍGUEZ Y RODRÍGUEZ, FLORENTINO, 'El método Decroly', *Anales de la Junta para Ampliación de Estudios e Investigaciones Científicas,* 18.16 (1925), 295–319

ROGERS, GAYLE, 'Translation', in *A New Vocabulary for Global Modernism,* ed. by Eric Hayot and Rebecca Walkowitz (New York: Columbia University Press, 2016), pp. 248–62

ROS, XON DE, *The Poetry of Antonio Machado: Changing the Landscape* (Oxford: Oxford University Press, 2015)

ROUMA, GEORGES, *Le Langage graphique de l'enfant* (Paris: F. Alcan, 1913)

ROURA I PARELLA, JOAN, *Conceptos fundamentales del pensamiento de Dilthey* (Havana: Universidad de La Habana, 1946)

——*Educación y ciencia* (Mexico: Fondo de Cultura Económica, 1940)

——'La educación viva', *Revista de Pedagogía,* 14.157 (1935), 9

——*La pedagogía de Eduardo Spranger* (Buenos Aires: Editorial Losada, 1942)

——*Spranger y las ciencias del espíritu* (Mexico: Minerva, 1944)

——'Les tres pedagogies', *Revista de Psicologia i Pedagogia,* 2.6 (1934), 164–89

ROURA I PARELLA, JOAN, and FELIPE PANIZO GAMBÓN, *Contestaciones al cuestionario de pedagogía de las oposiciones a Escuelas Nacionales* (Madrid: Imprenta Editorial Colón, 1923)

ROY HERREROS, PEDRO, *Planes escolares de la Villa y Corte: parques infantiles, excursiones escolares, escuelas al aire libre, colonias escolares y plan económico* (Madrid: Imprenta Municipal, 1929)

RUBIÉS, ANNA, *Aplicación del método Decroly a la enseñanza primaria* (Madrid: Publicaciones de la Revista de Pedagogía, 1929)

RUBIO, CHRISTIAN, *Krausism and the Spanish Avant-garde: The Impact of Philosophy on National Culture* (Amherst: Cambria Press, 2017)

RUBIO, RICARDO, 'Hay que enseñar a jugar', *La Escuela Moderna,* 20 (1901), 85–87

RUBIO MAYORAL, JUAN LUIS, 'Historia de la educación bajo la idea de las dos Españas (1931–1935)', in *Enseñanza, ciencia e ideología en España (1890–1950),* ed. by Manuel Castillo Martos and Juan Luis Rubio Mayoral (Seville: Diputación de Sevilla, 2014)

RUBIO LATORRE, RAFAEL, *Educación y educador en el pensamiento de Unamuno* (Salamanca: Ediciones Instituto Pontificio San Pío X, 1974)

RUEDA GONZÁLEZ, MANUEL, *Las colonias escolares y las escuelas al aire libre en su aplicación al mejoramiento de la salud y de la enseñanza primaria* (Palma: Rotger, 1915)

RUIZ, MARÍA JESÚS, 'Vieja tradición oral y nueva pedagogía: el teatro infantil de Alejandro Casona', in *La palabra y la memoria,* ed. by Pedro Cerrillo (Cuenca: Universidad de Castilla-La Mancha, 2008)

RUIZ AMADO, RAMÓN, *El modernismo pedagógico* (Barcelona: Librería Religiosa, 1925)

SACRISTÁN, JOSÉ M., 'El fenómeno eidético', *Revista de Pedagogía*, 6.61 (January 1927), 1–6

——'Libros: Germain (J.) y Rodrigo (M.): *Pruebas de inteligencia* – Madrid, La Lectura, 1930', *Revista de Pedagogía*, 9.108 (1930), 569

——'La teoría psicoanalítica de Freud', *Revista de Pedagogía*, 2.18 (1923), 201–06

SÁENZ DE LA CALZADA, LUIS, *'La Barraca', teatro universitario* (Madrid: Revista de Occidente, 1976)

SÁEZ MORILLA, MARIANO, *Introducción al estudio de la paidología y pedagogía moderna* (Pamplona: Artes Gráficas, 1922)

SÁIZ, MILAGROS, and DOLORES SÁIZ, 'La estancia de María Montessori en Barcelona: la influencia de su método en la psicopedagogía catalana', *Revista de Historia de la Psicología*, 26.2/3 (2005), 200–12

SALINAS, PEDRO, *Defensa del estudiante y de la universidad* (Seville: Editorial Renacimiento, 2011)

SALINAS DE MARICHAL, SOLEDAD, *El mundo poético de Rafael Alberti* (Madrid: Publicaciones de la Residencia de Estudiantes, 2004)

SALVAT-PAPASSEIT, JOAN, *Poésies complètes*, ed. by Joaquim Molas, 3rd edn (Barcelona: Editorial Ariel, 1981)

——*Selected Poems*, ed. and trans. by Dominic Keown and Tom Owen (Oxford: The Anglo-Catalan Society, 1982)

SÁNCHEZ CARAZO, JOSÉ IGNACIO, 'Joaquim Xirau: una filosofía de ultimidades' (unpublished doctoral thesis, Universidad Complutense de Madrid, 1996)

SÁNCHEZ DE MADARIAGA, ELENA, ed., *Las maestras de la República*, 7th edn (Madrid: Catarata, 2014)

SÁNCHEZ FREIJÓ, C., *Paidología e higiene escolar (Inspección médico escolar)* (Madrid: Editorial Reus, 1935)

SÁNCHEZ GARCÍA, REMEDIOS, ed., *La construcción de la identidad pedagógica española: entre la Institución Libre de Enseñanza y las Escuelas del Ave María* (Madrid: Editorial Síntesis, 2015)

SÁNCHEZ SARTO, LUIS, ed., *Diccionario de pedagogía*, 2 vols (Barcelona: Editorial Labor, 1936)

SÁNCHEZ TRINCADO, JOSÉ LUIS, *Pasión del arte nuevo* (Caracas: Grupo 'Viernes', 1940)

SÁNCHEZ TRINCADO, JOSÉ LUIS, and RAFAEL OLIVARES FIGUEROA, eds., *Poesía infantil recitable* (Madrid: M. Aguilar, [1934])

SANTAMARÍA ESQUERDÓ, FRANCISCO, *Los sentidos: lecciones de psicometría, dadas en la Escuela de Criminología de Madrid*, 2nd edn (Madrid: Suárez, 1918)

SANTULLANO, LUIS, 'La enseñanza del idioma', *El Imparcial*, 1 May 1923, p. 4

SANZ DEL RÍO, JULIÁN, 'Psicología del niño: el espíritu en el niño', *Boletín de la Institución Libre de Enseñanza*, 16.363 (1892), 81–83

SARTO, JUAN DEL, 'La Escuela Internacional Española', *Crónica*, 11 May 1930, pp. 31–33

SCARRY, ELAINE, *On Beauty and Being Just* (Princeton: Princeton University Press, 1999)

SCHULTZ, DUANE P., and SYDNEY E. SCHULTZ, *A History of Modern Psychology* (Boston: Cengage Learning, 2007)

SEGERS, JEAN E., *La percepción visual y la función de globalización en los niños*, trans. by Jacobo Orellana Garrido (Madrid: Espasa-Calpe, 1930)

SENSAT I VILÀ, ROSA, 'Momentos escolares', *Revista de Pedagogía*, 9.101 (May 1930), 196–204

——'La escuela al aire libre', *Revista de Pedagogía*, 8.85 (1929), 15–22

SERRANO, LEONOR, *La educación de la mujer de mañana*. ed. by María del Carmen Agulló Díaz (Madrid: Biblioteca Nueva, 2007)

——*El método Montessori* (Madrid: Revista de Pedagogía, 1928)

——*La pedagogía Montessori: estudio informativo y crítico* (Madrid: Sucesores de Hernando, 1915)

SERRANO PLAJA, ARTURO, '¿Por dónde se escapa el Sudeste? (poema de niños y poesía)', *Sudeste*, 4 (July 1931), 8

—— 'Juan Ramón-Tagore', *El Sol*, 21 February 1932, p. 2

SHUTTLEWORTH, SALLY, *The Mind of the Child: Child Development in Literature, Science and Medicine, 1840–1900* (Oxford: Oxford University Press, 2010)

SIERRA BLAS, VERÓNICA, *Palabras huérfanas: los niños y la guerra civil* (Madrid: Taurus, 2009)

SIMMS, EVA M., *The Child in the World: Embodiment, Time, and Language in Early Childhood* (Detroit: Wayne State University Press, 2008)

SINCLAIR, ALISON, *Sex and Society in Early Twentieth-century Spain: Hildegart Rodríguez and the World League for Sexual Reform* (Cardiff: University of Wales Press, 2007)

—— '"Telling it Like it Was"?: The Residencia de Estudiantes and its Image', *Bulletin of Spanish Studies*, 81.6 (September 2004), 739–64

—— *Trafficking Knowledge in Early Twentieth-century Spain: Centres of Exchange and Cultural Imaginaries* (Woodbridge: Tamesis, 2009)

—— *Uncovering the Mind: Unamuno, the Unknown and the Vicissitudes of Self* (Manchester: Manchester University Press, 2001)

SLUYS, ALEXIS, 'La cinematografía escolar', *Revista de Pedagogía*, 1.11 (1922), 401–10

SMUTS, JAN CHRISTIAN, *Holism and Evolution* (London: Macmillan, 1926)

SOLANA, EZEQUIEL, *Don Andrés Manjón: sus obras y doctrinas pedagógicas* (Madrid: Escuela Española, 1941)

—— *María Montessori: exposición crítica de sus métodos de educación y enseñanza* (Madrid: n.p., 1915)

SOLER I MATA, JOAN, 'The Rousseau Institute of Geneva's Influence on and Presence in Catalan Pedagogy in the First Third of the 20th Century', *Catalan Social Sciences Review*, 1 (2012), 58–87

SOMBART, WERNER, *Die drei Nationalökonomien: Geschichte und System der Lehre von der Wirtschaft* (Munich: Duncker & Humblot, 1930)

SORIA Y MATA, ARTURO, *Origen poliédrico de las especies: unidad, origen, reproducción y síntesis de las formas* (Madrid: Sucesores de Rivadeneyra, S.A., 1894)

—— *El talentómetro: reglas para construir un aparato medidor del talento* (Madrid: Imprenta de la Compañía Madrileña de Urbanización, 1902)

SORIANO, MARÍA, and CÉSAR JUARROS, 'El método de Rorschach en los niños', *Revista de Pedagogía*, 7.74 (February 1928), 66–69

SOSA, JESUALDO, *La expresión creadora del niño*, 2nd edn (Buenos Aires: Editorial Poseidón, 1950)

SOTO, JUAN B., *Las leyes mecanicistas del aprendizaje y la nueva psicología alemana (Gestalttheorie): estudio de psicología comparada* (Madrid: Espasa-Calpe, 1933)

SPENCER, HERBERT, *Education: Intellectual, Moral and Physical* [1860] (New York: D. Appleton, 1896)

—— *The Principles of Sociology*, 3 vols (New York: D. Appleton, 1897)

SPIRES, ROBERT C., *Transparent Simulacra: Spanish Fiction, 1902–1926* (Columbia: University of Missouri Press, 1988)

SPRANGER, EDUARD, *Las ciencias del espíritu y la escuela*, trans. and ed. by Joan Roura i Parella (Buenos Aires: Losada, 1942)

—— 'Idees fonamentals de la psicologia com a ciència de l'esperit', *Revista de Psicologia y Pedagogia*, 2 (1934), 125–38, 239–56

—— *Psicología de la edad juvenil*, trans. by José Gaos (Madrid: Revista de Occidente, 1929)

STEEDMAN, CAROLYN, *Strange Dislocations: Childhood and the Idea of Human Interiority, 1780-1930* (Cambridge, MA: Harvard University Press, 1995)

STEWART-STEINBERG, SUZANNE, *The Pinocchio Effect: On Making Italians, 1860–1920* (Chicago: University of Chicago Press, 2007)

SUÑER ORDÓÑEZ, ENRIQUE, *Herencia y educación* (Madrid: Julio Cosano, 1932)

SWANSON, LARRY W., and OTHERS, eds., *The Beautiful Brain: The Drawings of Santiago Ramón y Cajal* (New York: Abrams, 2017)

TAGORE, RABINDRANATH, *Gitanjali: Facsimile of the Original Manuscript* (Calcutta: Sahitya Samsad, 2011)

——*Recuerdos*, trans. by Zenobia Camprubí de Jiménez, ed. by Francisco Garfías (Barcelona: Plaza y Janés, 1983)

TAGORE, RABINDRANATH, and W. W. PEARSON, *Morada de paz (Shantiniketan)*, trans. by Zenobia Camprubí de Jiménez (Madrid: Fortanet, 1919)

——*Shantiniketan: The Bolpur School of Rabindranath Tagore* (London: Macmillan, 1917)

TERMAN, LEWIS M., *Genetic Studies of Genius: Mental and Physical Traits of a Thousand Gifted Children*, 4 vols (Stanford: Stanford University Press, 1925–1947), I (1925)

THOMAS, SARAH, 'Phantom Children: Spectral Presences and the Violent Past in Two Films of Contemporary Spain', in *Espectros: Ghostly Hauntings in Contemporary Transhispanic Narratives*, ed. by Alberto Ribas-Casasayas and Amanda L. Petersen (London: Rowman & Littlefield, 2016), pp. 101–16

TIERNO GALVÁN, ENRIQUE, *Humanismo y sociedad* (Barcelona: Seix Barral, 1964)

TOLOSA LATOUR, MANUEL, *El niño: apuntes científicos* (Madrid: s.n., 1880)

TOMÁS Y SAMPER, RODOLFO, *La psicometría en la escuela primaria (Técnica de paidometría)* (Madrid: Editorial Instituto Samper, 1936)

TORRE, JOSEFINA DE LA, 'Mediodía', in *Poesía infantil recitable*, ed. by José Luis Sánchez Trincado and Rafael Olivares Figueroa (Madrid: M. Aguilar, 1934), p. 7

TORRES, CECILIA DE, and SUSANNA V. TEMKIN, 'Chronology: Documentary Materials', Joaquín Torres-García Catalogue Raisonné, <http://torresgarcia.com/chronology/documentary_materials.php> [accessed 8 May 2018]

TORRES GARCÍA, JOAQUÍN, *Aladdin: juguetes transformables* (Montevideo: Museo Torres García, [2005])

——'Al Magisterio Nacional Primario: Propósito', *Biblion*, 2 (1933), 4

——*Torres-García, construcciones en madera*, ed. by Marc Domènec Tomàs (Madrid: Guillermo de Osma Galería, 2000)

TURIN, YVONNE, *Miguel de Unamuno, universitaire* (Paris: S.E.V.P.E.N., 1962)

TURRÓ, RAMON, *La base trófica de la inteligencia: conferencias dadas en la Residencia de Estudiantes los días 12 y 14 de noviembre de 1917* (Madrid, 1918)

UEXKÜLL, JAKOB VON, *Bausteine zu einer biologischen Weltanschauung: gesammelte Aufsätze*, ed. by Felix Gross (Munich: Bruckmann, 1913)

——*Umwelt und Innenwelt der Tiere* (Berlin: Julius Springer, 1909)

——*Ideas para una concepción biológica del mundo*, trans. by R. M. Tenreiro (Madrid: Calpe, 1922)

UNAMUNO, MIGUEL DE, 'Al hombre entero y verdadero', *Ahora*, 1 January 1936, p. 5

——*Amor y pedagogía* (Madrid: Espasa-Calpe, 1992)

——*Cómo se hace una novela* (Buenos Aires: Editorial Alba, 1927)

——'Confesión de culpa', *El Día*, 7 December 1917, p. 1

——'De la enseñanza superior en España', *Revista Nueva*, 1.18 (5 August 1899), 830–37

——*En torno al casticismo* (Madrid: Fernando Fé, 1902)

——'El niño es el padre del hombre', *El Sol*, 14 August 1932, p. 1

——*Recuerdos de niñez y de mocedad* (Madrid: V. Suárez, 1908)

UNED, 'Cambio de nombre del Centro de Zona *Andrés Manjón*', <http://portal.uned.es/portal/> [accessed 1 October 2018]

URMENETA Y CERVERA, FERMÍN DE, *La doctrina psicológica y pedagógica de Luis Vives* (Madrid: CSIC, Instituto San José de Calasanz de Pedagogía, Sección de Barcelona, 1949)

Valbuena, Cecilia, 'La obra de Elisa López Velasco: la enseñanza del dibujo orientada por la Escuela Activa', *Actas del XVIII Coloquio de Historia de la Educación*, 2.3 (2008), 261–73

Valdés, Mario J., and María Elena Valdés, *An Unamuno Source Book* (Toronto: University of Toronto Press, 1973)

Vaquero Cantillo, Eloy, *Las escuelas al aire libre* (Córdoba: n.p., 1926)

Verdier, Rafael, 'Aprendizaje y cultura', *Revista de Pedagogía*, 8.91 (1929), 295–301

—— *Cinco bolas y un misterio* (Málaga: n.p., 1973)

—— *De Uexküll a Decroly* (Málaga: Tipografía Ibérica, [1931])

—— 'Filosofía y educación', *Escuelas de España*, 2.1 (1930), 33–53

—— *La enseñanza de la ortografía en la escuela primaria* (Madrid: Diana, Artes Graficas, 1963)

—— *Nene* (Málaga: Paidós, 1960)

—— 'Notas para una pedagogía de base existencial', *Escuelas de España*, 1.2 (1934), 1–10

—— 'La pedagogía y la crisis de la psicología experimental', *Revista de Pedagogía*, 5.52 (1926), 152–58

—— *Zurdera y destreza* (Málaga: Instituto de Cultura, 1969)

Verdier, Rafael, and Víctor Argueta, *Ya leo: la lectura y la escritura por el método ideovisual*, 2nd edn (Málaga: 'La Española', 1935)

Verdier, Rafael, and Rafael Gutiérrez, 'Del hacer en la escuela: una unidad de trabajo escolar', *Escuelas de España*, 3.25 (1936), 12–29

Vidal, Fernando, *The Sciences of the Soul: The Early Modern Origins of Psychology* (Chicago: University of Chicago Press, 2011)

Vilanou Torrano, Conrad, 'La formación, entre el amor y la plenitud: de J. W. Goethe a Joaquín Xirau', in *Ideales de formación en la historia de la educación*, ed. by Javier Vergara Ciordia, Fermín Sánchez Barea, and Beatriz Comella Gutiérrez (Madrid: Editorial Dykinson, 2011), pp. 399–436

—— 'La Pedagogía, ciencia de segunda clase. (En torno a un informe remitido por Juan Roura-Parella desde Berlín en Febrero de 1932)', *Historia de la Educación*, 24 (2005), 463–84

—— 'Joan Roura-Parella and his Presence in the United States', *Journal of Catalan Intellectual History*, 1.2 (2011), 131–47

—— 'Juan Roura-Parella (1897–1983) y los orígenes de la pedagogía universitaria en Cataluña', in *Pedagogía y educación ante el siglo XXI*, ed. by Julio Ruiz Berrio (Madrid: Departamento de Teoría e Historia de la Educación, 2005), pp. 171–202

Vilariño, Octavio R., *La infancia y la naturaleza: estudio sintético de la influencia que ejercen, en el desarrollo orgánico e intelectual del niño, las colonias escolares, los jardines de la infancia y los campos de juego* (Madrid: Librería Médica, 1930)

Villar, Rogelio, 'Un gran progreso pedagógico: la educación por el ritmo', *La Esfera*, 2.79 (1915), 30

Viñao Frago, Antonio, *Escuela para todos: educación y modernidad en la España de siglo XX* (Madrid: Marcial Pons, 2004)

Viver, Darius Rumeu i Freixa, barón de, 'L'Institut d'Estudis Catalans', *La Publicitat*, 12 April 1924, p. 4

Vives, Juan Luis, *Tratado de la enseñanza*, trans. by José Ontañón (Madrid: La Lectura, 1922)

Wadsworth, Barry J., *Piaget's Theory of Cognitive and Affective Development: Foundations of Constructivism*, 5th edn (White Plains: Longman, 1996)

Whitebread, David, and others, *The Importance of Play: A Report on the Value of Children's Play with a Series of Policy Recommendations* (Brussels: Toy Industries of Europe, 2012),   <http://www.importanceofplay.eu/IMG/pdf/dr_david_whitebread_-_the_importance_of_play.pdf> [accessed 1 November 2018]

Widlöcher, Daniel, *L'Interprétation des dessins d'enfants* (Sprimont: Mardaga, 1998)

WITTMANN, BARBARA, 'Drawing Cure: Children's Drawings as a Psychoanalytic Instrument', *Configurations*, 18.3 (2010), 251–72

—— 'Symptomatologie des Zeichnens und Schreibens: Verfahren der Selbstaufzeichnung', in *Spuren erzeugen: Zeichnen und Schreiben als Verfahren der Selbstaufzeichnung*, ed. by Barbara Wittmann (Zurich: Diaphanes, 2009), pp. 7–20

WOLFF, WERNER, *Diagrams of the Unconscious: Handwriting and Personality in Measurement, Experiment and Analysis* (New York: Grune & Stratton, 1948)

—— *The Personality of the Preschool Child: The Child's Search for His Self* (London: William Heinemann, 1947)

WRIGHT, SARAH, *The Child in Spanish Cinema* (Manchester: Manchester University Press, 2013)

WYATT, JOHN, *Commitment to Higher Education* (Bristol: Open University Press, 1990)

XANDRI PICH, JOSÉ, *Concentraciones: cuarto y quinto grado o grado medio de la escuela primaria*, I: Letras (Madrid: Yagües, 1932)

—— *Niñerías: primer libro de lectura y lenguaje: grado preparatorio* (Madrid: [s.n.], 1943)

XIRAU I PALAU, JOAQUIM, *L'amor i la percepció dels valors* (Tarragona: Tipografia Sugrañes, 1936)

—— *Amor y mundo* (Mexico: El Colegio de México, 1940)

—— 'Bibliografies. Charlotte Bühler: Der menschliche Lebenslauf als psychologisches Problem. Verlag von S. Hirtzel, in Leipzig, 1933', *Revista de Psicologia i Pedagogia*, 1.1 (1933), 87–89

—— 'La concepción del mundo de Goethe', *Revista de Pedagogía*, 11.124 (1932), 157–63

—— 'Direcciones filosóficos: El idealismo', *Revista de Pedagogía*, 6.65 (1927), 209–15

—— 'Direcciones filosóficos: El realismo', *Revista de Pedagogía*, 6.71 (1927), 523–28

—— 'Filosofía y educación', *Revista de Pedagogía*, 9.106 (1930), 433–37

—— *Manuel B. Cossío y la educación en España* (Mexico: El Colegio de México, 1945)

—— *Obras completas*, ed. by Ramón Xirau, 4 vols (Barcelona: Anthropos, 1998)

—— 'La pedagogía y la vida', *Revista de Pedagogía*, 12.133 (1933), 1–6

—— *El pensamiento vivo de Juan Luis Vives* (Buenos Aires: Editorial Losada, 1944)

—— 'La psicología de la forma', *Revista de Pedagogía*, 5.57 (1926), 385–91

YOUNG, HOWARD, 'The Invention of an Andalusian Tagore', *Comparative Literature*, 47.1 (1995), 42–52

ZARAGÜETA, JUAN, *Conciencia y organismo* [offprint from the journal *Ensayos de Cultura Médica*] ([Madrid]: n.pr., 1932)

—— *Las directrices de la pedagogía de Juan Luis Vives* (Madrid: Imprenta de Editorial Magisterio Español, 1945)

—— *El estudio del niño para la cultura nacional* (Bilbao: Bilbaína de Artes Gráficos, 1919)

ZIMMERMANN, JENS, ed., *Re-envisioning Christian Humanism: Education and the Restoration of Humanity* (Oxford: Oxford University Press, 2016)

ZOZAYA, ANTONIO, 'La cuenta del golfo', *Vida Socialista*, 25 June 1911, pp. 4–5

ZULUETA, ANTONIO DE, 'Herencia y ambiente', *Revista de Pedagogía*, 6.69 (1927), 420–26

ZULUETA, LUIS DE, 'La vela en el horizonte: una pedagogía más moderna', *Revista de Pedagogía*, 1.1 (1922), 1–5

INDEX